NIETZSCHE
& THE JEWS

NIETZSCHE & THE JEWS

Exaltation & Denigration

SIEGFRIED MANDEL, PH.D.
FOREWORD BY RICHARD HUETT

Prometheus Books

59 John Glenn Drive
Amherst, New York 14228-2197

Published 1998 by Prometheus Books

02 01 00 99 98   5 4 3 2 1

Library of Congress Cataloging-in-Publication Data

Mandel, Siegfried.
    Nietzsche & the Jews : exaltation & denigration / Siegfried Mandel ; foreword by Richard Huett.
        p.   cm.
    Includes bibliographical references and index.
    ISBN 1–57392–223–4 (alk. paper)
    1. Nietzsche, Friedrich Wilhelm,—1844–1900—Views on Jews and Judaism.
2. Nietzsche, Friedrich Wilhelm,—1844–1900—Friends and associates. 3. Jews—Intellectual life. 4. Judaism—Germany. I. Title. II. Title: Nietzsche and the Jews.
B3318.J83M36   1998
193—dc21   98–21368
                                                             CIP

Printed in the United States of America on acid-free paper

Dedicated to Dorothy Mandel

Acknowledgment

Professor Weaver Santaniello's substantial contribution to the editing of this work merits deep appreciation. Through some vicissitudes she was ever graciously cooperative.

Contents

Foreword

Richard Huett

In light of Professor Mandel's extensive and encompassing Introduction, to add a substantial Foreword would be but "to paint the lily." Thus, brevity is the soul of sufficiency. What follows is an attempt to establish the book's essentials: that it is probably the fullest treatment of Nietzsche's relationship to Jews as individuals and Judaism as an institution; and it presents for the first time in depth the philosopher's attitudes toward them as *true ambivalence*, oscillating between praise and dispraise. Nietzsche had been Richard Wagner's apt and avid acolyte, matching the latter's virulent anti-Semitism until the philosopher's disillusionment with the composer for reasons more complicated than need be addressed here. The ensuing "great divorce" seemed to have opened Nietzsche's eyes to the several virtues of the Jews.

From the outset, when contemplating this work here, Professor Mandel, after extensive and intensive reading in the Nietzschean corpus (including primary and secondary material), had come to the conclusion that the philosopher's basic view of existence was characteristic of the very essence of the man: ambiguity, ambivalence, paradox; that the anfractuosities of his psyche constitute, arguably, the most complex figure in the history of Western thought. Thus it was, throughout the various stages of the book's composition, that he chose to employ the subtitle "Exaltation and Denigration," which became a leitmotif.

By using the inclusive conjunction "and" rather than "or" in its exclusive sense, the author indicates the true ambivalence in Nietzsche vis-à-vis the Jews. Others, in presenting their respective versions of the duality in Nietzsche concerning the Jews, have offered us a choice: The philosopher was either anti-Semitic *or* philo-Semitic—*in the final analysis*. But Professor Mandel contends it would be a mistake to come down on one side or the other; that the *real* Nietzsche had a full leg in each camp, and that the book's aim is "to liberate Nietzsche from his venerators and detractors."

Yet it is curious that despite what seems to be a convincing case for that belief, Professor Mandel appears to be one of a very few scholars to recognize what should be obvious to anyone even moderately familiar with Nietzsche the man and his works, to anyone not already predisposed to a *parti pris* position, that Nietzsche actually harbored *both* antitheses in almost equal measure.

But then we are reminded of Edgar Allan Poe's "The Purloined Letter," whose thesis is that matters can be *too* simple, *too* plain, *too* self-evident; that the stolen missive had been deposited "beneath the nose of the whole world, by way of best preventing any portion of that world from perceiving it."

I believe that the author has succeeded in defining his conception of Nietzsche as one who in his life and work exemplified Faust's *cri de coeur*: "Alas, two souls live within my breast," with equal weight. Nietzsche, "one of the intimates of Hell," Thomas Mann called him, was a battlefield of contending polarities: Dionysian versus Apollonian, good versus evil, light versus darkness, master morality versus slave morality—shuttling between them as circumstances dictated, until the referee, insanity, intervened to call the battle a draw.

It is this conception that distinguishes this book from all the others which gerrymander the philosopher and his thought. This "stacking of the cards" has had its conscious perpetrators: on the one hand, a Nietzschean anthology of philo-Semitic quotations, compiled by Benjamin De Casseres, and, on the other, vicious and egregious misuse of Nietzsche dicta by the Nazis. But there have been outstanding scholars who, in good faith, have concluded that the philosopher was either a philo- or anti-Semite.

While Professor Mandel has dug wider and deeper than any other scholar to prove his case, there have been a few who have intimated they were fascinated in seeing "both sides of the coin":

But the fact that opposed interest—in this instance, Jewish as well as anti-Semitic—could simultaneously harness divergently conceived notions of Nietzscheanism for their own purposes, will not come as a surprise to anyone familiar with the vagaries of Nietzsche reception. Ironies of this kind constitute the rule rather than the exception. For a crucial characteristic of the determinedly experimental and anti-systemic Nietzsche corpus was its congeniality to multiple and opposed interpretations. Some form of casuistry was, of course, endemic to the way in which these—and all—interested appropriations of Nietzsche operated. Nietzsche, clearly, was not identical with any appropriations made in his name. . . . But all those who appealed to his authority (and not just Jews and Zionists) were obliged to explain (or explain away) how Nietzsche, despite obvious contradictions or even hostility, was in effect compatible with one's favored position, perhaps its most enthusiastic representative. Placing Nietzsche within any "framework" entailed a filtering system in which desired elements were highlighted and embarrassing ones deleted or played down. Inevitably, the "real" or "deep" . . . Nietzsche had to be located and distinguished from the merely apparent ones.

(Steven E. Aschheim [1890–1939],
Nietzsche and the Nietzschean Moment in Jewish Life)

[There is] Nietzsche's gigantic diatribe against the ancient Jews as the poisoners of the wellsprings of human vitality, the perpetrators of the millennial disease of Judaeo-Christianity. One might be passionately opposed to the anti-communism of the McCarthy type without sympathizing with the Communists, anti-anti-Semitism might be compatible with indifference to, or dislike of, Jews; or—and perhaps this describes by and large Nietzsche's attitude—with an ambivalent mixture in which the negative sentiment remained somewhat preponderant, though it was perhaps increasingly interspersed and mingled with respect, admiration, and sympathy, especially for individual Jews.

(Peter Heller, *Nietzsche and the Jews*)

Nietzsche and Jewry! Doubtlessly one of the most interesting chapters in all of cultural history. No thinker has defamed and at the same time exalted Jews as has Nietzsche.

(Dr. Oscar Seligmann, a prominent Berlin rabbi in 1905,
five years after Nietzsche's death)

Forty years ago, C. P. Snow, the British novelist, scientist, and government administrator, in his *Two Cultures and the Scientific Revolution*

(1959), inveighed against the growing division between the humanities and the sciences. Even earlier on, John Dewey spoke of the "cultural lag" in our society and, with Snow, bemoaned this condition. Since then the chasm has widened exponentially, *Homo faber* far outstripping *Homo sapiens*.

Professor Siegfried Mandel was one of the decreasing number of those who bridge both cultures. Professor of English and Comparative Literature at the University of Colorado from 1962 until his death in 1993, he was also the compiler of the *Dictionary of Science* (1969) and the author of the vade mecum *Writing for Science and Technology* (1970).

His awards for achievements as an editor, translator, lecturer, and reviewer on extensively diversified subjects, are legion. In April 1993 Professor Mandel was invited by the Friedrich Nietzsche Society of Great Britain to deliver his paper "Nietzsche and the Jews: Exaltation and Denigration." He died a month later, depriving the world of scholarship, which he graced, of further rich contributions. In one of his final public utterances he enunciated the heuristic principle by which he was guided in preparing his *magnum opus*, this very book:

> To chart Nietzsche's failures and successes, especially in his attitudes toward Judaism and Jews—ancient and contemporaneous—one must avoid gerrymandering his biography, correspondence, and writings, and start again with renewed perspectives from the beginnings. . . .

In what proved to be his last communication to me, accompanying the manuscript, Professor Mandel wrote:

> Since I last talked to you I have completed the Introduction and body of my latest foray. . . . To know what Nietzsche meant one should not gerrymander his works. Correspondingly, I have gone through a vast amount of material to give a bio-critical, chronological, narrative review from a fresh angle to arrive at my destination—to do justice to the man, honestly. . . . By the time this opus reaches you, we will be in England for the Nietzsche conference of which I apprised you. But on our return, I'll call to find out if you've taken even the briefest look at my offering. . . . So off we go, knowing this packet will be in good hands.

I hope so, dear friend, I hope so.

Abbreviations

GT	*Die Geburt der Tragödie* (*The Birth of Tragedy*)
MA	*Menschliches, Allzumenschliches* (*Human, All-Too-Human*)
VM	*Vermischte Meinungen und Sprüche* (*Mixed Opinions and Maxims*)
WS	*Der Wanderer und sein Schatten* (*The Wanderer and his Shadow*)
M	*Die Morgenröte* (*Daybreak*)
FW	*Die Fröhliche Wissenschaft* (*The Gay Science*)
Z	*Also Sprach Zarathustra* (*Thus Spoke Zarathustra*)
J	*Jenseits von Gut und Böse* (*Beyond Good and Evil*)
GM	*Zur Genealogie der Moral* (*On the Genealogy of Morals*)
G	*Die Götzen-Dämmerung* (*Twilight of the Idols*)
A	*Der Antichrist* (*The Antichrist*)
EH	*Ecce Homo*
NCW	*Nietzsche contra Wagner*
WM	*Der Wille zu Macht* (*The Will to Power*)
KGW	*Werke. Kritische Gesamtausgabe* (ed. Colli and Montinari, ca. 30 vols.)
KGB	*Briefwechsel. Kritische Gesamtausgabe* (ed. Colli and Montinari, 18 vols. Berlin, 1975–)
KS	*Werke in drei Bänden* (ed. Schlechta)
ML	*Modern Library Edition: The Basic Writings of Nietzsche* (trans. Kaufmann)
UW	*Unschuld des Werdens* (*The Innocence of Becoming*)

Introduction

Every great philosophy has consisted of confessions and unconscious autobiography.

(Beyond Good and Evil, 6)

And, do you know what "the world" is to me? Shall I show it to you in my mirror?

(The Will to Power, 1067)

We who are homeless.—Among Europeans today there is no lack of those who are entitled to call themselves homeless in a distinctive and honorable sense: it is to them that I especially commend my secret wisdom and *gaya scienza*. For their fate is hard, their hopes are uncertain. . . . We children of the future, how *could* we be at home in this today? We feel disfavor for all ideals that might lead one to feel at home even in this fragile, broken time of transition; as for its "realities," we do not believe that they will *last*. The ice that supports people today has become very thin . . . we ourselves who are homeless constitute a force that breaks open ice and other all to thin "realities."

(Gay Science, 377 [1882])

Nietzsche, no mean parodist himself, would have derived gleeful pleasure from a novel published in 1960 titled *Mendelssohn Is on the*

Roof by the Czech writer Jiří Weil. Years earlier, the young Jewish writer had been captive in a transport to a concentration camp; he feigned death and escaped into hiding. His novel opens as an ambitious toady, a boastful Aryan, Julius Schlesinger, is given the order by authorities to remove the statue of the Jewish composer Felix Mendelssohn from the roof of Prague's concert hall. Afraid of heights, Schlesinger hires workers who then trudge around the roof listlessly, dragging a thick rope with a noose in search of Mendelssohn's bust. "Well, boss," they say to Schlesinger, "we're all set so tell us which statue." Uncertain, he suggests that the head-hunters look for a plaque with the word "Men-dels-sohn." There are no plaques, however. Schlesinger, who has taken a course on "racial science," then instructs the workers to use a ruler and find the statue with the biggest nose. Had not the "science course" advised that the biggest noses belonged to Jews? One of the workers uses a folding ruler and takes measurements, puts the noose around the neck of one statue and is about to topple it when Schlesinger, sweating with terror, screams at him to stop: "My God, it was Wagner, the greatest German composer . . . one of the greats who had helped build the Third Reich. His portraits and plaster casts hung in every household." Schlesinger asks, "Did that statue really have the biggest nose?" "You bet, boss," says a worker, "the other noses were just regular."

Nietzsche first loved Wagner and extolled him as his Pater Seraphicus; less than a decade later he was to excoriate the fallen father so relentlessly as the archenemy and anti-Semite as to contribute in a major way to the derailment of his own mind. Wagner became for Nietzsche the standard by which, and against which, he turbulently defined himself. On balance, he tried to distance himself from Wagner's diseased attitude toward Jews. I have no doubt but that Wagner was the decisive experience in Nietzsche's life, and that Wagner helped to crystallize negatively and positively Nietzsche's own attitudes toward Judaism and the Jews. He felt himself as victimized by Richard and Cosima Wagner as the many Jews who were exploited and abused by them.

There was irony in Nietzsche's belief that the illegitimate Richard possessed Jewish ancestry. Wagner, nastily, was called the Rabbi of Bayreuth by some journalists by virtue of his biological father, Ludwig Geyer; Wagner did not refute the rumors and Nietzsche slyly abetted anti-Wagner sentiments. Although a case for Wagner's Jewish ancestry was categorically unverifiable, Cosima's was undeniable; Nietzsche scared Cosima in that regard. Nietzsche was not above playing fast and loose with genealogical facts in other cases as well, when it suited his purposes.

In his association with the Wagners during the Tribschen and early Bayreuth days, Nietzsche was well acquainted with their "trinity of phobias": Jesuits, journalists, and Jews. Nietzsche was, like the Wagners, to harbor nothing friendly toward Jesuits (Catholics euphemistically), but took note of the powers ascribed by Wagner to journalists, critics, and Jews and eventually concluded that such lords of the national and international press, along with other nominally powerful Jews, could be enlisted in his revolutionary cause.

Biographically, a discussion of Nietzsche and the Jews can be divided justifiably into periods "before and after Wagner." Pertinent to Nietzsche's attitudes toward Jews and Judaism, did he have any Jewish friends or acquaintances as live sources for his *opinions*—prejudgments or prejudices—as he called them? Did his knowledge come from books? From personal experiences? What role did he grant or attribute to Jews regarding contributions to German life and culture? These are some critical questions worthy of exploration because Nietzsche devotes hundreds of passages—published and in note form—to the cultural, historical, religious, and social roles of the Jews, ancient and modern. Nietzsche's views, to say the least, are far from simplistic, and we find in his thought higher praise and lesser depreciation of Jews than in most anti-Jewish and even Jewish camps of thought during the nineteenth and twentieth centuries.

The rabid Nazi-advocate Curt von Westernhagen in his book *Nietzsche, Juden, Antijuden* (Weimar, 1936) ominously gloated that the day of reckoning had come: "the problem of Jewry is for us no longer a problem"; but the time had also come to expose the "defective personality of Nietzsche whose inordinate tributes for, and espousal of, Jews had caused him to depart from the Germanic principles enunciated by Meister Richard Wagner." The equally loyal Nazi professor Alfred Bäumler blamed the influence of Jews, namely, Dr. Paul Rée and Lou Salomé, for Nietzsche's aberrations. It didn't matter that Lou was not Jewish. The game of identifying people as Jewish was arbitrarily played by anti-Jews as well as by Nietzsche himself. Bäumler saw in Nietzsche's writings the prophetic heralding of the Führer Hitler.

In the Jewish camp, we find similar division of opinion in praise and

blame of Nietzsche. At the turn of the century the influential Jewish cultural spokesman Achad Ha-am deplored the alleged anti-Jewish Aryan-
isms of Nietzsche and exhorted Jews not to become young Nietzscheans.
"Jews," said Ha-am, "don't need the Zarathustrian super-man; Jewish tradition already has its ideal of the Zaddick, the righteous man for whose
sake the entire world has been created." At the other extreme, a decidedly unequivocal encomium comes from a recent and noted Hebrew
scholar, Professor Jacob Golomb of the Hebrew University of Jerusalem,
who esteems Nietzsche as a "philohellenic thinker, but more importantly
as a great philo-Semitic writer with a profound sympathy for, and
empathy with, the Jewish people."[1]

And we need to take note of what was said by Nietzsche's most reli-
able friend, protector, and Basel colleague, the church historian Franz
Overbeck. He and Nietzsche, Overbeck claimed, looked upon endemic
anti-Semitism with disfavor, "but . . . Nietzsche's slight dose of anti-
Semitism was not incompatible with philo-Semitism. When Nietzsche
speaks frankly about Jews his judgments far exceed any anti-Semitic
polemics in harshness."

At one point, Overbeck further suggested that Nietzsche's views constituted a kind of civilized anti-anti-Semitic reaction and that Nietzsche's fierce attacks on Christianity were predominantly grounded in
anti-Semitic sentiments. (Here we have an interesting nineteenth-century dilemma: Jews were routinely criticized for not accepting Christianity while Nietzsche loaded opprobrium on the Jews of antiquity for
having given birth to Christianity.)

The extremes of attribution to Nietzsche of ideas that express "philo-
Semitism" or shades of "anti-Semitism"—active or residually passive—
are matched by a more balanced position to which I subscribe and that
was first succinctly outlined by Dr. Caesar Seligmann, a rabbi and leader
of the Jewish-German liberal reform movement, who was typical of those
German-Jews who anticipated an optimistic future with full social and
cultural emancipation. In an elegantly written and reasoned book *Judenthum und moderne Weltanschauung*, published in 1905, he concluded:
"Nietzsche and the Jews. Doubtlessly one of the most interesting chapters in all of cultural history. No thinker has so defamed and also exalted
[ancient and modern] Jews, at one and the same time, as has Nietzsche."
From the scarce writings by scholars and critics on that relationship, one

would not suspect Dr. Seligmann of being right. But, indeed, he is. And so it is time to turn to Nietzsche's knowledge of Jews and Judaism through personal and other sources.[2]

Before and during his association with Richard and Cosima, one ought to consider Nietzsche's contacts with such Jews as Frau Privy Councillor Sophie Ritschl, Jacob Bernays, Dr. Paul Rée, and Lilli Lehmann, the noted singer who, as an insider and outsider of the Wagner entourage, gives us glimpses of both Wagner and Nietzsche in her autobiography, *Mein Weg*.[3] And in the Wagner postlude, one should consider his relationships with Siegfried Lipiner, Paul Lanzky, Josef Paneth, Helen Zimmern, Georg Brandes, Catulle Mendès, and others, including Dr. Bettman who came to Nietzsche's assistance during the time of his mental collapse in 1889. Of this roll call there was only *one* knowledgeable and self-identifying Jew: Jacob Bernays. Nietzsche's search for a personal source that would satisfy his deep desire to come in touch with a Jew aware of his heritage that went back to the awesomeness of the primal Yahweh, the biblical kings and prophets, was largely frustrated. For the most part he met atrophied Jewish intellects and inheritors remote from the sources of ancient power Nietzsche thought residual in modern Jews.

Of the many things I find remarkable about Nietzsche is *not* so much the host of controversial ideas he mustered, but the extent of his *emancipation from* conventions that made possible the adoption of "untimely" moral judgments or provocative substitute prejudices. His early home environment was of a placid order; it reflected a long line of pietistic, evangelical Lutheran pastors on both parental sides, the early death of his pastor-father, a super-pious mother, his sister, Elisabeth, and perpetually sermonizing maiden aunts. If a Jew had dropped into their home, he or she would have been viewed as an alien from another planet. All told, it would not have been surprising if Nietzsche had accommodated himself to the racist climate of his times—but he did not; instead, he confronted the apostles of religious, racial, and ethnic hate and cleansing: German nationalism bordering on xenophobia that, like rabies, infected so much of the nineteenth-century political and cultural body.

Though it is too intricate an attempt to trace every detail of Nietzsche's emancipation, a decisive step in June of 1865 occurs in a letter to Elisabeth, in which he explains the subjectivity of religious faith and concludes that *no* religion has a monopoly on absolute credence or the promise of salvation. With that declaration, he abandoned any pursuit of Christian theology for which his family had destined him, and instead turned to classical history, philology, literature, and philosophy, especially Greek and Roman—eventually seeing Jewish antiquity from those perspectives. Nietzsche entered Bonn University in 1864 at age twenty. In letters home and to friends, he occasionally echoed petty anti-Jewish stereotypical slurs, but a basically decent instinct allowed him to respond in kind to the heady intellectual freedom, a superlative faculty, and academic curriculum. The university replaced his lost home, something that underlay his constant lament. Professor Friedrich Ritschl, the renowned philological scholar, became his father-mentor. But more importantly from a personal perspective, Frau Sophie Ritschl, who was born Jewish, took Nietzsche under motherly wings, along with other of her husband's favorite graduate students. Frau Ritschl was the daughter of Dr. Samuel Guttentag, chief physician of Breslau's Jewish Hospital. Her social graciousness—a model of what Nietzsche held dear—captivated the young man and allowed him to display a warm gallantry toward the older woman who also gratified his need to have an audience for his musicianship, of which he was excessively proud.

An earlier protégé of Professor Ritschl, Jacob Bernays, became associate professor and chief librarian at Bonn in 1865. Bernays was of Jewish origin and an authority on Jewish Hellenistic literature. His father, Isaac (Chacham) Bernays, was a leading rabbi of the Hamburg Jewish community and a rare scholar.[4] Jacob Bernays not only resisted temptations at "conversion" and the benefits it would bring; he passionately clung to his father's orthodox ways.[5] Bernays exerted quite an impact on the young Nietzsche, which has been largely neglected in Nietzsche biographies. His ideas on Dionysiac rites paved the way for Nietzsche's first work, *Die Geburt der Tragödie* (*The Birth of Tragedy*, 1872); and his class lectures and informal advice, on campus, led Nietzsche to the significant work of the historian Edward Gibbon (*The Decline and Fall of the Roman Empire*). In addition, Nietzsche reviewed some of Bernays's work in the *Zentralblatt*, a scholarly periodical, praising the distinction, sensitivity, and importance of the writing.[6] He must have noted, too, that Bernays's uncompromising pride in his Jewish heritage and self-imposed demands and philosophical integrity made him a lonely man, a heavy price to be paid for the orthodox life he chose.

Although it has become a commonplace recounting how Professor Ritschl gained the chair of classical philology at the University of Basel for his favorite, Nietzsche, it must be remembered that the same year Frau Sophie fatefully introduced Nietzsche to the music phenomenon of the time—Richard Wagner. The Ritschls had transferred to the University of Leipzig to which Nietzsche loyally followed. There they became friends with the professor of philology Hermann Brockhaus and his wife, Ottilie, Wagner's sister. The women arranged a private party and Frau Sophie introduced Nietzsche to Wagner. Always on the lookout for acolytes, Wagner quickly ensnared the willing young man. Nietzsche's ego had expanded to the bursting point with the ascension to a chair at Basel and the hospitality the Wagners offered him throughout the following years.

Nietzsche's subsequent periods of voluntary servitude are well recorded, but in a short while he styled himself as a Prometheus unchained when he burst the bonds of Wagner who had become his tormentor and had inflicted incurable wounds and a "deadly insult." In a poem called "On Richard Wagner," he lashed out at the Meister as one overpowered by Christianity and sinking helplessly, poisoned at the foot of the cross:

> For long, I watched this play so weirdly shaped,
> Breathing an air of prison, vault, and dread,
> With churchly fragrance, clouds of incense spread,
> and yet I found all strange, in terror gaped,
> But now I throw my fool's cap o'er my head
> For I escaped!

For much of their relationship, Wagner and Nietzsche wore polite masks beneath which, however, seethed irreconcilables. Wagner's pro-German and anti-Greek sentiments were leveled against the insubordinate professor of Greek, and it served to be a significant cause of Nietzsche's lasting anger.[7] Wagner's anti-Semitism was to be another; yet it was also a masking factor in some respects.

For public consumption it did not take long for word to leak out from the Wagner Mecca in Bayreuth that it was Nietzsche's close companion, "the smooth Israelite Dr. Paul Rée," who was responsible for Nietzsche's departure from Wagnerian orthodoxy. Seemingly lost upon everyone was the fact that the excoriated "Jew Rée" had *fought* for the Fatherland and was wounded at the front during the Franco-Prussian war, while the jingoist Richard Wagner was cheering on the troops to destroy Paris—all from the safety of his Bavarian estate, subsidized by King Ludwig. Paul Rée, of assimilated Jewish descent, was terrified of being identified as a Jew; he was the perfect example of how brutally German society could impose a stereotype upon Jews to the point of turning a person of Jewish descent to self-loathing. During his decade-long association with Rée beginning in 1872, Nietzsche discreetly—despite his curiosity—stayed away from the subject with Rée. The story of their intellectual and personal relationship has its roller coaster aspects from happiest to pathetic periods, but the stimulus to Nietzsche's thinking and philosophizing was deeply rewarding. From the first, Rée turned Nietzsche toward the French moralists, the aphoristic method, and positivism, which emerged with Nietzsche's book, *Menschliches, Allzumenschliches* (*Human, All-Too-Human*, 1878).

In mid-1877, Nietzsche was the recipient of an epistolary courtship by a Polish-Austrian poetaster, Siegfried Lipiner. Nietzsche more than hinted that he was interested in Lipiner's Jewish background, but settled for an extended correspondence when Lipiner awkwardly sidestepped his Jewish origins. Nietzsche read Lipiner's closet-drama *Der entfesselte Prometheus* (*Prometheus Unbound*) and, like the other hasty critics of the day, called Lipiner a "veritable genius." Lipiner, a leader within a Viennese student circle, brought him the welcome tribute of an admiring young group, but more intriguingly opened autobiographical insights whose pathological nature fascinated Nietzsche with their similarity to his own. It is very possible that Nietzsche retained some of the fantasy images projected by Lipiner's long poem in progress called "Echo," and used them in his later *Die fröhliche Wissenschaft* (*The Gay Science*, 1882) and *Zarathustra* (1883–85). Nietzsche toyed with Lipiner's epistolary effusions, promising him a personal audience that never materialized. He brushed Lipiner off, however, when he heard of similar overtures that poet was making to his archenemy Wagner. Lipiner's venerative, maudlin, and emotionally smothering letters taxed Nietzsche's patience. Though he was in dire need of admiration, at that time he generalized Lipiner's attitudes as characteristic of Jews: an insinuative, parasitical quality that lacked modesty and personal distance. His greatest distaste, though, was reserved for Lipiner's metaphysical Christology and apologia for Christianity. It may have been one of the irritants that turned Nietzsche to reflections collected in his next book, *Morgenröte* (*Daybreak*, 1881), in which Nietzsche launches an attack on Christianity's denial of life, its emphasis on original sin, and all the Pauline paraphernalia of guilt and redemption. Against such denials of Eros and life, he posed the ancient Jews' love of the earthly life and disinterest in any hereafter. He also attacked scholars trained in philological methodology for not applying it to biblical exegesis and the "higher criticism," condemning the cavalier use of the Old Testament Bible to falsely validate the New. Section 205 of *Daybreak* is representative of the hymnic tribute to Judaism and Jews that marked Nietzsche's occasional and aggressive espousals of them. At the same time, he raises certain stereotypical fears about Jews, while providing extenuating reasons for Jewish flaws and perceived dangers to their hosts. *Daybreak*'s hymn is typical of Nietzsche's mix of exaltation and denigration of Judaism and Jews.[8]

Eventfully, in 1882, Nietzsche met Louise von Salomé of French Huguenot extraction, a young Russian beauty with intellect to match. His emotional involvement became so fierce that he thought of her as his *Erbin und Fortdenkerin*, his intellectual heir and disciple. His mother thought that the dilemma of her Fritz would have to end either with marriage or with suicide. Neither occurred; instead, he wrote *Also Sprach Zarathustra*. Lou became a source of contention between Paul Rée and Nietzsche, and Nietzsche vituperatively broke with both, but ultimately begged them to forgive his egocentric outbursts when they left him abruptly to live platonically in Berlin. He felt their loss deeply because with no one else had he ever been able to speak of himself as candidly, naturally, and spontaneously. Although Nietzsche eventually wanted the world to know that ideologically he and Rée were often light years apart, he never railed at Rée as a Jew.[9] This is in contrast to his charge against Bernays as a "clever Jew" (1872) when the young Nietzsche heard reports that Bernays commented that *The Birth of Tragedy* contained many of *his* ideas, except in exaggerated form.

A Jew Nietzsche was particularly pleased to meet in December of 1883, while living in his philosopher's cave in Nice, the busy French city on the Riviera, was the Viennese scientist Josef Paneth, who had admired

Nietzsche's writings as a graduate student and participant in a Viennese reading circle. Paneth was a familial friend of Freud and kept him informed of his conversations with Nietzsche. Nietzsche sorely felt his own lack of knowledge in the natural sciences and had hoped to engage in university studies after his retirement from Basel in 1879. Nietzsche averred that in discovering Greek thought he also learned of and adopted their "Mysterien-Glaube"—a cultic belief in the eternal recurrence of all things. For this consuming idea, Nietzsche hoped to find validation in modern science. While Paneth proved no help in that regard, he did recommend readings, especially the work of Sir Francis Galton, on the subject of eugenics. Germinations of Nietzsche's ideas are found in notes for a projected work, *Die Unschuld des Werdens* (*The Innocence of Becoming*).

Paneth had felt the stings of anti-Semitism unleashed by the Viennese, who needed their Jews and their professionalism but at the same time loved to hate them. "Nietzsche," Paneth wrote home, possessed a refreshing independence and integrity in regard to religion; "absolutely and categorically he is free from any anti-Semitic tendency." Nietzsche's sister cut this sentence from the published version of this letter. The absence of anti-Semitism was a litmus test for tolerance and liberality and good will as far as most Jews—including the unaffiliated—were concerned. In turn, Nietzsche regarded Paneth as a desirable link with a group he thought to be influential Jewish-Viennese intellectuals. But again Nietzsche was frustrated. Although Paneth had no inferiority complex, as did Paul Rée, he was culturally assimilated and completely distanced from the traditional religious world of Judaism. On the other hand, he did not resort to the devious devices of the ambitious Viennese convert to Catholicism, Gustav Mahler, who in a letter advised his Jewish friend Oskar Fried, also an orchestra director, to find a modus vivendi with "the anti-Semitic wretches, since we can do nothing about our being Jewish, our chief mistake."

Again, Nietzsche was frustrated that he was able to gain no knowledge of Jewish matters he was consistently curious about from Jews themselves. Paneth even rejected the idea of a revived Jewish state in Zionist terms, which Nietzsche seemed to favor, possibly envisioning a restoration of that ancient Israel he had admired in parts of the Old Testament—the nobility of kings, prophets, and warriors. Nietzsche was disappointed in Paneth's unresponsiveness politically and culturally. Their parting, however, was most amicable as Paneth returned to Vienna in May 1884, and Nietzsche retained a good impression of the vigorous mind and adaptability of Jews in contemporary circumstances.

Almost simultaneously with the loss of Dr. Paneth's company, another Jew, Paul Lanzky, ambled into Nietzsche's ken, a person who like Rée completely avoided insights into his Jewish origins (but who fifty years later was forcibly reminded of it by Mussolini). Lanzky was a strange person who combined scholarly pursuits, belles-lettres, and modest poetic talents and placed himself at the service of Nietzsche, calling him "Meister." That honorific title excited the philosopher as it gave him the illusion of receiving the tributes Wagner had formerly received from his courtiers. Lanzky was as protective of Nietzsche as Rée had formerly been, providing Nietzsche with companionship on demand or isolation as needed, but also embarrassment on two counts: Lanzky could be too motherly, something that Nietzsche detested as pity born of condescension, and he intruded into Nietzsche's privacy which consisted of physical and environmental bleakness. Also, Lanzky did not hide the inspiration he drew from Nietzsche's works and Nietzsche began to feel that Lanzky's published poetry parodied his own philosophy and nested parasitically within it. Again, he did not directly attribute Lanzky's personality to any Jewish traits, but, one day, he ordered Lanzky to stay away, as by this time he had similarly alienated most of his remaining friends.

This parting, too, was made easier by the sudden ego-lifting connection he established early in 1887 with the monarchical critic Georg Brandes, who enjoyed a pan-European reputation. Brandes maintained that the content of a philosophical book—whether right or wrong—was of lesser concern than the value of the man behind the book. *Does he deserve to be studied and contested?* Further, said Brandes, "No mature reader studies Nietzsche to adopt his opinions and even less to propagate them." From that perspective, Brandes regarded Nietzsche as the most vital and original contemporary thinker whose approach he called "aristocratic radicalism." Nietzsche was incensed by his sister's derogation of Brandes and replied acerbically that "naturally" Brandes was a foreigner and a Jew of intelligence who paid him serious attention. Brandes was no sentimental flatterer (as Lipiner and Lanzky had been), but mixed praise with undisguised social and political criticism of Nietzsche's philosophies and works, including *Jenseits von Gut und Böse* (*Beyond Good and Evil*,

1886) and *Zur Genealogie der Moral* (*The Genealogy of Morals*, 1887). Nietzsche repressed his usual irritability and basked in Brandes's flattery. Some of the unconscious sublimation, I believe, erupted into the harshest criticisms Nietzsche was to make of Jews and Judaism in one of his latest works, hidden from Brandes, part of a polemic in progress and titled *Der Antichrist*.

Brandes made it easy for Nietzsche to identify with him as an iconoclast and as a designated "Jewish" gadfly to his countrymen, as he wrote Nietzsche: "I am glad you find in me something serviceable to yourself. For the last four years I have been the most detested man in Scandinavia."[10]

Nietzsche well agreed with Brandes about the "hideous uniformity" existing in German life and institutions. As for contributing to Nietzsche's meager store of knowledge about Jews and Judaism, Brandes as an unaffiliated, marginal, and disinterested Jew left Nietzsche unsatisfied.[11] Even so, Brandes, an influential professor at the University of Copenhagen in Denmark, was responsible for Nietzsche's initial popularity. He started giving lectures on Nietzsche's philosophy shortly before Nietzsche's final breakdown.

When the peripatetic Nietzsche sought refuge from turmoil and retreated to Sils-Maria in the high mountains of the Swiss Engadine (in the late 1880s), he particularly enjoyed the company of Miss Helen Zimmern, "naturally, a Jew," whom he had met as early as his Wagner days. A decade earlier he had written his sister of the well-being he enjoyed there: freed from pain and stimulated to write: "It is as if I were in the Promised Land." He also wished to find his ultimate resting place there. God denied Moses his most fervent wish just as Lisbeth denied her brother's request; she was to do with his body and writings as she pleased: he was not buried at the "rock of Zarathustra's revelation" at Sils-Maria, but next to Pastor Nietzsche in back of the parsonage at Röcken.

In Sils-Maria, which he was fated to see for the last time, the philosopher who had enjoined Zarathustra's followers to take a whip when "going to women" enjoyed the sociability of a number of regular visitors to the town. Some were women of title as he unfailingly informed his correspondents. Among the women was Helen Zimmern. It would not have surprised Nietzsche were he to know that she eventually became one of his best translators. He spared no praise of her and wanted the "flatland Germans," especially his anti-Semitic sister, to know that Miss

Zimmern was at any rate, "not an Englishwoman but a sensible, intellectual Jew." Nietzsche's praise is all the more astonishing since Zimmern belonged to the phalanx of women's rights advocates intensely disliked by Nietzsche, Brandes, and Strindberg with whom Nietzsche had brief correspondence. Nietzsche's calculated attention to Helen Zimmern as a Jew has been overlooked by all biographer-critics.[12]

Exuberance and alternating paranoid depression marked Nietzsche's states of mind after descending from Sils-Maria to Turin. By September 1888, Nietzsche had driven himself to astonishing productivity within a short time: *The Wagner Case* and a compilation of previous essays for *Nietzsche Contra Wagner, Twilight of the Idols, The Antichrist*, and the rounding out of his baroque-expressionistic *Dithyrambs of Dionysus*. Among his rapidly shifting self-stylizations, he had seen himself as a haunted exile, an Oedipus yearning for a daughter like the young, spirited Antigone, and other martyred figures like the counterpoint figures of Jesus and Dionysus.

Nietzsche's psychological, philosophical, and polemical approaches were antipodal, increasingly so toward his later works. Jews and Judaism are praised, sometimes to the point of exaltation, and castigated, at times to the extreme of denigration. On the one hand, for instance, Nietzsche sees Jews as being the moral genius among nations; on the other, they suffer from delusions of grandeur and are the most curious and worst "Volk" upon this earth; "impertinent goodness is a phenomenon I have observed among Jews, Jews possess the art of adaptability and integration; there is the danger of the Jewish soul that sponge-like nests itself in others; they possess commendable filial piety, to wit, honoring father and mother; they possess dangerous traits [*Eigenschaften*]; they consider themselves the elect and are the best haters; anti-Semites cannot forgive them their spirituality; the Jew is a born man of letters, the actual lord of the European press and one who uses his powers with an actor's adroitness. And so bouquets and brickbats, praise of Jews and caterings to the fears of non-Jews, renegades, and socialist self-haters (like Ferdinand Lassalle and Karl Marx) proliferate with abandon . . ." (*UW*, 11, 994).

Jews, like all others, Nietzsche implied, can only be understood in terms of their inner contradictions and external opponents. Human conceptualizations come about through recognition of the relationship between opposites: good, evil; weak, strong. At times word-ideas harbor their opposites, with antithetical double meanings: *altus* means high and deep; *sacer*, holy and accursed.[13] Nietzsche brilliantly formulates the idea that things evolve from their opposites and ideas from their opposites and from comparisons; this is a cultural and not a biologically determined evolution, so that good evolves from evil, suggesting that the *Übermensch* (the superior man) may evolve from a present woefully deficient species of man.

Nietzsche was reaching the peak of his speculative powers when his world began to fall apart and he sank into the delusion that he had the fate of mankind in his hands in Turin during the last months of 1888. In uncanny fashion, the convergence with Jews in Nietzsche's life continued during his collapse into madness. He dedicated his last poems and "transmitted" his work to Catulle Mendès, a Jewish novelist, poet, and critic. And it was a Jewish person—now accurately identified as Dr. Bettman—who saved Nietzsche from an Italian asylum and helped guide him back to Switzerland and Germany where, ultimately, he was to rest in the arms of his mother, Franziska, who was convinced that her son had been "punished by God." All her life she had awaited the return of her prodigal child, a son who proclaimed himself a voluntary exile and wandering fugitive in search of a homeland, a figure akin to the Jew caught in a precipitous Diaspora, a prophet not heeded in his own country and who proclaimed the messianic *Übermensch* within a dynamic cosmos of eternally recurring events and time.

The poet W. B. Yeats once said, "I have often had the fancy that if there is some one myth for every man, which, if we but knew it would make us understand all he did and thought." I think that the Nietzsche "myth," in Yeats's sense, has a number of components: a mythical return to the earliest shelter of home—the Paradise quest; a snob striving for the regal, the noble that burgeoned into anti-democratic and grandiose elitist postures; the Miniver Cheevy complex—born too late, "untimely" in his own time, yearning for the role and age of the Greek philosopher attended by disciples and domestic slaves; the Nietzsche who aimed at transcending a Christian inheritance and the anti-Judaic legacy within; and, finally, the overcoming of the fatal fathers: the "magician-sorcerer" Richard Wagner, the spellbinding "Papa" Schopenhauer, the domineering mentor Ritschl, and the haunting retributive ghost of his biological pastor-father, Karl Ludwig, leading to the ultimate declination of the death of the greatest father: God. To chart Nietzsche's failures and successes, especially in his attitudes toward Judaism and Jews—ancient and contemporaneous—one must avoid gerrymandering his biography, correspondence, and writings, and start again with renewed perspectives from the beginnings at Röcken. "To be human," Nietzsche said, "means to seek origins."

Postscript: "Nietzsche's books acquired power; his name became a slogan. And yet, future generations will argue if his having lived will be our blessing or our curse."—Ferdinand Avenarius (Obituary in the *Kunstwart* periodical, 1890)

NOTES

1. Jacob Golomb, "Nietzsche's Judaism of Power," *Revue des études juives* 146–47 (July–December 1988): 385.

2. See ibid., pp. 353–85; Michael Duffy and Willard Mittelman, "Nietzsche's Attitudes toward the Jews," *Journal of the History of Ideas* 49 (1988): 301–17; Weaver Santaniello, *Nietzsche, God, and the Jews* (Albany: SUNY Press, 1994); and Robert C. Holub, "Nietzsche and the Jewish Question," *New German Critique* 66 (Fall 1995): 94–121, for recent discussions and textual analysis. Golomb describes Nietzsche as a "philohellenic thinker, but more importantly as a great philo-Semitic writer with a profound sympathy for, and empathy with, the Jewish people" (p. 35). Duffy and Mittelman conclude that Nietzsche strongly and consistently opposes anti-Semitism, and that "contemporary Christianity and contemporary anti-Semitism represent the vengeful ones who would prevent the *new* valuation by holding down the Jews" (p. 315). Santaniello highlights Nietzsche's consistent opposition to anti-Semitism (especially *Christian anti-Semitism*), showing how Nietzsche's (sometimes negative) critique of Judaism is primarily directed toward those elements giving rise to the offspring religion (Christianity). And Holub strongly emphasizes a historical approach to anti-Semitism specific to the 1880s, while holding that Nietzsche was free of racial prejudice, though ambivalent toward Judaism and even Jews. Mandel agrees with these thinkers that Nietzsche was not an anti-Semite; that is, Nietzsche did not support persecution of Jews—politically or otherwise; he opposed nineteenth-century racism and nationalism, and on a personal level, he did not regard the Jewish people with contempt. As Mandel shows, Nietzsche often regards the Jews with much respect and was drawn to many different aspects of

Jewish Scripture and culture, including the awesome power of the ancient Hebrews. However, because Nietzsche harshly criticizes certain aspects of Judaism—especially priestly Judaism (and its relationship to Christianity)—and because he aped some of Wagner's stereotypical slurs against Jews (especially in his early years), he did not, in Mandel's view, completely free himself from denigrative assumptions. Thus, Mandel does not regard Nietzsche as "philo-Semitic." All the writers mentioned above are aware of Nietzsche's complex stance toward the history of Judaism and Jews, and his opposition to German nationalism and anti-Jewish racism. Part of the difficulty of fitting Nietzsche into any one category is his novelty; thus, Golomb's careful qualification: "Should we yield to the present inclination to put *labels* [emphasis mine] on great men of spirit . . . we would label Nietzsche . . . as a great philo-Semitic thinker." Most of the erroneous charges against Nietzsche as an "anti-Semite" are due, of course, to the Nazi abuse of his writings in the 1930s and '40s and the popular conception that resulted from World War II propaganda. (Ed.)

But, as the wise old Greeks were fond of pointing out, "on the other hand," we have the judgment of Max Dimont, the author of the world-renowned *Jews, God, and History*:

> A whole school of apologists has recently arisen, making Nietzsche the ethical successor to the humanists. Nietzsche, however, with all due regard for his nervous, brilliant prose, is the "father" of Nazism, and his ethic is not the ethic of Torah and Testament, but the limited code of the Nazi. . . . His philosophy led, indeed, to a complete defiance of Christianity, to a complete reversal of teachings of Gospel and Decalogue. His works, the cornerstone of the Nazi state, were written during the decade before his insanity, and he died insane. It may be that he did not advocate what he wrote, but that he foresaw with the clarity of a prophet the morality of the new age ahead.

3. Lilli Lehmann (1848–1929), *Mein Weg* (Leipzig: Hirzel, 1913).

4. Isaac Bernays was also an ancestor of Freud's wife, Martha Bernays.

5. Jacob Bernays was even more orthodox than his father and believed that "Judaism would assume world-historic importance in the future, while Christianity proves itself to be too injurious with its accessories and therefore ephemeral." See Wilhelm Erman, *Geschichte der Bonner Universitätsbibliothek, 1818–1901* (Halle, S. A.: J. E. Karras, 1919), p. 207.

6. Among the works that gained a reputation for Bernays were his treatises on, and attempted reconstructions of, Aristotle's lost theory of comedy and discourse on dramatic tragedy. Bernays understood *katharsis* to be a medical term denoting the removal of physical impurities and not something signifying moral

purgation. In essence, as the historian Arnaldo Momigliano emphatically noted, "Bernays connected the cathartic process with the ecstatic practices of the Dionysiac rites. The way was open for Nietzsche—namely for his revaluative study, in *The Birth of Tragedy.*" Cf. Arnaldo Momigliano, *Jacob Bernays* (Amsterdam/London: North-Holland Publishing Co., 1969), p. 17; and Jacob Bernays, *Zwei Abhandlungen über die aristotelische Theorie des Drama* (1857; Darmstadt: Wissenschaftliche Buchhandlung, 1968).

7. An entry in Wagner's private diaries called *Das Braune Buch* (*The Brown Book*) showed him to be at complete variance with Nietzsche's admiration for the Greeks (after Nietzsche read to the Wagners in April 1873 from his monograph *The Tragic Age of the Greeks*). Wagner wrote in his defense of German culture: "What we can never—or in any language—understand about the Greek way, and what completely separates us from them, for instance, is their love—in—pederasty." Richard Wagner, *Das Braune Buch* (Zurich: Atlantis, 1975), April 1873 entry. One should be suspicious of Wagner's aggressive exhibition of masculinity; it hid a fear of homoerotic leanings—the fear of "the hidden sin"—and we note the festive male bondings in his operas and his vocal admiration of the young King Ludwig's beauty.

8. Cf. especially M, 205, 84.

9. Any retraction of praise for Rée's work or rejection of it had more to do with Nietzsche's inclination, by and large, to disguise, void, or minimize sources of borrowings and his intellectual indebtedness, as in the case of David F. Strauss, Ralph Waldo Emerson, and Edward Gibbon, among others.

10. Brandes continues: "Every day the papers rage against me, especially since my last long quarrel with Björnson, in which the German papers all took part against me. I dare say, you know his absurd play, *A Gauntlet,* his propaganda for male virginity and his covenant with the spokeswomen of 'the demand for equality in morals.' . . . In Sweden these insane women have formed great leagues in which they vow 'only to marry virgin men.' . . . I have read the three books of yours. . . . You are without doubt the most suggestive of all German writers" (letter, January 30, 1888). Brandes was too hard on Norwegian writer Björnstjerne Björnson (1832–1910), a Nobel Prize recipient. The versatile public figure, after all, spoke out against crippling religious and political dogmas and defended Alfred Dreyfus (in the infamous Dreyfus Affair) against the most vicious anti-Semitic attacks launched on the French scene.

11. Georg Brandes's "An Essay on Aristocratic Radicalism" and the Brandes-Nietzsche correspondence are contained in his *Friedrich Nietzsche,* trans. A. G. Chater (London: Heinemann, 1914). This volume has been utilized for my discussions along with Brandes's *Creative Spirits of the Nineteenth Century,* trans. R. B. Anderson (New York: Crowell, 1923).

12. The biographies by Walter Kaufmann and Ronald Hayman largely ignore this woman; Curt Janz pays her due tribute as does Franz Overbeck in his recollections published in condensed form in the *Neue Deutsche Rundschau* in 1906. Rarely mentioned as well is that despite his reputed misogyny, Nietzsche sided with Burckhardt *against* a majority of Basel University male colleagues in a failed test case over admission of females to graduate studies.

13. Such ideas were in circulation through the translated works of the Scots philosopher Alexander Bain (ideas arise through comparison), Karl Abel's monograph, *The Antithetical Sense of Primal Words,* and books by Rudolf Kleinpaul. Dr. Kleinpaul, who was to become the father of semiology, was a Leipzig University classmate and friend of Nietzsche. Freud expressed his indebtedness to all these persons for his dream interpretations and that of jokes. Although Nietzsche did not say so, his notions imply that the Jewish-anti-Semite and the Wagner kind evolved in opposition to what they chose to identify as "Jewish."

Nietzsche made the containment (and relationship) of opposites and contrasts a cornerstone of his thinking: ". . . As it did two thousand years ago, the philosophical question still persists as to how something can originate from its opposite [*Gegensatz*]; for instance, the rational from the irrational, the sentient from the inert [the organic from the inorganic], logic from illogic, disinterested viewing from greedy desiring, as well as altruism. . . . Metaphysical philosophy has ended these difficulties by denying the origin of one from the real other and assuming a supernatural source. Historical philosophy says that no longer are there opposites. Strictly speaking neither are there selfless actions [*unegoistisches Handeln*] nor a completely disinterested sideline observing—both are merely sublimations [*Sublimierungen*] in which the basic element appears in quick passing (*Human, All-Too-Human,* I, 1).

1

Prophecy at Röcken

RÖCKEN

Dear to Pastor Karl Ludwig Nietzsche's heart were three gifts of divine and monarchical favor: a family line of Lutheran clerics, the benevolence of his royal patron, and a first son. Somehow, Prussia's King Friedrich Wilhelm IV had taken note of Karl Ludwig, a tutor in the household of the Duke of Altenburg, and appointed him pastor of the small Saxony village of Röcken. Then, born to the pastor and his young wife, Franziska, was a son whose birthday coincided with the king's. No event could have augured better for the boy's future, and the pastor made several entries in the family's baptismal churchbook: Friedrich Wilhelm Nietzsche, son, born October 15 [1844]; baptism, October 24; Luke 1:66.

The pastor's christening speech brimmed with joy and devout thanks for "the most beatific moment of my life, sacrosanct work blessed in the name of the Lord to whom I dedicate my child in honor of my royal patron." Karl Ludwig envisioned a great future for his son, with distinctions that would go far beyond those ecclesiastical honors bestowed on himself by the king. He projected his son's role as that of John the Baptist heralding the advent of Jesus. The pastor's untimely death five years later, in 1849, was to spare him a confrontation with his mature son's self-arrogated titles of Antichrist and supreme Immoralist.

The New Testament passages in Luke referred to in Pastor Nietzsche's baptismal dedication have uncanny ramifications. The Gospel foretells the coming of Jesus the Messiah, and is a doubling of the Old Testament's prophecy of Israel's imminent Redeemer. Yet, for Friedrich Nietzsche, the *Übermensch*—no theological figure—was instead chosen to have a redemptive role for humankind. In addition, whereas Pastor Nietzsche compared his son's role with that of John the Baptist, Nietzsche, in turn, would later compare his father to Zechariah.

In Luke, the glad tidings concerning the births of Jesus and John are conveyed: The angel Gabriel tells the righteous Judaean priest Zechariah that his elder and barren wife, Elizabeth, will bear a son, John; months later, Gabriel also announces to the Virgin Mary that through the Holy Spirit she will bear the Son of God, Jesus. Supernaturally inspired, Elizabeth named their son; and when the peasant people of Judaea asked, "What will the child be? For the hand of the Lord was with him," his father Zechariah prophesied: "Blessed be the Lord God of Israel, for he has visited and redeemed his people . . . and you, child [John], will be called the prophet of the Most High; for you will go before the Lord to prepare his ways, to give knowledge of salvation to his peoples in forgiveness of their sins. . . ." (Luke 1 and 2).

Just how well Nietzsche knew the words of Luke and the attributions of his father's hopes for continuing the clerical lineage is seen in a passage intended for his last testamentary book, *Ecce Homo*, where he overtly compared his father—or his father's self-image—with the priest-prophet Zechariah. Both Zechariah and Pastor Nietzsche preached: one to the peasants of Judaea and the other to the peasants of Röcken. Nietzsche writes: "I consider it a great privilege to have had such a father: the peasants for whom he preached . . . said of him that this is what an angel must well have looked like. . . ."[1]

The Luke citation was typical of the ones Christian theologians used to create linkages, equations, and identities between the misnamed "Old" and "New" Testaments to foretell the coming of a king-Messiah, Jesus. This was a practice Nietzsche was to condemn as unphilological and his preference was with the Old Testament, for aesthetic reasons as well. Luke's rendering is bare bones, but here is the Old Testament Zechariah:

Rejoice greatly, O daughter of Zion! . . . Lo your King comes to you; triumphant and victorious is he, humble and riding on a donkey . . . on that day his feet shall stand on the Mount of Olives. (Zech. 14:14f.)

The minor post-exilic prophet Zechariah preached in the style of Ezekiel, prophesying the restoration of the nation of Israel and the advent of the Messiah.[2] Similarly, there are passages in Nietzsche's writings about Jews that correspond to the tone and message of the ancient preacher. For instance, in Zechariah's prophecy, the high priest is wearing a horned helmet symbolic of the Lord's weapon to be raised against those who have scattered Judah. It is related that the Lord will inscribe a stone tablet to reestablish Joshua and the Jews in their land. Zechariah's visions are apocalyptic and Edenic, the Lord is beyond good and evil: he is Lord who purposes evil when provoked and is pitiless, but nonetheless shows compassion when so moved. Satan and the angels stand at his side as in the story of Job.

Regarding Hebrew Scripture, Nietzsche early on absorbed its images and magic, its symbolism, hortatory language, and fiery pictorializations. Zechariah's graphic dream sequences and many supernatural visitations through dreams; the priestly-oracular and hallucinatory; the autosuggestions; parables, abstractions, and riddles abound: What are the four chariots, coming from between two bronze mountains? The seven lamps with seven lips? Answer: the seven eyes of God, ranging over the earth. The "covenant" will be restored and Gentiles will cling to the robe of a Jew, saying, "we have heard that God is with you" (8:20). Seraphim and idols are to be destroyed, "so that they shall be remembered no more" (13:2) on the day of Israel's renewal. Such were the literary features of Old Testament Jewry that Nietzsche eventually came to extol and cherish beginning with his *Human, All-Too-Human* (1878). Even so, he would also be intent on destroying the "old tablets" and substituting Zarathustra's. It is the fierce tribal God Yahweh—awe-inspiring and pitiless—that Nietzsche was to admire and to emulate in eradicating idols he defined as ossified ideals.

NIETZKY ANCESTRY

With more than a fair share of vanity, the immediate Nietzsche family and their relatives subscribed to the fiction that their ancestry dated back to Polish nobility with variations on the name Nietzky. It was a compensatory fantasy for their genteel middle-class status, and Franziska was ever priming her son and daughter to strive upward in associating with people who were "vornehm," of good breeding and social standing. Among forebears of recent vintage, however, they could point to only one distinguished person—Friedrich August Ludwig Nietzsche. In 1817, the University of Königsberg awarded him a doctorate in theology; subsequently he rose high in the educational and religious bureaucracy as a staunch public advocate of the monarchy and citizens' duty to it, condemning such plebeian subversions as the French Revolution. His grandson, Friedrich, was to agree by condemning the Revolution as a priestly-Judaean victory.[3] The doctor of theology gained a reputation for incisive intelligence, and his book *Gamaliel, or the Everlasting Survival of Christianity* (Leipzig, 1796) defended and explained the theological basis of Christianity with stylistic vigor.[4]

In view of Nietzsche's concern with ancestry it is fair to assume that he knew his grandfather's work. In fact, F. A. August Nietzsche's wife, the widowed Erdmuthe (1778–1856), was the grandmother who played a dominant role in the young Nietzsche's upbringing at Naumburg; he was nicknamed "Fritz" after a son by her first marriage. That son died at the age of two, just as did Nietzsche's brother, Josef. To add to the coincidences that gave Nietzsche the feeling of *déjà vu* or recurrence, grandmother Erdmuthe's father (Pastor Krause) died when she was four years old, nearly the same age as Nietzsche at the death of his own father.

The *Gamaliel* book has engaged the attention of few Nietzsche biographers—and its dogmatics do not need any special attention here. But the title figure should give one pause because Gamaliel (like Zechariah) appears in the Old and New Testaments, and one of his disciples, the apostle Paul, was to suffer scorching condemnation by Nietzsche. Gamaliel was a grandson of the famous Rabbi Hillel, a liberal among Pharisee leaders. As we are given to understand in Acts, Paul addressed fellow Jerusalemites autobiographically: "I am a Jew, born at Tarsus in Cilicia, but brought up in this city at the feet of Gamaliel and educated according to the strict manner of the law of our fathers and of Gamaliel" (5:34f.; 22:3). It is clear that Gamaliel was Paul's preceptor and it was precisely Paul against whom Nietzsche discharged his resentment as the "inventor" of Christianity. In effect, Nietzsche was to break decisively with the theology of his distinguished forebear and grandfather.

In order to keep what he regarded as "recollections of myself" for later use, Nietzsche resolved to write a diary. He began in 1856 when he was twelve years old and continued in fragmentary fashion until 1869 when he received the call to a university chair of classical philology and as a gymnasium teacher of Greek, at Basel, Switzerland. The main thematic and unifying elements of the autobiographical and repetitious fragments consist of lamentations for losses: his father, his brother, his home, the loss of sexual innocence; domestic feminine suffocations; surrogate father figures. Notably, they contain a record of unsettling nightmarish dreams. The religious and ideological underside of his thinking, however, was contained in poems he called "terrible" and in various confidential letters. All these give us a chart of his antipodal swing from saccharine religiosity to harsh ideological rebellion, from piety to impiety, from provincialism to worldly perspectivism. They finally reveal the rejection of Christian theology and Judaic monotheism as Nietzsche moved ideologically and emotionally to remove worlds of belief and to explore primitive Yahwehism and Greek paganism.

Although life with his father was short, the memory of those five years pursued Nietzsche into his last writings. In fact, from early on, the father became a Damonion, an inner voice, as it were, possessed by prophets (Hebrew, Christian, and Greek), madmen, or poets. Pastor Karl Ludwig liked having his "little friend" Fritz in his studio and fostered his moody child's inclinations to hear improvisatory music on the piano. Music, composing, always remained a deep emotional necessity for Nietzsche.

The antimonarchical events and revolutions of 1848, political unrest and types of anti-Christian manifestations caused Pastor Nietzsche "all kinds of peculiar visions." But most troubling was a condition the family did not want to accept as progressive brain disease to which the pastor lingeringly succumbed on July 27, 1849. The pastor had to cease giving Fritz lessons when his speech lost coherence and his eyes rolled frighteningly. Those last days profoundly depressed the child's imagination and memories. Karl Ludwig's death, at age thirty-six, shattered his twenty-three-year-old wife and widow, Franziska Oehler Nietzsche. According to Nietzsche's younger sister, Elisabeth, although her mother was attractively marriageable, Franziska was more akin to a stern older sister to both of her youngsters. Nietzsche biographer Carl Janz believes that Fritz was grateful for his mother's refusal to remarry. But her disinclination, evidently, was pathologically determined. Her own diary entries speak of her aim to keep alive a truly indissoluble union with "the man of my heart" into eternity, a mystical eternal continuation of marriage: "Yes, dear God, let me become better and more devout from day to day, so that I may enjoy the delight of a heavenly reunion, my only consolation."[5]

In return for her devotion, Franziska expected Karl Ludwig to intercede for his earthly family and to provide guidance from on high. During times of stress, it was not unusual for her to closet herself in order to converse with her deceased husband.

A tragedy that struck almost as hard as the death of his father was the totally unexpected death a year later of a younger brother he loved: Josef died of teething cramps in January 1850. With chilling, Gothic detail, Nietzsche later was to claim recollection of a premonitory dream he had the night before Josef's death:

> ... I heard the sounds of the church-organ, as if at a burial. When I noticed what the cause was, there suddenly appeared a grave and out of it emerged my father in a death-shroud. He hurried into the church and soon returned with an infant in his arms. The mound of the grave opened; he stepped into it and the cover once again sank back over the opening. At the same time the upsounding organ tones subsided and I awoke. The day after, little Josef became unwell, had cramps, and died in several hours. Our anguish was immense. My dream fulfilled itself completely.[6]

In the absence of documentation, we do not know if this was invented retrospectively or was the vague recollection of an anticipatory anxiety-dream triggered by the earlier traumatic loss of his father.

We have a clue also that as a boy Nietzsche was overwhelmed by his mother's intense grief and imitated it unconsciously. According to Franziska's diary entries—which resembled common folklore superstitions—she believed that her husband had returned from the supernatural world to fetch their twenty-two-month-old son, Josef. Fritz's dream had the same ghostly visualizations; Karl Ludwig was transformed literally by Nietzsche into Hamlet's father-ghost, a presence that remained with Nietzsche in varieties of demonic outer and inner shapes. Here was the onset of pathological—not theological—imaginings he himself termed the shadow, the Doppelgänger, the *tertium quid;* the dialogic and prophetic voice within and without; the voice that in 1882 announced to him the revelation of "the eternal return."

THE MOVE TO NAUMBURG

The loss of his paternal home in Röcken hurt terribly, and even here the deceased played an uncanny role in the family's future. Before he died, Karl Ludwig expressed the wish that Franziska, like the biblical Ruth protected by the God of Israel during the days of the Judges, return to her husband's people. More prosaically, Karl Ludwig had judged his mother-in-law to be too worldly and an altogether common woman. Leaving Röcken, the imaged Eden, was the beginning of Nietzsche's homelessness, a rootlessness he associated with the wandering Jew as the family moved to the city of "philistine virtuousness": Naumburg.

Karl Ludwig had anticipated that under the watchful female eyes of *his* seventy-year-old mother, Erdmuthe, and his spinster sisters Rosalie and Auguste, who were in their thirties, Fritz's upbringing would be narrowly religious and thus in keeping with the late pastor's habits of mind and living. What, in fact, did he bequeath to his son? A correct bearing, fastidiousness in manners, an essential shyness, and a pose that hid a deep insecurity toward women. The pastor's enjoinders, echoed by the family, aimed for upward striving and "nobility." Inoculated with the germs of snobbery, Nietzsche was to divide people into classes who were either "vornehm"—refined, aristocratic, well-bred—or "pobelhaft"—belonging to the crude herd, of the mob; his literary models were Shakespeare's nobles and their contempt for the plebeians.

At Naumburg, Fritz and his family were fortunate to be accepted by good society, without condescension, and to have his musical and academic talents furthered. To all appearances he acted like the "little pastor" he was nicknamed by classmates, making the proper obeisances to religious and social conventions through his school days to 1858, and then through the rigorous six-year Pforta: a prestigious, elitist, Lutheran prep school he attended on a scholarship. There was an underside to Fritz's life: he became a master at masking; and this facility is important because he came to attribute to the Jews masks and masking as major attributes of their status as survivors and as dissimulators, like himself: "I found it really impossible to feel at home any place other [than Röcken]. To part from a village where one has experienced much happiness and pain, and to leave the dear graves of one's father and little brother . . . (autobiographical fragment, 1858).

The strong element of Nietzsche's introversion was perpetuated in fantasies and dreams. He found similarities in Dostoevsky's novel *The Possessed* (sometimes translated as *The Devils*), which he read twenty-eight years after leaving Röcken. Nietzsche attributes his own problems to the same feelings of uprootedness displayed by the novel's protagonist, Stavrogin, the son of a domineering mother, who is caught up in a revolutionary movement, is debilitated by an inability to love, and proclaims the idea of man-as-god in diametrical opposition to Christianity's God-man concept. Nietzsche reasons that his own life similarly began with being unhoused ("unheimisch") and continued with being estranged ("unheimlich"), with maskings and evasions of reality that caused anguish and mental conflicts.

Pforta's monastic-academic setting and the loss of home moorings gradually prompted a drift from religious beliefs, and yet the struggle was hard. Nietzsche's necessary dissemblings are best illustrated by token public gestures he made in his Pforta graduation speech in which he piously thanked God, King, and Fatherland, and promised to bring them honor and love in the future. In his private poetry, however, he was subverting the authoritarianism of the school and theological orthodoxies. We may note a confessional poem directed "Dem unbekannten Gott" ["To the Unknown God"], precisely dated September 7, 1864, the last day of his Pforta incarceration. The poem begins with the lone poet's search for a God who, ironically, was also without a home. The title of the poem typifies Nietzsche's love for hide-and-seek references. He assumes one's knowing of Paul of Tarsus' finding an altar with the inscription "To an unknown god": a God who "commands all men everywhere to repent because he has fixed a day on which he will judge the world in righteousness by a man whom he has appointed . . . by raising him from the dead" (Acts 22:23, 31). Paul's theology of repentance, judgment, resurrection, and submissiveness was to be anathema to Nietzsche, but as early as this poem he turned to Old Testament imagery to validate his battle with a personally defined god in order to know him in his own depth, as did Jacob. The poet Nietzsche declares, "I want to know you, Unknown One."

In this connection it is worth recalling Genesis 32:22. After Jacob wrestles with the angel his name is changed to Israel. "For you," said the angel, "have striven with God and with men, and have prevailed. . . . So Jacob called the name of the place Peni'el, saying, 'For I have seen God face to face, and yet my life is preserved.' "[7] Indeed, the supercharged atmosphere of religiosity in which Nietzsche had been reared caused him to claim that as a twelve-year-old he had seen God in his hallowed glory, but despite the vision, had also composed his first philosophical essay about the origin of evil and of the devil, with the thesis that if God were self-created, he could only accomplish creation through the representation of his opposite. Much of such early writing, if indeed it existed in the form Nietzsche claimed retrospectively, was destroyed by his sister, Elisabeth.

NOTES

1. At the end of December 1888, from Turin, Nietzsche sent his publisher Georg Naumann in Leipzig substitute copy for section 3 of the chapter "Warum ich so weise bin" "Why I am so clever") of *Ecce Homo* already in proof stage. The substitution was never honored because it contained derogatory characterizations of his mother and sister; it is a section which we will return to later. See Mazzino Montinari, "Ein neuer Abschnitt in Nietzsches 'Ecce Homo,' " *Nietzsche Studien* (1972): 381–82.

2. Who was meant by the Messiah is discussed extensively in Joseph Klausner, *The Messianic Idea in Israel* (New York: Macmillan, 1955).

3. See *On the Genealogy of Morals*, section 16, for the context of Nietzsche's views.

4. *Gamaliel, oder die immerwahrende Dauer des Christentums* (Leipzig, 1796).

5. Quoted in Reiner Bohley, "Nietzsches christliche Erziehung," *Nietzsche Studien* (1987): 185; the entire article, pp. 164–96 and others by Rev. Boley in NS of 1976, 1980, 1987, and 1988 are indispensable for an understanding of Nietzsche's earliest milieu against which he rebelled.

6. Insistently, and with little variation, this scene is recapitulated in Nietzsche's "Autobiographical Accounts" from 1856 to 1869, contained in Karl Schlechta's edition, vol. III, pp. 9–154.

7. Jacob's name signified "the supplanter" of Esau's birthright. Israel's name signified "God rules." In the battle, the divine being had to retreat because of the oncoming sunrise, indicating anthropologically the remote antiquity of the story; Nietzsche was fond of the primal aspects of myths and legends.

2

Of Surrogate Fathers
and a "Rabbi" at Bonn

BONN AND THE SEARCH FOR TRUTH

In 1864, the twenty-year-old Nietzsche enrolled at the University of
Bonn in theological and philological studies; in the former, mainly to
please his family. His aversion to theology in the abstract and in practice
grew to the point that he refused to go to Easter communion with his
family when visiting Naumburg on a semester break in 1865—his mother's
tears and remonstrances notwithstanding. Aunt Rosalie blamed the influence of Shakespeare and other literary figures for the undesirable influence,
but noted that all great theologians had periods of crisis. She counseled
avoidance of vows, patience; lovingly she also gave Fritz some breathing
room and hoped that he would eventually make the "right" choice.

A major turn in his intellectual emancipation from Naumburg's doctrinaire mentality is marked in a letter to his sister, who at the time idolized her Fritz, suggesting that she join him in a new manner of freethinking he had adopted: the religious and cultural relativism of Mon-
taigne and Lessing. He chided Lisbeth for the naive, girlish tone and
content of her letters and suggested that if she wanted to follow her dear
brother into higher intellectual realms, she would have to make an
unforced and serious choice between habituation to deep-rooted views

about the world, God, and atonement held by family and society, and the difficult, convention-defying search for truth—"even if it were to be most repellent and ugly." Nietzsche writes:

> Suppose that since childhood we had believed that all salvation flows from someone other than Jesus, perhaps Mohammed; would it not be true that we would have gained the same blessings? Certainly, belief alone and not the objectification behind belief blesses us. I point this out to you, dear Lisbeth, only to disprove the most common means of evidence relied upon by orthodox people who derive the infallibility of their belief from subjective, inner experience. Every true belief is indeed infallible; it achieves whatever the particular believing person hopes to find in it, but faith does not in the least offer support for establishing an objective truth.
>
> Here, people's paths diverge: Do you wish tranquillity of soul and happiness, well then, believe; do you wish to be a disciple of truth, well then, search. . . . On this serious foundation I will build an edifice that will be all the gayer for it. (June 11, 1865)

Indeed, the revaluation of norms and the relativism of religious faith gave evidence in Fritz's letter of his "search." Later, he honed his observations further: "Wherever the strength of a belief strongly steps into the foreground, we must infer a certain weakness of demonstrability and the *improbability* itself of that belief" (*Toward a Genealogy of Morals: A Polemic*, III, 24, 1887; original italics).

Lisbeth was caught between wanting to please her unconventional brother-tutor and Naumburg convention steeped in family piety. In the long run, however, the only thing she would have in common with her brother was a strongly developed streak of expediency dictated by personal vanity; but it was unlike her brother's in that his was directed toward an elusive search for "truth."

This search for truth is a refrain in Nietzsche's writings and was influenced by writers of the eighteenth-century Enlightenment from Locke to Lessing.

Theodore Gotthold Ephraim Lessing (1729–1781), a pastor's son born in Saxony, turned from theology to philosophy and literature. His philo-Semitic writings possessed an originality and elegance that intrigued Nietzsche. As a model stylist and thinker, Lessing aimed to remove old religious prejudices, belief in biblical miracles, and the divinity of Christ; in his advocacy of reason, he developed a Spinozistic pantheism. He thought that truth was a divinely shrouded mystery— deadly if unveiled—but that the search for it was one's highest priority.[1] Profoundly stimulating to thinkers from Goethe to Nietzsche was Lessing's landmark essay on the aesthetics of Greek art and literature, *The Laokoön*; but for Nietzsche, Lessing was of further significance, for he reinforced Nietzsche's admiration for Shakespeare's "barbarous greatness" (Lessing's phrase) and was a model for liberal attitudes toward Jews. In that respect, Lessing assumes an historic role. His play *Die Juden*, written in 1749, was the first creative literary effort in modern times, by a Christian, to portray a Jew sympathetically as a refined and cultured individual. And his celebrated drama, *Nathan der Weise* (*Nathan the Wise*) (1779), which Lessing wrote out of his profound admiration for Moses Mendelssohn, served as a challenge to Christian intolerance.[2]

The story of *Nathan* is effective in its simplicity: In Jerusalem during the Third Crusade, Saladin, commander of the Saracen, asked the benevolent and reputedly wisest Jew of the city: "Which is the true religion—the Christian, the Mohammedan, the Jewish?" Nathan replied with "a parable of the ring." A father who loved his sons equally had two replicas made of a magic ring and bestowed a ring upon each son so that no one was able to tell which was the original ring. It is difficult to imagine today the sensation caused by Lessing's parable of tolerance in *Nathan der Weise*. To those sympathetic toward Jewish dilemmas, it gave positive reinforcement. However, to anti-Semites then and since (most notably to Wagner, and then a line extending into nazified Germany), it was incitement to anger. For many liberals, the play's message epitomized the philosophy of enlightenment.

In his "emancipation letter" to Lisbeth, Fritz had paraphrased Lessing's belief in the importance of the quest for truth and, in his own ecumenical extension of Lessing's parable, had made Moses part of a triumvirate with Jesus and Mohammed. Actually all this was an extension of an essay he had already written, "Über das Christentum" ("Concerning Christianity," 1862), in which he expressed the aim to reconstitute his life, to struggle and find an inner source of strength rather than accept the outer-directedness of Christianity; he expressed displeasure with church theology exemplified by the resurrection and God's incarnation in man.[3]

He acknowledged that "such demolition" was easy, but asked if it were possible to build constructively upon the rubble.

The young Nietzsche struggled with questions of faith, and his conclusions were not of a simplistic kind of atheism or even agnosticism, but decisive personal credos in the Emersonian vein (he was fond of quoting from translations of Emerson). He boldly declared his independence from God: "Submission to God's will" and "humility" (*Demut*) are often nothing more than covers for cowardly fearfulness and avoidance of meeting's one's destiny with decisiveness. Nietzsche can never be accused of humility, lack of decision making, or intellectual cowardice. He formulated his critique of Christianity lucidly and outlined the premises that could have made religion and Christianity palatable:

> When we begin to recognize that only we are responsible for ourselves and that any recrimination about missed opportunities in life should be directed against us rather than any higher powers, we then can cast aside the outer shell and let the grounding ideas of Christianity seep into blood and marrow. Christianity is essentially a matter of the heart; only when it has embodied itself in us and has become integral disposition, does a human being become a true Christian. . . . That God has become man, points only to the fact that man is not to seek bliss in the eternal but to ground his heaven on this earth. ("Free Will and Fate," 1862)

The essence of Nietzsche's ideology is captured in this essay, as is his inclination toward earth and human-centered cultures of antiquity: the Jewish and Greek. He was not to give up his old, given faith without a thorough struggle, but slowly the influence of works like Emerson's *Nature* dominated, and he became increasingly troubled by Christian assumptions that to him bordered on presumption:

> Today I heard a stimulating sermon by [Naumburg's chief pastor, F. A. Wenkel] on the topic of "Christianity, the Faith That Has Conquered the World"; it was intolerably arrogant toward non-Christian people, and yet it was very clever. Actually, he repeatedly substituted something else for the word "Christianity" that nevertheless rendered his correct sense. When he replaced the phrase "Christianity has conquered" with the phrase "the feeling of sin (or a metaphysical need) has conquered the world" that for us would contain nothing offensive, but

one ought to continue logically and say, "the true Hindus are Christians," and also conclude that "true Christians are Hindus."

. . . If Christianity means "belief in an historical event" or in an historical person, then I will want nothing to do with that kind of Christianity. If, however, it simply refers to a need for redemption I can still value it highly and don't even take it amiss that it seeks to discipline philosophers whose number is so negligible anyway relative to the uniform-mass of those craving redemption. . . . (to Carl von Gersdorff, April 7, 1866)

The last sentence and similar ones in other letters have been taken by some as evidence that Nietzsche did not relinquish totally a principle basic to Judeo-Christian thinking—redemption. Actually Nietzsche acknowledges the *psychological* actuality and power of impulses that strive for *liberation* from torments: *Erlösung* (redemption) is liberation; but he shuns supernatural terminology and explanations. Redemption is rejected along with the notions of sin and punishment; Nietzsche called them "monsters." We can only surmise the depths of his traumas that called forth such anger, feelings of guilt and shame. "Let us do away with the concept *sin*" (M, 202) was to become a drumbeat in his writings.

In his prolific reading and psychological needs, Nietzsche turned to Greek antiquity—a "natural" world without inhibitions. During his years at Bonn and Leipzig from 1864 to 1869, the experience of antiquity became alarmingly real to him, particularly the realm of Dionysus, a realm of deeper reality—dream-reality with intuitive visionary faculties to be fully born years later in *The Birth of Tragedy*. Although Nietzsche abandoned theological studies with a sense of relief, he, again by force of circumstances, was to lead a double life that he managed to control with masks as he probed into forbidding areas. Like Jacob wrestling with the angel, Nietzsche had to cope with inner demons—spirits or *daimones*—that played a great role in Greek thought, folkways, and philosophy.[4] During the years 1868–69, Nietzsche recorded in one of his autobiographical fragments an occult visitation: "What I fear is not the terrible figure behind my chair, but its voice: yet not even its voice but the terrifying unarticulated and inhuman tone of that creature. Yes, if it would only speak like humans speak!" (KS, III, 148). Such voices—predominantly of the ghostly father—images of Dionysus, or other hallucinations and alter egos—soon played decisive and creative roles. He decided to exploit himself psychologically as his own guinea pig by analyzing his divided self and his induced disembodied states of consciousness. Carl Jung diagnosed Nietzsche's neurosis as an attempt to reconcile his inner selves; Jung was somewhat off the mark, because Nietzsche found mental excitement not in reconciliation but in the warring and contentious activity of his other selves. By the time Nietzsche wrote *Morgenröte* (*Daybreak*, 1881), the idea of the demon had become a key concept: "The demon of power . . . not elemental life necessities, not covetousness [but] the love of power is mankind's demon ["die Liebe zur macht ist der Dämon der Menschen"], the demon lurks and waits and demands to be satisfied" (M, 262).

Until April 1869, when he assumed the chair of philology at Basel, Nietzsche was trying to accommodate many personal and academic demands in Bonn and Leipzig and still follow his own inclinations; the earlier games of masking resumed. The ersatz fathers of Naumburg are replaced by two powerful surrogate figures: one dead but intellectually alive and inspiring—Arthur Schopenhauer; the other, an acknowledged European authority in philological disciplines, Professor Friedrich Ritschl. The young man's discovery of Schopenhauer's *The World as Will and Idea* (first published, 1818) proved exhilarating:

> One day in the antiquarian shop of old man Rohn, a completely unfamiliar book came to hand and I paged through it. I don't know which demon whispered to me, "Take this book home with you." With that book, I saw a mirror in which the world, life, my own disposition were reflected with terrifying grandeur. . . . The need for self-knowledge, yes, self-laceration, seized me powerfully. (KS, III, 133)

"Papa" Schopenhauer became Nietzsche's stylistic mentor with his strong, flexible, informal, challenging expressiveness and inquiring intellectuality. This was precisely what Nietzsche needed at the time because, as he put it, his education lacked male guidance and "my father, a Thüringian country clergyman, died much too early."

THE RITSCHLS

Friedrich Wilhelm Ritschl's family originated in Bohemia, but encountering discrimination, its members left in search of a more congenial environment in which to practice their Protestant faith. His father had served as preacher and professor at Erfurt, exhibiting religious toleration in reaction to the persecutions endured by his ancestors. The young Ritschl followed in his footsteps. In 1833 and 1836, the thirty-two-year-old Ritschl was vacationing and hiking in the Warmbrunner mountains, where he met the three daughters of the Breslau physician Dr. Samuel Guttentag—chief of the city's Jewish hospital—and fell in love with the youngest, Sophie, precocious and handsome. Dr. Guttentag prevailed with his insistence that they observe a long courtship. Sophie, at fifteen and baptized like her sisters, agreed and the couple decided to marry in August of 1838 on Goethe's birthday. Their honeymoon journey to relatives and family in Switzerland, and from Breslau to Frankfurt, also included a meeting with his publisher to see his book on the Roman dramatist Plautus through the press; its publication helped Ritschl obtain an academic position, penurious though it was, at the University of Bonn through the efforts of Dr. Johannes Schulze, who thought that no one could better fill the philological duties at the university. Ritschl amply met Schulze's expectations and came to regard him as his spiritual father and mentor. He never forgot that relationship and used it as a model in relating to two of his favorite students—protégés and prodigies: Jacob Bernays and Friedrich Nietzsche.

Despite his carping, Nietzsche was fortunate in Leipzig to have found an enveloping, protective, and socially "vornehm" family—the Ritschls, and soon he was able to count himself a favorite son with them and their academic circle. Nietzsche reciprocated by proving himself worthy of such trust and acceptance. His rigorous training at Pforta was a factor in his ability to distinguish himself as a budding scholar and to become the leading spirit of the graduate student "Philological Club," something that greatly pleased Professor Ritschl.

This no doubt also impressed Frau Sophie Ritschl, who became the first in a line of mother figures for Nietzsche. She readily overshadowed the limited, provincial, and pietistically strangling Franziska, whose main role at this juncture was to send to Naumburg care packages for the young scholar and tend to his shipped trunks of laundry. In his autobiographical diaries, we find an entry that typifies what was to be an unvarying sensitivity for Frau Sophie Ritschl's feelings and his knowledge of her Jewish origin. Referring to the "uncouth manners" of Franz Hüffer, a fellow classmate,[5] Nietzsche writes:

> One time when the two of us were invited to the Ritschl family, Hüffer heaved his top-heavy body around on a chair that was unaccustomed to such a load; it creaked loudly, and Hüffer lustily shouted: "Oho, that thing is not kosher," a word that must have caused acute discomfort for Frau Ritschl who was born Jewish and later in life baptized. . . . (KS, III, 138)

In Bonn and in Leipzig to which Nietzsche had fatefully followed his teacher Ritschl, the familial relationship grew closer in time. Nietzsche was the first graduate student thought scholarly enough to be encouraged and then to be published in the prestigious journal Ritschl edited, *Das Rheinische Museum für Philologie*. When Nietzsche lectured on the poems of Theognis of Megara, Ritschl asked for a revised manuscript for publication. "After this," Nietzsche wrote in his dairy, "my self-esteem soared up to the clouds. . . . For some time I went around in a state of delirium." Ritschl was the *living* father while Nietzsche kept a photograph of his own deceased father, Karl Ludwig, over the piano in his small apartment, along with that of Schopenhauer and a reproduction of a painting of Jesus.

At times, Fritz lapsed into the kind of fashionable social anti-Semitism natural to another friend, Hermann Mushacke, who railed against Berlin Jews during Nietzsche's visits there.[6] But, on the whole, we find among the mass of letters to his family and friends only a few that carry any petty and objectionable remarks about Jews. In a peevish mood, he wrote from Leipzig,

> Dear Mama and Lisbeth,
>   . . . Food at restaurants here is hardly edible. On top of all this, the place swarms with repulsive, soulless apes and other merchants, so that I heartily yearn for an end to this intermezzo. Finally, with Gersdorff[7] I found a tavern where one does not have to endure butterfat and Jewfaces and where we are the only regular guests. It is a place recommended by Mushacke. . . . (April 22, 1866)
>   (Signed "Fr. W. N., someone who is ready for war")

A few days later, also from Leipzig, he wrote to Mushacke, ". . . the food everywhere is very bad as well as expensive; at the theater there always was an African woman and Jews and their compatriots wherever one looked" (April 27, 1866).

Two years later in a letter to his mother and sister, he indulges in small talk, mentions Ritschl's friendliness, and then falls into a glib refrain of prejudice against commercialization and Jewish exemplars:

> Today finally, the [Leipzig city fair] has come to an end, and with that we have been happily rescued from the butterfat smell and the many [visiting merchant] Jews. At the [boarding house] table was a Frenchman, as well, a Monsieur Flaxland whose language, I really don't understand. . . . (October 18, 1868)

Clumsy and insensitive as these remarks appear, they were taken for granted by their recipients. The stereotypical figure of the Jewish merchant was for Nietzsche the symbol of the materialistic industrial-mercantile world of Leipzig where the term "money lender" or "money changer" had—as elsewhere—been transformed to "banker" and "financier." Aversion to Jews in general was not far from the young Nietzsche's unexamined feelings.

Ritschl's academic reputation was formidable at the time Nietzsche began to enjoy a mentorship that led to publications in Ritschl's scholarly journal, which were to provide Nietzsche with the equivalent of a Ph.D. But he wrote to his friend Mushacke, who either brought out the worst in Nietzsche or whatever was boiling within, that he was beginning to lose interest in rigorous philological research. Philosophy was to take its place. At one point, Nietzsche had sensed Ritschl's displeasure when he had not followed his advice about taking a certain seminar, and he complained in a letter to Mushacke, "Such people [as Father Ritschl] after all, are tremendously arrogant . . . and we may come to a parting of the ways" (letter, April 27, 1866). Ritschl could be domineering and drive himself to exhaustion; he would tolerate no academic sloth or bureaucratic politics, but on the other hand was unreservedly generous with deserving and needy students. Such irascibilities and mood swings were part of Nietzsche's personality, too.

For some time, Nietzsche's interests and reading at private and university libraries had taken directions incompatible with strict philology.

At the same time, he slipped deeper and deeper into the pagan world of antiquity, the mystery cults, and pursued the god of masks, the protean Dionysus, and associated figures—Father Pan, Bacchus, the wise old prophetic Silenus, an ancestor of Dionysus. Compendious works had been published on cultural anthropology and theoretical exegeses of Greek mythology by respectable academicians—precursors of James Frazer, Jane Harrison, and other Cambridge scholars. Available to Nietzsche were the voluminous works of F. G. Welcker (*Griechiche Götterlehre*), as well as the work of Karl Otfried Muller of Göttingen, C. A. Bottiger, Friedrich Creuzer, C. A. Lobeck, and F. Max Muller.[8]

Among these scholars, Nietzsche found an enthusiasm for pagan Greek culture, mythology, and literature that by comparison made theological studies look pale. Theology, he concluded, "chokes God." On the contrary, he came to extol pagan antiquity as "eine Welt ohne Sündengefuhl"—"a world without a concept or sense of sin" (*FW*, 146). He identified with the Dionysian masks and that of Greek actors as activities of dissimulation—"Verstellung," artistic deception to be enjoyed as a form of willed deception and creative tension.

During his early academic career, Nietzsche's mentor Professor Ritschl had been similarly attracted to the bacchic mysteries, cultism, and anthropological resources; but he turned against such pursuits and even discarded most of his writings that had utilized those sources, repenting of what he called his youthful follies and strayings from philology and unconscionable dabblings in symbology.[9] Nietzsche for the same reasons was attracted to such inquiries, but repressed them until they blossomed into his path-breaking *The Birth of Tragedy*. In that respect, among other factors, Jacob Bernays was to be a stimulant.

If we quickly summarize the years at Bonn (and Leipzig) and look ahead somewhat, we note uncanny patterns of recurrence in Nietzsche's life: the acceptance and love by a father and eventual reciprocal abandonment and losses. The one person who was never to disappoint him was his mother-confidante, Frau Ritschl. His clandestine pursuit of knowledge led him into the labyrinthine underworld of antiquity and the Dionysian cult. Of immediate importance, though, were two figures on the academic scene: Professor Ritschl and Jacob Bernays who, along with Nietzsche, was a protégé of Ritschl's. Bernays, an Orthodox Jew, is rarely acknowledged in Nietzsche biographies.

JACOB BERNAYS

Long before Nietzsche's arrival in Bonn, Jacob Bernays had become one of Ritschl's favored graduate students who was welcomed by Frau Sophie as well. He was the eldest son of Isaac ben Ja'akov Bernays, a Portuguese Jew, who, during the brief period of Napoleonic liberalization in Europe, had studied at the University of Würzburg, published an acclaimed study of the biblical Orient, *Der Bibel'sche Orient* (1821), and at Hamburg assumed the post of Chief Rabbi. He preached in German, following the demand made of Jews by Goethe and others. Rabbi Bernays set for himself the goal of bringing Orthodox and Reform Jews into communal contact. (Among the poor fringes of the Reform wing of the Jewish community was Heinrich Heine who was distantly related to the Bernays family. Heine had studied law at the University of Bonn and in 1825 converted, a conversion on paper that proved satisfactory to no one: Christians would never say a mass for him nor would Jews honor his death with the ritual Kaddish mourning. For Nietzsche, the self-exiled Heine in Paris would be his mirror image of the outsider, society's "other.")

At Bonn, Ritschl took Jacob Bernays under his wing and sheltered him from his undergraduate days to 1848, when he obtained his doctorate. From the start Sophie Ritschl made Jacob feel at home and teased him for his orthodoxy which prevented him from having meals at her home; she eased his essential social shyness. It was not long before he gained attention among scholars with a fruitful methodological approach to the study of the pre-Socratics and his expertise in Jewish-Hellenistic literature. He was given an adjunct lectureship at the university and was an assistant editor of Ritschl's philological journal. At the same time, his publications, lectures, and research ranged from Heraclitus and Lucretius to Maimonides and Spinoza ("did I not belong to Spinoza's people whose inheritance includes a portion of cheerfulness?" Bernays asked). What gave Bernays's reputation its immediate impetus was his attempted reconstruction of Aristotle's lost theory of comedy and a treatise on Aristotle's discourse on dramatic tragedy, much of which was illuminated by Bernays's understanding of Aristotle's concept of *katharsis*, a medical term indicating the removal of impurity and the purge of excess, and which influenced Nietzsche's *Birth of Tragedy*.[10]

Bernays's published ideas spread quickly among scholars and Hellenists in Germany and England. It was the imagined Dionysian experience of pre-Homeric times that Nietzsche regressed to in his imagination and became its recurrence; for him it was not to be a cathartic, healing process but something altogether catastrophic. Beyond personal and seminar contacts with Jacob Bernays, Nietzsche not only knew his work but also commented on it in the *Literarisches Centralblatt*, edited by Professor Friedrich Zarnke in Leipzig. In reviewing Bernays's work on *Die Heraklitischen Briefe* (1869, *Heracleitean Letters: A Contribution to Philosophical and Religious Literature*), Nietzsche complimented "the sensitive manner of everything this author [Bernays] has written with distinction."

Bernays's advice and class lectures on Edward Gibbon were admired on campus and guided Nietzsche to translations of *The Decline and Fall of the Roman Empire*. (Gibbon, "the lord of irony," was a favorite also of Bernays's father). For Nietzsche's thoughts about Judaism and Christianity, Gibbon's work was to be magnetic.

Prussian ministerial appointments to university professorships, in Bernays's time and later, excluded Jews, but when it became evident that Ritschl's arduous schedule required relief, he turned to his illustrious student and recognized scholar, Bernays, who accepted the offer of an associate professorship and the post of Chief Librarian at Bonn, having been denied a full chair at Breslau and Heidelberg.

Bernays overcame the slights and his own reluctance by thinking of the advantage he would gain by having an academically broad audience of students and colleagues for his work, seminars, and lectures. We have firsthand recollections about Bernays from an intriguing source, namely, a fellow Pforta alumnus of Nietzsche and later a formidable enemy who envied Nietzsche academically: Ulrich von Wilamowitz-Moellendorff. Moellendorff writes of Bernays:

> Personal contacts with the "Rabbi," as [Bernays] was called by the students, were interesting and contributive to one's education. He was not only a strict [Orthodox] Jew . . . but put his Jewishness on display with pride; even in the comic neglect of his appearance, there lay a conscious alienation. It was a unique kind of prideful nobility that repelled most people. As for myself, I felt somewhat intimidated because everything about him was genuine, everything had style, even his undis-

guised despisement of the Christian "daughter-religion," as he put it. He directed me toward Plutarch's *Moralia*, saying, "Only when you have correctly read these writings can you claim to know Greek."[11]

Wilamowitz's attitude toward the "Rabbi" alternated between carping and praise, but in an article for the *British Journal of Philology* (1868), he unambiguously expressed deep gratitude. Nietzsche, unlike Wilamowitz, was greatly interested in the philosophy of antiquity and came closer to sharing some of Bernays's views.

For a brief time, Bernays was a lecturer at Bonn and then for twelve creative years taught at the Breslau Jewish Theological Seminary until returning to Bonn. Though academic doors were closed to Jews, they could open slightly if one were to become a "Taufjude," a baptized Jew. Liberal Christians (like the great historian Theodor Mommsen, a friend of Bernays) and Gentile atheists urged this course upon their Jewish colleagues as a way of giving a token of loyalty to German institutions, a form of rationalization that minimized the act of conversion by proposing that the individual is greater than his professed religious beliefs. Bernays's close friend Georg Bunsen, son of the Prussian envoy to England, urged him to convert and make it possible for a German university to give him a chair, or, failing that, to emigrate to Oxford. Bernays declined Bunsen's invitation. He stated that "if Jesus himself were reborn, as a Jew, he of all people, would not bring himself to convert" to Christianity . . . or to conform to the "herd," the compact majority. However, Jacob Bernays's brother Michael, a brilliant Germanist and literary historian, *did* convert and twenty years later was instated with a university chair at Munich. The whole family mourned him as "dead," following a Jewish Orthodox tradition.[12]

Nietzsche in his initial gleanings of the Jewish character noted a life-affirming pride and fine-honed mind as defining the personality of Bernays. What was it that allowed the Orthodox Jew to pursue and exhibit his scholarly talents in a restrictive Prussian-Protestant environment, as well as in an exclusively Gentile academia? The French critic Marthe Robert suggests that in the field of the humanities the cult of antiquity was widespread among Germans as well as among Jews (particularly among, though not confined to, assimilated Jews), and thus provided a neutral ground on which Gentiles and Jews could meet. A Jew associated with antiquity could approach the Gentile world without the fear of being insulted and rebuffed; specializing in ancient learning was a respectable discipline that offered the Jew a way out of the ghetto.[13]

For a Jew it was easier intellectually to be a citizen of Greece or Rome than of modern Germany or Austria. The assertive refusal to be intimidated as a Jew was a phenomenon Nietzsche observed in Bernays—the powerful will to live as a Jew, to endure, and to remain a Jew (in name) within a hostile setting. Nietzsche was to generalize this "will" as a Jewish instinct and he repeatedly applauded it as typical of the historic effort to stay alive in history, unlike the ancient Greeks.

Aside from the shared interest in the cult of antiquity, Bernays drew Nietzsche's attention to Gibbon's style and historic sweep and to readings in Spinoza and other sources in which the young Nietzsche found yeast for his formative thinking. Bernays was the only Jew Nietzsche had ever met—or was to meet in his lifetime—who was profoundly aware of his own heritage and unapologetically proud of it. Although humble in the face of scholarship and learning, Bernays was almost arrogant in his demands for excellence. Ultimately, he was a lonely man.

SCHOPENHAUER

A repetitive pattern of strong attraction to people and ideas and then a violent repulsion is discernible in Nietzsche's encounters: Schopenhauer's works were no exception. In mid-July 1866, Nietzsche wrote to Mushacke: "Since Schopenhauer removed the blinders of optimism from our eyes, one sees more sharply. . . . Who would not be proud to be a Prussian?" One would hardly have guessed that his enthusiasm for Schopenhauer would actually turn into its opposite—and precisely because of the very pessimism he initially praised. But cause for greater astonishment still is Nietzsche's vision twenty-two years later of an ideal genetic *mix* of the Prussian Junker's dignity with that of Jewish intelligence and instincts. To be sure, no Jewish or Gentile thinker was *ever* to entertain that kind of vision: one that would categorically meet with ridicule by anti-Semites. The distance traveled over those years is a vintage Nietzschean story.

In Schopenhauer Nietzsche found a bracing individualistic style and a primer on how to write with lucidity, fluency, and persuasiveness. Schopenhauer had the stamp of genius, though denied due recognition, even by the academic world and the brokers he had alienated: Fichte, Schleiermacher, and Hegel. But slowly his reputation was beginning to take hold. Nietzsche could not help but observe that the Schopenhauer surge came about largely through the effort of Jews—German and English—and their perceptiveness. Helen Zimmern, a Jewish writer, was Schopenhauer's first English biographer (in 1876) and a subsequent translator of Nietzsche. And Dr. Julius Fraunestädt persuaded the Brockhaus firm to reprint Schopenhauer's *World as Will and Idea*, and also made the philosopher's ideas accessible to a large audience with his book *Brief über die Schopenhauersche Philosophie*, in 1854. Even so, Schopenhauer's prejudices toward Jews were severe; and, in his perpetual pessimism, he actually *condemned* them for their "joyfulness." Zimmern writes:

> His [Schopenhauer's] hatred of the Judaic element was as strong as that of Kant; he branded Jews as confirmed optimists, and traced Spinoza's optimism to this root. "The Jews are a joyous nation full of love for life. Spinoza was always cheerful." This dictum [or indictment] Schopenhauer held with obstinate persistence and it recurs perpetually in his writings.[14]

The usefulness of Jewish critics, professional journalists, and intellectuals was something Nietzsche was to be immensely conscious of in his own cause. As for Richard Wagner's obsessive anti-Semitism, Nietzsche was to put blame on the influence of Schopenhauer, but this proved to be only a pale explanation for a complicated phenomenon.

How greatly personal dispositions can shape a philosophical worldview is illustrated here. Schopenhauer's mother, a writer herself, blamed his ill-humor and sullen laments about a "stupid world" for the nightmares he had caused her and she refused to live with a son who, as an acolyte of Buddhistic pessimism, slept with a pistol under his pillow. Wagner, who loved animals more than he did humans in general, placed the same charge upon Jews as did Schopenhauer and became a vociferous antivivisectionist. Nietzsche, for a time, accepted Schopenhauer's characterization of Jews but turned their "love for life" into an inestimable virtue rather than a debit. Nietzsche felt that personality and the style of one's work are of one cloth, so that the exuberant eccentricity of Schopenhauer reveals his epigrams and life to be synonymous. We find points of biographical similarity between Schopenhauer and Nietzsche: a pietistic upbringing among stern women, the devastating loss of a father early in life. Schopenhauer satisfied his conscience by following his father's wishes, though only for a short time, while Nietzsche quickly dropped theology and became a candidate for guilt feelings heightened by a fear of retribution for abandoning the biblical faith of his ancestral tribe.

Schopenhauer's book title *World as Will and Idea* encapsulates his theory: The universe is my subjective interpretation of what presents itself; everything within it is driven by a blind, irrational, and purposeless will or impulse—a pantheistic life-force that rules out a monotheistic being; the intellect is an instrument of the will to life and is not superior to the instincts, and every aspect of life is subject to inexorable necessity and had to occur. Schopenhauer hoped to attain Nirvana, a release from a life in which one has no choice or purpose; he felt that it was better "*not* to be than to be." This was a view that Nietzsche soon rejected along with Schopenhauer's view of the world as cosmically evil. But Nietzsche was in sympathy with Schopenhauer's ideological hostility to established religion and shared his physical justification for eating to fuel the mind. They also shared a horror of "mob rule and its danger to the elite." But there were Schopenhauerisms with which Nietzsche parted company, such as Schopenhauer's notion that Christianity (its ethics but not its mythologies) belongs to the old true sublime belief of humanity, as opposed to the false, ignoble, noxious optimism embodied in Greek heathenism, in Judaism, and in Islam.[15]

In essence, Schopenhauer's subjective agreement with Buddhistic teachings urges an extirpation of desire—if not life itself—and the mortification of every passion. Nietzsche was slow in formulating a counter-response; it was precisely the heathenism or paganism in the religions that Schopenhauer despised, which Nietzsche found to possess a culture, optimism, and naturalness of instinct that civilization subsequently "tamed" in order to domesticate the human animal. For Nietzsche, becoming "more natural" means becoming more profound, self-confident, mistrustful, or nonmoral "like nature." He spoke of the courage of regaining natural drives; retrospectively, he confided this to his notes (*WM*, 124, 1887) as drives that he recognized in himself, repressed, and diverted. His self-knowledge and psychosexual autobiography were discharged mainly into his poetry and he masked it in his writings. Eroticism in his visualizations was the upshot of unfulfillment. In the Old Testament, Greek tragedies, and the historical background to Euripides' *Bakkhai*, for instance, and their Oriental past and legacies he found a naturalness and spontaneity of sexual response denied him in his Naumburg upbringing. His mother's eyes were turned heavenward toward her deceased Ludwig; his grandmother and aunts in black and concealing Victorian dress were female mysteries to him; and his sister, submissive to his substitute fatherly pedagogies and male superiority, overwhelmed him with girlish flatteries and sentimental doe-like affection which initially soothed his ego. But these enveloping and smothering females did not ready him for the real world of girls and women.

ROCKING THE GOLDEN CRADLE

Of the friends made at Pforta, Nietzsche was most comfortable in sharing his most personal thoughts with Paul Deussen, also a pastor's son. During their religious confirmation at Pforta, they knelt together and swore allegiance to Jesus and pledged lifelong dedication to him. That proved to be a passing phase for both friends. When at Bonn years later, Nietzsche urged his friend to shed his theological bearskin and to join the ranks of philologists and Schopenhauerians, and to cut through the "Hebraic fog" between them (September 1866). In a long, serious, and mature letter addressed to his friend Fritz, Deussen touched on matters that would be of vital concern to Nietzsche.[16] In this long letter which resembled a scholarly essay, Deussen was convinced that the fiery, fantasy-rich Oriental and Semitic imagination was superior to the rational Indo-Germanic mind:

> . . . The Bible offers us, aside from the indispensable Hebrew language, a double interest, namely, historical and philosophical. Primarily in evidence: The Jewish people stand so unique in history because of its constituted order as well as its fate, through its long antiquity as well as its ancient ancestors and its deep well of ethics that penetrated through all Oriental barbarism, so that it greatly repays to recover its history. . . .
> (August 1866)

Interestingly enough, as Nietzsche began to explore biblical texts rigorously from a philosophical perspective, with especial antagonism reserved for the New Testament, Deussen's interests turned to Indology; he became a foremost authority in Oriental religions and the philosophy of the Upanishads. What keeps Deussen contributive to Nietzsche's biography, however, is his retelling, in his memoirs, of a confidential account his friend gave him concerning a trip to a brothel:

> One day in February of 1865, Nietzsche travelled alone to Cologne, let himself be guided by a porter to sites worth seeing, and then finally asked to be led to a restaurant. The porter however took him to a bordello. "I saw myself surrounded suddenly," Nietzsche told me the next day, "by a half dozen apparitions in spangles and costume-gauze, who looked at me expectantly. Speechless, I stood stock-still for a moment. Then instinctively, I quickly headed for a piano—as if it were the only being there possessed of a soul—and I struck several chords. These freed me from my state of petrifaction and I successfully made my way into the open air."[17]

Only a pastor's son could believe such a far-fetched story told by another pastor's son. The need to appear righteous and to prove their resistance to sexual temptation prompted the retelling of the story. Deussen wanted to be helpful to Nietzsche's reputation for chasteness (a dubious myth also fostered by his sister) and told the story as objective proof of his friend's aloofness, and their loathing of tavern songs about kissing the lover's "red mouth." On the other hand, Deussen noted that his friend expressed no aversion to the idea of marriage and even bragged that he would wear out at least three wives. Between such pieties and exaggerations, it is no wonder that biographers became confused.[18]

Nietzsche placed blame for his identity confusions and maimed sexuality on the black-frocked pietistic oppressors who, for a long time, kept him in a confining "Golden Cradle," which he was determined to violently rock: "The free spirit will always breathe easier when he has finally made up his mind to shake off those maternal cares and protectiveness with which women around him dominate" (MA, 429).

What kept Nietzsche from feeling totally isolated during his graduate-student days was his meeting Erwin Rohde, son of a Hamburg doctor, handsome and of mature bearing.[19] Because of their obvious companionability and common interest in Greek literature and history, Ritschl dubbed them "the Dioscuri" (the twin striplings of Zeus). "Together," wrote Nietzsche, "we are no twosome [*Zweiheit*] but a true and genuine monad, pitting a shared loneliness against the world." With his newest and dearest friend, he planned to leave the factory work called philology—"an abortion of the goddess of philosophy"—and its overseer Father Ritschl, "the panderer who wants to keep us ensnared." Here was ingratitude toned down by jest. Nietzsche wanted to say farewell to the tedium of scholarship and to share with Rohde a wandering-student life, "studying and worshiping at the altar of the high priest Schopenhauer." Their first stop would be Paris, a city at the opposite pole of small-town Naumburg "virtue."

Such were the dreams while passing the days of October 1868, when Nietzsche was stationed near Naumburg as a volunteer with the 21st Battalion, Field Regiment Nr. 4. He styled himself a "cannoneer"—and as the best among thirty other cavalrymen—riding his fiery steed "Balduin." Pleasantly exhausted after drills, stable cleaning, and hard riding, he fell into a reverie and the magic of anticipating a Sonnabend, a sabbath of respite "like that of the Hebrews" who invented that beautiful story . . . (to Rohde, February 1–3, 1868; Gen. 1–3:22).

The particular Old Testament allusion is to recur in self-satisfied Nietzsche phrasings: the seventh day on which God rested from his creations and thought them "very good." The prevalence of "seven" as a sacred coefficient in Bible texts was evident to Nietzsche as was the special dignity given the idea of the "seventh,"[20] and the "optimistic" aura in which the primal Yahweh basks in his stellar creations. Creativity and the pursuit of life as art and not as a preoccupation with ethics, Nietzsche concluded, was the attraction held out by Paris where Heinrich Heine had found a home in exile as a writer.

The National Library in Paris could give academic legitimacy to Nietzsche's vision of a stay in that city, and, he limned seductive pictures for Rohde. Next to Father Schopenhauer, Jacques Offenbach, the popular German-Jewish composer and French citizen, was elevated to sainthood. A Leipzig performance of "Sankt" Offenbach's *La belle Hélène* sent Nietzsche into raptures and he hummed tunes from that opera bouffe. *Fair Helen* appealed to Nietzsche for its *vie parisienne* lilt no less than for its humorous parody of government and theology.[21] The flouncing of ruffled petticoats by the heel-kicking cancan dancers created a veritable phantasmagoria for the excitable young Nietzsche, conjuring up Dionysian maenads, the engauzed brothel women of Cologne, and the brash Parisiennes. "To learn the divine Cancan," to imbibe nectar-absinthe, to make Paris the school of life and experience, and with a few friends perhaps to found a German expatriate colony were objectives Nietzsche devoutly wished for.

NOTES

1. "We possess art," Nietzsche was to say, "so that we do not perish of the truth," *GT*, 3.

2. Howard M. Sachar, *The Course of Modern Jewish History* (New York: Vintage Books, 1959; 1990), p. 30.

3. In an essay "Fatum und Geschichte" ("Fate and History," Spring 1862), Nietzsche laid the groundwork for his new thinking: the structure of Christianity is based only on assumptions and not history, mankind is only a step in universal evolution, we have been led astray for two thousand years by foolhardy presumptions, "free will" is nothing more than the extreme power of fate—a view that brought him closer to Greek philosophers.

Particularly contributive is George J. Stack's *Nietzsche and Emerson, An Elective Affinity* (Athens, Ohio: Ohio University Press, 1992). Professor Stack meticulously examines the intersection of Nietzschean and Emersonian thoughts and illustrates how Emerson's "surprisingly radical thought entered the bloodstream" of European philosophical existentialism through Nietzsche.

4. Insightful perspectives on the subject are best found in E. R. Dodds, *The Greeks and the Irrational* (Boston: Beacon Press, 1951; reprint, 1957).

5. Franz Hüffer (1845–1889), a fellow student in Leipzig, became a musicologist and subsequently resided in London. Dr. Hüffer reported to German newspapers about the music scene in London.

6. Mushacke (1845–1906), later a professor at Hildesheim.

7. Carl von Gersdorff (1844–1904), a friend of old.

8. A useful overview of the encyclopedic research and interpretations by some of the scholars noted here is found in Professor H. J. Rose's introduction to *A Handbook of Greek Mythology* (New York: Dutton, 1959).

9. For critical and biographical information see Otto Ribbeck, *Friedrich Wilhelm Ritschl: Ein Beitrag zur Geschichte der Philologie* (Leipzig: B. G. Teubner, 1879-81), particularly vol. I, 159f. and vol. II, 948ff.

10. Jacob Bernays, 1824–1881. See Arnaldo Momigliano, *Jacob Bernays* (Amsterdam/London: North-Holland Publishing Company, 1969), p. 17. Similarly recommended is Hans I. Bach, *Jacob Bernays: Ein Beitrag zur Emanzipationsgeschichte der Juden und zur Geschichte des deutschen Geistes im neunzehnten Jahrhandert* (Tübingen: Mohr, 1974); Michael Fränkel, *Jacob Bernays: Ein Lebensbild in Briefen* (Breslau: Marcus, 1932). Fränkel dedicated the book to Sigmund Freud, whose wife, Martha, was a niece of Bernays. Freud expressed appreciation for the Jewish intellectual inheritance left by Bernays and was particularly taken with his medical interpretation of catharsis. Since he called psychoanalysis "a cathartic method," he probably knew of Bernays's work much earlier. Freud, who had been accused of unacknowledged borrowing from Nietzsche, was undoubtedly delighted to find Nietzsche's hands in Bernays's cookie jar. Freud sent a copy of the collected Bernays letters to Arnold Zweig, a friend and novelist, with a note saying that Bernays's "attitude toward the Jewish and Christian faiths is worthy of attention, also his affectionate relationship to Paul Heyse. I beg you to read this little book" (November 27, 1932). Paul Johann Ludwig Heyse (1830–1914), a relative of the Mendelssohns, was the first German to win the Nobel Prize for literature (1910) as a prolific novelist, dramatist, and translator; his mother was Jewish but he was in total ignorance of both Jewish and Christian traditions. A warm personal friendship developed between him and Bernays. In a letter to the critic Georg Brandes, February 19, 1888, Nietzsche complimented him for knowing Heyse's works.

11. Ulrich von Wilamowitz-Moellendorff, *Erinnerungen, 1848–1914* (Leipzig: Koehler, 1928), pp. 87f.

12. See, "Die Bruder Bernays," in Franz Kobler, ed., *Juden und Judentum in deutschen Briefen aus drei Jahrhunderten* (Vienna: Saturn Verlag), pp. 288–94; p. 292, Bernays's letter to Bunsen.

Bernays's situation in mid-century was similar to Freud's thirty years later. And Freud's assessment in *My Life and Psychoanalysis* held true for both men: "above all, I found that I was expected to feel myself inferior and an alien because I was a Jew." Rejecting the label of "the other," the alien, Freud found a prideful predecessor—a person different from his own passive father—in Bernays.

13. See Marthe Robert, *From Oedipus to Moses: Freud's Jewish Identity*, translated by Ralph Mannheim (New York: Anchor Books, 1976), pp. 28ff.; 56; 187–88.

14. Helen Zimmern, *Schopenhauer: His Life and Philosophy*, rev. ed. (London: Allen & Unwin, 1932), pp. 103–104.

15. Ibid., p. 174.

16. Paul Deussen (1845–1919) in his various books, including *Sutras des Vedanta* published during the 1880s, avoids any mention of Nietzsche. Introduced by Nietzsche to Schopenhauer's works, Deussen became a lifelong disciple and president of the German Schopenhauer Society. Nietzsche and Deussen parted ideological company when Deussen asserted the New Testament and the Upanishads to be humanity's noblest, complementing products of religious consciousness.

17. The incautious bordello story is recounted in Paul Deussen's informative *Erinnerungen an Friedrich Nietzsche* (Leipzig: Brockhaus, 1901).

18. Controversy reigns. That Nietzsche's sexual drive must have been abnormally low is the conjecture offered by Ronald Hayman, *Nietzsche, A Critical Life* (New York: Oxford University Press, 1980), p. 64; on the other hand, others like the biographer H. W. Brann, *Nietzsche und die Frauen* (Leipzig: Meiner, 1931), p. 24, believe that Nietzsche's sexual desires were even stronger than usual in males but they were repressed and sublimated. In any case, what inhibiting fastidiousness Nietzsche possessed is owed to Franziska Nietzsche's hygienically vigorous regimentation of Lisbeth's and Fritz's lives.

Certainly applicable retrospectively to the Cologne episode is the aphorism: "Of all, the most sensual men flee from women and must martyr their bodies" (M, 294). Even more telling is the blunt assertion in his last testament, *Ecce Homo*: "I am a disciple of the philosopher Dionysus, and would much prefer being a satyr than a saint" (*EH*, Pref. 2). And, according to Nietzsche, "In Dionysian intoxication there is sexuality and voluptuousness" (WM, 799).

19. Erwin Rohde (1845–1898) became professor of classical philology at Heidelberg and author of the book *Psyche*, which continues to maintain his reputation: it omits any reference to works by his friend Nietzsche.

20. M, 205, is to the point.

21. The modern musicologist Paul Henry Lang, *Music in Western Civilization* (New York: Norton, 1941), p. 1006, describes it as "being surprisingly Greek in spirit."

3

Encountering the Maestro of Anti-Semitism: Wagner

MEETING THE MEISTER

Nietzsche's student life in Leipzig was compartmentalized and severely strained by the public and private masks he alternatively wore. There had been an uneasy truce after his mother, Franziska, had warned him about being a disgrace to his deceased pastor-father with his cavalier attitudes toward theology. They managed to paper over a fierce altercation of 1862 but he never forgave her.[1] He had indeed turned for motherly understanding to Frau Sophie Ritschl, upon whose genial nature and graciousness he practiced his social gallantry in visits and letters, showing his affection in gentlemanly ways and enjoying theater-outings in her company. But his unresolved and clandestine sexuality in a prurient world made him feel uncomfortable with women, an awkwardness he did his best to disguise with brief periods of effusive pursuits of actresses.

His intellectual conflict sharpened between philological slave labor, at which he was superb, *and* philosophizing in the manner of Schopenhauer and living the free-lance life of Heine in Paris. He naively underestimated the range of scholarly learning that went into Schopenhauer's patient writings and the horrendous sacrifices Heine had to make to pursue his life in Paris. Deussen suggested that at the time another question lay unresolved. After their joint reading of David Friedrich Strauss's secularized *Life of Jesus*, Nietzsche told him that such rationalistic treatment had "serious consequences": "If you give up Christ, you also have to give up God."

Right after Pforta his "freethinking" took on new dimensions, but enmity toward Christianity, its morality and prayers, was still subdued. Toward what ends Nietzsche's flounderings in Leipzig might have led is intriguing but made irrelevant by two events that were to shape his life decisively: his fateful meeting with Richard Wagner and, upon graduating from Leipzig, his astonishing appointment to a chair of philology— a discipline he had begun to despise—at the University of Basel.

Professor and Frau Ritschl were intimates of another academic family, the Orientalist Hermann Brockhaus and his wife, Ottilie, Wagner's sister, and it was in her home that the spark was ignited between Wagner and Nietzsche. The sequence that led up to the event had its peculiar "theatricality" so dear to Nietzsche's heart and sense of fate. He reported to Rohde that on October 27, he had heard a performance of Wagner's *Tristan* prelude and the overture to *Die Meistersinger*, and that he could not bring himself to "remain cool, critically speaking," toward Wagner's music. Strongly connected with this is his recollection of a Sunday spent with the Ritschls the last week in June of 1868, which Nietzsche described as "a day of . . . grace and sunny warmth, a memory of the best" that he preserved from his lonely life at Leipzig.

The fifty-year-old Sophie Ritschl, Nietzsche's "muse" and "feminine inspiration," made him feel part of the family and encouraged his performing and improvising on the piano. Frau Ritschl had shared with him some of her favorite reading, including a little book by Louis Ehlert, *Briefe über Musik an eine Freundin* (*Letters about Music, to a Lady Friend*), who pointed to Wagner not only as an original composer but also as the creator of incessantly declamatory characters. Nietzsche readily agreed; and, upon invitation played from the piano score of Wagner's *Die Meistersinger* for Frau Sophie.

In a letter to Rohde, Nietzsche grandly called Frau Ritschl "meine intime Freundin" (my intimate woman-friend) (letter, August 6, 1868). She brought out a buoyancy concealed by the young man's stiffly serious exterior. In a thank-you note to her, he wrote:

—Highly esteemed Frau Privy Councillor,

. . . I've not succeeded in disguising from you my inclination for discord. Certainly you have already a terrible sampling of it? The cloven hoofs of Wagner and Schopenhauer do not let themselves be disguised easily. But I will improve. And when once again you will permit me to play the piano for you, I will shape tones that recall that beautiful Sunday . . . and you will hear how much that recollection means to me, a poor musician, Friedrich Nietzsche. (July 2, 1868)

Only a gallant sure of being a favorite with Frau Sophie would permit himself such verbal flippancies, playing satyr and displaying an ebullience suited to a twenty-year-old male. But unconsciously, beneath the pagan mask was a pagan disposition, a fierce interest in Dionysian cultism.

Between that heady personal exchange with Frau Sophie during the summer and events in the fall, much had transpired, and Nietzsche duly wrote an exceptionally long letter to Rohde. He began by recounting his inaugural semester-talk at Ritschl's graduate philological society, at which he had asked his friend Heinrich Romundt to check on his lecture performance—style, voice, delivery, dramatic effect—as he talked about satire and the cynic Menippus. "And behold," said Nietzsche in the style of the Genesis Yahweh, "kala lian," "it was very good." His pleasure at seeing the light at the end of the academic tunnel as a student was eclipsed by a note he found asking if he wanted to meet the celebrated Wagner in person. Nietzsche then summarized for Rohde how Wagner initially learned of Nietzsche:

. . . Wagner visited his relatives in Leipzig, strictly incognito; the press had no wind of it. . . . In Frau Ritschl's presence, Wagner played the *Meisterlied*, and the good woman tells him that she already knows this song well, *mea opera* [my doing]. Pleasure and astonishment on Wagner's part; he expresses his supreme wish to get to know me, incognito. . . . Sonnabend [Saturday] was proposed. . . . During those days my mood possessed the euphoria of fiction . . . verging on a fairytale. (November 9, 1868)

Nietzsche then tells Rohde of a grotesque interlude during which he lost a battle with a tailor's apprentice over a new suit and a bill he was unable to meet. He wanted to be appropriately dressed for "Richard," already named familiarly, but never again afterward—ever.

Finally, at the Brockhausens, Nietzsche conveys that Wagner, during their first encounter, put on quite a show: Naturally he wants to know how young Nietzsche became familiar with his music, he curses all misperformances of his operas and praises the ones that succeeded, he pokes fun at conductors, laughs at academic lackeys, crudely mimics Leipzig dialect, entertains his hosts with vocal and piano parts from his *Meistersinger*, reads draft extracts from his autobiography, and brags in superior fashion about how the "little" king of Bavaria—Ludwig, his benefactor—respectfully addresses *him* as the "great" German composer Richard Wagner.

Nietzsche did have an opportunity to talk to Wagner about their common favorite, Schopenhauer, who, according to Wagner, was the only philosopher to understand the essence of music (he apparently pushed under the rug uncomplimentary remarks Schopenhauer had made about Wagner's music many years before). Without realizing it, Nietzsche in his letter to Rohde captured the dimensions of Wagner's ego that he himself would not match until after he was to serve as a scholar-in-waiting to the Meister. Toward the end of the letter, Nietzsche turns his attention to his friend Rohde and proposes that they collaborate on a history of Greek literature.

CHAIR AT BASEL

Close on the heels of this memorable soirée, Nietzsche's mentor Professor Ritschl confided that he had recommended Nietzsche to the search committee at the University of Basel for its vacant chair of philology. Ritschl put his prestige on the line, saying that his protégé was the most mature graduate student he had seen during his thirty-nine-year academic career —energetic, healthy, nonpolitical. Basel made its offer; they had been looking for a young scholar with no excessive salary needs and whose career held promise of greatness ahead. Nietzsche, at age twenty-four, was at a crossroad: study of the natural sciences at the University of Paris with Rohde and the Cancan nightlife *or* the once-in-a-lifetime chair, though in the field of philology, a scholarly discipline he had begun to excoriate. Ultimately, he sadly deceived himself and others by continuing the emotional and intellectually dissociated lifestyle he himself called "Verstellung"—dissimulation—and accepted the position.

Vanity and the lure of instant prestige triumphed over what were the inner wishes confided to his twin Rohde. The faculty at the University of Leipzig felt that honor demanded that its prize student be given a doctorate on the basis of already published philological monographs and other works—although, to his credit, Nietzsche offered new research work for a dissertation. The envy, if not rancor, that emanated from other academicians was damaging to Nietzsche in the long run.

Nietzsche had new calling cards printed up and urged his friends to trumpet the good tidings; he answered well-wishers humbly but was enraged when his old friend Deussen responded with a lack of satisfactory deference. Nietzsche declared their friendship at an end due to Deussen's temporary "mental derangement." Here begins Nietzsche's megalomania. In keeping with his new position, the young professor reminded his family that he wanted to be treated with new respect and even asked his mother to find a manservant for him. Franziska's frugality put a quick end to such pretensions; she had periodically reminded him that it would be his duty eventually to provide for his bereaved mother and sister; and now the time had come. A fortuitous bonus came with Nietzsche's move to Basel: Wagner issued a standing invitation to have the young man visit nearby Lucerne and continue their acquaintance.

Though busily drafting his required inaugural address for Basel,[2] he found time to visit Wagner in Lucerne at his Tribschen peninsula estate with its idyllic setting at the lovely Vierwaldstattersee—a locale that was to become Nietzsche's "Isle of the Blessed" in contrast to the comparatively drab life at Basel. There were to be more than twenty pilgrimages to Tribschen during the three years between May 1869 and 1872, when Cosima and Richard Wagner moved permanently to their mansion named Wahnfried ("freedom from turmoil") in Bayreuth, where the Wagner opera-theater, cult, and court were to flourish.

For Wagner and the divorcée Baroness Cosima von Bülow, people were worthy collectibles to the degree that they could serve as personal and professional subordinates: only people of superior talent were encouraged to apply. With Nietzsche's ascension at Basel, he became a desirable and usable academic commodity, mouthpiece, and ally. In short order, two rooms were put at Nietzsche's disposal. As before, he needed a father-figure to venerate and fear. Reverently, he moved to the head of the Tribschen line by observing all due tribute to the Meister but also styling himself as one of the choirboys to his "seraphic" Father Wagner: the Redeemer.[3]

Nietzsche was never mistaken in his first impressions of Wagner as a "fabulously lively and fiery" person who spoke rapidly, was witty and entertaining—characteristics absent in Nietzsche himself and all his friends, and thus enviable and refreshing. One assumed that Wagner, like Schopenhauer, was entitled to the eccentricities that often accompany genius. Nietzsche wanted to believe in Wagner and at first coupled his own efforts in an ambitious—if not arrogant—adventure as jointly advancing German culture. The route from Nietzsche's veneration of Wagner and the unmasking of him, from mutual admiration to bitter recriminations, is worth traversing briefly because it tells us much about Nietzsche's attitudes toward Jews, Judaism, and Wagner's relentless anti-Semitism. When the break came a decade later, the love-hate relationship was to persist even in absentia, with the difference that Nietzsche had to murder not only the father image but also what he considered to be the archetypal anti-Semite. His conception of anti-Semitism was to be based on everything he saw operative in Wagner's thinking and behavior.

Not to be ignored either is Cosima's anti-Semitism which worked in harmony and tandem with Richard's. What is astonishing is the fact that Nietzsche, though enveloped over the years by the virulent anti-Semitism of his newly adopted "Pater" and his Meisterin, was not *completely* damaged by it. In his *Ecce Homo*, he retrospectively regrets the anti-Semitic contaminations that he had echoed for a time under the influence of the Wagners; but, in fact, he was not able to completely obliterate Wagner-inspired stereotypes and denigrating assumptions.

At the time, it was easy for Nietzsche to convert his friend Baron Carl von Gersdorff to Wagnerism; Gersdorff was disdainful of Jews anyway.[4] As a new Wagner acolyte, Nietzsche told Gersdorff:

> Our "Jews"—and you know the circumference of that concept—hate the idealistic art of Wagner that relates him most strongly to Schiller's glowing, high-spirited battle for the day when "men shall be noble." . . . It is an infinite enrichment of life really to have come to know genius at first-hand. . . . (March 11, 1870)

This note was typical of Nietzsche's attraction to genius and of Wagner's antagonism to so-called Jewish opponents he himself had created. Nietzsche ignored the fact that Jews open-mindedly and in great numbers supported Wagner's avant-gardisms and Germanisms, and the Meister resented Jewish approval when it exceeded that of *bona fide* Germans.

THE JEWS IN MUSIC

At this time the impressionable Nietzsche aped Wagner's slurs against Jews. Shortly before Nietzsche's first visit to Tribschen, Wagner successfully made news and assured himself of a public imbroglio in March of 1869 with his republication of the monograph *Das Judenthum in der Musik* (literally *The Jews in Music*, originally published in 1850).[5]

Although Cosima agreed with every touch of scurrility in the polemic, she was uncomfortable with the added public attention it would draw to their unmarried state, her pregnancy, and their background as illegitimate offsprings. Beyond that, she also felt that it was unproductive to antagonize Jews more than necessary. Her apprehensions were justified: Nietzsche did not directly involve himself in the matter but duly reported to Cosima that *Die Meistersinger* was hissed in Mannheim, and *Lohengrin* had to be postponed in Berlin; Tribschen was the recipient of many adverse news reports. What had triggered Wagner's decision to republish the diatribe was that he sought to rationalize his unpopularity with the press, which he regarded as Jewish.

Wagner, who could never be accused of brevity in his operas or writings, delivered himself of a 6,600-word diatribe, "Explanation of *Jews in Music*." His main accusatory points were embellishments of ideas that had obsessed him for decades: in the daily presses in Germany, France, and England, Jews were responsible for the frivolous treatment of every one of "my artistic achievements"; they indulged in running ridicule of Liszt's inventive designation of himself as a "Zukunftsmusiker"—a musician of the future—while the persecution and hereticizing of himself were also orchestrated by the Jewish press and other "Jew-agitations"; Jews aborted incipient and honest discussions of his theoretical writings. He complained of the deleterious, alien intrusion of Jews in post-Beethoven German music and in the Germanic aesthetic system, and their displacing the "blond German aesthetician." Adherents of "pure Jew-music" allowed every calamity—à la Offenbach—to express itself over German artistic essence. Specifically, he repeated his attack on the undesirable intrusion of Jewish essence into *our* art, arrogating to himself and like-minded compatriots the definition of German culture. Wagner trumpeted the claim that intelligent Jews with hearts in the right place— although certainly belonging to the "enemy camp"—responded posi- tively to his instructional messages. His "letter" concluded with a pes- simistic—if not ominous—outlook about any possibilities of Jewish assimilation:

> I am absolutely clear about one thing: . . . the Jews have gained ascen- dancy over our spiritual life—as evidenced by deviations from and fal- sifications of our highest cultural tendencies. . . . Whether or not the decline of our culture could be stemmed by a forcible ejection of that fragmenting alien element [Jews], I cannot tell because for that purpose some forces [*Kräfte*] not yet known are required.

With alarm, Wagner pointed to the danger of "alien Jews" in the host body of a Germanic-Aryan "folkish community." At any rate, the Jew was incapable of expressing, especially in music, the "völkisch" ideology of the German people. In effect, Wagner turned the activities of music and art into racial affairs. What makes it difficult to ignore Wagner's writings on Jews, and his followups in 1870, as "aberrations" are the facts that they were *not* aberrations but calculated incitements to active big- otry that became handbook sources for fascists and anti-Semites, most notably such Wagnerians as Hans von Wolzogen and Curt von Western- hagen who carried the Wagner message straight into the Hitler era.[6] Yet Nietzsche, too, was not unaffected by Wagnerisms, phraseologies, and vituperative terminologies of the Meister. With Wagner, Nietzsche let his face be his mask, as he confessed, and while acquiescing to his biases, Nietzsche would silently—or as an "enemy"—(as the Wagner-court biog- rapher Westernhagen would claim) deceitfully write of the Meister: "The tyrant in Wagner accords legitimacy to no other person than his own and his circle. The danger to Wagner is great when he gives no credit to Brahms . . . and the Jews" (*UW*, I, 259).

Elsewhere in his notebooks Nietzsche writes:

[Wagner] failed completely to perceive the situation of 1848: he enmeshed himself in the Revolution, lost wealthy patrons, seemed to socialists to be a renegade, and generally caused fear. He [also] insults Jews who in present-day Germany possess the most money and own the press. At first, he had no vocational reasons, later his insults were acts of revenge. (January 1874, *UW*, I, 250)

Though critical of the tyrant Wagner and pointing to his vengeful-ness, Nietzsche does not disagree with him about alleged Jewish money-power and their "possession" of the press, catering to perceived and bogus stereotypical fears of Jews.[7]

Generic hatred of Jews was a canker that tragically affected Wagner's first marriage. In an anguished letter to Richard on May 1850, Wagner's wife, Minna, spoke of the two years since she had dared to disagree with an early version of *Jews in Music*: "You 'defamed people' who basically have done you kindness, and in your wrath, you punished me so hard that you never again allowed me access to your works."[8] Among the "defamed people" from their shared, poverty-stricken Paris days was the Jewish composer Giacomo Meyerbeer. In 1845, Wagner inadvertently confessed to the music critic Eduard Hanslick that he and Minna in Paris "had a wretched time, and without Meyerbeer's help we might have starved." For all this Wagner perversely set out to punish both Meyerbeer as a Jew and Minna as a wife lacking in homage to his opinions. The character of Wagner, or the absence of it, hardened from those moments on. And Nietzsche was to draw firsthand conclusions about psychological reactions to indebtedness and the phenomenon of resentment.

The question of Jewish participation in German life and culture was a contemporary topic, and what caused Wagner to jump into the fray was the critical assessment from some quarters about his musical indebted-ness to the Paris-based Jew Meyerbeer. Such talk had to be squelched. He wrote plainly of this to Franz Liszt:

I nurtured for some time a suppressed resentment against this Jewish business, and this resentment is as necessary to my nature as gall is to the blood. The immediate cause of my intense annoyance was their damned scribblings. . . . I have struck home with terrible force . . . pre-cisely the sort of shock I wanted to give them. For they—bankers and Philistines . . . —and not our princes—always remain our masters.

Meyerbeer is a special case as far as I am concerned: it is not that I hate him, but that I find him infinitely repugnant. This perpetually kind and obliging man reminds me of the darkest . . . period of my life, when he still made a show of protecting me . . . we were treated like fools by patrons whom we inwardly deeply despised. (April 18, 1851)[9]

Wagner's ingratitude was pathological.[10]

Wagner presumed to act as spokesman for the German "folk's unconscious feeling of revulsion against Jewish nature," and his anti-Jewish vocabulary repetitiously aimed to differentiate between "our" German *Volk* sensibilities and "their" Hebraic repulsiveness. Wagner helped to draw the subsequent battle lines between the German "we" and the Jewish "alien-other." His code words were no longer disgruntled pejoratives but weapons of destruction. They were triggers to riot: *Volk, volkstümlich*, we, they, German culture, foreign Jewish language and nature. Wagner cruelly toys with his subject, alternating between jocularity and scurrility and appealing to emotions rather than reason.

One hesitates to continue the abusive Wagnerian catalogue, but it is necessary in view of the fact that Nietzsche in his writings was to react positively and negatively to all these Wagnerisms that became planks in anti-Semitic platforms. Wagner makes the mock-claim that "we fought for the abstract principle of emancipation of the Jews but really have no real sympathy for their person"; as usurers, they amass money without performing real work; the Jew dominates and the sons of Israel will rule as long as money is power (*Macht*); they will promote commercialism in the arts; their genius for money had been cultivated during a two-thousand-year period so that their blood now sticks to money. Modern art suffers from Judaization (*Verjudung*) and we need to expose what we hate about Jewish "nature" in order to excise it. The Jew has his own god and in the eyes of every European nationality possesses something odious. We wish to have nothing to do with someone of his physiological appearance. We cannot conceive of a Jewish actor on stage as being able to represent a hero or lover without appearing ludicrous. His language is that of a foreigner, it is something acquired and not of the native-born. He is rootless, possesses a dead Hebrew language and is alone with his Jehovah. He is incapable of creating works of art; he can only imitate. His speech with its peculiarities of Semitic expression and shrill Jewish intonation repels us with its hisses; it becomes intolerable for us. When we hear a Jew speak, we are offended by his every lack of purely human expression—its babble cuts a ridiculous figure. They are like parrots and dabble in arts like foolish birds. Jewish music-makers possess a peculiar Jewish speech and sing-song with impertinent stubbornness. Jews never possessed their own art and therefore never a life with the contents of art. Hearing this grotesque synagogue art, one is seized by its yodeling and gurglings; its melismata are wondrous jargon without expression. The educated Jew in our society has made excruciating efforts to erase all traces of his origin; in many cases, and for practical reasons, through Christian baptism, but this has led to his isolation in a society he has not understood and to whose history and development he is indifferent.

To prove his "objectivity," Wagner mildly praises the safely deceased Mendelssohn and allows his intellectual creditor Heinrich Heine—"the spirit of negation" who maligns decent Germans—*some* talent because he scourged his Jewish compatriots; Wagner deliberately skirted Heine's baptismal conversion. If there is to be redemption for Jews they must, like Ludwig Börne, *cease* to be Jews. Through their self-destruction and rebirth they could become undifferentiated from "us," but, Wagner declared: "Jews, remember, only one thing redeems you from the eternal curse placed upon you: the salvation [*Erlösung*] of Ahasuerus—his death [*Untergang*, destruction]!"[11]

This tract verbalized the anti-Jewish sentiments of Wagner's times and invited Jews to self-destruct instead of waiting for some "unknown-as-yet" forces to obliterate them. Minna Wagner was fully justified in being aghast at the slanderous attack by Richard upon people who had benefitted him, but this was a debt he wished to abrogate; it was an unconscious declaration of bankruptcy. Nietzsche eventually was to see what raw emotions hid behind Wagner's theatrical facade and was to see him as the arch anti-Semite to be countered. An intriguing parallel in the lives of Wagner and Nietzsche presents itself: Wagner's early lack of recognition fueled an anger that was discharged against Jews and an entity he disparagingly called "Jewish music," while the mature Nietzsche vented his resentment against Germans and Christians for not acknowledging his works in contrast to some discerning Jews. But Wagner and Nietzsche had one activity in common: the desire to enact cultural revaluations and revolution.

Ironically, like dispossessed Jews, Wagner was an involuntary wanderer, one step ahead of incarceration for alleged revolutionary activities and one step ahead of a legion of creditors from Paris to Vienna. In a bleak mood resulting from his impecunious lot and lack of recognition, he wrote to his future father-in-law, Franz Liszt: ". . . I must make people afraid of me. Well then, I have no money, unlike [Meyerbeer], but I do have an enormous desire to commit acts of artistic terrorism" (June 5, 1849).

How apt that phrased intent is!—"Ich habe ungeheuer viel Lust, etwas künstlerischen Terrorismus auszuüben"—an irresistible urge to overpower and intimidate. Wagner always sought easy targets, Nietzsche rarely. Both had combative streaks, and for Nietzsche not even Wagner's death assuaged his hatred for the composer.

In a number of notes, Nietzsche devoted some attention to music and generally praises the music, musicians, and intellectuals for whom Wagner had had a dislike. Quietly, Nietzsche was preparing to launch a guerrilla attack on the reputation of the deceased Wagner whose ghost kept haunting him. The damning notations would have had the intended effect of irritating the Meister, had he lived. Even the mere thought of this afforded Nietzsche the pleasure aimed for by his *ressentiment* feelings. Nietzsche's choice of Jewish names, therefore, was deliberate—Mendelssohn, Offenbach, Bizet, Heine, Varnhagen:

> For a chapter on "Music." . . . It is an error to consider what Wagner created as possessing *form*; it was formlessness. The possibility of *dramatic construction* is still to be sought. . . . In praise of *Carmen* . . . Mendelssohn: an element of Goethe in him . . . that also came to perfection in Rahel [Varnhagen][12] and her glittering intellectual salon in Berlin at the turn of the nineteenth century, and, in a third, namely Heinrich Heine. (WM, 835; probably 1886)

German Jews felt that their devoted attachment to Goethe—an acknowledged culture hero—would facilitate their own assimilation or entrance into German culture and they made of Goethe more of an emancipatory "genuine humanist" than he deserved, considering his slighting of Frankfurt Jews. For anti-Semites, Heine came to be the Jewish symbol and representative of the detractors and destroyers of German "values"; but Jews, ignoring some distasteful denigrations of them by Heine, saw him as a Jewish-German integrative force as did Rahel Varnhagen. More needs to be said later about Nietzsche's passion for Bizet's *Carmen* when it is used *contra* Wagner.

> . . . Offenbach has even more right to the title of "genius" than Wagner. Wagner is heavy, ponderous: nothing is more alien to him than moments of exuberant perfection achieved by this buffoon [*Hanswurst*] Offenbach . . . but perhaps the term "genius" means something entirely different. (*WM*, 384; 1884)

Nietzsche uses the words and concepts of buffoon and satyr interchangeably at times and identifies with both. Buffoon (in German *Hanswurst*, clown) appears strange, except in context. Like the word "idiot" in a Dostoevskian sense of "innocence," unselfconscious or "holy" naiveté, buffoon is applied to Offenbach,[13] Heine (and his "divine sarcasm"), Shakespeare, and himself ("a buffoon, not a saint, but a satyr"). In sum, wrote Nietzsche, how much must a person have suffered in order to find it necessary to be a buffoon?" (*EH*, II, 4). To suffer and to laugh—though he indulged the former more than the latter—were co-requisites for Nietzsche's philosophy of life. Offenbachiana was considered a new form of musical burlesque or spirited buffoonery, and Rossini called Offenbach the "Mozart of Paris."

> In the sphere of art, the Jews have grazed the border of genius [*das Genie gestreift*] with Heinrich Heine and Offenbach, that most sophisticated and exuberant satyr, who keeps to the great tradition as a musician and who—to ears that are not deaf—is a real relief from the sentimental— and at bottom the *degenerate* [*entarteten*] composers of German romanticism. (*WM*, 832; Spring–Fall 1887)

Ironically, the words *Entartung* and *entarten*—degeneration, degenerate —from Wagner on into the Nazi era became anti-Semitic weapons against designated opponents and nonconventional art. Nietzsche resists going the full length of praise and allows the Jews only to "graze" the border of genius. But which other thinker of his time had gone even that far? The more favorably Nietzsche speaks of Heine in his works, the more he has begun to identify himself egoistically and biographically with him.

Wagner had been dead for some five years when Nietzsche decided to wield his polemical rapier and kill the censorious father-figure once more; "the deadly insult," as described earlier, would not die.[14] Against Wagner it was an unending act of exorcism that Nietzsche was to advance with a motto from Horace—"ridendo dicere severum" ("to say the serious in a vein of laughter")—in *The Case of Wagner, a Musician's Problem* (1888). In his preface, Nietzsche calls Wagner a "sickness" in himself, which he had to overcome, an indispensable sickness—combining good and evil—that is a philosopher's "bad" conscience and puts "a vivisec-tionist's knife" to the claimed "virtues," the "good conscience of one's times" (J, 212). He opens with an assertion that critics have turned into a question, ". . . It is not merely pure malice when I praise Bizet . . . at Wagner's expense . . . ," and he puts "Wagnerizing" on the same level of danger as Judaizing, Christianizing, or any other kind of proselytizing.

Further,

> Yesterday—would you believe me?—I heard Bizet's masterpiece [the *Carmen* opera] for the twentieth time . . . such a work transforms one into a "masterpiece." . . . [It marks] the first principles of my aesthetics: "Whatever is divine moves on light, dancing feet."

Carmen, he says, is the opposite of Wagner's "polyp in music"—"the infi-nite melody, the counterfeit lie of the 'great style.'" Was Nietzsche merely spiteful in posing Bizet against Wagner? It seems not, when we consider that already at Bayreuth after viewing Wagner's *Ring*, Nietzsche sadly saw it as "the death throes of a last great art." His love for the gypsy Carmen and the opera is explained as going beyond melodrama and tragedy:

> I know of no instance where the tragic joke that forms the essence of love is expressed so compactly and transposed—with terror—into a for-mula like Don Jose's concluding cry: "Yes. I have killed her, I—my adored Carmen!"

It is the tragedy of possessive love that blindly demands reciprocity,[15] and it is the instinct that goes beyond love and hate to kill the object of one's love—a drama played out in Nietzsche's symbolic murder of a long line of father-figures, a younger brother, and ultimately God. Nietzsche said that "Wagner in his operas misunderstands love"; indeed, for Wagner "love is primarily spiritualized sexuality"; for Nietzsche it is the battle between the sexes for possession.

First commissioned by the Opéra Comique, *Carmen* was presented in music-and-play form and was coldly received by Parisians in 1875; but transposed to Paris's Grand Opera, it attained worldwide acclaim for its swift, vital, and dazzling rhythms and powerful dark tones. Bizet had been converted to Wagnerism late, but Wagner, seeing the opera performed (perhaps in its original form) in Vienna in November of 1875, sniffed an upstart rival—or worse, a genius—and termed the opera "interesting for the glaringness of the modern French manner"; and Cosima chimed in by dismissing it as a work "of much tastelessness."

Nietzsche fell passionately in love with *Carmen* in December of 1881 and immediately adopted it as a utilitarian antithesis to the "brutal Teutonisms" of Wagner's operas. Nietzsche readily admitted to friends that in his preference also resided "Bosheit"—a touch of malice—in promoting *Carmen* and Bizet over Wagner; after all, "Pietro Köselitz," the composer he had dubbed as a welcome "Gäst," or guest, turned out to be a dismal failure as the opera composer Nietzsche had chosen to dethrone Wagner. Although Bizet, suffering heart problems, died several months after *Carmen*'s premiere, Nietzsche was not aware of it until years later. At the instigation of Georg Brandes, Nietzsche found Bizet's widow Geneviève's address, wrote her a handsome note, and had a copy of his *Wagner* book sent to her.[16] He was delighted to learn that she was the daughter of the prominent Franco-Jewish composer Jacques Halévy and later to find, in 1886, that Hermann Levi, the Jewish conductor abused and exploited by Wagner, also was an enthusiastic admirer of Bizet, a composer of Spanish-Jewish ancestry. All these genealogical tidbits would be inconsequential were it not for Wagner's anti-Semitism and caricatures of musicians of Jewish origins. Bizet, defensive in the face of anti-Semitism, wrote in 1867 that to inquire of an artist his passport is "a police method: The artist has no name, no nationality . . . he is a genius or he is not . . . we must appreciate the qualities which he has."[17] The absence of such cosmopolitan sentiments in Wagner did offend Nietzsche.

Carmen, as Nietzsche told Lou Salomé, had a profoundly calming effect upon him, while his friend Resa von Schirnhofer, who was in Nice in 1884 and in Nietzsche's company at a bullfight (palliated by Nice's laws that prohibited horses and the killing of bulls in the arena), tells of the animated and electrifying effects of *Carmen*'s music upon her host. As a postscript, Nietzsche, approaching madness in late 1889, claimed, "I am Prado," the real-life Don José who killed his lover. Perhaps in his mind there lodged a scenario of the unfaithful Lou-Carmen and himself the rejected Don; much of his antipathy toward women in *Zarathustra* had to do with his Lou experience.

Early on, Nietzsche's combative lust was used in defense of Wagner as displayed in a strident assault on a writer who had won great public attention with his books *The Life of Jesus* and *The Old and the New Faith*, namely, David Friedrich Strauss—"a typical cultural philistine . . . with an influential role in the dominant pseudo-culture of Germany." Strauss had made unflattering remarks about Wagner's music and the Meister felt that retribution was in order; Nietzsche jumped into the breach with his essay "David Strauss, The Confessor and Writer" (1873).

Nietzsche's truncheoning succeeded in pleasing the Meister. (Much later an embarrassed Nietzsche was to claim that he attacked the cause and not the man.) Despite Nietzsche's dismemberment of Strauss's works —which Bernays also thought empty of content—Nietzsche was in sympathy with Strauss's rejection of supernatural and mystical beliefs such as the resurrection, but more significantly he went along with Strauss's charges against Christianity that its roots derived from the objectionable, Oriental soil of Judaism and its feminized nature: charges supported by other writings of the day, all having an anti-Judaic tinge.[18]

The extent to which Nietzsche was irritated and stimulated by, and actually indebted to, Strauss has not been fully assessed, but a sampling will help to identify some points—particularly the Judeo-Christian phenomena—on which they agreed and differed. Strauss completely secularized Judeo-Christian Scriptures and history; but he did not seek to "destroy anyone's church" since for countless people it was still a necessity (8). Nietzsche, however, increasingly was to advocate such extirpation, regarding institutional religion (and the state-church) as hypocritical. Strauss devoted a chapter to the question, "Are we still Christians?" Although both said "no," Nietzsche was to go farther and declare that Jesus was the most "Jewish Jew" and "in truth there was only one Christian and he died on the cross" (A 39). The apostles—the "Verschnittenen" (who divested themselves of material goods)—preached a cult of poverty and beggary, said Strauss, and Nietzsche depicted *that* as typical of *chandala,* the "untouchable" caste, ripe with resentments. Strauss praised the sentiments of pity, mercy, and neighborly love toward all people (even enemies) as found in Buddhistic teachings and those by Rabbi Hillel well before Jesus (93), whereas Nietzsche saw those alleged virtues as false sentiments: pity was an intolerable acceptance of condescension, a patronizing attitude; one must be hard and pitiless even against oneself.

Strauss joined his thinking to nineteenth-century stereotyped equations between alleged feminine and Oriental-Jewish "debilities." Nietzsche was, on occasion, to diverge from this view. But mostly he was to reject the virtue Strauss attributes to Jesus in taking over Judaism's belief in monotheism and also the laws, "interpreting them more spiritually and purifying them." According to Strauss, Jesus transformed the strict God and Lord into "a loving and forgiving father and herewith gave the religious conduct of people a kind of freedom and joy unknown in Judaism" (61). Nietzsche did not care for this "transformation" of God into a benign being. He preferred the omnipotent patristic Yahweh, beyond human invention and morally neutral in an indifferent universe and nature.

While Wagner spewed diatribes against Jews, Nietzsche, even while under the Meister's power, set up for his main target not the Jews but institutional Christianity. After Wagner's conversion to Christianity, and Nietzsche's rejection of Wagner *and* anti-Semitism, Nietzsche was in a position to have a field day flinging his most ferocious arrows against Christian anti-Semites.

FAMILY HISTORY AND THE TRIBSCHEN DAYS

Wagner became for Nietzsche a great specimen for significant psychological observations and theorizings, particularly the concept of *ressentiment* as a key dynamic force in human behavior. With growing concern Nietzsche saw in the Meister the forces of resentment and rancor that embraced envy, hate, jealousy, and vindictiveness. Nietzsche used the French word *ressentiment* because it contains important nuances. *Ressentiment* propelled Wagner's diatribe against *Jews in Music* as it did his views of the press. His fear and loathing of the press no doubt was grounded in the wicked lampooning his works and person received ceaselessly throughout his career from nearby Munich, Berlin, Vienna, and the more distant Paris, St. Petersburg, and London. There was reciprocal antagonism between Wagner and critics who complained of hours-long abuse of eardrums, torture of singers and musicians, bombastic texts with unattractive ding-a-ling rhymes, and tedious allegories. Nor was his fraudulent ethnomusical mythologizing forgotten, but it was—ironically—a large *Jewish* audience that passionately supported his music and financially and managerially assisted the founding and continuance of Wagner benevolent societies. Some anti-Semitic cartoonists ignored the fact that Wagner himself was an ardent anti-Semite and ridiculed him as the "Rabbi of Bayreuth" who extracted usurious prices from his mainly Jewish audiences.[19]

Wagner was painfully aware of the press cartoons and particularly those caricatures that illustrated his Semitic features, with gleeful views of his profiled nose.[20] He was quite aware of and sensitive to rumors that his biological father, Ludwig Geyer, a part-time actor and painter, came from Jewish ancestry. It may be that Wagner's ostentatious anti-Jewish crusades had the further objective of refuting rife public beliefs (eventually and vindictively exploited also by Nietzsche).

Cosima, an illegitimate child, was an active partner to Wagner's aggressive prejudices, and also had similar anxieties concerning her ancestry, but with a more tangible basis. Her mother, Marie d' Agoult, had left her husband, Count Charles (whom she wed in 1827), to become Franz Liszt's mistress.

Marie's father and Cosima's grandfather, Viscount de Flavigny, had been a page to Marie Antoinette. Because both his parents perished by the guillotine, he reestablished himself by marrying the daughter of Simon Moritz Bethmann, a Jewish banker of Frankfurt on the Main, where Marie was born in 1805. Four years later, Flavigny returned to France with his family, to live there until his death, when Marie was in her teens. For a time, Cosima's mother lived in the Frankfurt household with her Jewish ancestors who were to become an embarrassment to her daughter, Cosima. Cosima vehemently referred to Frankfurt as "abominable" because of its Jews. She had a difficult childhood; and when her mother and Liszt's affair ended, Marie (temporarily) returned to her husband, Count Charles.[21]

Cosima eventually was abandoned to the strict tutelage of several surrogate mothers and developed a toughness that would stand her in good stead for the rest of her life. She was nicknamed "the stork" in contrast to her beautiful mother, Marie, and was determined to exceed her mother in two things: a career of writing and finding and holding a husband whose genius she would further. Cosima, of course, succeeded in the latter, discarding the predictably competent orchestra conductor Baron Hans Guido von Bülow (1830–94) for the composer-genius of the future, Richard Wagner, twenty-four years older than herself, and taking with her two Bülow-fathered children and three by Wagner.

Cosima's betrayal of Bülow brought her deep guilt feelings, generating nightmares. Even so, her cuckolded husband continued to show more love—if not masochistic devotion—for Wagner rather than Cosima, after the debacle. Ultimately, Cosima was to have no regrets. In her ambitious and valuable diaries and prolific letters, she fulfilled herself as a writer, though limited to a single subservient cause: promoting the grandeur of R. (Richard). In the diaries, any trace of ancestry is studiously avoided; "the Franco-Hungarian-Jewish Cosima"[22] had *no* intention of being anything *but* German, despite her dominant French upbringing or more removed Jewish ancestry.[23]

During Cosima's lifetime, the Bethmann family of bankers, still in existence in Frankfurt, had long been assimilated. Several of the Bethmanns became distinguished diplomats, emissaries, philanthropists, and contributors to communal causes; in the role of public figures they were helpful to politically harassed Frankfurt Jews, and they were met with racial slurs by vocal anti-Semites as well as by small-business owners and workers who feared Jewish competition.[24]

It was a measure of Cosima's psychological problems that she would not be proud of such romantic, powerful, and accomplished forebears—a line founded by Netherland Jews—but such identifications were out of the question for her new life enclosed by anti-Semitic and religious fervor; at the Meister's request, she had converted from the Catholicism Richard loathed to the Protestantism he really did not believe in. Deep down, Cosima kept faith with her Catholic indoctrination.

At Tribschen, affairs were heading for a crisis with the public and Wagner's royal benefactors, and *that* could not be blamed upon any Jewish conspiracies. The unconventional Cosima von Bülow and Richard Wagner ménage scandalized the Swiss and the Bavarian public. Tourists to Lucerne were said to have trained their binoculars on the

Tribschen estate to gawk at the famous adulterers. Every so often Cosima joined her husband, von Bülow, on his concert tours but the deception fooled no one. Cartoonists had a field day with the paunchy, five-foot-tall Wagner.

Since Nietzsche was unable to attend Richard and Cosima's wedding ceremony (on August 25, 1870),[25] nor the belated baptism of the year-old Siegfried, Cosima kept him informed in detail: "Siegfried was not at his best behavior during the baptism [September 4]. At first, he babbled and finally—when the Holy Ghost descended—he cried. But now, he is a Christian, and if he did not give the priest much joy, I hope that he will be true to the Savior on the cross."[26] Nietzsche, who during the Pforta period had already renounced all forms of religious prayers, and then had steered toward a relativistic philosophy and a pre-Hellenistic paganism, carefully avoided any potential religious controversy that could offend Meisterin Cosima. As for Richard Wagner, as Ernst Newman notes, he was what he wanted to be at any given moment and followed his own laws: "He was by turns Christian and Freethinker and Christian again, republican and royalist, lover of Germany and despiser of Germany, anti-Semite (in theory) and [Newman has tongue in cheek here] pro-Semite (in practice). . . . He never had any objection to accepting money from Jews, or to calling on their assistance in the production of his operas."

All three—the Wagners and Nietzsche—disguised many of their differences for as long as they possibly could in order to find a common ground, and, bluntly put, to exploit each other for self-serving purposes.

There could have been no greater contrasts than between the mandatory air of religious tolerance in the academic household, graciously presided over by Frau Sophie Ritschl, and the confused bigotries at the Wagners' "royal court." Cosima was deeply immersed in theology, the New Testament commentaries of H. E. G. Paulus (author of *Das Leben Jesu*, in two volumes), and the writings of the Bayreuth Deacon Dittmer, all in preparation for her official conversion to Protestantism on October 31, 1872. She took religion seriously—often to her husband's derision; in chivalrous silence Nietzsche sympathized with her in the face of Wagner's natural malice. Still, her main task vis-à-vis Nietzsche was to train the young professor of Basel as an acolyte in the service of Meister Richard. Her letters charted their increasing intimacy in contrast to the formal household graciously presided over by Frau Ritschl, and the change of salutation from "esteemed Professor" to "God be with you, dear friend." She coaxed him with the flattering reminder that even the children were looking forward to the next visit from "Herr Nü—tzsche." The transition from membership in the Ritschl family to that of the Wagners was like falling into the iron net of a spider, but Nietzsche was more than willing to welcome yet another surrogate family situation.

Nietzsche's pattern of submission to persons and ideologies, immersion, and rebellion or revaluation is, of course, illustrated in his relationship to Wagner. Less than a week after meeting Wagner, Nietzsche was ready to join the court-chorus in hymnic adoration of the seraphic Meister with a calculatedly awe-stricken and ingratiating letter to warm the cockles of any divinity's heart,

> Much esteemed Sir,
>   . . . I have dared count myself among the *pauci* [select few] in this unperceptive world, when it comes to understanding your personality in its totality. . . . [W]e impoverished Germans have been robbed overnight, so to speak, by all conceivable political miseries, philosophical nonsense, and aggressive Judaism. To you and Schopenhauer, I owe thanks for my holding steadfast to the earnestness of the Germanic race and to a deepened contemplation of our riddlesome and perplexing existence.

Without coercion, Nietzsche fell into lockstep with Wagner's anti-Jewish phobias. He noted that the most elevated moments of his life consisted of meeting him, and in Wagner that great brother-in-spirit, Schopenhauer, according them equal religious veneration. He apologized that his vocation kept him chained to his "Basel dog house" (to Wagner, May 22, 1869).

Indeed, Nietzsche felt welcome in the new family circle and remained so while in the posture of servitude. He was encouraged to talk about his works in progress and to hold mini-lectures; their evening readings and conversations ranged prodigiously.

Wagner had plans for Nietzsche's familial future. It was easy for Wagner to assume a father-figure role, having been born the same year as Nietzsche's father in 1813, making him thirty-one years older than Nietzsche. Though Wagner felt that his music was immortal, his perennial ailments reminded him of his mortality, and so he had a vision of

weaning Nietzsche from his chair at Basel and enlisting him as his chief
propagandist and as educator-tutor for his favorite and biological offspring, Fidi and Siegfried. Nietzsche did try his hand at writing a "Mahn-
ruf "—an epistolary and apostolic letter of "appeal to the German public"
to rally behind Wagner's cultural aims. Wagner's court council, however,
found it stilted and unsuitable for publication and Nietzsche was urged to
go on a lecture tour instead. Soon Nietzsche saw himself and his sister as
objects of exploitation, and feeling fit neither to be a foster father to Fidi
nor a public propagandist for Wagner, he had to define the space he
needed to maintain between himself and the Wagners without jeopar-
dizing the rare honorific intimacy that had been granted. There were
even occasions when Wagner entrusted Cosima to Nietzsche in escorting
her to events in Wagner's honor.

Nietzsche was enormously stimulated by Cosima's attentiveness and
she was the single audience to whom he dedicated a number of essays and
some musical compositions, hoping to gain the Meister's plaudits. When
he formulated the injunction "Become who you are," he meant the drive
toward music ever since he was in knee-pants, and his desire for philosophizing that seized him with his discovery of Schopenhauer. He thought
and hoped that both musical and philosophical desires could be satisfied
in the company of Richard and Cosima. During his paradisiacal euphoria
at Tribschen, on Cosima's birthday, he wrote a piano piece called "Pro-
cessional Song"—my "Dionysian manifestation," he said privately—and
was permitted to perform it for the incredulous Wagners.

Privately, as Nietzsche learned, Wagner laughed at Nietzsche's heartfelt offering at the piano and acidly called the piece for four hands an
"underhanded music score." Nietzsche also sent his "Manfred" improvi-
sations to von Bülow who returned it with undiplomatic contempt for
what he deemed Nietzsche's "rape of the Muse." Nietzsche reluctantly
accepted such rebuffs, putting on a good face and promising not to go
near a piano again for some time. Here was a reception of his musical gallantries far different from Frau Sophie's.

THE BIRTH OF TRAGEDY
OUT OF THE SPIRIT OF MUSIC

All this did rankle, but Nietzsche put petty thoughts aside for the moment and gave compositional shape to his idealized visions of Schopenhauer and Wagner as an incarnation of the Greek spirit of antiquity. He particularly lauded what he interpreted as a revival of Dionysian elements in the music of Wagner, hence the title *The Birth of Tragedy Out of the Spirit of Music*, appearing in 1872. Nietzsche conflated Wagner's *Tristan* with what he believed to be a modern parallel to the development in Greek antiquity: the Dionysian cult as the ultimate source of the Greek chorus, impelling the development of a theater that produced the great Greek tragedies: "Music is the real idea of the world, drama, its reflection" (*GT*, 21). With Wagnerian flourishes, Nietzsche grandiloquently proclaimed: "No one shall obliterate our faith in the imminent rebirth of Greek antiquity . . . the hope for the rejuvenation and purification of the German spirit through the fire-magic of music . . . this Dionysiac life and rebirth of tragedy" (*GT*, 20). The "fire-magic" imagery, as will become evident, clearly displays Wagner's influence and language.

The Birth of Tragedy immediately infuriated philological scholars who saw no evidence for the extravagant speculations that religious cultism, the Dionysian, and music gave rise to drama, and that the natural, spontaneous, unbridled, ecstatic, and dissolvent elements shaped by Apollonian genius gave a work of art its individuation and harmony. Since we cannot reconstruct with precision the role of music in ancient Greek drama, Nietzsche's essay remains essentially brilliant psychological theorizing that did, however, in the later nineteenth century (and beyond) engender scholarly revaluation of Greek civilization not as a paradisiacal period peopled with skylarking Greeks of noble simplicity, calm grandeur, and gaiety (*Heiterkeit*), but as a people and culture deeply torn by major mythopoetic forces. Of course, this was a highly charged projection of Nietzsche's own internal drama exacerbated by association with the Wagners.

At Basel, he worked diligently within a rigorous academic schedule for a small student body at the university, and at the Gymnasium gave a number of public lectures, among them "Homer and Classical Philology" and "Socrates and Tragedy"; he was quickly rewarded with a promotion to full professor. Fortunate, too, was the gaining of new friends, among them the reclusive historian of Renaissance culture, Jacob Burckhardt, and the scholarly historian of church history, Franz Overbeck. Nietzsche temporarily shrugged off one keen disappointment: the university did not permit him to play "musical chairs"; the philologist wanted to switch to the vacated chair of philosophy, but the request was denied.

At Tribschen an entirely different psychodrama unfolded. The Wagners were ecstatic with the publication of *The Birth of Tragedy* in which Nietzsche gave Richard's music and aims an aura of academic respectability.[27] At that stage of his life, Nietzsche was able to endure the strains of a divided public and private self: a Basel professor with a *superior* pose toward his family and friends, and the *subservient* pose at Tribschen, which barely held in check the urge to enact the Oedipal slaying of the vulture-father. It may come as a surprise that Nietzsche's revulsion toward the powerful genius-father figure simmered so early in his relationship with Wagner, but the musicologist P. H. Lang expresses the situation precisely:

> Wagner found a disciple. . . . But this disciple was much more dangerous than his enemies. As long as there was contact between the creative activity of these two, [Nietzsche's] admiration was boundless. A break was inevitable as soon as Nietzsche's critical faculties were brought into play and he began to examine his own ideas . . . he had an almost morbid ability to sense a false tone, an insincerity. Such uncanny clairvoyance is the characteristic of those fanaticists of truth who educate themselves by vanquishing the many evil inclinations and passions seething in themselves . . . the disciple had to abandon his master the very minute he discovered that Wagnerian heroism was the heroism of an actor, that the Wagnerian mythology was a theatrical myth.[28]

Significantly, *Wagner musicalized myth while Nietzsche philosophized myth.* Yet the bonds—despite psychological strains and stresses—were so profound that they did not give way "officially" until nine years later, in 1878, with Nietzsche's publication of *Human, All-Too-Human* which included attacks on the masked Wagner but also, almost mockingly, pro-Jewish panegyrics.

Wagner's duplicitous attitudes toward rivals dead or alive who possessed technical mastery of music, soon became evident to Nietzsche and he was to associate this with the psychology of envy basic to attitudes of anti-Semites generally. Although Wagner did not hold Nietzsche in high esteem as an amateur composer, Cosima knew precisely how to prey and play on Nietzsche's personal vanity, particularly his musical divagations. While the Meister pointedly ignored Nietzsche's wishes for a professional opinion of a twenty-minute piano piece he had composed for and dedicated to Cosima, she smoothly wrote to him: "Your comparison of the religious choral dance with the tragedy of a Beethoven allegro is bold and is on target, proving to me once again how deeply musical you are" (June 24, 1877).[29] Though not coming from a peer scholar, Cosima's flatteries found a home; Nietzsche was enraptured. The collection of Cosima-Nietzsche letters from 1869 to 1877 is an extended testimonial to how much they were in need of each other's epistolary support; they possess surface politeness and avoid ideological clashes. Regrettably, most of Nietzsche's letters to Cosima were destroyed by her when Nietzsche became a heretic to the Wagner crusade.

Nietzsche had kept Cosima informed of his correspondence with Frau Sophie, and Cosima diplomatically tried to wean him away by offering him the comfort and congeniality of a surrogate family. But she made it clear that she regarded herself as equal to the challenge of intellectual dialogue. In the letters certain refrains can be heard insistently: religious pieties, German chauvinism, pointed anti-French abusiveness, and sentiments directed against Jews ranging from the phobic to the condescending. Attacks on the Meister—whatever the source—were mainly, of course, inspired by Jews as far as Cosima was concerned: "The more I see how the Jews—and lamentably also the Germans treat our friend [Richard Wagner], all the more fervently do I wish that our Tribschen refuge may never be torn away from us."

Most of her day, Cosima said without intentional blasphemy, was devoted not to the gods but to God [Richard], and Nietzsche was to understand this to be an undeviating principle. She and Nietzsche appeared to enjoy gathering gossip—even unpleasant regalements—for each other. Rumor had gotten around that the gibberish song of the *Meistersinger*'s villain-baritone was Wagner's malicious parody of an old Jewish synagogue song which became a signal for audience hissing.

Wagner had been courting trouble with his thinly disguised antagonism toward an enemy he himself had created, namely, the influential music critic Eduard Hanslick, portraying him in the role of the fraudulent singing "master" Beckmeister (pejorative for "carper"). Wagner's program for "artistic terrorism" included counterattacks on formidable opponents for the sake of gaining attention. As great an opera as *Meistersinger* undoubtedly is, it is not free from racial bias.[30]

A SQUARE IN THE WAGNER CIRCLE

Gradually, Nietzsche was introduced to the rest of the growing Wagner entourage, not the least of whom was the adolescent, cigar-smoking Karl Tausig, an acclaimed Jewish-Polish pianist. Wagner welcomed male company into his home where his family, except for his favorite, Siegfried, consisted of females, and the unlikeliest bond with Tausig took hold. To the anti-Semite Wagner, the Jewish Tausig became like a son, his "beloved angel of the piano" [*Klavierengel*].[31] Among his effective tasks were to produce piano scores transcribed from Wagner's operas and to recruit patrons and subscribers for the Bayreuth theater and the first planned festival which he helped to found. In her diaries, Cosima noted on September 7, 1872, Richard's response to Tausig's early death: "R. [Richard] unwell, but he writes the epitaph for Tausig's grave, which I find wonderfully moving." Without being unduly sarcastic, one might point to comparable sentimental tribute accorded by Wagner to some of the domestic pets he buried. Tausig's death was generally attributed to a case of typhus, though some uncertainty is introduced by a later diary entry: "Richard maintains that it was the *Jews [in Music]* essay which destroyed . . . Tausig, for he has Jewish blood in his veins" (January 27, 1874). The word "destroyed" (*vernichtet*) points to the self-destruction Wagner wished for Jews.

Nietzsche remembered Tausig best for his prompt responses to any Wagner request, whim, or command with "wird besorgt"—"it's done" or "your will be done." What was Nietzsche to make of Wagner's "love" for Tausig and his loathing for the Jewish blood in his veins? One simply makes exceptions for certain Jews and one may still condemn their racial characteristics. On a historical scale, there has always been that exempted and exploited group of "Schutzjuden," the protected Jews.

In Cosima's diaries we find ample references to Wagner's dream-haunted fears of being assassinated by Jews,[32] as well as her own para-noiacally induced ones; neither of them examined the contents and causes of those nightmares. Not Wagner's conscience or honest convic-tions dictated his attitude toward Jews, but personal whims and momen-tary needs. Contradictions were irrelevancies to his mind: *he* dictated what was appropriate behavior, not only toward Jews but to all other per-sons as well.

Just as Nietzsche sacrificed David Friedrich Strauss on the altar of Wagner's prejudices, he ingratiatingly did the same with Heine's works. Inspired by Wagner's praise of *The Birth of Tragedy*, he planned an expanded introduction.[33] He subtly wanted to enlist Wagner to agree with him about "the falsity of the Greek-serenity views" commonly held vis-à-vis the Greek world, and he wanted to help Wagner lead the "German rebirth of the Hellenic world." But first it would be necessary to reject what he claimed was Heine's view of Greek art as "bequemer Sensualismus" (placid, comfortable and, by implication, decadent sensu-alism as against the "healthy sensualism" Nietzsche wished to ascribe to the Greeks). But Heine as early in his writings as the *Helgolander Briefe* (1830) confessed to being a secret Hellene as well as an admirer of the Jewish Old Testament and in his Ludwig Börne book characterized Shakespeare as, at once, Jew *and* Greek—a symbiotic play of Greek "art" and Jewish "spirituality." In other words, Heine thought opposites func-tioned creatively as a form of complementariness: a mutuality like the model of the Dionysian and Apollonian. Nietzsche's emotional and intellectual relationship to Heine took on many different shades of attraction and repulsion throughout his life.[34] In 1870–72, though, Niet-zsche's failure not only to acknowledge Heine's ideas but to come close to falsifying them resembled Wagner's own rejection of debts; even more, he aimed to prove that he was a worthy ally against Wagner's "enemies."

When Nietzsche began to realize that Wagner's mythologized Teu-tonism was incompatible with his own pre-Hellenic Dionysianism, and as their relationship became increasingly aggravated by Wagner's schizo-phrenic exhibitions and congenital boorishness, it was only a matter of time before familial bonds ruptured painfully. But there were other con-tributing events.

Goaded by his sister, who appealed to his manliness and German allegiance, her Fritz joined the Franco-Prussian War in late 1870. The neutral Swiss allowed him leave as a noncombatant medical orderly for the Prussians. Nietzsche, who has been branded as a war propagandist and lover of war, quickly became disenchanted when the bloody reality of war set in with its stench, horrors, and disease. He wound up sick with diphtheria and disaffected with and wary of Prussianism. Cosima had wanted him to stay away from the war; he was too valuable on the Wagner homefront. As Wagner's nationalistic jingoism—an amalgam of rabid anti-French and anti-Jewish tones—rose, Nietzsche's fell and he took a noticeable turn favoring French culture. He had to hide these inclinations so as not to offend his Tribschen family.

Of the intimates admitted to the Wagner household, the noted singer Lilli Lehmann gives us glimpses of the Meister in her autobiography, *Mein Weg*. Although an admirer, she took Wagner to be too old at sixty-two to be educable in respect to his habits of "cruel joking," and recalled that Wagner's "xenophobia was undisguised."[35] Lehmann also reminisced briefly about her first contact with Nietzsche:

> Sometimes I sat with Friedrich Nietzsche who glorified Wagner ecstatically, speaking quietly and softly. At that time he knew nothing as yet of the "wicked old sorcerer" Wagner [parodied by Nietzsche in *Zarathustra*, IV].

Although Nietzsche still cherished letters from Frau Sophie Ritschl, who commented with pleasure on her young friend's early academic lectures, Cosima had become her substitute. Nietzsche, naturally, sent Father Ritschl a copy of what he had hoped to be his first publishing triumph, *The Birth of Tragedy*. Perhaps at first, he thought that the tribute to Wagner would please his old mentor. But Nietzsche had misunderstood. The Brockhaus-Wagner connection brought Ritschl briefly in contact with Wagner, but Ritschl actually sided with Wagner mainly because his university colleague Otto Jahn, with whom he engaged in a bitter personnel-hiring squabble, was an anti-Wagner critic. Ritschl had made it known that his favorite pupil Nietzsche would soon become Europe's foremost philologist with a full-length book in any of the subject areas he had worked on while under Ritschl's aegis. But *The Birth of Tragedy* intentionally ventured into Greek cultic areas that Ritschl had closed off as taboo, and regretfully he considered the book a nonscholarly "dizzy aberration" and declined to be its godfather. Unsuccessfully, he advised Nietzsche to publish a sturdy scholarly defense to answer attacks on the book, without denigrating philology.[36] Sophie restrained Vater Ritschl from completely disowning his favorite protégé; but Nietzsche pushed him into unwilling responses with his repeated requests for reaction to what he regarded as his manifesto. Nietzsche desperately wanted Ritschl's approbation, but never received it. Their correspondence almost ceased and Cosima solicitously tried to minimize and bridge the loss that ensued for Nietzsche.

Yet, whenever the opportunity presented itself, Cosima exploited rifts that developed between Nietzsche and others. On December 7, 1872, Nietzsche wrote to Rohde.

> . . . My book [*The Birth of Tragedy*] actually has been out of print in Leipzig. The latest [news] is that Jacob Bernays has explained that the book's points of view are his, but only strongly exaggerated. I find that divinely sassy coming from this educated and clever Jew; at the same time, it is a jolly sign that "the cunning ones of the country" have a sense of how the weather blows. The Jews are everywhere, and even here they are in the vanguard. . . . (December 7, 1872)

Bernays, it should be remembered, was the other stellar protégé of Professor Ritschl and one who never abandoned scholarly research. Nietzsche was ironic and disturbed about the disaffection he had created among former Leipzig faculty, but from Wagner he learned that one buries debts without acknowledging them. He sent the same report about Bernays to Cosima and she clucked echoingly. The Wagners, however, on several occasions invited Jacob Bernays's converted brother Michael to their home.

When Ritschl died in 1876, Nietzsche was psychologically unable for some time to write to the widow, his benefactress, and express his genuine sorrow. This sentiment, one might conjecture, was mingled with a touch of parricidal guilt at the passing, as Nietzsche wrote, of "the last of the great men, the father of a very great time." Nietzsche regretted that his own illness prevented a more demonstrable "sacrifice to the dead" at Ritschl's grave and a public tribute to him (letter to Sophie Ritschl, January 1877). Superstitiously, Nietzsche feared that his failure at "sacrifice" would raise another father-ghost to haunt him.

While Nietzsche during his years of bondage conveniently suppressed much of Wagner's unpleasantness, he had a chance to observe and psychologically analyze other capitulants, such as the composer Peter Cornelius (1824–74), who, in 1862, was invited to share a "marital-like" arrangement with Wagner but declined. Cornelius, like Nietzsche, was also eventually "excommunicated" from the Wagner clique. Although different reasons prompted Cornelius's and Nietzsche's severance from Wagner—the former simply refused to be a complete Wagner yea-sayer —there was a common ground. Cornelius, despite difficult economic straits, managed an optimistic and joyful pleasure in his artistic strivings and familial relations; and Nietzsche, too, was driven by a lust for life— a Dionysian overcoming of fatalities.[37]

In his association with Wagner, Nietzsche saw the ideologue and artist Wagner cultivating an apocalyptic vision. It was more accurate than Cosima had imagined when she reported Richard's progress toward "composing the end of the world."

APOCALYPTIC VISIONS

During his visits to Tribschen, Nietzsche had unrestricted access to Wagner's published works, manuscripts, and most correspondence to account for his familiarity with the Meister's views. A boisterous raconteur, Wagner was on stage at all times and loved to embellish his life stories for an audience of intimates or a stream of chosen guests. His autobiography, *Mein Leben*, was composed with considerable artistic license. Some very delicate matters that could have put Richard in an even more damaging political and personal light were toned down or eliminated, as they were from Cosima's diaries or those letters saved for publication— certainly those from Richard and most from Nietzsche were destroyed. Still, some prejudicial material survived purgation or surreptitiously found its way into private collections. There was nothing in Wagner's outpourings that was less than immodest or provocative. Wagner spoke of "fire cures" and revolutions that would "burn the monster Paris to the ground," and he gave the young Nietzsche much to think about: to agree with and much ultimately to reject, and to style himself the antipode of Wagner. Early on, in 1850, Wagner wrote in a personal letter to Theodor Uhlig (1822–1853, an old friend of close political persuasion, composer and member of the Dresden court orchestra):

> With complete level-headedness . . . I assure you that I no longer believe in any other revolution save that which begins with the burning down of Paris: no more June [1848] battles will be fought there . . . these are no longer prison cells in which they are turned to beasts.—Does that alarm you? . . . Strong nerves will be needed, and only true human beings will survive the revolution . . . whose humanity is the product of need and the most grandiose terror . . . our redeemer [*Erlöser*] will destroy with furious speed all that stands in our way! When?—I do not know . . . but . . . the coming storm will exceed all earlier ones . . . of February 1847. . . . We need a fire-cure [*Feurkur*] in order to remedy (i.e., destroy) the cause of our illness. . . . Shall we then return to a state of nature. . . . God forbid! Man is a social, all-powerful being only through culture . . . live a life of enjoyment . . . active enjoyment is what matters (letter to Theodor Uhlig, October 22, 1850).[38]

With black humor, Wagner ends the letter to Uhlig with the injunction not to jiggle the night lamp and set his bed on fire. Not to be ignored in the letter are the paranoid *ressentiments* that find violent expression in the apocalyptic wish of a cleansing "fire-cure": first Paris, the city that had failed to capitulate to him and grant him recognition, and then the Jews within it, whom he decided to blame for his misadventures. In his unconscious and in his dreams, there smoldered for most his life such feelings for a "Feuerkur," a wish for a cure by fire, which in reality, burst like an abscess in December 1881.

On December 10 Vienna's Ringtheater was engulfed in flames just before the curtain was to go up on Offenbach's *The Tales of Hoffman;* more than four hundred people, many of whom were Jewish, perished. Cosima reports casually (December 17) that "the fact of 416 Israelites perishing in the fire did not heighten Richard's empathy for the disaster." Cosima continues to say that the next day Richard told her about a recent performance of Lessing's *Nathan the Wise*, during which an Israelite in the audience shouted "Bravo" when an actor onstage said that Jesus also was a Jew. Richard reproached Lessing for "this piece of insipidity," and when Cosima replied that the play seemed to contain a "peculiarly German kind of humanity," he responded:

> But not a trace of profundity. . . . One feeds the impudence of these char-
> acters by having truck with them, and we . . . do not openly express such
> opinions in front of Rub[instein], about those Jews [burned] in the [Ring]
> theater, 400 unbaptized and probably 500 baptized ones. [Richard] says
> with impetuous jocularity that all Jews should be burned to death [ver-
> brennen] at a single performance of Nathan. (December 18)

Wagner, self-styled "plenipotentarius of destruction," was an inspiration only some forty-five years later to "der Führer" who nearly succeeded in immolating Paris and the Jews. We owe the survival of Wagner's inhuman expression of wishes to Cosima's diaries which—ironically— she never intended for publication. To keep their friendship, Nietzsche ignored Wagner's and Cosima's pleasure at the humiliation of the French and wish for their destruction. During the Franco-Prussian war, Wagner dreamed of a burning Paris, while Nietzsche had yearned to visit it for his own pleasure and intellectual rejuvenation—and he was to return to that dream later when he met Lou Andreas-Salomé. While Wagner carried on endlessly about Jews, Nietzsche responded with later reprisals of mockery at the display of mean-spirited anti-Semitism embodied in the dogmas proclaimed by Wagner and his apostles.

Nietzsche, by inclination and also having been infected by Wagnerian indoctrination, had clearly been on the verge of succumbing to a politicized advocacy of German culture. It took him a while to realize that Wagner's idea of "German" was utterly xenophobic. Wagner's pro-German and anti-Semitic thoughts were often published in his propaganda organ, the Bayreuther Blätter. Ultimately, however, Wagner was not able to persuade Nietzsche that the dichotomy between Germans and Jews was the critical contemporaneous or historical problem; Nietzsche, instead, was to follow Heine's earlier lead that posed the historical drama as one between the Greek-Hebraic and the victorious Judeo-Christian. Nietzsche, more than any other contemporary, understood how Wagner's anti-Jewish phobias infected his prose works and operas. And this understanding preceded his own serious responses and interpretations. Like other Wagner followers he, at first, fell under the nihilistic spell of the joyous renunciation of life, the attraction of pyromania and sexuality, the *Liebestod* motifs,[39] Schopenhauer-Buddhistic denial of the will, submission to the cyclical ring of destruction and regeneration (*Anfang* and *Untergang*), and the purifying fire-cure necessary for the renewal of humankind. Here was Wagner's inner, emotional autobiography. With the perishing of his alter ego, the spectral Flying Dutchman, he had hoped to gain "peace and salvation"; instead, Wagner wrote:

> . . . too late now! for me there is no longer any possibility of redemption—except for *death*! Oh how happy I should be to die in a storm at sea—but not on my sick-bed!!! Indeed—I should be glad to perish in the flames of *Valhalla*! Mark well my new poem [the *Ring* cycle]—it contains the world's beginning and its end! I must now set it to music for the Jews of Frankfurt and Leipzig—it is just the thing for them. (to Liszt, February 11, 1853)

Wagner's obsession with annihilation linked to Jews was to define for Nietzsche the irrational nature of anti-Semitism: *Wagner was its embodiment.*

Nietzsche's negative reaction to features of Wagner's music and anti-Jewish ideology was kept in temporary abeyance while he was still in the Meister's thrall and in the web of the Schopenhauer who had brought them together. Wagner was permanently wedded to—while Nietzsche was to divorce himself from—such Schopenhauerian creeds that optimism was an undesirable "Jewish superstition"; that the Semitic religions—Judaism and Islam—were too much this-world-oriented in comparison with the spiritual, otherworldly orientation of Buddhism, Brahmanism, and "true Christianity"; and that Judaism was the affirmation of the will to life at any price and hence the drive that accounted for the Jews' dominance in Europe.

Neither Schopenhauer nor Wagner took vows of poverty in line with such theoretical professions of Christian otherworldliness—and professions are all they ever remained for Wagner who needed luxurious and sensual stimuli for his works. Nevertheless Wagner, like his contemporary Jew-hater Karl Marx, identified Jewish influence as perniciously worldly and destructive in spirit. As far as Nietzsche was concerned, he was to laud the worldly optimism of Jews, which accounted for their survival despite historical odds; he compared their worldly aims with that of the Greeks, and he was not hypocritical about the positive values of wealth and the goals it could assist in achieving. The "Mitleid," or pity, piously preached by Wagner and Schopenhauer, Nietzsche thought to be a weakening and inimical sentiment without moral values; he fiercely inveighed against it. There is no doubt, though, that he accepted uncritically Schopenhauer-Wagner fears and allegations of Jewish power, yet his solution was to seek an alliance with it.

When the Wagners moved from Tribschen to Bayreuth in 1872, they founded a new home for themselves and a temple for the Meister's operas. For Nietzsche the move was as great a blow as the loss of his childhood Röcken, despite the death traumas experienced there. The Wagner-Nietzsche bond was loosening. The professor was no longer the star guest and the Wagners were too preoccupied with financial and production problems to pay more than perfunctory attention to Nietzsche. In a way, he was relieved and was free to form other friendships.

NOTES

1. Nietzsche's amanuensis Heinrich Köselitz (renamed Peter Gast), about whom more later, voided a manuscript passage he thought unjust in *Ecce Homo*, Nietzsche's last "confession," in which he said that "to believe myself related to such a canaille as my mother and sister would be blasphemy against my divinity. ... What I have experienced from them fills me with unspeakable horror. My mother and sister constitute the profoundest objection to an 'eternal recurrence,' always my own catastrophic thought." The restored passage and its history is found in Mazzino Montinari, *Nietzsche Lesen* (Berlin: Walter de Gruyter, 1982), pp. 120–68.

2. The inaugural talk given May 17, 1869, on "Homer and Classical Philology," praised philologists for bringing Homer into the public domain, but criticized them for not crediting the poetic genius that gave birth to the Homeric works. He sent a copy of the talk to Frau Sophie ("my always well-wishing audience") as a Christmas present and joshingly asked her to "hide" it if possible because he was fearful of her husband, "my strict teacher and taskmaster." She fondly replied a few weeks later with reciprocal confidence, praising his spiritedness and intellect and signaling readiness to receive all his future contributions.

3. This is a literary reference to the mystical chorus at the end of Goethe's *Faust*.

4. Nietzsche was to regret the number of friends he brought into the Wagner fold during his initial enthusiasm; his greatest personal loss was to be his sister, Lisbeth.

5. See Erich Leinsdorf's incisive review of *Selected Letters of Richard Wagner*, edited and translated by Stewart Spenser and Barry Millington, *The New York Times Book Review* (May 15, 1988), pp. 7, 9. Leinsdorf notes that the title *Das Judenthum in der Musik* should properly be translated as *The Jews in Music*.

6. The official guidebook of the Lucerne Wagner-Museum, published in 1983, unembarrassedly calls *Judaism in Music* a famous, major cultural and literary study; p. 16 of the English edition.

7. From Nietzsche's notebooks kept during the time of composing his main works we glean ideas in germination and expansion. There is an indication that he intended them as sources for a book to be called *Die Unschuld des Werdens* (*The Innocence of Becoming*). *UW* will designate reference to these notes, published in the major German editions of his works and conveniently in *Friedrich Nietzsche, Die Unschuld des Werdens, Der Nachlass*, ed. and comp. Alfred Baeumler, vols. 1 and 2 (Stuttgart: Alfred Kroner, 1956). Baeumler was, like Elisabeth, a Nazi; caution should be observed when using the notes, which often lack proper punctuation, quotation marks, context, and so on. The date given for the notebook entries in parentheses are approximations by the editors of the Grossoktav edition, vols. 9–16, published by the Nietzsche Archive. The notes were kept from the early seventies to the mid-eighties, and display some discrepancy at times between Nietzsche's private thinking and published writings. In the notes, he was severely critical of himself for having abetted Wagner's causes. More often than not, however, these untranslated notes were incorporated into the published versions with or without shadings.

8. Burrell Collection, p. 391.

9. Eric Werner, "Juden um Richard und Cosima Wagner: Eine Konfrontation nach einem Jahrhundert," *Oesterreichische Akademie der Wissenschaften* (1984), no. 36, p. 139. Werner's monograph is indispensable for an overview of Jews in the Wagner orbit. The author makes it clear that Wagner opposed any kind of "emancipation" for Jews.

10. Ernest Newman, *Wagner as Man and Artist* (New York: Vintage Books, 1960), p. 246. As Wagner biographer Ernest Newman aptly comments, Wagner "might have forgiven Meyerbeer for writing 'poor' music; but he could never forgive him for being a rich banker," for having inherited wealth, and for being one

of Wagner's creditors. In effect, he made Meyerbeer the Jewish scapegoat for his own early failures. Wagner continually railed against the wealthy classes though without having them (and less monied friends) to sponge on successfully, he would never have achieved his goals. Perhaps to compensate for his lack of money to subsidize his operatic ventures, Wagner developed an insatiable appetite for luxuries. His fawning and wheedling forced him to use deceptive ploys in his one-way vituperations and he often loathed himself for them, but he turned his wrath on the "benefactor" instead. The obsession not only with money but with the idea of it drove him to far-out rationalizations with particular virulence against Jewish entrepreneurs and bankers. He never relinquished his early anarchistic resentments against all capitalistic land owners and the monied Church as well. In a letter to an old friend of the family, Dresden stage designer Ferdinand Heine, Wagner aimed to put his views "in philosophical dress" but declined into a plaintive argument that money is the most decisive power in life, money *is* God because he has command over money, in the absence of which "I do not consider myself to be God" (December 4, 1849). Such tasteless grumblings formed the subsoil for *Jews in Music*, signed "Freigedank" (independent thinker), but he quickly gave up the disguise and relished the avalanche of criticism and praise that his bigotries elicited.

11. Wagner had precedents for his hate-mongerings and he escalated anti-Jewish propaganda found in the public domain. Politics and economic discontent peaked in demands that Jews as an alien people not be granted civil rights in a dominant Christian-German state and that medieval badges be required so that Germans not be misled by the outer appearances of their Hebraic enemy: Germany's salvation could only come with the extirpation (*Untergang*), root and branch, of Jews and their eviction from Germany. A brief summary of literature that appealed to the popular imagination may be found in Ismar Elbogen and Eleonore Sterling, *Die Geschichte der Juden in Deutschland* (1966; Frankfurt, A.M.: Athenäum, 1988), chapter 7, "Die Restauration."

12. Rahel Varnhagen von Ense, Rahel Antonie F. Friederike (1771–1833), and Heine, both as Jews and disillusioned converts and pariahs, had struck up a friendship as "outsiders" to both the Jewish and the Gentile worlds. Yet a sense of Jewish identity was ingrained in the baptized Heine and he promised Rahel consolingly that he would be "enthusiastic for the cause of the Jews and their attainment of equality before the law. In bad times, which are inevitable, the Germanic rabble will hear my voice ring resoundingly in beer halls and palaces." See Hannah Arendt, *Rahel Varnhagen. The Life of a Jewish Woman*, trans. Richard and Clara Winston (New York: Harcourt, Brace, Jovanovich, 1974), p. 227. A number of Berlin's literary salons were presided over by "Jewish" women

of culture, notably Rahel Varnhagen and Henriette Herz. A "Jewish" designation is appropriate for Rahel because the unhappy convert was never regarded as anything except the "other." "To cease being a Jewish woman meant being uprooted"—a price she felt might have been too high; see Elbogen and Sterling, *Die Geschichte der Juden in Deutschland*, p. 167. Mrs. Herz, though no convert, liberally took Christian lovers.

13. Jacques Offenbach (Jacob Levy Eberst, 1819-1880) embodied the spirit of *la vie parisienne*; he was the son of an Orthodox Rhineland cantor; Offenbach's casual conversion in Paris was a matter of social expediency and facilitated a favorable intermarriage.

14. That this is no exaggeration may readily be seen in a letter to Malwida von Meysenbug in which he confessed that Wagner's death put Nietzsche in a terrible state of mind, but the event would prove a relief in the long run. For six years he had condemned himself to silence toward Wagner, whom he had deservedly honored and loved, although Wagner had "insulted me in a most *deadly* fashion [Wagner trumpeted the charge that Nietzsche, like other young intellectuals, had suffered masturbatory derangement]. . . . Had Wagner lived longer, oh what could have transpired between us! I can string awesome arrows on my bow, and Wagner is the sort of person who could be *killed* with words." (February 21, 1883)

15. Kaufmann, ML edition, p. 615 notes Goethe's derivation of the same idea from Spinoza's *Ethics* (V, 19): "Whoever loves God cannot will that God should love him in return." Nietzsche's ideas on the subject are variations of the Spinoza-Goethe dicta; Rainer Maria Rilke later made them the cornerstone of his life and works. Oscar Wilde pithily phrased matters, "all men kill the thing they love . . ." (*The Ballad of Reading Gaol*, 1898).

16. Brandes, aware of Nietzsche's misogyny, teasingly wrote that the charming widow with a *tic* remarried (a French lawyer, Straus) and did not remain "true to her God [the composer]—any more than the Virgin Mary, Mozart's widow, or [Napoleon's] Marie Louise" (letter, October 6, 1888).

17. Gdat Saleski, *Famous Musicians of Jewish Origin* (New York: Bloch [1927] 1949).

18. The page numbers in parentheses after Strauss's statement refer to those in David Friedrich Strauss, *Der alte und der neue Glauben*, 11th ed. (Bonn: Emil Strauss, 1881).

19. The anti- and pro-Wagner spectacles even a century later remain unedifying.

20. See the compendious collection in Ernst Kreowski and Eduard Fuchs, *Richard Wagner in der Karikatur* (Berlin: B. Behr's, 1907).

21. Robert W. Gutman, *Richard Wagner: The Man, His Mind, His Music* (New York: Harcourt Brace, 1968), pp. 211–12. Gutman is severe with the person of Wagner, but fair to the estimate of his music.

22. Newman, *Wagner as Man and Artist*, p. 394.

23. Martin Gregor-Dellin and Dietrich Mack, *Cosima Wagner's Diaries*, vol. I, 1869–1877, vols. I, II (New York: Harcourt Brace Jovanovich, 1978–1980). The English edition is enhanced by more informative annotations than the original. For the Cosima and Liszt backgrounds, helpful assistance comes from Dietrich Fischer-Dieskau, *Wagner and Nietzsche*, trans. J. Neugroschel (New York: The Seabury Press, 1976); Victor Seroff, *Franz Liszt* (New York: Macmillan, 1976); Alan Walker, *Franz Liszt*, 2 vols. (New York: Knopf, 1983).

24. Tracking Cosima Wagner's background relative to the Bethmann family is fascinating. Their names are not found in the recent study by Alexander Dietz, *The Jewish Community of Frankfurt: A Genealogical Study, 1349–1849* (Cornwall [England]: Vanderher); a detailed historical view is obtained from Wilfried Forstmann, "Studien zur Frankfurter Geschichte" (Frankfurt, a.M., thesis), 1971, and *Simon Moritz von Bethmann, 1768–1826: Bankier, Diplomat und Politischer* (Frankfurt a.M: Kramer, 1973).

25. Cosima's diary entry reads: "May I be worthy to bear Richard's name and that Hans von Bülow, far away from me, may lead a happy life."

26. The complete entry from the baptismal register of the Como Cathedral is given by Alan Walker, *Franz Liszt*, vol. 1 (New York: Alfred Knopf, 1983), p. 248. Cosima's diaries, September 27, 1877: Cosmòs, "My Patron Saint."

27. Wagner, posthaste, appropriated Nietzsche's language and images, and claimed that the book's basic ideas had already come from him by way of a watercolor he possessed, at Tribschen, by the painter Buonaventura Genelli (1798–1868) and called "Dionysos, von den Musen des Apollos erzogen" ("Dionysus educated by the Muses of Apollo"). In fact, the watercolor did inspire Nietzsche but he saw in the Apollo figure conducting a choir of muses a vainglorious Wagner and in the dark-brooding phallic Hermes-figure, a Dionysian alter ego, the spirit of subterranean creativity. For an analysis of the parallelism of Nietzsche's work and Genelli's watercolor, see my essay "Genelli and Wagner: Midwives to Nietzsche's *The Birth of Tragedy*," *Nietzsche-Studien* 19 (1990): 212–29.

28. Paul Henry Lang, *Music in Western Civilization* (New York: Norton, 1949), pp. 879–80.

29. *Die Briefe Cosima Wagners an Friedrich Nietzsche*, Pt. I, 1869–1871, Pt. II, 1871–1877, Erhart Thierbach, ed. (Weimar: Nietzsche Archive, 1938–40). Thierbach's annotations are very useful biographically.

30. How the past shades compromisingly into the present is acidly illustrated in the following historical footnote found in Gutman's *Wagner*, where he tells of the Nazis' choice to mount *Meistersinger* in celebration of their annual party day in Nuremberg. Wagner had written to Bülow in 1866 that he wanted *Meistersinger* produced in the city it celebrated because he was outraged by the erection in Nuremberg, opposite the monument to Hans Sachs, of "an imposing synagogue in purest Oriental style." Gutman writes that Wagner's indignation was to find redress some decades later when the Nazis demolished this Jewish structure stone by stone. Gutman critically notes that Wagner propagandist Richard Stock, in his *Richard Wagner und die Stadt der Meistersinger* (1938), could, in all conscience, proclaim the life goals of Wagner to be fulfilled on that day when the Führer set forth the Nuremberg race laws in the war against modern Jewry. Gutman adds: "nor did Stock forget to condemn the 'Halbjude' Eduard Hanslick, and to quote in derision his review of the *Meistersinger* premiere." Gutman notes: "That the Nazis chose to mount *Meistersinger* made many well-meaning people lament the evil purposes to which scoundrels can put great art. However, in this case no distortion was necessary," pp. 221–22.

31. Ebert, p. 286. During his tenure with the Wagners, however, Cosima called him "Malvolio," a caricature of her father, Liszt, his teacher, and a figure without any individuality.

32. Cosima to Nietzsche, April 13, 1871. Here we find a typical persecution-complaint, where the persecutor sees herself as a victim.

33. See the "Vorwort an Richard Wagner," February 1871, posthumous fragments, *KGW*, III, 366–70.

34. The chapters on Heine and Nietzsche in Sander L. Gilman's *Inscribing the Other* (Lincoln: University of Nebraska Press, 1991) are vital to an understanding of Nietzsche's changing image of himself vis-à-vis his perception of his "other"—Heine; Heine himself saw his "other" in the poet Byron.

35. Lehmann, *Mein Weg*, p. 212.

36. Ritschl correctly assessed Nietzsche's defection from philology. In the projected new foreword to *The Birth of Tragedy*, Nietzsche wrote, "In the hands of philologists, antiquity breaks to pieces."

37. We need only point to one of the many near-disasters. During Nietzsche's service as voluntary reservist with the Prussian cavalry artillery, he violently jumped on his horse—his trusted Balduin—and practically impaled himself on the saddle horn and tore breast muscles; agonizing suppurations of the chest followed and he faced a series of operations. But he rejected medical intrusions and in essence healed himself; during the Franco-Prussian war as well, he endured sicknesses that would have destroyed lesser constitutions. Sheer

willpower that he later came to designate as the will to overcoming the self was the mainstay of a physiological, intellectual, and emotional drive.

38. John N. Burk, ed., *Richard Wagner Briefe. Die Sammlung Burrell* (Frankfurt a.M.: S. Fischer, 1950); Stewart Spencer and Barry Millington, eds. and trans., *Selected Letters of Richard Wagner* (New York: Norton, 1988).

39. Nietzsche's ingrained Naumburg modesty and sexual repression surface in his writings and most clearly in a letter to Malwida von Meysenbug: "My aim as advisor of conscience to German musicians is to plant the deepest hate against the disgusting sexuality of Wagnerian music" (October 20, 1888). "Music," he also said, "is a woman."

4

A New Rée-ality and the Breach with Bayreuth

RÉE-FLECTIONS

Quite out of the blue, in Basel at the beginning of May 1873 appeared an old Leipzig University friend Heinrich Romundt, a member of the philology club of which Nietzsche had been the guiding spirit. Romundt stayed on at Basel for three years as an adjunct lecturer in philosophy and fortuitously brought with him a friend, Dr. Paul Rée. Both immediately audited seminars given by Nietzsche—one on the pre-Socratic philosophers. Soon, the new friends joined the small Basel social circle in which Nietzsche moved. Rée was the second son of a Jewish family from Hamburg; his father owned an estate in Pomerania. Though his father wanted Paul to study law, a profession more accessible to Jews than was academia, he turned to philosophy and obtained a doctorate at Halle with a dissertation on Aristotle's *Ethics*. During the Franco-Prussian war, he patriotically enlisted and in 1870, as an infantry soldier, was wounded at Gravelotte and discharged from the army.

The friendship between Nietzsche and Rée was to extend through a decade fateful to both. By way of contrast to the exploitation of Jews at Tribschen and Bayreuth, Nietzsche's relation with Rée for the most part was to be of personal and intellectual collegiality—except when Nietzsche needed to retreat into a shell of contemplation. Rée, using the language of the French moralistic aphorists typified by La Rochefoucauld, pithily said, "The art of conversation is difficult. One risks boring another person by speaking, and boring oneself by listening." With each other Nietzsche and Rée found satisfying conversational compatibilities; neither was bored. If Nietzsche was curious about Rée's ethnic background, he gave no hint of it by asking overt questions. He sensed Rée's disinclination for the subject and respected Rée's avoidance of it. Because of the total assimilation of the Rée family to German culture and society and total alienation from any Jewish tradition, Paul Rée had not the foggiest notion of what was meant by a Jewish heritage. Although Nietzsche has left only sketchy characterizations of Rée in his letters and works, we do know that Rée was not oblivious of or unselfconscious about his origins. In fact, social pressures and rampant stereotyping of Jews did take its toll. Rée suffered greatly, as we learn from the insights of a person who lived with him longest and enjoyed his domestic confidence:

> I, too, have frequently observed half-Jews who have suffered because of their mish-mash situation. This dividedness in itself could hardly be termed pathological because it is just as normal as a limping person who has a long and a short leg. But to see someone limp with two healthy legs as did Rée—! Being a Jew completely and finding in himself something deficient to identify himself with, something that despicably and contemptuously contradicts his own person—I never saw this in anyone else to the same degree. (Letter, Lou Andreas-Salomé to Ferdinand Tönnies, December 7, 1904)[1]

So wrote Lou Andreas-Salomé to a mutual friend, the sociologist Ferdinand Tönnies, who met Lou and Paul Rée in Berlin. She added that on one occasion, during Rée's lifetime, she had made similar remarks to Rée. When he realized that she had not at all been conscious of his being Jewish, he was so embarrassed that he promptly fell into a dead faint in front of her eyes. He was shocked at not being taken for the instantly recognizable stereotyped-alien or "other." The kind of oppressive social conditioning Rée—like other Jews—accepted became painfully evident to Salomé:

The few times when Jews in our company were not recognized by him instantly as such . . . created incidents whose ludicrousness and horror defied description. Such disquietude motivated his behavior more than any Jew I became familiar with.

This violent self-effacement [*Sichvergessenwollen*], self-rejection, suppression caused the thinker in Rée to shun the emotional and personal. Yet . . . he was not as narrow as one might suppose; however, the door that led out was tightly closed . . . but it allowed communication of intimate matters, as if through a keyhole. And towering high above all walls there grew an almost ethereal goodness out of this painful self-hate [*Selbsthass*]. No one knew this better than I who nested within it as did a fledgling bird in its mother's shelter.[2]

Lou understood, earlier than did Nietzsche, the psychopathology of the westernized, rootless Jew Rée in an alienating world, exemplified by Wagner's Pavlovian training of Tausig, Rubinstein, Levi, and Porges. Neither she nor Nietzsche would associate biological heredity with Jewish character, as did Wagner (and Carl Jung later) with the myth of the inborn racial soul. Nietzsche, for instance, consistently attributed problems not so much to the Jews—ancient or modern—per se, as to their confining, retributive social and political environments. Though conscious of Jews, Nietzsche never made Rée feel self-conscious about his Jewish background or attempted to associate it with any of Rée's beliefs or actions. Uniquely, however, Lou was one of the first non-Jewish modern thinkers to use the term *Selbsthass* (self-hate) conceptually and to see its specific dynamic activity in the personality of Rée. I am not sure that "self-hate"—Lou's diagnosis of Rée—is entirely appropriate. Ordinarily, Jewish self-hate manifests itself in forms of Jewish anti-Semitism—and of that there was no trace in Rée's correspondence or writings; but there was a distinct absence—if not absolute avoidance—of pro-Jewish sentiments such as we find among Nietzsche's first major writings.

In a pioneering study of the subject, Theodor Lessing finds the psychology of the Jews to be typical of any oppressed minority, although there was no other in Germany.[3] Rée could not be called a "Grenzjude" either, that is, a marginal Jew who belongs to neither his ethnic nor host culture (the styled term "host" itself being a condescending chauvinistic designation). The "marginal Jew" is outside the border of society by either necessity or choice; and, at the very least, Rée, unlike Heine,

Kafka, Theodor Lessing, Hermann Levi, Karl Kraus, Jacob Wassermann, and a host of others, possessed no Jewish cultural milieu to identify with or to react against. Ironically, though insecure himself, he was able to provide five years of protective companionship for Lou—after the friendship with Nietzsche ended—that nurtured her intellectually and allowed her at the same time a protected celibate existence; though she did not marry him, Rée gave her a nested security but himself suffered an internalized insecurity as both a male and a Jew. He had her to blame for the former and himself for the latter.

PSYCHOLOGICAL OBSERVATIONS

The fall 1875 semester at Basel brought a major helper into Nietzsche's life, a young student with amateur musical talents, Heinrich Köselitz. Nietzsche soon rebaptized him "Peter Gast" (a guest who came to stay as amanuensis, copy transcriber, and general factotum), and in him Nietzsche had a volunteer disciple, an unpaid replica of Wagner's satellites. He joined Nietzsche's small circle of friends just as they were reading a book called *Psychologische Betrachtungen* (*Psychological Observations*), and with pleasure they guessed correctly that the voice of the anonymous author was Paul Rée.[4] Nietzsche liked the mischievous humor displayed on the title page: "From the literary remains of ****" and an epigraph, "l'homme est l'animal méchant par excellence." He and Rée were to share a dim view of the wicked human animal. Nietzsche immediately sent off a letter to "My dear Dr. Rée": "Even if you were to publish nothing other than these maxims that instruct the mind, they will have served your purpose richly" (October 22, 1875).[5]

Inscribing a copy of the book for Nietzsche, Rée credited his new-found friend as the source of inspiration while Nietzsche called the first period of their friendship "the time of my "Rée-alism." Clearly, Nietzsche was heading toward a manner of philosophizing and seeking similar to that which he complimented in Rée: psychological realism, objective observations of human actions, and the discernment of their underlying motivations. The primary result was to be the psychopathology of everyday life analyzed in his incipient *Human, All-Too-Human*; there he credits Rée's book with hitting the "bull's-eye of human nature" (MA, 36).

Rée's book is a collection of aphorisms or maxims grouped around a number of topics, mainly on books and authors; human actions and motives; women, love, marriage, religious matters; the subject of vanity. Rée had taken for his models the French "moralists" from La Rochefoucauld to Chamfort and Vauvenargues. Of course, Nietzsche was not unacquainted with aphoristic moral generalizations by way of the aphoristic mode from the biblical Book of Proverbs; the Greek and Roman writers in the genre, the classical Stoics Epictetus and Marcus Aurelius; Pascal in the seventeenth century; and, through Rée, the later French moralists with their ironical view of life. Nietzsche was becoming increasingly conscious of style as a formidable means of getting at experiential truth, human wisdom, and folly. His failing eyesight limited his reading capabilities severely, so that scholarly research was to be out of the question, yet philosophical "psychologizing" and the poetization of ideas became his compensatory strength. And Nietzsche's recall of what he had read was almost total.

Not being able to find a niche in academia, Rée had no particular love for it, hence: "Pedants shine like the moon—with borrowed light; the brain of many of them is drowned in learnedness." Much that was caustic about Rée's collection seems petty and the misogynistic tones were based less on experience than on male conceit. The Basel bachelors chuckled over the "reflections" that smacked of jejune cleverness: "Every woman values highest those manly attributes missing in her husband." "Handsome women are proud of their conquests, ugly ones are proud of their virtues." "Life-long marriage is a useful but also an unnatural institution." "Girls who have no men are pained more by the thought that others believe them to be incapable of snaring one." "No one would covet his neighbor's wife if he knew her as well as his neighbor does." Yet the observations dealing with belief, envy, vanity, malice, religion, egoism, aggression, love of neighbor, and morality were like flint-sparks that ignited a welter of ideas and connections in Nietzsche's mind. Rée's *Observations* are loaded with such provocative axioms: "Belief and unbelief contribute no inherent moral qualities but solely opinions." "We would not believe ourselves immortal if the opposite conviction were congenial to us." "Priests support religion because it supports them." "Behind every emotion is a mosaic of motives."

If Nietzsche's ideas more and more were clothed in elitist radicalism and cynicism, they found early support in the stylized *Maxims* of the Duke de La Rochefoucauld and the *Réflexions* of Marquis de Vauvenargues. The duke and marquis had ample opportunities to observe the courtier and salon society of their world and the year-round court games of sex and politics. Nietzsche faced an entirely different and bourgeois milieu in Naumburg and Basel, yet he extracted the essence of the French cynics' reflections and applied them freely to his contemporaries and to historical persons. There is no doubt of Nietzsche's idealization of the French seventeenth-century aristocracy; in his notes he compared favorably ancient Greek culture and the Age of Louis XIV over against the egalitarian French Revolution and its "continuation of Christianity."[6] Ethics as a substitute for religion engaged Rée's attention and proved attractive to Nietzsche. But Nietzsche, unlike Rée, was to go on the attack against certain elements of Christianity and Judaism, using subversive techniques handed him by the moralists. With honed wit, La Rochefoucauld encouraged redefinition and revaluation of values he thought to be pernicious platitudes. The assertion that "love of justice in most men is only a fear of encountering injustice"[7] could be attributed to either La Rochefoucauld or Nietzsche, as could the rejection of the idea that human aims or motives can possibly be "selfless" or pure.

RUMBLINGS IN BAYREUTH

In July 1876, Wagner responded to the publication of Nietzsche's *Untimely Meditations* IV: *Richard Wagner in Bayreuth*: "Friend! Your book is tremendous! —Wherever have you gained such knowledge of me?" The answer was obvious: from Wagner himself—his library and personal archive. What Wagner enjoyed in Nietzsche's monumental eulogy that celebrated his sixtieth birthday and the dedication of the Bayreuth opera-theater in May 1872, was the placement of Wagner's name among the constellation of the great from the Greeks to the moderns—Goethe, Schiller, and Schopenhauer; the extolling of the magic, the sorcery of his dramas, "the most moral" myths as in the *Ring,* and the loyalties of its characters like those of Schiller with their selfless fidelity steeped in a mood of holiness and sublimity. The ecstatic prose is rendered suspect, however, by the private notes Nietzsche was writing concurrently (and published posthumously). The effulgent printed praise reminds one of La Rochefoucauld's observation that the lover loves not so much his object but his own emotion. That was true of the Nietzsche who was absolutely spellbound by Wagner's genius, tyranny, and the Wagners' flatteries of their prize Basel professor.

In his Wagner tribute, Nietzsche's comparisons range through heroicism, martyrdom, and victory, and pictured Wagner's self-satisfaction. He portrayed Wagner as an incarnation of Alexander the Great at the height of his world conquests, possessing a lust for power that overcame pitfalls and adversity, resulting in a triumphal return to a society that had cast Wagner out to the gypsies. He gave Wagner—the embattled artist— a martyr's crown, as Nietzsche himself was to assume it vis-à-vis the Germans. But amid exaggerations in the essay there also was some cautionary wording: "It is true that a person like Goethe creates a greater sense of comfort around him . . . whereas Wagner's torrential stream of power may perhaps inspire fright and repulsion" (section 3).

Veneration of and antipathy against Wagner had been at war within Nietzsche ever since the Bayreuth festivities. One major reason he was to give for the final break in 1878 was Wagner's anti-Semitism. But this was only part of a larger picture. Most Wagnerians gave themselves over to the spirit of Bayreuth with grim seriousness or with sincere but amused detachment—like Lilli Lehmann, who was entertained by the fact that horses whinnied and dogs barked wildly when the Yo-ho to-ho-yo cries of the Valkyries reverberated through the town. Was it the music and text or the atmosphere of Bayreuth that alienated Nietzsche? Critics are at odds about this. One gathers that Nietzsche was distinctly put off by the philistine and carnival atmosphere, as well as the commercialism that turned the festivities into a travesty of Greek solemnities and not the revival he had envisioned. Disillusioned, he criticized the Wagnerian theater as a gross form of cultural nationalism. Nietzsche realized that Wagner was serious when, in his writings, he had demanded that Germans do honor to their German composers, with himself at the helm. And it was to be only a matter of time before a tormented and conflicted Nietzsche had to free himself from the latest and most powerful father and Fatherland figure yet. Inadvertently, Wagner helped him to that decision.

Wagner knew that Nietzsche's first and deepest love was for music and that Nietzsche sublimated music to his philological and philosophical works. Nietzsche was not allowed to have musical opinions other than the ones dictated by the Meister. One embarrassing incident in particular made Nietzsche aware of Wagner's arbitrariness. Nietzsche had been impressed by Brahms's music at a performance in Basel's Münster Cathedral. He bought a copy of a musical score bound in red leather and placed it as a gift on Wagner's piano. This acted on Wagner like a flag to a raging bull. He exploded, hurled the manuscript away, and inveighed against the "Jewish" Brahms; of course, it did not matter that Brahms was not Jewish—Wagner decided who fitted the pejorative and who would be granted dispensation. Nietzsche maintained a discreet silence but took note of what he was to characterize as the prototypical anti-Semitic Wagner. In the subterranean drama of Nietzsche's mind, he had already committed parricide: In a title-illustration to his own *Birth of Tragedy*, he is Prometheus who slays the vulture, a surrogate sent by the father. The seraphical image and the mean father image proved to be two sides of the same coin. Wagner's bullying tactics, after a time, were things that Nietzsche found as hard to take as had another favorite of Wagner, Cornelius. Wagner wished to have his courtiers in his presence on demand.

Cosima diplomatically wrote Nietzsche that the children noticed the empty place at the table set for him, while Wagner would chide his impermissible absences. Wagner wrote to Nietzsche:

> Among other things, in my life I have never found such male get-togethers as you have them on evenings in Basel. If all of you are hypochondriacs, then there is not much worth bothering with. It seems though that the young bachelors need women . . . but where to find them without stealing? . . . I believe that you must marry or compose an opera. One as well as the other will help you; but marriage, I consider the better thing for you.[8]

The letter, if Wagner indeed sought to draw Nietzsche to him, had the opposite effect. Nietzsche stayed away for almost two years.

The arrogance of this letter lacked neither humor nor brutality in Wagner's self-revelation and its callous disregard for Nietzsche's sensitivities. In compressed form, he made invidious comparisons, putting Nietzsche in his place, taunting him with his musical inferiority and Wagner's own success with women. Wagner likened art to a woman to be conquered. He was serious when he told Cosima, "I had hoped to have written all my work before I was forty; I assumed that the sexual urge, with which all productivity is connected, would last until then" (*Diaries*, August 20, 1871); in fact, it lasted to his dying day.[9] The skilled eroticism of the charismatic Wagner became plainly evident to a Nietzsche whose Dionysian impulses were severely confined to his imagination and mainly projected into suggestive poetry.

Wagner's self-stimulation by means of mirrors, luxurious bedding, silks, and perfumes went as far back as his Paris years; with Cosima, he shared a love for fineries and elegant costuming that accented their grand airs. "*Décadence*," Nietzsche called it, and the word became an important part of his vocabulary. Wagner's advice to Nietzsche about stealing women, marriage, and homosexual implications was painful, especially since one impetuous marriage proposal by Nietzsche to a young music student, Mathilde Trampedach, had failed. While Nietzsche made dour aphoristic pronouncements on sex and allowed himself furtive lapses, Wagner pursued his satyric appetites with exploitative and rationalized abandon.

Nietzsche's distance from Bayreuth, however, did not lessen his eagerness to get reports about its alarums or to discuss his reactions as reported by one of Nietzsche's students, Louis Kelterborn, in whom he had first instilled an enthusiasm for Wagner. Kelterborn noted that Nietzsche thought of himself as a co-worker with Wagner for a higher German culture, but he later dropped the remark that Wagner was one of "those greatest persons who in certain areas are very small and cannot tolerate being reminded of this by others."[10] Of the operas, Nietzsche maintained consistently that *Tristan* was "the most complete and pure expression of Wagner's genius." In Basel, Kelterborn was introduced to Dr. Rée in the living room (semi-darkened to spare Nietzsche's eyes) of a Basel domicile comfortably arranged by Nietzsche's sister, Lisbeth. There were occasions when Nietzsche lent his sister to the Wagners as a combination governess and tutor to their children when they were away on music engagements. Lisbeth was pleased with this social boon and bond, and was flattered to be able to advise Cosima on such matters as how to pickle cucumbers.

The extent to which Nietzsche hoped to gain a confidante even more intimate than Sophie Ritschl is clear in a trusting letter sent to

Cosima on her birthday, December 19, 1876 (a letter that only came to light in 1964). Just as he had intimated his Dionysian inclinations to Frau Sophie, he now hinted at his heretical drift from Schopenhauer (and one might also substitute Wagner for Schopenhauer's name): "Do you not wonder when I confess to gradual but now sudden differences with Schopenhauer's teachings? Even while I wrote about Schopenhauer, I could not agree with his generalizations and dogmatism."[11]

Despite a small student body, both at the university and gymnasium at Basel and small seminars, teaching duties and lengthy schedules weighed heavy on Nietzsche and when illnesses wore him down, he was glad to be relieved of the 1876 spring semester. He spent time with friends, with reading and writing. After he had made a presentation of his dithyrambic Wagner essay to the Meister and attended the July and August Bayreuth rehearsals, he fled the festival, writing to his sister: "I long to escape . . . I have a horror of the long art-evenings—yet I listened to the *Walküre*." Escape he did, but Lisbeth urged his return and he stayed for a few more weeks and heard the first public Bayreuth performance of *Rheingold*. During that time, with unconscious resentment, he started work on his "subversive" book, *Human, All-Too-Human*. In the company of Rée, Nietzsche quickly returned to Basel.

The friends spent three October weeks in Bex in the Swiss Canton of Waadt. Rée recollected, "After a fashion, here were the honeymoon weeks of our friendship . . . the isolated little house, the wooden balcony, and the grapes—the picture of a rounded entity."[12] To his mother, Nietzsche wrote, ". . . the most lovely Fall days, together with Rée, the incomparable."

Rée had to leave for Pisa, and Nietzsche on his way to join him met a young woman, Isabella von der Pahlen—later the graphologist Frau Ungern-Sternberg who in 1902 wrote a memoir, *Nietzsche im Spiegelbild seiner Schrift* (*Nietzsche Reflected in his Writings*). She remembered Nietzsche's monologues as they went sightseeing in Pisa and particularly his views on eugenics as the duty of the state to prohibit by law marriage for unfit persons. Rée brusquely took her aside to warn her that Nietzsche needed to avoid nervous excitation. Rée well knew that Nietzsche was stimulated by attentive daughter-like younger women; Sternberg had declared herself to be a *libre penseur*, belonging to the independent thinkers and French moralists of whom Nietzsche was fond.

SORRENTO

Nietzsche was graciously granted a year's sick leave from Basel, this time with almost full salary; colleagues covered his courses. He promptly dictated a letter to Malwida von Meysenbug, the conservative suffragette he had met at the Wagners, telling her he was delighted to accept her invitation to be a guest and to recuperate at the Gulf of Naples.[13] He wrote that "Dr. Rée [whom she had not as yet met] would like to accompany me, with your consent?" (September 26, 1876). He added another companion to the list, a young writer, poet, and law student at Basel, Albert Brenner.

By design, the Wagners had decided to leave their troubled financial affairs behind in Bayreuth and embark on a family trip from September 14 to December 20, with a brief stay in Sorrento where Nietzsche was to winter with his friends. Before Nietzsche left Basel, Wagner asked him to kindly procure for him some underwear from the Basel firm of C. C. Rumpf. Was Nietzsche's reply (September 27, 1876) perhaps tongue in cheek in regard to the errand? "Most esteemed friend, you gave me pleasure with the small task that you assigned me—it reminded me of the Tribschen days." Nietzsche, as if to say "thanks for letting me run out to buy your underwear," continues: "At the moment, I have time to think about things distant and near while sitting much of the time in a darkened room, suffering from neuralgia, and taking atropine treatments for my eyes." Nietzsche thought that it would be good for his friend Wagner to get away from the Germans and visit Italy, where he had gained his inspiration for the *Rheingold* music. He told him also about his intended trip to Italy for reasons of health.

In the letter's last paragraph, Nietzsche sent his heartiest wishes to Wagner and Cosima, and included a slur about the "Jew Bernays." Nietzsche's slur indicated that he had retained his grudge against Bernays and at the same time could not resist catering to Wagner. If Nietzsche, at the time, knew that Rée, too, was Jewish, he did not let on but recommended to Cosima that she read his book and the writings of the French moralists. She promised to do so and sympathized with the annoyance directed toward Bernays.

Malwida had rented the Villa Rubinacci in Sorrento, with comfortable working and resting quarters for everyone and less expensive than the hotel chosen by the Wagners for their stay. Malwida's and Wagner's entourages joined in day-excursions and long social evenings, all of which proved more taxing and wearying to Malwida's friends than to the Wagners who were used to long evening routines. On October 31, all parties toasted Malwida at a birthday celebration. Cosima's diary entry for November 1 mentions a visit that includes not only friend Nietzsche "run down and concerned with his health" but also a "Dr. Rée whose cold and precise character does not appeal to us." She adds that "upon closer observation we [she and R.] discovered that he must be an Israelite." Cosima's sharp nose had sniffed out what she instinctively felt to be a Jew. And thereafter she set the tone for Bayreuth's attitude toward Rée.

Sometime before the Wagners left on November 7, Richard and Nietzsche met for private talks and walks. Nothing is known directly of what transpired—a deep silence cast a pall around everyone. In her biography of her brother, Lisbeth surmised that Wagner had donned a mask of piety and offended her brother by not honestly admitting his capitulation to audience tastes; and further that Wagner's life-denying and Catholic-romantic *Parsifal* stood in contrast to her brother's life-affirming ideals. What she left unsaid—though her brother did not—was that Wagner's cardboard *Teutonic* gods, heroes, and heroines and the pagan *Greek* ones whom Nietzsche revered never had much in common in the first place. Wagner, the atheist, hiding behind a religious mask, represented the height of hypocrisy as far as Nietzsche was concerned; but he never dared tell this to the Meister straight out. Cosima, according to her diary, reread Nietzsche's "Wagner in Bayreuth" essay and despite the hagiographical emanations knew that earlier she had glossed over subsurface dissonances.

After Sorrento and their mutual disillusionment, contact between the Wagners and Nietzsche nearly vanished, and in her diaries Cosima was writing him off as deficient in "loyalty"—which meant usefulness and subservience to "R." In the real-life drama played out in the Wagner and Nietzsche camps *all* were accomplished actors.

In Sorrento, a harmonious and productive atmosphere prevailed after the Wagners' departure. Rée was at work on his next book, *Ursprung der moralischen Empfindungen* (*The Origin of Moral Perceptions*), Malwida was busy with a novel as was Brenner with his fiction, and Nietzsche made progress on his *All-Too-Human*. Their joint outings were as bracing as their long discussions—including biblical texts—that roamed far and wide but were linked to their work. Nietzsche saw in this creative circle a prototype of a monastic order modeled on Greek schools of freethinkers. The Sorrento idyll lasted until April 10, and despite the usual Nietzschean bouts with illnesses, Nietzsche, at year's end, felt enriched by new inner experiences. Within the next two years, different ideologies and personal interests were to widen the gap between Wagner and Nietzsche; they were not destined to meet again personally, but even at a distance they were to inflict serious wounds upon each other. Ultimately it was Wagner who totally rejected his former friend and unforgivable defector. Quite as unbridgeable as their parting was their perception of Jews and Judaism.

PARSIFAL AND ALL-TOO-HUMAN

The following January of 1878, the Wagners sent Nietzsche a handsomely bound copy of *Parsifal* that the Meister teasingly inscribed to "dear friend" Nietzsche but with the added request that the book be forwarded to Nietzsche's colleague and closest friend, the Basel church historian Franz Overbeck. Nietzsche read Wagner's preface and libretto and was displeased by the cultic will to death. In letters to friends he ridiculed the libretto as having been written in a style suggestive of a translation from a foreign language; as being in the service of reactionary Catholicism; as employing hysterical heroines—Madame Bovary types, actors with contorted throaty cries whose theatrics contained purely fantastical psychology—"No flesh," Nietzsche proclaimed, "and too much blood of sacramental communion." But Nietzsche did not retract his earlier admiration for Wagner's long, motivic introduction to the *Parsifal* theater drama. The grueling Nietzsche-Wagner vendetta had begun.

With thanks—and some malice aforethought—for the *Parsifal* libretto, Nietzsche sent his *Menschliches, Allzumenschliches (Human, All-Too-Human)*, to the Wagners, oddly hoping that the Meister would bestow his blessings upon it and that the Meisterin Cosima would grant it "intelligent favor." He drafted letters never sent to the Wagners explaining that he felt like an "army officer storming the barricades" with his philosophical aphorisms and the series of carefully extended essays. At first, he intended to publish the book by hiding behind a pseudonym in order to "provoke sober, nonpartisan discussion." Although Nietzsche had edited the book to tone down what Wagner might consider personally offensive, there was a deafening silence from Bayreuth. Just as Nietzsche had miscalculated the effect of *The Birth of Tragedy* on Father Ritschl, he again committed sacrilegious subversion—this time against Pater Seraficus Wagner by demanding acceptance of gospels developed by a filially subversive Nietzsche. Was Nietzsche deliberately or unconsciously courting rejection in order to be free to strike out on his own intellectually assertive paths, after realizing that Wagner was incapable of granting him equal status? Indeed, the Wagner who had gained European acclaim had little reason to make room on his throne for a Basel professor recognized more for his eccentricities than for any widely acknowledged publications. The subtitle of Nietzsche's *All-Too-Human* (spring 1878) tells us of his stance: "A Book for Free Spirits" or independent thinkers; "the good European" freed from the vice of German nationalism. Independence from Wagner had been arrived at painfully; privately, Nietzsche claimed splitting headaches from rehearsals and performances of Wagner's music and his disillusionment with their contents as causes for his escapes from Bayreuth (1876). Intellectually, he saw Wagner as one of "the acrobats of the higher spirits" who toyed unconscionably with religious ceremonials and symbolism of "The Last Supper" with his *Parsifal* (1878). Nietzsche disqualified Wagner as the German equivalent of Aeschylus, an honorific title he had placed upon him earlier.

Nietzsche believed that Wagner was creating forgeries that catered to public, religious pieties. It was a pity that there was apparently no dialogue between the two on these pointed charges because actually Wagner had characterized contemporary religion to be so enfeebled and artificial that his *own* art would justifiably serve as a substitute. Nietzsche aimed to do the same later with his *Zarathustra*.

In the meantime, Nietzsche realized that his defense and sacralization of Wagner was a misguided but all-too-human impulse to idealize persons and ideas. Henceforth he would aim to discard at least one consoling belief daily (letter to Louise Ott, September 22, 1876). Stimulated by his friend Rée's book on psychological observations, he would now concern himself with the subconscious motivations of human actions; he came to the insight that all of our valuations are at best rationalizations of our personal interests.[14] Intriguingly, he postulated that self-observation is a mode of universal knowledge and experience.

Nietzsche's publisher, Ernst Schmeitzner, talked him out of the idea that *All-Too-Human* ought to be issued anonymously and reminded him of Wagner's dictum that controversy is good publicity for book sales. As it stands, the title expresses Nietzsche's disillusionment with and also recognition of human foibles: "In truth, even the greatest I found all-too-human," was an observation by Zarathustra that spoke of Wagner. Nietzsche let the publisher have his way, softened his aggressive intent, and substituted the words "artist" and genius" when he meant to indict Wagner. He redefined the theoretical relation between the artist (Wagner) and the thinker (Nietzsche): "the artist has a weaker morality than the thinker when it comes to recognizing truths" (146). In his *Nietzsche contra Wagner* (compiled in 1888 and first published in 1895), he retrospectively claimed that mentally he had already broken with Wagner during the *Ring* performances of mid-1876, being heartily sick of Wagner's aesthetic pretensions, crude anti-Semitism, and pious posturing (". . . the outwardly conquering hero Richard Wagner is in reality a lamenting *decadent,* [lying] broken at the foot of the cross . . ."). To the horror of Cosima, Nietzsche also defamed Christianity by attributing to it an immoral theology and debilitating myths; and finally—to the dismay of both Richard and Cosima—he praised his Jewish philosopher-friend Rée and certain aspects of Jews and Judaism. He meant what he said, and also abrasively challenged the Wagners' anti-Semitism.

Nietzsche dipped freely into the writings of Heine, and it is pertinent to note a brief excerpt from his *Geständnisse* (*Confessions*) with its defense of Jews and accusatory tone against their persecutors, and then to compare it with a well-known section in Nietzsche's *All-Too-Human.* Heine writes:

> Hatred of the Jew in antiquity has the same origin as that which the proletariat has today for the rich. And hence their persecution, exclusion from property ownership, being damned, hated, and murdered legally; in olden days such murders were covered by a religious blanket and it was said that one must kill those who once killed our Lord God. Curious! It was precisely that nation which had given the world a God and which during its entire history lived and breathed devotion to God that was maligned as a deicide! (*Geständnisse,* 1852, 1854)

In *All-Too-Human*, the obliteration of national boundaries, echo Heine's reflections:

> Incidentally, the entire problem faced by Jews exists only within nation-alistic states; insofar as everywhere here Jews' successful participation and higher intelligence—acquired during the long schooling of their suffering from generation to generation—and the consequent amass-ment of capital, of spirit and will was so huge that it had to incur envy and hate-filled measures in the form of literary indecencies in almost all of our nations . . . making Jews scapegoats for all conceivable public and private misfortunes and leading them to the slaughterhouse.[16]

With *All-Too-Human* come the first of Nietzsche's more explicit summa-tions, diagnoses, and recommendations in his developing attitudes toward Jews and the social dilemmas they incurred by living among Euro-pean nations: narrow nationalism has artificially excluded Jews from social acceptance, something that can be solved by transforming nation-alistic mentality into that of a cosmopolitan "good Europeanism"; envy and hate have made Jews scapegoats for nations' problems; the idea of racial purity is detrimental to a strong racial mix to which the Jew can contribute greatly. To the argument that Jews have dangerous character-istics—as Wagnerian anti-Semites asserted—Nietzsche agrees, but coun-ters that Jews, like other people, have no monopoly on unpleasant char-acteristics; moreover, he reminds his readers that "we" Europeans share in the guilt of making "them" what they are and of having led them to the slaughterhouse. Nietzsche reminds Europeans of the historical, intellec-tual, and religious debt they owe to the Jews through the legacy of Christ, Spinoza, and the Old Testament. These views are Nietzsche's interpreta-tion of historical data. The weakest but not the least interesting of his assertions is his linkage of Judaism and Greek culture. At the time of this writing Nietzsche first held out hope that Germans would act as "media-tors" and like the English and French accept the Jews, their intelligence, and their economic abilities schooled during long periods of suffering.

The Wagners' reaction was predictable. Richard's fury knew no bounds and shortly thereafter he forbade the mention of Nietzsche's name in his own august presence. Nietzsche's book had arrived at a bad moment—Wagner was in the midst of writing an article that claimed

"Rossini bad; Brahms, Schumann mediocre . . ." and here was "friend" Nietzsche joining the enemy and praising Jews, neglecting—if not denigrating—the genius Wagner. "I can understand," Cosima says, quoting Richard, "why [the Jew] Rée's company is more congenial to him than mine: *Human, All-Too-Human* consists of 'Rée-flections, pretentious ordinariness,' an evil book prompted by evil feelings."[17] And Wagner imperiously told Cosima a month later that "all those," like Nietzsche, "who are not with us are at liberty to go." Cosima and the Bayreuth apostles took the Meister's cue and ascribed Nietzsche's defection and adoption of heresies to the contributive influence of Dr. Paul Rée, "a smooth, very cool Israelite." The Bayreuth *Blätter* launched articles attacking Nietzsche, and in November Nietzsche asked that he be taken off the subscriber list; Richard agreed and was pleased that Nietzsche had finally understood Bayreuth's displeasure.

Nietzsche felt "excommunicated" (May 31, letter to Gast) but one also senses some relief on his part as if deep down he had really wanted the rupture. Wagner could not resist glancing into Nietzsche's book occasionally, and Cosima thought it regrettable for him to continue with the "bad" book that ridiculed her wifely submission to the Meister. The book was a thorn in Richard's side and he was intent on proving the "perverseness" of its author and later on exposing what he insisted to be Nietzsche's "secret perversity" as a bachelor and professor of ancient Greek morality. Among Nietzsche's friends, opinions were divided on the merits of the book, its advocacy of "racial" mix and social integration of Jews. Rée "devoured" the book enthusiastically, yet there is no sign that he overtly contributed to Nietzsche's interpretation and understanding of Jewish aspects that Rée himself had avoided for discussion. It certainly was unheard of for someone of Nietzsche's academic position and social background to speak of Jews as favorably as he had. Even Voltaire, to whom Nietzsche had dedicated the book and praised as the spirit of the Enlightenment, was a formidable anti-Semite who especially excoriated the Old Testament that Nietzsche singled out for praise. There was no discernible Gentile or Jewish model for Nietzsche's positions, and it accounts for much of the wishful attributions of philo-Semitism to his works; *All-Too-Human* did give the impression of going far beyond any generalized tolerance and communal acceptability of Jews.

THE DEADLY INSULT

Although Nietzsche claimed that anti-Semitism was the cause for his break with Wagner (at the Bayreuth Festival in 1876), it actually largely involved a very personal matter despicably exploited by Wagner (in 1877), which preceded the last and final exchange of *Parsifal* and *All-Too-Human* (in 1878). A brief review of an unfortunate series of violation of confidences yields somewhat the following sequence. Baroness Malwida von Meysenbug had had a long and friendly acquaintance with Wagner since 1855 and a short and motherly one with Nietzsche, and she valued both highly as friends. With fake solicitude Cosima had inquired of Malwida about friend Nietzsche, and was told that Nietzsche had been advised urgently by a Sorrento doctor to consider marriage. At the same time, a letter from Nietzsche told the Wagners that he had consulted Dr. Otto Eiser, in Frankfurt, who had expressed concern about his health. Dr. Eiser was a confirmed Wagnerite, so he was not surprised to receive a letter from Wagner's Bayreuth aide Hans von Wolzogen. Dr. Eiser answered and Wagner took charge, continuing the correspondence by means of a long, solicitous letter, in which Wagner assessed Nietzsche's physical and emotional condition:

> . . . As for the fateful question that concerns the health of our friend N., I feel an urgent need to inform you, briefly and decisively, of both my opinion and anxiety—but also of my hope. In my attempts to assess N.'s condition, I have been thinking for some time of identical and very similar experiences which I recall having had with certain young men of great intellectual ability. I saw them destroyed by similar symptoms and discovered quite clearly that these symptoms were the result of masturbation. Guided by these experiences, I observed N. more closely and, on the strength of these traits and characteristic habits, my apprehension became a conviction. . . . One thing that struck me as being of great importance was the news I recently received to the effect that the doctor whom N. had consulted in Naples advised him first and foremost—to get married. . . . I believe that I have said enough to enable you to make a serious diagnosis along the lines I have indicated. . . . (October 23, 1877)[18]

Wagner, the physician manqué, also recommended cold hydropathic cures for Nietzsche, which reminds one of his mother's prescriptive hygienic measures during his childhood.

Eiser, in complete violation of physician-patient confidentiality, wrote Wagner to the effect that as far as he knew Nietzsche *did* follow his Italian doctor's advice and engaged in coitus several times so that the truth of his accounts "is not to be doubted and . . . proves that our patient is not lacking the capacity to satisfy his sexual drive in a normal way." Further, reported Eiser, Nietzsche never had syphilis but did incur several gonorrheal infections when he was a student.

The contents of the Wagner-Eiser exchanges became part of the Bayreuth gossip mill, and Cosima crowed that she knew all along that Nietzsche was a "Geck," a dandy, a fop, and worse, with his "unnatural" characteristics. Even Nietzsche's publisher, Ernst Schmeitzner, had gotten the news from Bayreuth but withheld the outrageous rumors from Nietzsche and his friends. To put himself in the "right light" in the whole affair, Dr. Eiser wrote to a colleague in explanation of why Nietzsche defected from Wagner. Eiser stated that he knew Nietzsche's defection was complete when, in his office, he informed the philosopher of Wagner's letter. An hysterical outburst was the consequence, and Nietzsche was completely out of control.

Nietzsche remained silent for a while after his outburst against what he termed Wagner's "deadly insult." Pederasty would have been an ancient Greek convention, but onanism was a biblical sin that the medical profession and the Victorian lay public assumed with certainty was the road to mental derangement and the madhouse. Except for telling a few friends of a vague Wagner perfidy, he decided that suppression of Wagner's actual derision was the better part of valor; he had no other options. Only after Wagner's death in 1883 did he write the most scathing books about Wagner, attempting to kill the Pater Seraficus over and over again. In the meantime he had the satisfaction of dispatching his heretical *All-Too-Human* to the Wagners (begun in 1876; published 1878), knowing inwardly at that point that it would bring them no joy.

Whatever reservations Nietzsche had about openly declaring his ideological severance from Christianity disappeared with his rejection of Christian mythology and theology; he had already dismembered the conservative "rational Christianity and philistinism" of Strauss. Much earlier, Jacob Bernays had characterized the Strauss book as empty of content. Among the opening fusillades in section 113 of *Human, All-Too-Human*, Nietzsche expresses incredulity at the retention of untenable beliefs and the subscribing, by gullible people, to assertions by a crucified Jew. Were his ironic thrusts anti-Semitic (or anti-Judaic), or were they meant to ridicule Christian anti-Semites? They possess elements of both here. Whatever the aim, Nietzsche rarely discusses Christianity or Judaism without noting their intertwined features:

> *Christianity in the guise of antiquity.* On a Sunday morning when we hear the old bells growling, we ask ourselves: Is it still possible in this day and age? This is intended for a Jew crucified more than two thousand years ago, who said that he was the son of God. Proof for such an assertion is missing.[19]

The depth of Nietzsche's eventual revulsion for Wagner can best be explained by the strength of the early attractions and uniting affinities: their demonic drivenness; the irreparable loss of fathers in childhood and consequent feelings of aloneness and homelessness; and both identifying themselves withe the exiled and wandering Jews. Nietzsche's poetry is filled with such laments, and Wagner is not far behind. Wagner identified with the legend of Buddha and the extirpation of consciousness, and sanctification at the moment of renunciation. For Wagner, the teachings of Buddha made us "one" with all living things through compassion (*Mitleid*). It is a tantalizing possibility that the figure of Buddha that Wagner could not shape into musical and dramatic representation was among the subliminal sources of inspiration for Nietzsche's *Zarathustra* or the *Übermensch*.[20] Regardless, with the exchange of *Parsifal* and *All-Too-Human*, the Wagner-Nietzsche bond was eternally severed, although, as Nietzsche realized, their names would be linked together in history.

NOTES

1. Lou Andreas-Salomé, *Lebensrückblick,* ed. Ernst Pfeiffer (Frankfurt a.M.: Insel, 1968), pp. 241–48; see notes 75–80.

2. Ibid., pp. 242–43.

3. Theodor Lessing, *Der jüdische Selbsthass* (Berlin: Jüdischer Verlag, 1930). Lessing had a traumatized childhood; his parents taught him that he was a "good Jew"—German, secular, and nonreligious—in contrast to others. He learned to swallow the anti-Semitic stick with which he was beaten in life and identified

with the aggressor, dishing out opprobrium in turn to other Jews. Eventually, he began to understand his own self-hate and studied the phenomenon in Paul Rée, Karl Kraus, Otto Weininger, Maximilian Harden, and Arthur Trebitsch. Lessing's political outspokenness prompted a Nazi death squad to murder him in 1933, after he had accused Germany of regression to the Dark Ages.

4. Paul Rée, *Psychologische Betrachtungen* (Berlin: Carl Dunker, 1875).

5. *KS*, III, 1114.

6. *WM*, 940.

7. This quote belongs to La Rochefoucauld. See the engaging introduction and selections translated by Louis Kronenberger, *The Maxims of La Rochefoucauld* (New York: Modern Library, 1959).

8. Elisabeth Forster-Nietzsche, *Wagner und Nietzsche: zur Zeit ihrer Freundschaft* (Munich: G. Müller, 1915). English edition, *Wagner and Nietzsche*, p. 213.

9. Wagner's opera libretti were thematic autobiographies of his own love life and the transformations are quite evident: Mathilde Wesendonck/Isolde; Cosima/Brunnhilde; Judith Gautier/Kundry. Wagner egotistically associated himself with stealers of wives or betrotheds: Gunther (*Götterdammerung*), Lohengrin, Tristan, the Dutchman, Tannhauser. Wagner laid claim not only to the wives of his ostensible friends but also to their purses. Almost all those husbands proved to be willing victims, except for Monsieur Laussot who threatened to blow Wagner's brains out if he did not distance himself from his wife, Jessie Laussot: Richard promptly vanished. Catulle Mendès (the Jewish-French poet who divorced Judith Gautier) masochistically remained a strong propagandist for Wagner's music, in spite of Wagner's trysts with his wife.

10. Wilhelm Hoppe, ed., *Friedrich Nietzsche Werke und Briefe, Historisch-Kritische Gesamtausgabe*, vol. 4, *Briefe* (Munich: Beck), p. 352.

11. Mazzino Montinari, *Nietzsche Lesen*, pp. 40–42.

12. Janz, *Friedrich Nietzsche*, I, 471.

13. Baroness Malwida von Meysenbug (1816–1903) was a women's rights activist banned from Berlin for associating with revolutionaries. She went to London and then returned to the Continent in 1862. She authored the widely read *Memoirs of an Idealist*. For Nietzsche she became his last important mother figure. Malwida's long friendship with both Wagner and Nietzsche was spoiled by Wagner's sullen, private ridicule of her and Nietzsche's rejection of her ultimately as a Wagnerite.

14. This prefigures Freud's *Psychopathology of Everyday Life*.

15. "How I Broke away from Wagner," sec. I; *VM*, sec. 3.

16. See *MA*, 475, for the lengthy essay cited here only in part.

17. The same diary entry (June 24, 1878) also notes that Lulu (Daniela,

Cosima's daughter by her first marriage to Hans von Bülow) writes of good news from London: "An Israelite," a Herr Seligmann of Cologne, is subsidizing the London production of the *Ring*.

18. Curt von Westernhagen, *Richard Wagner* (Zurich: Atlantis, 1956), pp. 527–29. Westernhagen was a Nazi propagandist.

19. MA, 113; see also M, 114. This passage could also be seen as directly ridiculing Wagner, for although he was not a church-going Christian, he vehemently denied Jesus' Jewish origins (attributing Jesus' roots to Adam, not David). (Ed.)

20. By way of Schopenhauer, Wagner was drawn to Buddhistic philosophy and mythologies, a subject explored by Wolfgang Osthoff, "Richard Wagners Buddha Projekt, 'Die Sieger': Seine ideelen und strukturellen Spuren in 'Ring' und 'Parsifal,' " in SL 3 (1983): 189–211, Archiv für Musikwissenschaft, Wiesbaden. Nietzsche's insight into Wagner's psychology was enhanced by studying the rough sketches Wagner made between 1850 and 1857 for projected operas involving Parsifal, Jesus, and Buddha, dramas in which compulsive eroticism and revulsion from it are resolved. In the sketch for a contemplated opera "Die Sieger" (The Victors), Buddha himself was to become the hero "completely divested of all passion" (*Venetian Diary*, October 5, 1858).

5

The Lipiner Interlude

PROMETHEUS UNBOUND

If Nietzsche's preference for the personal and intellectual companionship of Dr. Paul Rée, the "cool Israelite," displeased Wagner, another
Jew was to enter Nietzsche's life, though briefly. In Vienna, among
German-speaking and German-cultural enthusiasts, university students
formed reading and discussion clubs, most prominent of which was the
"Pernestorfer Circle"[1] whose members stemmed mainly from upper-
middle-class assimilated Jewish families. Desperate to prove their German identity, they espoused "volkisch" movements whose exclusionary
programs, ironically and invariably, culminated in anti-Semitism. The
Pernestorfers agitated for a revived German culture and inveighed
against "materialistic, rational science" and ossified "Wissenschaft" (academic learning). They adopted Schopenhauer, Wagner, and Nietzsche as
lodestars, and their intellectual hunger fastened peculiarly on Nietzsche's
rhetoric in "Schopenhauer as Educator" (1874), which exhorted the
individual to join a mighty community solidified by a common culture;
to extinguish one's "ego," and to become "as one with the community
and nature." They bought into the idea of a cult of genius and the metaphysical meaning of culture. Preening themselves as political activists,

they unwittingly fell into the trap of seeking a cultic genius-leader and other anti-democratic and anti-liberal, elitistic models. In Schopenhauer's and Nietzsche's works, they found the prototypical myth of Dionysian communality and reconfigured it into a pan-Germanic chorus of "Deutschland, Deutschland über Alles" that was sung at some of their more fervid meetings.

The incandescent star on the group's horizon was the poet Siegfried (Solomon) Lipiner (1856–1911),[2] who adopted the name of the Wagner opera-hero. He was born into a Polish-Jewish family at Jaroslaw, a town near Galicia's city of Lemberg, but as a young man he decided totally to disown his family and Judaism and to study philosophy at Vienna. In 1876 the twenty-year-old Lipiner published an epic poem Der enfesselte Prometheus (Prometheus Unbound) that stirred the admiration of Austro-German literati who hailed him extravagantly as "a new Goethe." Essentially, the poem is a paraphrase of and commentary on Nietzsche's monograph "On the Advantage and Disadvantage of History for Life," as well as The Birth of Tragedy whose title-page illustration shows Prometheus breaking his chains. Lipiner's allegorized figures represent the war between dry academic learning and the fiery will of Dionysian rebellion that intuitively cuts closer to the essence of reality than does the intellect. He sent a copy of the book to Nietzsche at Sorrento during the philosopher's stay with Rée, Malwida, and Brenner, but apparently the packet strayed. Early in June 1877, Rée brought Nietzsche up to date. In letters, as in close companionship, Rée acted like a solicitous and protective mother hen, upbeat and gossipy:

> . . . Rohde's betrothed is a bewitching creature: modest, graceful, perhaps not dumb[3] and very much in love—let's not say any more. . . . Yesterday a Herr Lipiner from Vienna visited with me. He is the source of the complimentary packet for which we waited in vain in Sorrento. Content: the unbound Prometheus. He "hungers for you." But he is not an appetizing person. I was evasive about your address, yet I fear that you will not escape his hot yearning. He also knows the Observations. He asked me if you and I were of dissimilar opinions. I believe that my answer was very good. I said, matter-of-factly, that you had opinions similar to mine but aside from that you had a great number of opinions to which I had no affinity. (Rée to Nietzsche, early June 1877)

Rée's catty reference to Rohde's betrothed was just as inappropriate as his negative characterization of Lipiner; others have described Lipiner as "unprepossessing" in appearance but a good conversationalist and public speaker with a dynamic range. But the idea of a stranger—and a Jew at that—laying claim to Nietzsche upset Rée. Diplomatically, he also wanted to deflect any hint of Nietzsche's indebtedness to his own ideas. Rohde heard from Rée that Nietzsche intended to give up his professorial post because of health problems and he hastened to dissuade his old friend-in-arms, as well as to mention Lipiner. Rohde writes:

> Do bear for a while longer the pain of fulfilling unsatisfying [academic] duties . . . is it not your clear duty to use your great gifts on behalf of the young and to educate them!— . . . I will marry in August and probably go to Paris.
>
> Incidentally! The other day, a Herr Lipiner was here, a friend of the lecturer in philosophy Volkelt [Dr. Johannes V., at Jena]. He is one of the most bowlegged of Jews but not without entirely unsympathetic, timid and sensitive features in his horrific Semitic face. He is a great admirer of your writings, a member of a Viennese "Nietzsche Society"; he literally raves about you and was certain of having sent you his book *Der enfesselte Prometheus*. I was to enquire if you had received it and if not, he will send you a second copy immediately. Please let me know soon and eventually make . . . "Prometheus-Lipiner" the happiest of all bowlegged Jew-boys. He has the advantage of not seeking a university lectureship despite his impoverished circumstances. (Rohde to Nietzsche, June 29, 1877)

Rohde, like Lisbeth and Franziska, was worried about Nietzsche's potential abandonment of his prestigious Basel position. What would become of him? Rohde's deliberate mention of Paris was a barely disguised reminder that it was Nietzsche who had aborted their planned escape from academia to Paris when the Basel temptation of a professorship offered itself. The careless anti-Semitic tone of Rohde's letter apparently was not inhibited by his own friendship with Rée; but his decamping to the Wagners was abundantly clear.

Lipiner sent Nietzsche a replacement copy of his *Prometheus* with a cover letter that closed with the fervid declaration, "no one can more deeply venerate and love you than I—. Lipiner" (from Jena, August 3, 1877).

We have a fragmented copy of Nietzsche's reply of August 24, 1877, to Lipiner's letter and his reaction to the Lipiner book:

> Well then; from now on I do believe that a real *poet does indeed exist.*
> . . . Do tell me then, without inhibition, in respect to your origins, how
> you stand in relation to the *Jews*. In fact, in recent times, I have had
> numerous experiences that have aroused my *very great* expectations of
> young people of this origin. I must beg postponement of a meeting until
> my next book appears, [but then] I would quite urgently wish for a per-
> sonal encounter: Before that, many preliminaries would be needed in
> order to avoid misunderstandings—and I have very little time.

The contents of a number of other Nietzsche communications indicate that at first Nietzsche was pleased with the fervent declarations of admiration by incipient followers whose Jewish backgrounds he did not fail to be impressed with. In a postcard to his mother, a day after he had answered Lipiner's letter of August 3, Nietzsche wrote that he had received "indescribable pleasure" from Lipiner's poetry and added: "It is of the first rank; a true poet notwithstanding. . . . That he is estimable also as a human being is an overabundant and sudden gain for me as well (to Franziska, August 25, 1877).

Apparently, Lipiner had made a favorable impression when he personally approached Franziska in Naumburg and asked for her son's photograph and address, wishing to get in touch with him to express his admiration and to send his Prometheus book. Lipiner again is favorably referred to by Nietzsche in a letter of August 28 to Rohde:

> Quite recently because of the "Unbound Prometheus," I experienced a
> genuine festival-day. If that poet [Lipiner] is not a veritable genius, I no
> longer know what the word means: everything is wonderful, and it
> seems to me as if, in that work, I meet my elevated and idealized self. I
> bow deep to one who can experience such things inwardly and project
> them outward. . . .

Lipiner's *Prometheus*, with its personally inscribed, venerative dedication, broke down Nietzsche's inhibitions—to judge from Lipiner's September 10 letter to Nietzsche. Its responses allow us to reconstruct partially what was excised by Frau Elizabeth Förster-Nietzsche when she published the

version of her brother's letter to Lipiner, dated August 24 (cited earlier).
Lipiner artlessly dodged, but finally acknowledged, Nietzsche's question
about his Jewish origin:

> Nietzsche, my dearest Nietzsche, how can I find words to thank you?
> You call yourself powerless? If you could have seen me—forlorn and
> tired—when my dear lady friend handed me your letter (which because
> of my frequent wanderings could not be sent in pursuit of me). . . . I
> revived with tears at the thought that perhaps the heart of my Niet-
> zsche was no longer alien and indifferent to me—You would have truly
> praised your power. . . . What you fear, has already been conquered in
> me. Do not mock! I well know that at twenty-one one has not tri-
> umphed. But I was in hot contention and have looked terror in the eye
> without being turned to stone. What more can happen to me? I can, I
> will suffer and bleed, be torn with doubt; but I will never perish.
>
> I read the first five songs [of the poem "Echo"] written in Elgersburg
> to Rohde; he found them . . . "absolutely splendid"; but I tossed the writ-
> ings into the fire and started all over again; they no longer pleased me.
> My surroundings are friendly; yet, actually, I have no friend; I wend my
> way lonely. . . .—My Jessie is a splendid woman, yet to be happy without
> making another happy, that I am incapable of. Yes, if I could only love
> without being loved! I would be much better off. What can I, the
> unhoused, offer her clear-eyed child's soul? (September 10, 1877)

Toward the end of this rather lengthy and poetic letter, Lipiner finally
addresses his ancestry: "I am a Jew." He then asks Nietzsche about his
views toward Lagarde and his whereabouts,[4] and quickly changes the subject, stating that he longed "indescribably" for Nietzsche's work *Human,
All-Too-Human*: "Could I not proofread your book? I would be deliriously
happy if you were to permit it. Just let Schmeitzner send it to me at the
above address. In that way your eyes and I will both benefit."

It was balm for Nietzsche's bruised ego to receive solicitude and veneration—though he was categorically to despise the former as "pity" and
welcomed the latter as he had seen it operate among the Wagner circle
at Tribschen and Bayreuth. Now he had *his* Jewish tribute-givers, Rée and
Lipiner, in competition with each other. Lipiner's letter closed with an
expression of sympathy for Nietzsche's eyes. Rée, several months earlier,
had expressed his empathy for Nietzsche's eye condition and also claimed

that he, too, suffered similar irritation.[5] Lipiner knew of Rée's concern for Nietzsche and wanted to make certain to match it.

ECHO

Some personalized confessions in Lipiner's August letter to Nietzsche matched Nietzsche's own autobiographical experiences: terrifying nightmares, the personified inner demon or alter ego, the recurrent and demanding ambiguous ghost figure—paternal and androgynous—a disembodied viewing of himself, and the warring and divided inner selves.[6] For Lipiner, these were preconditions for creativity, and Nietzsche, as never before, perceived them as his own. Lipiner's poem "Echo," as symbol and personified subjectivity, struck a chord in Nietzsche. It is the myth of Pan, who, because of unreciprocated love for the nymph Echo, sends madness upon shepherds who tear her to pieces so that only her voice survives, or the version in which the frigid youth Narcissus rejects the nymph's love—she wastes away to a whisper and he is punished by drowning in his own image. As Lipiner psychologically understood the myth, it expressed his own and—though he did not know it—Nietzsche's notion of unpossessive love, as Lipiner expressed in his letter: "If I could only love without being loved!"[7] Lipiner's influence is reechoed four years later in Nietzsche's *Gay Science*, in an aphorism titled "Within Solitude": "When one lives alone, one neither speaks nor writes too loudly because one fears the hollow reverberation—the criticism of the nymph Echo.— And all voices sound differently within one's solitude" (*FW*, 182).

Unlike Wagner, Nietzsche could not afford to support assistants; he had to rely on voluntary amanuenses of independent though moderate means like Peter Gast, Paul Rée, and others, so that repeated offers by Lipiner to render help proved to be impractical in view of his frankly admitted impecunious circumstances. Above all, I think, Nietzsche feared Lipiner as a dangerous and demanding pathological alter ego.

To celebrate Nietzsche's birthday on October 15, 1877, Lipiner orchestrated greetings and tribute from the Vienna Pernestorfer student circle. Nietzsche's writings, no doubt, had an impact on young intellectuals in rebellion against their bourgeois elders, for on April 19 he also entertained a request from a Prague student group. Years before, it had received from Nietzsche a copy of *Die Geburt der Tragödie aus dem Geiste der Musik*—"that now belongs to the most-read books in our library," said a representative of the group; now they requested a copy of Nietzsche's "Richard Wagner in Bayreuth." Flattering though such attention was, Nietzsche could not cultivate these students nor a Berlin Nietzsche circle of believers;[8] he simply had no public relations, propaganda, and finance ministers in his orbit as did Wagner, and he was not inclined to forge such links: "Nothing is farther from my mind than to make proselytes—no one has more strenuously *warned* of the dangers to independent thought . . ." (to Reinhart von Seydlitz, May 13, 1878). Yet, Nietzsche did not ignore a tributary and respectful Pernerstorfer letter signed by leading members—mainly of Jewish background—who promised to live up to the model that Nietzsche laid out in his "Schopenhauer as Educator."

Not to be outdone by the groups' co-signed "collective letter," Lipiner added one of his own and repeated earlier requests. Again, he referred to the agonies accompanying his "Echo" poem. Having found sustenance in Nietzsche's latest letter (not preserved), Lipiner expressed empathic sentiments: ". . . what threatened you, threatens me. . . . For God's sake, if at all possible, let me know that it no longer threatens! I suffer along with you, enormously—! (November 3, 1877, to Nietzsche). Lipiner offered to put himself completely at Nietzsche's disposal in Basel, for at least a month, as he could financially manage it. However, Nietzsche was unable to accept such hysterical subservience and to endure contact with a person suffering psychological traumas similar to his own. Lipiner also enclosed nine stanzas from section eight of his "brooding" "Echo" poem. Of greater interest than the tortured and strained verses is the introductory prose description that prefaces the section:

> The coffin of the bewitched Echo is guarded by an enormous snake whose poison nourishes every evil spirit in the world. Whoever has felt its bite has experienced in his bosom all earthly pain. . . . Dion, the hero and singer, vanquishes the snake but his body, wracked with pain, is transformed from that of a powerful youth into a wounded old man. . . . (Lipiner to Nietzsche, November 3, 1877)

Lipiner's allegorization of personal anguish is later imaged and replicated in the snake-and-shepherd scene in *Zarathustra*; Nietzsche's and Lipiner's poetic psychopathology meshed.

Within the next two months, Nietzsche gathered from Lipiner that he was gravitating toward Wagner and holding fast to Schopenhauer. Nietzsche, the third of Lipiner's deified trinity, could not help but regard the poet's maneuver as anything but heretical. Nietzsche writes to Seydlitz: "Lipiner, judging from a letter [not extant] he wrote to me, is a good Wagnerian; incidentally, one would almost wish that he would rewrite *Parsifal* once more" (Nietzsche to Seydlitz, January 4, 1878). But Nietzsche did not make a clean break; in fact, he sent Lipiner on some errands and still did not discourage him from believing that he would be called to Basel to serve Nietzsche, the object of his veneration whom Lipner addressed as "My fervently adored."

Lipiner invited Nietzsche to spend the summer in the Austrian Alps where he would protect his recuperation in solitude and himself keep a solicitous distance. It was a foolish and unrealistic promise on the part of Lipiner. When *All-Too-Human* was published, Lipiner quietly expressed his disappointment at the pragmatic psychologizing found in Nietzsche's book, but kept his disenchanted views from Nietzsche; further, he was distressed by Nietzsche's bellicose departures from Wagner and Schopenhauer. The spring of 1878 was not a particularly easy time for Nietzsche in regard to health and friendships; he complained of "the peculiar estrangement of many acquaintances and friends": there had been the break with the Wagners and the Bayreuth circle, the death of his young friend Albert Brenner, the marriages of old comrades, a bitter row with Gersdorff, the coolness of Rohde who was not altogether happy with *All-Too-Human*, and the impending dissolution of a joint housekeeping arrangement in Basel with his sister. Rée and Gast were not appreciated and not proven sufficient during that time. Lipiner was a tempting curiosity Nietzsche could not afford despite his serious initial interest in the young Jewish poet who turned out to be considerably *less* Jewish than Nietzsche had initially hoped. In gossipy Basel, he could not, at any rate, risk the kind of relationship that Lipiner had craved. He let the correspondence lapse, gave no further encouragement for a meeting, and got matters off his chest by not addressing Lipiner, but rather, by asking for opinions about Lipiner from his newly found aristocratic friend, Baron Reinhart von Seydlitz:

> . . . I would very much have liked a word from you about the impression
> Lipiner made upon you. Actually, with his repeated attempts to com-

mandeer my life from a distance, making it impossible therefore through advice and deed to do so. Something of that sort, I despise: none of my friends would dare to propose such bold measures. Lack of shame—that's what it is. Thus, one must keep such a one at arm's length; friendship could be possible, though partly. . . . (May 13, 1878)

Lipiner's worshipful advances were matched only by his maudlin sentiments that taxed Nietzsche's desire and tolerance for admiration, but still Nietzsche excused him on dubious grounds:

A long letter from Lipiner that says much for him but is of unbelievable impertinence toward me. I am now rid of the "admirer" and his circle— and heave a sigh of relief. His progress lies close to my heart, but I do not confuse him with his Jewish characteristics [*Eigenschaften*] for which he is not to blame. (Letter to Franziska and Lisbeth, August 13, 1878)

By accident of birth, Lipiner cannot help being Jewish and acquiring those "characteristics." Here, Nietzsche does not completely disown Lipiner, but ascribes his defects or Jewish characteristics to a stereotypical cause—a heredity for which he cannot be held personally responsible.

Although he clearly shuns Wagner's irrational hatred toward Jews, Nietzsche does share contemporary attitudes, especially Wagner's, toward supposed ingrained Jewish "Eigenschaften," or traits.[9] Nietzsche placed great importance upon heredity as a formative personality factor; but in the case of Lipiner, he failed to see that Lipiner was typical of the young intellectual Jew alienated from, and totally ignorant of, his cultural heritage and at the same time rejected, or not accepted, by a political, national, and Christian society. Lipiner's typical marginality helps to account for his desperate—if not pathological—attempts to prove his distance from Jewishness and eagerness to ingratiate himself with the cultural idols he created in Schopenhauer, Wagner, and Nietzsche, who formed ersatz figures for a family and religion he had jettisoned.

LIPINER AND WAGNER

Not being admitted to Nietzsche's intimate circle inclined Lipiner to move toward Wagner at a time when Nietzsche was attacked by his former idol in the *Bayreuther Blätter*—attacks to which Nietzsche responded belligerently.

If Nietzsche did not have his own way with people, quite often he would transform them into enemies to contend with agonistically, resulting—in the case of Wagner—in a kind of masochistic joy; he needed and craved opposition worthy of his challenge and polemical counterattack. In that respect, Nietzsche could be a naive and awkward tyrant.[10]

Malwida von Meysenbug tried to keep her friendship with Wagner and Nietzsche in balance, so that she conveyed her enthusiasm for Lipiner to both men. And between September 1878 and the following mid-January (as briefly recounted in Cosima's diaries on five occasions) there ensued an odd flirtation between Wagner and Lipiner. Lipiner sought to make himself useful to the Meister and, reciprocally, Wagner tested Lipiner's utility value and wished to determine if he would fit into the company of his kept "Israelite pets"—as he waggishly called the Jewish collective—the Porges brothers, Rubenstein, and Levi. Here the difference between Wagner and Nietzsche is crucial: while Wagner consistently ridiculed Jews, Nietzsche consistently reserved his ridicule for anti-Semites.

In September, Wagner read Lipiner's lecture, "Über die Elemente einer Erneuerung religiöser Ideen in der Gegenwart" ("On the Elements of a Renewal of Religious Ideas in our Time"), published as a pamphlet by the enthusiasts of the Viennese Student Circle. Though a quagmire of aesthetic religiosity, Lipiner's monograph flattered Wagner to no end, especially with its long extract from *Parsifal*. Lipiner saw the Angst-tormented, desire-driven, and "hounded" person universalized in the figure of Kundry yearning for redemption that would absolve her death-seeking, sinful soul. Wagner was intrigued and intuitively right about Lipiner: here was an example of the Ahasuer-Jew seeking redemption himself as Wagner had ordered in his *Jews in Music* tract. He requested an article from Lipiner on *The Flying Dutchman* (the wandering Jew incarnate) for the *Bayreuther Blätter* periodical, an article that would, in a popular vein, incorporate Wagner's philosophy. Wagner also requested Lipiner's presence at the Bayreuth court. As usual, however, Jews irritated Wagner's spleen. Richard tested and found Lipiner's pedantic writings unsuitable for his periodical and even expressed "disgust" with Lipiner's published appreciation of Wagner's old monograph on *Art and Revolution* (1849). Cosima's description of Richard's divine displeasure is grimly comic:

"Lipiner is discussed and condemned by R., whose right eye flashes fire, his left is inwardly contemplative" (*Diaries*, November 10, 1878). Extolled by Lipiner as an artist who replaces the high priest, Wagner rebuffed his latest Jewish acolyte.

Not knowing what went on in the privacy of Wahnfried very likely saved Lipiner from suicidal thoughts. He did not realize Wagner's depths of paradoxical resentments against those to whom he owed the most: Jewish sponsors and audiences, the conductor Levi, and the like. If only audiences other than Jews would appreciate Wagner was a plaint that the Wagners voiced privately. One particular diary entry sums it all up and marks affinities as well as differences between Wagner's and Nietzsche's views:

> Friend Levi stays behind after our other friends have gone, and when he tells us that his father is a rabbi, our conversation comes back to the Israelites—the feeling that they intervened too early in our cultural condition, that the human qualities which the German character might have developed from within itself and then passed on to the Jewish character have been stunted by their premature interference in our affairs before we have become fully aware of ourselves. The conductor [Levi] speaks of a great movement against the Jews in all spheres of life; in Munich there are attempts to remove them from the town council. He hopes [and we only have Cosima's word for Levi's self-condemnation that follows] in twenty years they will be extirpated root and branch, and the audience for the *Ring* will be of another kind of public—"we know differently"!

Cosima notes that she and Richard discussed the "curious" attachment individual Jews had for him. This is all the more curious when taking into account Wagner's openly expressed hope for their demise.

Some Jewish Wagner-connoisseurs were able to follow Verdi's example and praise the absolute technical genius of Wagner and the advances he made in the state of the art while at the same time despising the man-monster composer. Or, it may be that some of them were more cosmopolitan and receptive to new and bold ventures while others followed what they assumed to be the coming "German" fashion. Of course, a good deal of the Jewish response to Wagner's anti-Semitic diatribes and operas was negative and justifiably defensive. The enlightening dialogue recorded between Cosima and Richard ends with the rueful acknowledgment of Jewish taste and the large number of devoted Jewish followers. Richard says with clownish banter: "Wahnfried will soon turn into a synagogue" (Cosima's *Diaries*, January 13, 1879).

Lipiner took his rejection by his idols Nietzsche and Wagner in stride; he was utterly alien to both their worlds and his social and financial standing was without redeeming qualities. Lipiner's rhapsodies on Wagner's *Parsifal* in his "religious-renewal monograph," also sent to Nietzsche, validated Nietzsche's view that Wagner had deserted to the "foot of the cross." By the same token, Lipiner's courtship of Nietzsche and incomplete allegiance to Schopenhauer offended Wagner. Lipiner, who earlier had scorned academia, became more realistic; took a doctorate with a safe dissertation on Goethe's *Faust*; became a librarian (*Reichsrat*) and wrote a verse play, *Adam: A Prologue to a Christ Trilogy*, in which Adam theologically prefigures the coming of Christ. With this drama, he completed his turn from early Jewish childhood training in Poland to poetical Christology in Vienna. He converted to Protestantism in 1891 and in 1894 he was rewarded with a governmental promotion to librarian of the Austrian Parliament until his death in 1911. Lipiner is reputed to have filled the prestigious post of "Regierungsrat" with distinction. No pictures of him are extant in the portrait archives of the Viennese institution he served.

THE "POLISH JEW"

As a practicing poet but also as a model of the intellectual "Ostjude," the immigrant Jew from Eastern Europe, Lipiner brought his abilities to bear in translating from his native Polish to his adopted German the great epic poem *Pan Tadeusz* (1834) by Adam Mickiewicz, a story of the Polish nobility's fight in 1811–12 against Russian incursions. Lipiner brought the poem to Nietzsche's attention, and he apparently put it aside until years later when the memory of it resurfaced. Once his friend Overbeck mentioned the name Mickiewicz, floodgates opened and Nietzsche wrote to Overbeck,

> Your reference to Mickiewicz came opportunely, I am embarrassed about knowing so little about the Poles (who, after all are my "an-

cients"!)....Chopin does me good....About Lipiner, I recently heard something very precise: outwardly he is a "successful person" but aside from that he possesses the typical shape of the present-day obscurantist, had himself baptized, is an anti-Semite, is pious (recently he attacked Gottfried Keller[11] venomously and accused him of "lacking true Christianity and faith"!). Lipiner is reputed to have ruined those young people who have come under his influence by driving them toward "mysticism" and causing them to despise scientific thinking. He is a person with many "practical" ulterior motives, and opportunistically takes advantage of the trend of the times. My information comes from a natural scientist in Vienna [Josef Paneth], who has known Lipiner since childhood. (Letter to Overbeck, April 7, 1884)[12]

In his notes, Nietzsche pays the same backhanded compliments to Lipiner as he did Heine. Any compliment is diluted with the Wagnerism that they bear the taint of being "foreigners." Wagner was inspired by meanness, Nietzsche by social and intellectual habit. The difference, then, is one of degree and ingrained insensitivity. Nietzsche writes:

> Jew—I single out for distinction Siegfried Lipiner, a Polish Jew who knows how to imitate the varied European forms of lyricism down to their most charming nuances—"almost genuine"—as a goldsmith would say. (*UW*, I, 543)

> Mimicry—a talent possessed by the Jew. "A suiting oneself to forms"— and therefore an actor, and therefore a poet like Heine and Lipiner. (*UW*, I, 544)

Nietzsche's mentioning Heine in the same breath as Lipiner puts Nietzsche's literary judgment in severe doubt. Lipiner turned out to be an absolute nonentity by even the least of critical standards, but it does emphasize the absolute subjectivity of Nietzsche's thinking. Lipiner was only as important as Nietzsche's momentary use of him and his identification with him, especially his foreignness; Nietzsche regarded himself as a perpetual alien after the loss of his father's home.

Not "the real article" but good "imitation" was Nietzsche's private verdict in respect to the Jewish Lipiner and Heine. These seem hardly to be philo-Semitic views, but neither do they completely disparage either "Jew" or "actor" since Nietzsche acknowledged for himself and Wagner the necessity and compulsion to assume the role of actor and to adopt chameleon masks.

Lipiner managed to magnify his relationships with Nietzsche and Wagner and gained more influence than he might otherwise have had over Vienna's academic youth. Among Jewish intellectuals in Vienna, none of his friendships was more important than that with Gustav Mahler. But then, Mahler possessed the same psychological debilities.

With Rée either in attendance or close by through correspondence, Nietzsche had no need of Lipiner, and so things rapidly wound down in that respect. The case of Lipiner had no tragic outcome as did the pathological suicide of Wagner's Joseph Rubinstein and other tormented Jews like another suicide, Otto Weininger, who rejected his Jewish origins and converted.

To close out the Lipiner story, Wagner had found Lipiner insufficiently subservient, and Nietzsche whistled him down the wind because Lipiner turned into a Wagnerite and anti-Semite. The latter designation had been earned because Lipiner had made the theologian Paul de Lagarde a competitor to Nietzsche in his affection and strongly urged Nietzsche to read the vociferous Lagarde. That theologian's major message to bigots placed the blame for industrial inequities and political liberalism upon Jewish influence; he condemned "Judaization" (*Verjudung*) of Germans by Jewish bacteria that needed to be exterminated so that with their demise (*Untergang*) Germany could be saved.

Interestingly enough, Nietzsche himself had catered to Cosima's bigotries in 1873 and had asked her to read Lagarde's *Kirche und Staat*, a book that espoused a nationalistic church. Subsequently, Nietzsche's first flush of enthusiasm for Lagarde turned to indifference; Lagarde was to be discarded along with Lipiner.

NOTES

1. William J. McGrath, *Dionysian Art and Populist Politics in Austria* (New Haven: Yale University Press, 1974), gives a rounded account of this group.

2. Siegfried Lipiner (1856–1911). Basic data on Lipiner's career may be found in H. von Hartungen, "Der Dichter Siegfried Lipiner" (diss. Munich, 1935); William J. McGrath, *Dionysian Art and Populist Politics in Austria* (New

Haven: Yale University Press, 1974); entries in *The Blackwell Companion to Jewish Culture, Encyclopaedia Judaica,* and *Oestereichisches Bibl. Lexikon* (1972). Paul Natorp's introduction to *Siegfried Lipiner: Adam, Ein Vorspiel [und] Hippolytos, Tragödie* (1913; Bern: H. Lang, 1974), pp. 3–13. From 1861 active in Vienna literary circles and studied at Leipzig and Vienna universities, and pursued doctoral studies and journalistic work briefly, and took certification in librarianship. He wrote poetry and unperformable dramas; he enjoyed an intermittent friendship with Gustav Mahler, and was known as a translator of Polish literature; an official record of conversion to Protestantism appears in 1891, though Josef Paneth told Nietzsche that it occurred earlier.

3. Rohde's planned defection into marriage made Nietzsche unhappy, as Rée knew it would, but Nietzsche overlaid his feelings with charm in a letter to Rohde on August 28, cited above.

4. Paul Lagarde (1833–1921) caught Nietzsche's attention with his book *Das Verhaltnis des deutsche Staates zur Theologie, Kirche, und Religion* (*The Relation of the German State to Theology, Church, and Religion,* 1873). Lagarde, an anti-Semite and professor at the University of Göttingen, advocated a German national church, something that apparently appealed to Lipiner, who was to convert to Protestantism in 1891. For discussion, Nietzsche, at that time (mid-1873), had sent Lagarde's book to Cosima Wagner.

5. See Paul Rée's letter to Nietzsche, July 2, 1877.

6. Lipiner writes: "I speak of an inner enemy. During the past half-year, he has tortured me terribly. . . . He can turn every one of my joys to gall and shorten my youth, and he can, like an immobile nightmare, burden my soul while I speak with words of joy from the depths of my being as he rises like a ghost, confusing my speech, shaking my voice, martyring and numbing my heart so that it is severed from the speech of my mouth. . . . Finally at the height of my yearning, I must break into peals of childish gaiety—the terrible ghost stands before me revealed as a well-known magnificent woman that I had already espied in my first childhood dreams; all torment is forgotten, and magically transformed she stands before my gaze and I before her joyous one. And I give her many names because I do not know the real one. Now she appears to me as 'echo'—and that is the name of the poem also I am working on."

7. This psychological Nietzschean demand is taken over in Rainer Maria Rilke's works. Nietzsche paraphrased Lipiner: "Das Verlangen nach Gegenliebe ist nicht das Verlangen der Liebe, sondern Eiteleit und Sinnlichkeit" ("The demand for reciprocal love is not love's demand but that of vanity and sensuality") (*UW*, I, 926).

8. His future brother-in-law, Dr. Bernhard Förster, a strident anti-Semite, belonged to the Berlin Nietzsche group.

9. Heredity as a "problem of race" and parentage is emphasized in Nietzsche's thinking. See, for instance, *J*, 264. Heine, read assiduously by Nietzsche, self-demeaningly referred to Jewish traits that not even *The Baths of Lucca* (a huge, satiric metaphor for baptismal waters) could cleanse.

10. Giorgio Colli aptly discusses Nietzsche's tendentious psychological warp in regard to erstwhile friends like Rohde, Wagner, and Lou von Salomé; *Nach Nietzsche* (Frankfurt a.M.: Europäische Verlagsanstalt, 1980).

11. Gottfried Keller (1819–1890), a noted Swiss writer, was a philosopher of atheism in the vein of Ludwig Feuerbach (who held that only material security and not religion can bring happiness to mankind). Keller possessed an intense feeling of love for life and had contempt for beliefs in a hereafter. His philosophy, novels, and stories were admired by Nietzsche.

12. More about Josef Paneth, Nietzsche's source, later. Paneth occasionally attended reading-circle lectures in Vienna, sessions at which Freud reportedly also was present. Born in Vienna in 1857, Paneth could not have known Lipiner during his Polish days. Paneth was a physiologist and histologist, a friend of Freud until altercations about Nietzsche parted them. He died in 1890 of tuberculosis.

6

Emancipation and Exile

THE WANDERER AND HIS SHADOW

The dominant note of *Human, All-Too-Human* is a disillusionment that marks the beginning of wisdom: "Truly, even the greatest I found all too human," as Zarathustra was to put Nietzsche's accelerating revaluing of persons and ideologies—Schopenhauer, Wagner, Christianity, Judaism. His earlier idea that art can redeem life is abandoned along with Wagnerian art. "Wagner," he declared, "is a splendid vestige."

The magnetic attraction exerted by Wagner upon Jews like Lipiner—as well as the many patron societies in Germany and Austria—was a puzzle to Nietzsche. He underestimated the extent to which some "emancipated" or assimilated Jews felt that their embracing of the nationalist cult and "culture" spearheaded by Wagner would bring them acceptability in turn, a serious delusion encouraged by wishful thinking. Nietzsche attempted to formulate some rationale to account for the cool distance in Jewish-Gentile relations:

> It is typical of Jews to exploit opportunities in relationship to other people whose boundaries they approach and proclaim familiarity. . . . This makes them importunate [*zudringlich*, i.e., insistent, pushy]. All of

139

us do wish to be inviolable and yet give the impression of being ap-
proachable. The Jews go counter to this national and individual not-
wanting-to-be-touched . . . and they are hated for it. (*UW*, I, 717)

Lipiner's "importunities," no doubt, contributed to such caustic observations in Nietzsche's notebooks. As a corollary, sarcastically he attributed
teeth-grinding hysteria and emotional disturbances to "inherent
Semitic" characteristics that therefore give "the Semitic races a better
understanding and approach to Wagnerian art" (*UW*, I, 331).

Not only was this Nietzsche's dim bird's-eye view of what energized
Wagner's Jewish entourage and his Jewish audiences, but it carelessly
echoed vintage nineteenth-century racial theorizing that associated
alleged Jewish pathology with female uterine hysteria. For a thinker of
Nietzsche's depth to subscribe to such conventional nonsense may be
attributable to his criticism of Jewish Wagnerites who seemed to him to
represent a contradiction in terms. Nietzsche's *ressentiments* were unconsciously formulating an attack on Wagner as a Jew, which breaks out
years later. Nietzsche remarked that we welcome certain circumstances
that give us an excuse to break with people with whom we no longer wish
to associate. The anti-Semitism endemic to Wagner was among sufficient
reasons to seek breathing room between himself and the composer. At
the same time, Nietzsche's spirit of agonism and contest demanded fair-
ness in contention, and he saw only vulgarity in the anti-Semite who
unsportingly takes advantage of the defenseless:

> Young people whose achievements are not commensurate with their
> ambitions look for things to destroy out of a spirit of revenge—mostly
> objects, persons, social classes, races, which cannot retaliate in kind:
> those of more honest inclination wage war directly or seek duels. The
> better person seeks an opponent of equal strength. And so, the fight
> against the Jews has always been a sign of the worse, more envious, and
> more cowardly of types: and whoever now participates in such a fight
> must inwardly bear a vulgarian sentiment. (*UW*, I, 676)

Back in the chafing academic harness at Basel, Nietzsche completed
"Assorted Opinions and Maxims" in continuation of *All-Too-Human*,
and it was published in February 1879. His anger against Wagner had not

abated and he delivered himself of anti-Wagner resentments in aphorisms such as "Bitterest Error":

> It offends us beyond forgiving when we discover that where we were convinced we were loved we were in fact regarded only as a piece of household furniture and room decoration for the master of the house to exercise his vanity upon before his guests. (VM, 74)

In addition artillery shells were lobbed against Wagner's Teutonic pretensions. Nietzsche scorned Wagner's appropriation of the old Germanic sagas, the ennoblement of their strange gods and heroes who actually are "sovereign beasts of prey invested with magnamity and life-weariness" (VM, 171). The lingering effects of his break with Wagner, the mixed reception of his aphoristic book, the confinements of academia, migraine attacks—all assailed him with a force that brought him to the brink of death; the fact that his illnesses were psychosomatic, of course, did not lessen their severity and danger. Lisbeth was summoned to Basel in April and Nietzsche had no choice but to withdraw from the university. In June 1879 he retired on a pension arranged for by his well-wishers and adequate for his modest future needs for about a decade. The years of restless wanderings began. Although Nietzsche was not a Swiss citizen, having broken his residence requirements by Prussian service as a medical orderly in the 1870 war, the Swiss did provide him with a visa that allowed him unrestricted travel on the continent—and so he became the good European and cosmopolitan for which he had chosen the Jews as models.

Released from the university Nietzsche was able to draw a deep breath, vacationing with his sister near Bern, and then alone at St. Moritz, where he polished the manuscript of the final sequel to *All-Too-Human*, appropriately called *The Wanderer and His Shadow* (*der Wanderer und sein Schatten*) in 1880. In it he continued to "unmask" pretentious commonplaces and to unsettle settled minds. Among the aphorisms, we find one titled "Felix Mendelssohn" that Nietzsche knew would infuriate Wagner if brought to his attention: "Mendelssohn's music is the music of good taste for everything good: it is far ahead of itself and so much of it is of the future!" (WS, 157).

At St. Moritz Nietzsche succumbed to a mid-life crisis:

I am at the end of my thirty-fifth year. . . . Dante had his vision, expressed in his poem. Well, I am in the middle of life and so "surrounded by death" that it could seize me any hour. . . . I feel as if I have *completed* my life's work. (Letter to Gast, September 11, 1879)

This self-dramatization was accompanied by the request that Gast review *The Wanderer and His Shadow* before sending it to the printer. Nietzsche apologized for not joining Gast in Venice and thought it more salutary to return to the "nearness of mother, home, the scene of childhood memories." And that was a psychological mistake. He returned to Naumburg in October and suffered severe traumas experienced during "the most sun-deprived days of my life"; and he wrote Rée that he wished "for a life together with you in my Epicurean garden." Nietzsche idealistically envisioned male, intellectual companionship based on the models he saw in Greek antiquity, where females were notably absent. Rée obligingly spent most of January with Nietzsche in Naumburg—a compromise of sorts between practicality and vision. Then Nietzsche put distance between himself and his mother, Naumburg, and even his sister. He sensed that he had come down in her estimation when he lost his prestigious professorial position and had become an "unattractive little creature" in her eyes. He felt the need to prove himself all over again, to banish the old ghosts, and to find a substitute for his lost idyll: the imaged Tribschen-Eden. Until March 1882 he wandered restlessly through Italy and Switzerland and with incredible persistence continued his thinking, living, and writing in tandem.

In June 1881, Nietzsche published *Morgenröte* (*Dawn*, *Daybreak*), after having completed its writing far from Naumburg, the citadel draped in piety and virtue. Perfectly expressive is the book's subtitle, *Gedanken über die moralischen Vorurteile* (*Thoughts on Moral Prejudices*), that is, prejudgments and convictions—religious, social, ethical; reason versus unexamined unreason or faith. His primary axiom stated that convictions are not synonymous with truth or proofs nor does the principle of "utility" prove or negate morality. The 575 entries of varying length were written in notebooks during walks and hibernations in locales from northern Italy's Riva southward to Venice and Genoa. His devotee Peter Gast made clean copies of the entries for Nietzsche's revision prior to sending the manuscript to the printer.

Interestingly, Rée was not involved in any discussions and perhaps that had something to do with the apparent random sequence of the thought entries and his very strong, uniquely Nietzschean views on features of Jews and Judaism as integral or related to Christianity:

> ... The Jews felt differently about anger [*Zorn*, wrath] than we do and have pronounced it holy, and therefore it possesses the darker majesty of man with whom it originated and who raised it to a height unimaginable by a European: they fashioned their angry, holy Jehovah in the image of their holy prophets. Compared with them, the great European ragers are but pale, second-hand creations. (M, 38)

To the question of good and evil, good and bad conscience, Nietzsche devotes more attention in subsequent works. The relativity of moral sensibility among Greek, Jewish, and Christian cultures is briefly described, indicating his own preferences: the Greek penchant for the contest and contention, the agon in every phase of Greek life, was adopted as his own method of intellectual inquiry. Nietzsche's admiration for the Old Testament is encapsulated pithily in his view that "the darker majesty" of the primal, wrathful deity "Jehovah" was created by the Jews and their holy prophets. This Nietzschean image—almost Dionysian—of an awe-inspiring God differed drastically from the popularized image from Voltaire's to Nietzsche's time.

Here, I believe, the prototypical figure of a majestic, powerful God who could, if he wished, destroy humankind root and branch and yet who benevolently restrains himself from abusing this might, this figure eventually becomes—with the death of God—the *Übermensch*. From here on Nietzsche will unfavorably contrast the New Testament with the Old, standing uniquely alone in that respect from thinkers and theologians of his time. He will contrast St. Paul's doctrinaire theology with Jesus' ethics which he commends in part but finds psychologically naive in its egalitarianism and with its enjoined "love of neighbor"; he places Jesus in the category of what the Greeks called the *idiotes*, the holy fools. Nietzsche ignores Matthew's Jesus who came not in peace but with a sword (Matt. 10:34). But while Nietzsche has some praise for the instinctive and unassuming aspects of Jesus' life and teachings, he has nothing but vitriol for St. Paul. Like other secularists, Nietzsche thought Paul to be the real founder of Christianity and the historic person who distorted Jesus' teachings by introducing a theology of sin and redemption—doctrines Nietzsche despised categorically, taking them as personal affronts.[1]

Yet, in a psychologically complex way, Nietzsche partly was to identify himself with features of both figures. He could never accept the alleged pacifism and egalitarianism preached by Jesus nor the dogmatic supernaturalism of Paul. Like the Greeks he could understand conceptions about the immortality of the soul but not about the raised and resurrected body or the new, imperishable mystical body envisioned by Paul and the promised resurrection after death.[2] But he was held spellbound by the visionary Jew: Paul's vision on the road to Damascus and the power of its revolutionary subversion of old beliefs and consequent reformulations of beliefs.[3] Unconsciously, the prophetic role was being prepared for the revelations of Zarathustra later in the retreats of caves and mountains, and Nietzsche's own at Sils-Maria.

In aphorisms such as "Christian revenge upon Rome," Nietzsche slowly begins to develop both his "revenge motif" and the cross as its symbol. He has in mind Jesus' admonition, "He that taketh not his cross and followest after me, is not worthy of me" (Matt. 10:38–39), and other such strict demands:

> Christianity . . . gathered together into one concept "world" and "sin." It revenged itself upon the Roman empire . . . foretelling the imminence of the world's end, finishing Rome's importance. One took revenge by dreaming of a Last Judgment,—and the crucified Jew as a symbol of salvation was the deepest mockery directed against the magnificent Roman praetors in the province, because now they appeared as the symbols of misfortune and of a "world" ripe for destruction. (M, 71)

Nietzsche's tone in his essayistic reflections is tinged with mild mockery, the Voltairean savagery lies in the future; the arguments advanced here are still reasonably presented—in contrast to an all-out assault found in later writings.[4] To Gast, he wrote of being mindful of his own pastoral forbears: "Christianity is the best part of an idealistic life I pursued since childhood and I have never been mean-spirited toward it in my heart" (July 7, 1881). At any rate, Nietzsche comes back to Pauline dogmatics and contrasts them with that of primitive Christianity, the Greek, and the Jews, "that strange folk" who clung to life and were a people he could admire but also ridicule:

> Ultimately, though, only a very few have been selected, a fact that the elect cannot help but note arrogantly. With others among whom the drive for life was not as strong as it was with Jews and Jew-Christians [Christian Jews], and where the prospects of immortality were indubitably deemed more valuable than the prospect of final annihilation, there the heathen (and the not altogether un-Jewish) addition of hell became a wished-for working tool in the hands of missionaries. . . . (M, 72)

THE CHOSEN PEOPLE

In no uncertain terms, Nietzsche took to task what he deemed to be fraudulent philological scholarship. Himself a former scholar specializing in textual transmission, he was indignant at cavalier revisionisms and arbitrary and inaccurate handling of texts. And he also had in mind the kind of theological prefiguration acrobatics practiced not only by theologians but unlicensed poets and overt apostates like Siegfried Lipiner, who followed the precedent of evangelists who fervently realigned or reimagined events in Jesus' life to coincide with Old Testament "prophecies." Missionary proselytizing, from whatever quarter, Nietzsche rejected with editorial anger. In the "Philology of Christianity" he writes:

> However strenuously Jewish scholars protested, the Old Testament was interpreted as speaking of Christ and only of Christ, and especially of his cross; wherever a piece of wood, a birch-switch, a ladder, a twig, a tree, a willow, a staff is mentioned it is taken to be a prophetic allusion to the wood of the cross. . . .
>
> The church did not recoil from enriching the text of the Septuagint (for instance, Psalm 96, verse 10) in order to be able later to exploit the smuggled-in verses in the sense of Christian prophecy. Since they were engaged in warfare, they had thoughts only of opponents and not of honesty. (M, 84)

One particularly long essay (M, 205) is a prime example of Nietzsche's juxtaposition of exaltation and denigration that deserves close attention. Nietzsche writes:

Of the People of Israel. [*Vom Volke Israel.*] To the drama which the next century invites . . . belongs the deciding point about the fate of European Jews. One can now understand completely that the Jews have thrown their dice [*würfel geworfen*, cast their lot] and crossed their Rubicon: it now is really up to them either to become the lords of Europe or to lose Europe, just as long ago they lost Egypt when they confronted a similar either-or. In Europe, however, they have experienced eighteen centuries of schooling that no other people can duplicate; it so happened that the experiences of a horrendous trial period [*Übungszeit*, period of tribulation, of probation] has been of greater benefit to the individual than to the community. Consequently, the mental and spiritual resources possessed nowadays by Jews are extraordinary. Even during times of distress, more rarely than any other Europeans do they resort to drink or suicide in order to escape from a deep dilemma— options that lay close at hand for the lesser-gifted. In the history of their forefathers, every Jew had a treasure-trove of examples of coolest deliberation and steadfastness in terrifying situations overcome by subtle cunning and exploitation of misfortune and coincidence; their courage under the cover of piteous submissiveness, their heroism in *spernere se sperni* [despising one's despisers] exceeds the virtues of all saints. For two thousand years, one wished to make them despicable by treating them with contempt and denying them access to honors and everything honorable in order to put them deeper into demeaning vocations, and truly with such proceedings they have not managed to become cleaner. But contemptible? They have never ceased to believe that they were destined for the highest things, and similarly the virtues that attend all sufferers have never deserted them. Their manner of honoring parents and children, the reasonableness of their marriages and marriage customs give them distinction among all Europeans. Relative to this, they knew how to derive a feeling of power and eternal revenge [*der Macht und der ewigen Rache*] from precisely those occupations left to them (or those to which they were abandoned); one must say even in extenuation of their usury that without this occasional pleasant and useful tormenting of their despisers, it would hardly have been possible for them to retain self-esteem for long. It is certain that respect for ourselves is bound to the fact that we can dispense retribution [*Wiedervergeltung,* retaliation, reprisal in matters of good as well as evil things]. All things considered, [Jews] are not easily moved to extreme actions because they possess liberality, even a liberality of soul [*Freisinnigkeit der Seele*] that comes with the education gained by frequent changes of residence, of climate, of customs of one's neighbors and oppressors; they possess by far the greatest experience of diversity of living among peoples, and even in the throes of passion they exercise a caution born of their experiences. Their intellectual suppleness [*Geschmeidigkeit,* feline litheness and grace] and sharpened wit [*Gewitztheit,* shrewdness, polished wit] have made them so self-confident that they temper their emotions; even in times of most bitter distress, they have not found it necessary to exert physical strength as common laborers, porters, agricultural serfs in earning their bread. One can tell from their manners [*Manieren,* habits, attitudes] that no one has ever planted in their souls chivalrous and noble feelings or equipped them with admirable bodily weaponry: thus something insistent [*zudringliches,* pushy, importunate] alternates with an often tender, almost often painful submissiveness. But now, since from year to year they inevitably intermarry with the highest nobility of Europe, they will soon gain a goodly inheritance of manners in body and spirit; in a hundred years they will appear sufficiently genteel [*vornehm*] so as not to make them feel ashamed of their subservience to their [Jewish] masters. And that is precisely the point! And it is for that reason that a settlement of their affairs is premature! They themselves well know that a conquest of Europe and any kind of forcefulness is not to be contemplated: It may well be that somewhere along the line, Europe, like a fully ripened fruit, will fall into their hands if they choose to be receptive. Meanwhile, they find it essential to excel in all fields of distinction in Europe and to be counted among those in the front ranks until they themselves become the judges of what is excellent. They will be acknowledged as discoverers [*Erfinder*] and as guides [*Wegweiser*] for Europeans and will no longer offend their sensibility [*Scham*]. As for the fullness of accumulated great impressions that Jewish history signifies for every Jewish family—a richness of passions, virtues, decisions, renunciations, battles, victories of all kinds—where shall this find an outlet if not in great intellectual people and works! On the day when Jews are able to point to such precious gems and golden vessels as their work, in contrast to the briefer and less profound experience of European nations incapable of matching that of the Jews;

when Israel transforms its eternal vengeance into an eternal blessing,
then again will arrive the seventh day on which the ancient Jewish
God may rejoice in Himself, in his creations, and in his chosen
people—and all, all of us will want to rejoice with him! (M, 205)

This particular essay, a rich source and example of Nietzsche's extenuation of perceived Jewish behavior and his praise of Jewish cultural contributions to Europe, has drawn praise; but only selective and discre-
tionary quotations make the thrust "pro-Jewish." Without intending to,
Nietzsche played into the hands of those demagogues who postulated a
Jewish God (the Old Testament God admired by Nietzsche for his awesome archaic might) against a benevolent "Christian God." On the surface it appears to be a huge encomium and hymn of exaltation, but a cautious reading shows exaggerations and huge dangers. Wagner, with
malice aforethought, warned about Jews being the masters of Europe,
while Nietzsche, without due alarm, posed the same theory clothed as
fact, with the dubious parallel that their ancestors could have taken over
Egypt in biblical times. Jews were cunning, schooled in persecution,
hardened by it, pretending to be submissive but biding their time to get
back at their tormentors. With fake saintliness they turned the tables and
even in their practice of usury found occasional pleasure in tormenting
their tormentors. Nietzsche either forgot or did not know that debts
owed to Jewish lenders were not frivolous matters; most often in Europe
the debts were wiped out along with the creditors through murder and
expulsions. A common canard leveled against Jews was that they did not
soil their hands with work, something that neither Wagner, Nietzsche,
nor their forebears did. But in order to survive, the mass of Jews worked
manually in cities and villages as laborers and farmers extensively
throughout Russia and Austro-Poland, wherever they were permitted to
do so; not every Jew was a merchant or banker. A measure of emancipation, it is true, brought some German Jews into prominence in the professions. (Nietzsche's friend Dr. Paul Rée could not find a job in academia, and we have already noted the discriminatory examples of Jacob
Bernays); yet, literary salons held by cultivated Jewish ladies enhanced
German cultural life, while intermarriage in monied Jewish circles and
conversions gained momentum. Nietzsche generously allowed that given
time some noble feelings and manners would supplant the unattractive

"traits" Jews had no time or opportunity to shed. Nietzsche praised Jewish family life that welded its community and he especially commended the obligatory honoring of mother, father, and children. Singling out those specific Old Testament commandments seems puzzling, except that they contrasted sharply with the demands attributed to Jesus in respect to those who wished to follow him: ". . . I have come to set a man against his father, and a daughter against her mother. . . . He who loves a father or mother more than me is not worthy of me" (Matt. 10: 34–36).

Against such harsh divisiveness, Nietzsche posed and praised a Jewish liberality of mind, spirit, and great intellect. Further, Nietzsche allays any fear that the Jews will want to exert their potential for mastery, but he already has damaged that credibility by raising the specter of Jews as masters and by catering to rampant fears about them. Nietzsche's prose rises to what appears to be a philo-Semitic crescendo that praises the historic accomplishments of Jews above those of European nations, but then it is undermined by a conditional "if and when": "when Jewish vengeance is transformed . . . then all of 'us' will want to rejoice." Then the outsider will be accepted. No doubt, this is far better than Wagner's conditioned "acceptance" of Jews, welcome only with their extinction. Nevertheless, setting any conditions on what common decency and communal goodwill would demand is itself condescending. Nietzsche will elaborate, farther down the road (in *The Genealogy of Morals*), what he means by vengeance, that is, in his mind, the Jewish Pauline-Christian offer of the crucified Jesus as a "bait" that poisoned humankind. How such a "vengeance" can be transformed into a blessing is indeed left to conjecture. Wagner and other laypersons and some theologians not only rejected the Jewish God but they also de-Judaized Jesus and transformed him into an Aryan. Elisabeth and Bernhard Förster, Nietzsche's impending and undesired brother-in-law, argued that God and His son could not be Jewish; Nietzsche argued the reverse. His response to such willful Aryanizations was unequivocal: "If one would wish to assert that the Teuton was preconceived and predestined for Christianity, it would be extreme impudence. . . . Why should it be that the inventions by probably the two most Jewish Jews ever—Jesus and Paul—are so congenial to Germans—more so than to others . . . ? (*UW*, II, 908).

The phenomenon of "conscience" held a fascination for Nietzsche and he went much deeper in his psychological explorations than did his friend Rée. Since conscience can be good or bad, what constitutes either condition? What prompts one to evil deeds, even in the absence of necessity? What is the relation of morality and conscience? Concern with such questions surfaces repeatedly in Nietzsche's thinking and investigation of human prejudices and errors. Immediately prior to the aphorism quoted above, Nietzsche turns his irony against the users of "good conscience" who burn [good] books, Jews, and heretics in servicing their lust for power:

> What in our time accounts for the excessive impatience that turns people into criminals under conditions that would have seemed more likely to produce the opposite. . . . Along with this impatience and this lust, there reappears the fanaticism called power-craving and comes to the fore; in former times it had been inflamed by a belief that one possessed the truth that . . . one could dare to be inhuman with a good conscience (to burn Jews, heretics, and books at the stake, and to wipe out higher, much higher cultures, such as those extinguished in Peru and Mexico). The method of the power-hungry has changed but the same volcano still glows as unrestrained lust and impatience demand their victims: and what one formerly "did for God's sake" one now does for the sake of money, that is to say, for the sake of that which now yields the highest sensation of power and a good conscience. (M, 204)

What one can observe best of Nietzsche's attitude toward Jews in the late 1870s is a sympathetic tolerance rather than an unqualified acceptance of them as communal citizens.

Nietzsche had wanted to herald the coming of a new dawn in his life with the exposure and destruction of long inherited and residual prejudices; hence *Morgenröte* and its subtitle, *Thoughts on the Origin of Moral Prejudices*. Once these encrustations had been cleared away, he was ready to journey in search of new visions and become a *Versucher*—a philosopher who pursues an experimental approach and is not afraid to treat himself as a subject. He continued using the unsystematic but sharp-probing aphoristic mode to challenge and question all absolutes. All this upsurge aimed to overcome Nietzsche's personal debilitation and cyclic depression in a joyous affirmation of life as he shed Schopenhauer's pessimistic outlook and negativity.

Nietzsche's next book, *Die fröhliche Wissenschaft* (*The Gay Science*),[5] resonates with a kind of *sprezzatura* or buoyancy and sunniness inspired by his recuperation in the southern Mediterranean; and it is called upon to be Nietzsche's new guide to life. Partly, he also referred to the troubadours of old who roamed Europe like free spirits among whom Nietzsche wanted to count himself in his post-professorial peregrinations. Science (*Wissenschaft*) and art (*Kunst*) are compatible; in his theory of the relation of opposites, they possess mutuality.

Except for the summer of 1881 spent in Sils-Maria, which was to become Nietzsche's Holy of Holies, he stayed in or near Genoa, Sorrento, and other southerly places of rest where he wrote poems called "Lieder des Prinzen Vogelfrei" ("Songs of Prince Free-as-a-bird").⁶ The songs celebrate his release from Basel and his footloose wanderings in the south of Italy. When he chose to he could summon his "incomparable and most considerate friend" Rée and enjoy "the stimulus of a twin-star" (*Sternenfreund*); or he could summon Peter Gast; or, as he did on occasion, fend them and others off to preserve his "holy solitude." With Rée he could be "ridiculously happy at having found a small stretch of earth to share," and he could vow never to relinquish the hope of living together "in my Epicurean garden" to "learn something" from Rée, as he rhapsodized in various letters written in 1879. Among his longer stays was a half year in Genoa from November 1880 on; then to Vicenza, Sils-Maria in the summer of 1881; then back to Genoa, where in January 1882 he was imbued with a feeling of radiant health and recovery and busily at work on *The Gay Science*; and then on to Messina, a locale to which he dedicated poems called "Idylls from Messina." Book Four of *The Gay Science* is called "Sanctus Januarius," and he hails the new year: "I still live, I still think: I still have to live, for I have to think" (*FW*, 276). Curiously, the pagan Nietzsche compares himself to Saint Januarius, but an identification may have emotional validity without facticity.

In the "fairest month of January" 1882, Nietzsche rejoiced with his "Sanctus Januarius." He basked in well-being as he and Rée bathed in the cold waters and both lay on the Genoese sands, "happy like two sea urchins in the sun," watching the quick slitherings of lizards. And like the holy Saint Januarius of Naples whose reliquary of congealed blood in a vial allegedly liquifies during feast days, so Nietzsche's blood coursed in him recharged. But his enthusiasm was not directed into Saint Januarius's religious channels; on the contrary, Nietzsche had other perspectives of feeling, gravitating inexorably toward the non-Judaic and the pre-Christian paganism of Greece, as he had made clear in his *Morgenröte* aphorism:

> What does our chatter about Greeks amount to! What do we understand about their art, the soul of which is the passion for naked, manly beauty! That viewpoint, mainly, gave them their perception of female beauty. And so they possessed a perspective entirely different from ours. And similarly their love toward women: they venerated differently and they despised differently. (M, 170)

It was bold, heady—if not risky—for Nietzsche to refer to Greek *manly* passions. But in the Ligurian-Genoese setting Nietzsche styled himself a new Genoa-born Columbus "not only geographically," as he wrote his sister. He left unsaid what he meant by "geographically" and his new adventures; when left to his own devices, he ventured to the former Greek colony of Taormina at the slope of Mount Aetna in Sicily, with its remnant of a typical ancient Greek theater he had visualized in *The Birth of Tragedy*. Sun-drenched and exuberant, he composed visions of dancing gods who shed clothes and shame.[7] These neo-Greek surroundings and bronzed bodies of young music-making men whose companionship was available in and out of barges (as he pictured in one of his erotic poems) may have brought Nietzsche's latent bisexuality to the surface, in addition to the furtive liaisons with peasant girls Rée indiscreetly told about. He was so stimulated by experiences in Messina and Taormina that he wanted Rée to accompany him on a visit to North Africa's Biskra.[8] Offhandedly he mentioned to his sister that he had a yearning to see the desert lands, camels, oases, and other exotica. That Biskra was a known paradise for Europe's bisexuals was something left unsaid; Rée, sufficiently guilt-ridden by simply having been born a Jew, did not take Nietzsche's bait. Gast, who was jealous of Rée and his companionship with Nietzsche, hinted darkly that he knew more about the man he served as a disciple, but swore to his Austrian girlfriend Cäcilie Gusselbauer that he would evermore be silent, and he kept his vow even after Nietzsche's death.

The contents of *The Gay Science* are so diverse as to defy attempts at major groupings of thoughts. But Nietzsche's overriding aim was exploratory as he notes in a passage titled "In the Horizon of the Infinite": "We have left the land . . . burned our bridges" (FW, 124). It takes courage to travel without solid ground underneath and to venture into the infinite, to discard all cherished prejudices and beliefs, and to demystify the world and universe and to live without deifying them; that is the path from "morality to wisdom." And wisdom, before it is gained, Nietzsche said, exacts a painful price, as Oedipus learned. Nietzsche repeats things he has said before, but in *The Gay Science* he places special emphasis on Germans, Jews, women, and the relationship of Christianity to Judaism. His tone ranges from the polemical to the reasoned and rhetorically oscillates between opinion and the opinionated.

One's fiercest obsessions are the hardest to disgorge and so Nietzsche returns to them perhaps too insistently. In respect to Wagner and Schopenhauer, he burns his bridges many times over, demonstrating the difficulty and need for the disciple to seek freedom from his masters. Discipleship has its problems of which not even Wagner could free himself. Schopenhauer's anti-Jewish prejudices reinforced Wagner's: "Wagner is Schopenhauerian in his hatred of the Jews to whose greatest deed he is not able to do justice: Christianity! After all, the Jews are the inventors of Christianity" (*FW*, 99).

The impact of religious environments and theological preaching upon a young Nietzsche attempting to come to grips with his sexual and intellectual identity was as severe as it was generally for creative and original thinkers, as best expressed in Joyce's own *Portrait of the Artist as a Young Man*, Rainer Maria Rilke's *Malte*, or poignantly in Simon de Beauvoir's Catholic experiences. Her loss of faith and spiritual crisis match Nietzsche's guilt-ridden duplicities and consequent sense of guilt and sin.[9]

By and large, not until the late 1870s did Nietzsche stop his pretending, but never was he to abandon a sense of "sin" and he blamed Judeo-Christianity for originating it as a concept and psychological weapon of terror. In the "Origin of Sin," Nietzsche writes:

> Wherever Christianity has dominated and whenever it took hold as a feeling, sin prevails as a Jewish sentiment and invention, and with this in mind, all of Christian morality has aimed "to Judaize" the entire world. Indeed, the extent to which this has succeeded in Europe may be acutely sensed by the degree of alienation from Greek antiquity—a world that was without the concept of sin. . . . [The notion that] "Only if you repent will God be gracious unto you" would have made a Greek

laugh irritably; he would have said that this sentiment belongs to the
feelings of a slave. . . . (FW, 135)

If Nietzsche's Jewish friend Dr. Paul Rée had any sort of awareness of
Judaic thought, he might have been able to counter some of Nietzsche's
grossest misconceptions in this mini-essay. In the main, if Nietzsche wished
to ridicule the human creation of a God who wanted humans to grovel in
order to elevate divine self-esteem and honor, that was Nietzsche's satiric
privilege. But it is another matter when he simplistically reduces Judaic
concepts of sin that stress ethics over theology. Ethically speaking, sin is
the failure of humans to live up to their having been created in the image
of God. It is an implied partnership. In biblical thought, humans and God
are not "antithetical," as Nietzsche claims. Rather there is a possessive
analogy in parental terms; Jews are the children of God, not slaves, but
"sons [and daughters] of God" (Deut. 1). That relationship demands a
sense of modesty and self-esteem, not a sense of guilt. Further, Judaism,
unlike early Christianity, never preached subservience to any would-be
master, any human sovereign or state. Nietzsche is correct that Greek philosophy in antiquity had no sense of "sin" or repentance or wrongdoing;
Jews, however, regarded repentance and redress—though practiced
without public display—as a matter of ethical necessity. For Christians, sin
required a savior (John 14:6); for Judaism, it did not. By and large, "sins"
against humanity could be dealt with no less harshly than those against
God. In brief, "sin" had biblical significations that Nietzsche ignored.

Few designations have caused Jews throughout the ages more hostility and consternation than of being "the chosen people." The question
still is, chosen for what? In the context of Deuteronomy (12–16), Moses
admonished Israel that they were chosen to keep in all respects the commandments he brought down from Mount Sinai, to love, fear, revere, and
serve God with heart and soul: God "had a delight in your fathers [Isaac,
Abraham, Jacob] to love them" and He "chose their seed [descendants]
. . . above all peoples." The prophet Amos, however, warned sternly that
to be chosen and not to obey would merit retributive punishments
(Amos 2:2). In the "Chosen People," Nietzsche writes:

The Jews who regard themselves as chosen from among all nations no
doubt have a talent for morality (for they possess the ability to despise

the human within themselves more than any other people)—those Jews take the same pleasure in their divine king and saint as did the nobles in Louis the XIV. The French nobles permitted themselves to be stripped of all their own power and personal splendor and became contemptible. In order to put aside such ignoble feelings, it became necessary to create a royal brilliance, a kingly authority and power without parallel and to which only the nobility had access. When they raised themselves to privileged positions and the heights of the court, their view from above made everything below appear contemptible, and they put themselves above any pangs of conscience. And so they deliberately created a sky-towering monarchical power base that became the final steppingstone for their own power. (*FW*, 136)[10]

Nietzsche adopts analogies and psychological motivations as means for his messages, leaving historical and philological scholarship far behind:

A Jesus Christ was possible only in a Jewish landscape; I have in mind a landscape over which hovered continually the threatening and magnificent thundercloud of a raging Jehovah. Only here could a rare and sudden sunbeam pierce the dreadful and lasting nocturnal day and appear like a miracle of "love" and as the ray of a "grace" least merited. Only then could Christ dream of his rainbow and a heavenward ladder on which God descended to mankind; everywhere else was undisturbed weather and unclouded sun-induced lethargic routine, and the commonplace. (*FW*, 137)

The tone set here toward Jesus is mild; it was to become increasingly virulent and critical toward Christianity and the "priestly" aspects of Judaism; yet in one of his last works, *The Antichrist*, he regards Jesus as a free spirit (using the word "somewhat tolerantly") and upholds the ancient Jewish God: Yahweh.[11] Excoriation of what Nietzsche considered prudery and hypocritical moral conventionality in Judaism and Christianity became pronounced, especially during his time in Messina and Taormina when he felt himself transported back to ancient Greek times. Was he creating a Miniver Cheevy type* of wishful regression to supposedly more "spontaneous" life-loving times? In that respect he was untimely, i.e., born at the wrong time and place.[12]

---

*See note 1 to Appendix I.

Nietzsche lamented the fact that "the superior culture of the ancient world in the South" had been barbarized through an excessive mixture of "Teutonic barbarism" and Christianization (*FW*, 149). The fearsome and awesome Yahweh was a figure he could admire, but not the "Orientalized" god who demands reciprocity in love and who conditions his love on obedience (*FW*, 141). Clearly he had mixed feelings, and was haunted by all his authoritarian fathers—the deceased pastor, Ritschl, Schopenhauer, and Wagner (*FW*, 140):

> If God had wanted to become an object of love, he would have had to avoid the role of judging and justice-dispensing: a judge, and even a merciful judge, can be no object of love. The founder of Christianity, as a Jew, was not sufficiently sensitive to that fact. (*FW*, 140)

Nietzsche's emancipation from Wagner and the Circle brought him to insights that were novel during his time; it is clear that he struggled, and would continue to struggle, with issues of Judaism, Jews, Christianity, anti-Semitism, and of course, Wagner. Although Nietzsche felt the "great liberation" from his former mentor, as time went on, his polemics against Wagner did not cease but rather became more outspoken. He had freed himself from Wagner physically, but never emotionally. After Wagner died (in 1883) at the time of *Zarathustra*, Nietzsche's revolt against him and what he stood for would become even more pronounced.

NOTES

1. See the clear discussion of "The Rise and Rescue of the Jesus Sect" (50 B.C.E.–250 C.E.) in Paul Johnson, *A History of Christianity* (New York: Atheneum, 1976), pp. 36–67. Johnson sees Nietzsche's anti-Pauline invectives as typical of attacks on Christianity, culminating in Nazi fulminations against "the evil rabbi Paul" (p. 35). But whether Paul "originated" or "rescued" Christianity, historically the results were the same.

2. Two different approaches to Nietzsche's evaluations of Christianity may be seen, for instance, in F. A. Lea's *The Tragic Philosopher* (London: Methuen, 1957), and Karl Jaspers's *Nietzsche und das Christentum* (1938; Munich: Piper, 1947). Both disagree with Nietzsche, Lea superficially and Jaspers (who sees a secret Christian in Nietzsche) profoundly.

3. See especially M, 68. With this psychological biography of Paul, Nietzsche charts his own which parallels his wrestlings with tradition, identity, sexuality, and a sense of sin in response to his revaluation of pietistic Lutheranism.

4. It may well be that Nietzsche sensed his devoted friend Gast's extreme discomfort on a visit to Venice where he dictated portions of *Morgenröte* to him and launched his critiques of Christianity. He very well could have struck an unspoken bargain: Gast was not to play piano scores of Wagner operas that made Nietzsche ill and, in turn, Nietzsche would implicitly rein in some of his views. Also, Nietzsche perhaps did not want to take any chances of wounding the sensibilities of Rée, one of his few remaining helpers, with excessively critical estimates of Judaism and Jews. This can explain why some of the unpublished notes for the "Innocence of Becoming" project were harsher than any published reflections at the time or in his correspondence.

5. The book's motto is drawn from Emerson: "All things are befriended by the poet and sage, all experiences are useful, every day is holy, all people divine," and Nietzsche's variation: one must accept the necessity of facing life's dangers bravely and even court them. See the discussion by Stack, *Nietzsche and Emerson, An Elective Affinity*, pp. 50–55.

6. To be declared "vogelfrei" is a colloquialism that refers to being regarded as an outlaw; Nietzsche thought of himself accurately as an outsider, a loner.

7. Later codified in *Zarathustra*, I, "Of the Friend"; III, "Of Old and New Tablets," sec. 2–3: "There I picked up the word *Übermensch*." Nietzsche returned to the analogy of nudity and morality with as much candor as the Victorian era would permit and augmented *The Gay Science* with Book V, sections 343–83, published in 1886, after *Zarathustra* and *Beyond Good and Evil*: ". . . It seems that we Europeans cannot do without the masquerade called clothes. . . . 'Moral man' is dressed up . . . veiled with moral formulas and concepts of decency. Disguised by morality, man is a sick, tame, weak animal" (*FW*, 352). Modern Europeans, unlike Greeks of old by implication, are frightened by nudity.

8. It was André Gide, who, styling himself after Nietzsche with his novel *The Immoralist*, made the journey and discovered his suppressed homosexuality.

9. "I had stopped believing in God . . . but my case was aggravated by deception: I still went to Mass and took Holy Communion. I would swallow the Host with complete indifference, and yet I knew that according to the faith I was committing a sacrilege. I was making my crime all the worse by concealing it; but how could I have dared confess it?" Simone de Beauvoir, *Memoirs of a Dutiful Daughter* (New York: World Publishing, 1959), pp. 146–47.

10. Typical of detractors of the "chosen people" assumption is Arnold J. Toynbee, who calls it the most constant and "notorious historical example" in

Jewish history of "the idolization of an ephemeral self," perpetuating the "error" in discovering the one true God and claiming spiritual eminence. Nietzsche regards the "chosen" concept with a touch of amusement, but Toynbee in line with denigrators of Jews speaks less as a historian than as an Arabist who was employed in the (British) Royal Institute of International Affairs. See A. J. Toynbee, *A Study of History*, vol. 4 (New York: Oxford University Press, 1939), pp. 262f.

Among living societies Toynbee sees "Jews and Parsees [Zoroastrians]" among history's "fossilized relics"; he claims that Judaism holds a contemptuous attitude "toward its successful Christian offspring" while the Christian Church holds "an uneasy and ambiguous attitude" toward Jewish ideals and monotheism and aniconism (lack of religious images). To Toynbee's credit, he proposes that so-called Jewish racial characteristics "are not racial at all but are due to the historical experiences of the communities in question." This is something Nietzsche agreed with. The revivals of the Hebraic "relics" are due not to superior biological endowments but to the ability to rise to challenges through unprecedented efforts. Toynbee was encouraged to this view by Nietzsche's ideas on Jewish survival—an overcoming of self and adversaries.

11. Cf. A, 25, 32.
12. Cf. FW, 139.

7

Of Lou, Zarathustra, and the Wandering Jew

Lou

One might readily speculate that Nietzsche could have remained indefinitely in the nearness of Genoa, Messina, and the Sicily in which he felt at home, comfortably almost incognito, among all the things that suggested Greek antiquity to him. But a new episode opened up for him, beginning with gaiety and ending with even greater hurt and disappointment than his experience with Wagner. And this episode was to be of only six months' duration: the shattering encounter with Lou von Salomé. The twenty-one-year-old Lou, like many of her German-speaking group of Huguenots, felt confined in the foreign enclave of Russia's St. Petersburg and yearned for her student days in Zurich. Her father was a general in the Russian army—a respected official—and throughout his life Lou was the apple of his eye. She was a superbly adept student of the humanities and impressed her teachers at home and the university. But soon she wanted to be on her own and came to Rome where, in the salon of Malwida von Meysenbug, she was introduced into a circle of suffragettes, but she took a greater liking to the personable Paul Rée who had given a philosophy lecture to the young ladies. Soon she was to make of him an inseparable platonic companion. Rée against all better judgment and with the encouragement of Malwida who, unsuspecting of Nietzsche's clandestine doings in Messina, pitied Nietzsche's loneliness and lured him to Rome to meet Lou. Rée's letter to Nietzsche has not survived, but its enticements must have been astonishing. Nietzsche answered Rée on March 21, 1882: "Greet this Russian for me, if that has any purpose. Yes, I lust for this species of soul. Yes, I shall now look forward to plunder, and with what I have in mind for the next ten years, I will need her! An entirely different chapter would be marriage—at the most I could agree to a two-year marriage. . . ."

Nietzsche was so badgered by family, some friends, and, earlier, Wagner, that the unconventional philosopher was ready to capitulate for convention's sake. He rushed to Rome for a prearranged meeting at St. Peter's. Lou's memoirs recall that Paul Rée was sitting in a confessional booth where the light was good, working on notes for a book, while Nietzsche's first words to Lou were, "From what star have we fallen to meet here?" Was this mere pedantic gallantry, "his studied, elegant posture," or a stellar compliment to Rée who had brought them together, as one biographer suggests? Lou claims that she was surprised how quickly Nietzsche had wanted to make himself a "third member of our alliance and to form a Trinity." Both vied for her hand in marriage. Nietzsche meant for Rée, however, to act as an intermediary. In her memoirs, Lou relates that she and Rée diplomatically invented the excuse that if she married, her widowed mother would lose her state pension. Rée, loyal and fiercely attached at the time to Nietzsche and Lou, ignored a psychological truism he himself put to paper in his book *Der Ursprung der moralischen Empfindungen* (*The Origin of Moral Perceptions*), 1877, p. 142: "All burning desire is warlike: no two humans can yearn for the same object without feeling enmity toward one another." And he also recognized an inherent masochistic element, "Yearning—for the person who yearns—is itself a painful sensation and one's awareness of it is pleasurable."

No one eventually was to be left unscathed by Lou's appearance on the scene. Pert, stunning in her black student dress with its high neckline, jocularly known as the nun's dress, and her hourglass figure corsetted in the Victorian fashion, causing spells of illness that alarmed her friends, she dominated events. Malwida had extolled Lou to Nietzsche as an extraordinary girl of philosophical bent and practical idealism and a delightful conversationalist, but she soon feared that she would lose the

Trinity's friendship and warned Lou not to abandon the apostolic role she was to set for women's emancipation. Malwida pleaded with Lou not to enter into an impossible "neutral threesome" with Rée and Nietzsche; nature, Malwida shrewdly advised, "will not allow itself to be mocked."

Malwida was all in favor of Lou going to Bayreuth to hear Wagner's *Parsifal* during its premiere performance on July 26. Hungry for first-hand news from Bayreuth, Nietzsche welcomed the opportunity for his sister, Lisbeth, to accompany Lou. He had kept Lou a secret from his sister and mother, but in a letter composed by Lisbeth, she has her brother say that young Miss Lou von Salomé "is plain, but like all plain girls, has cultivated her mind in order to be attractive" (letter, April 1882). True, Nietzsche was near-blind, but not totally. He had good reasons, however, not to make his sister jealous. Because of the welcome help Elisabeth had given him during childhood and in setting up joint domestic households when he needed her during his professorial career, he had affectionately given her the nickname "Llama"—a creature known to be a beast of burden. But llamas also are known to spit venomously, turn ferocious, and be capable of killing wild coyotes. He was soon to realize her less admirable qualities. Torn between loyalties to Bayreuth, where she was called "Aunt Elisabeth," overseeing the Wagner home and children during some of the pair's tours, and tending to her brother's predictable illnesses at other times, her problems were compounded when she was courted in Naumburg and Bayreuth by a fateful suitor—Dr. Bernhard Förster.

Fritz had not been able to convert his sister to his freethinking style, and she was discomfited by blasphemous aphorisms in *All-Too-Human* that ridiculed Christians—especially anti-Semitic Christians. She was tolerated in Bayreuth as a trophy, despite her brother's banishment. Most painful of all, Elisabeth felt her life slipping into spinsterhood, an intolerable fate. Her aunts and mother had taught her that a woman's life was to be directed entirely to marriage or self-sacrifice. Like others of her time, she was intimidated by a manual of advice by Johann Abel, assiduously read by mothers and young women.[1] This alarmist admonished his female readers: "Don't let vanity stand in your way to marriage—you blossom at twenty-two and then fade; after that only your material possessions will be attractive." Lisbeth, with the experience of having been Fritz's domestic partner and having no possessions of her own, was terrified of becoming, in Abel's words, an unused household utensil. Marriage would set her free from the "clutching" of her brother and her mother, Franziska. She unsuccessfully engaged in a campaign to marry Fritz off and to cease being a domestic surrogate. But she did not have Lou Salomé in mind as a candidate for Fritz's hand.

Lisbeth and Lou went to Bayreuth for the *Parsifal* performance; there Lisbeth felt herself a wallflower in comparison to the vivacious Lou and entertained some fears that Lou was too attentive to the person to whom she was about to be engaged. Dr. Bernhard Förster, about Lisbeth's age, had been a schoolteacher in Berlin. Initially an admirer of Nietzsche, he readily matched Meister Wagner's anti-Semitic prejudices and beliefs in Aryan superiority. He gained public notoriety by verbally and physically assaulting a Jewish tram-passenger in Berlin and organizing a petition drive that garnered some two hundred thousand signatures, urging Chancellor Bismarck to adopt measures against Jews in the press, on the stock market, and in the civil service, and to stop Jewish immigration. As a precondition for marriage Elisabeth allied herself with Förster's racial Aryan-Christian cause that she called "socially mainstream," and she did it with fervor and new-found conviction. She had made her choice, at the moment, between her beloved Fritz, "changed" by Rée, the subversive ironist Jew, and the new Förster-Wagner axis. Although Wagner subscribed totally to the anti-Semitic program he reinforced, and perhaps inspired, in Förster, he did not sign the petition in 1880 because he was still hoping for financial support for Bayreuth from Chancellor Bismarck. To the end, Wagner remained an opportunist and would let others carry out his "cleansing" program. Fritz was appalled by his sister's defection to the enemy camp, and did not appreciate her desperate desire for a new life before it was too late for her as a woman.

Nietzsche became increasingly envious of the closeness between Rée and Lou and her visits early in 1882 to Rée's parental estate in Pomerania to the point that Lou resented his ploys to drive a wedge between them. Yet her wish to benefit from a great male intellect and her aim to further her own creative talents overrode any misgivings. After returning in July from Bayreuth, an ugly quarrel ensued between Lisbeth and Lou and led to an enmity on the latter's part that was to survive by decades the death of Nietzsche. Nevertheless, Lisbeth agreed to act as chaperone for Fritz and Lou during their contemplated stay at Tautenburg in Thuringia. In short order, however, they rid themselves of any sisterly supervision.

From August 7 to 26, according to Lou, they figuratively talked themselves to death from morning to night, "like devils heading toward dangerous abysses on dizzying paths." Both were shaken to their depths by what they discovered in each other. They found that no subject was taboo in their intellectual intimacy and confidence, including the touchy question of bisexuality—the fact that two souls can reside in one breast. Lou was to mature sexually only much later, but even now she was able easily to ward off Nietzsche's awkward and sensual gallantries. His embarrassment helps to explain the acerbity of his later diatribes against her. Their talk-fests resembled free-wheeling psychoanalytic sessions, and much of the past welled up in his memory. Lou surmised that Nietzsche's losses of father and God compelled him to search for surrogates and that his was a deeply religious nature. She predicted that, "We will live to see him as a prophet of a new religion that recruits heroes as disciples." Nietzsche confirmed that much of their talk centered on religion, and the connection becomes clear when we recall that Nietzsche had started to work on his *Zarathustra* at the time. To Lou he was to first confide the revelation he received at Sils-Maria, as important as any in the history of humankind's prophets and visionaries. Zarathustra was to be a kindred projection of his alter ego. With quiet terror, he solemnly revealed to Lou that a year earlier, in early August 1881, he walked along the shores of Lake Silvaplana, in the Swiss Engadine Mountains, 6,000 feet above sea-level, "far above all things human, beyond man and time." At the high-towering boulder near Surlei, he halted and there the figure of Zarathustra "overpowered me," and the ideal of an eternal recurrence of the same became imprinted in his mind as the highest affirmation of life that could be achieved by humans. The suggested analogy was that of an "eternal hourglass" that revolved to return rhythmically and cyclically with exactitude all that had ever transpired. Nietzsche imputed a sense of Dionysian immortality to his *déjà vu* experiences, and coupled with the eternal recurrence belief was his resolute willingness to accept and love life as an *amor fati*. Here, with finality, he cut the umbilical cord to Schopenhauer and Socrates who had regarded life as a discardable illness.

Lou gathered that Nietzsche took his identity experiments, his illnesses, and revelation-auras as means to knowledge, while she was trying to employ rationality as a means to her understanding of phenomena. In Lou's company, though not in Rée's, Nietzsche's remembrances would plunge deep into childhood. But what Lou wanted was to escape from similar memories of her own: "That," she recalled . . . "prevented me from ever becoming one of his disciples." While rejecting the idea of discipleship and the greater personal involvement that Nietzsche hoped for, she did accept his intellectual tutelage. She benefitted from his theories of style of which he was a master and what she described as the filigreed web of his philosophical and psychological thinking. She had problems, though, with his Dionysianism which she thought resembled Christian mysticism, "a coarsely religious sensuality—a false pathos that abandons truth and the honesty of emotions."

Finally, Lisbeth's intrigues reached defamatory levels as she accused the Russian Lou of immoralities that no Germans would permit themselves. Fritz, she complained, had become like the books he wrote under Rée's influence. She floated rumors that Lou was Jewish, which, of course, would serve as an explanation for her brother's deviations from proprieties.[2] Lisbeth contacted their mother, who again warned Fritz against being a disgrace to his deceased father. Nietzsche, realizing that Rée and Lou had become closer to the point of excluding him, was in turmoil; confused, he turned against Lou—"sharp-witted like an eagle," with whom he had previously wanted "to elope to Vienna alone"—and called her a "she-monkey with false breasts"—which proved to be a tragic prophecy.[3]

Lou and Rée left for Leipzig to avoid any further unpleasantness, but later in 1882 Nietzsche briefly visited them, without achieving a longed-for reconciliation; and, after October, he was to see neither of them again, though they were to continue life in his consciousness. The void in Nietzsche's life was even greater than his loss of Wagner and Cosima, and it brought him dangerously close to suicide.[4] Nietzsche wrote with sincere anguish because with them he could be himself. He distanced himself for a time from his sister and mother and decided no longer to live in Germany, taking refuge instead for months in Rapallo where his writing, as always before, was to prove his lifeline. *Also Sprach Zarathustra: Ein Buch für Alle und Keine*, as its subtitle indicates, was to be a book for everyone and no one: For everyone, in the sense that here was a revelation of a new way of life for humankind's future, and for no one in that the substrata were full of riddles and deeply autobiographical, but unobtrusively so for the common reader. On one point Lou was surely wrong when she thought that *Zarathustra* was Nietzsche's decline into madness; the book, she said, was a philosophical extravaganza with ecstatic poetizing and sermonizing.

ZARATHUSTRA

Nietzsche called *Zarathustra* the "fifth Gospel"—albeit a pagan-Dionysian yea-saying gospel—heralding one who overcomes and transcends humanity in the same way that humanity has transcended the ape; namely, he heralds the *Übermensch*, a self-disciplined warrior, a powerful and wise elitist who will supplant Judaic and Christian ethics with new codes. Coincident with his adoption of the eternal recurrence theory, Nietzsche acquainted himself more intensely with the writings of the heretical Jewish philosopher Baruch Spinoza; he exclaimed, "I have a precursor!" In a sense Spinoza's *amor dei*—the love of a universal divinity, a form of ethical pantheism—became a corollary to Nietzsche's own *amor fati*—the acceptance of everything that life has given us—and became related to the eternal return of the same: "That something like Spinoza's "amor dei" could be experienced recurringly is a great event in itself . . ." (*UW*, I, 615).

"God," Spinoza had asserted, "is at one" with the workings of nature, and to love one is to love the other, striking hard, in essence, against traditional Jewish and Christian doctrines. Nietzsche writes:

> I hardly knew Spinoza; instinct prompted me *now* to reach out for him.
> Not only that his tendencies are entirely like my own, namely, to make
> knowledge the *mightiest* of passions. I find myself linked with five main
> points of this abnormal and most lonely thinker's teachings . . . : he
> denies free will, purposiveness, a moral world order, the non-egoistical
> [altruism], evil; although our differences here are enormous, they are
> accounted for by contrasts of time, culture, and [gains in] knowledge. *In
> sum:* my solitude that has often deprived me of breath . . . on moun-
> tainous heights has now at least become an abode for two.—Curi-
> ous! . . . (Letter to Overbeck, July 30, 1881)

There are, said Spinoza, no chosen people among nations or God's favorites. Nietzsche similarly had courted opposition, but unlike the anathematized Jewish-Dutch lens-grinder and philosopher who turned down a university post at Heidelberg in 1673, Nietzsche was largely ignored in his own time, something that galled him to the end. "Zarathustra, the godless," was variously designated by Nietzsche as his shadow, his mouth-piece, his son, his alter ego, his Doppelgänger, a disembodiment, or as one possessed by Dionysus. While it was dangerous heresy for Spinoza in his seventeenth-century Sephardic community to talk about God in deistic terms or as an immanent force, the way had already been prepared for Nietzsche's public by Ludwig Feuerbach (1804–1872) and others who proposed naturalistic explanations for God and religion: humans have created God and the gods, and not the other way around. Therefore, if God or the gods were dead, and humans were their murderers, they would have the arduous responsibility of creating substitutes—including the *Übermensch*. "We need a new voice," claimed Zarathustra, "that speaks of the meaning of the earth" and not the heavens.

Zarathustra dismisses Jewish and Christian "fables" by scurrilously imitating the language of "once upon a time":

> Once, long ago, the year of our Savior, I think,
> The Sybil spoke without a drink,
> How awful all things go.
> Decay! Decay! The world never sank so low,
> Rome became a whore and bordello stew,
> Rome's Caesar turned into cattle, while God became a Jew.
> (Z, IV, "Conversations with Kinds," 1)

Although Zarathustra wants to bring new valuations into play and destroy the old commandments, he does recognize the positive features of the ancients that can serve as models for reconstruction; those positive features embody a way of transcending the human all-too-human self, through self-discipline and control, all summed up in a will to power that is more important even than Schopenhauer's idea of a will to life.

Among a number of nations, the Greeks, Persians, Jews, and Germans, Zarathustra found redeeming elements that would allow them to be the harbingers of the *Übermensch*. Among the Greeks may be seen the following ideals and injunctions, a drive for power and the pursuit of greatness: "You must emerge always first and excel above all others." In contrast to the Judeo-Christian injunction to love one's neighbor, the

Greeks exemplify the noble ideal to love one's friends: "never shall your envious soul love anyone except your friend." As for the ancient Persians, morality and physicality were their inscribed ideals: "Speak the truth and excel with bow and arrow—that seemed . . . both estimable and difficult [for the Persian nation] from whom I take my name." On the Jewish tablets the desire for moral superiority is prescribed: "Honor your mother and father and obey their will unto the roots of your soul—this was the commandment that [the Jewish] nation adopted and with it became mighty and eternal." For the Germans, ancient or modern, Nietzsche singled out the following injunction: "Practice loyalty and for its sake pursue honor and risk your blood, even for evil and dangerous things. Disciplining itself and self-taught, the [German] nation became pregnant and heavy with great hopes."[5]

To the Jews of the Old Testament, *Zarathustra* attributed a moral power that underwrote their perpetuity. Nietzsche was to emphasize the point that whoever gives honor to things, *creates values* as well (J, 160).[6] These are the valuable residues of antiquity, but even Zarathustra of ancient Persia has undergone a transformation and is the prophet of a radicalized and changed mission. He no longer poses a dualism, but a principle "beyond good and evil."

When Zarathustra, the wanderer, was thirty years old, analogous to the traditional age of Christ when he began teaching,[7] he came down the mountain carrying a Promethean message and met an old saint, an anchorite, who had not yet heard that "God is dead." God's death had been preceded by the death of the Great Pan, Bacchus, and the other pagan gods: humanity's faith in the gods and the God of Judaism and Christianity had died, and it was Zarathustra's mission to fill the void and speak to the people: "*I teach you the Übermensch.* Man is something that should be overcome."

Without hesitation, Jung claims Nietzsche to be identical with Zarathustra, but it also is a problem to find Nietzsche among the tangle of archetypes. The figure of Zarathustra is as expansive as that of Walt Whitman, who poetically claims to contain multitudes. He is possessed, as were the followers of Dionysus, and he becomes an instrument of prophecy, of the inner demons and voices that bring on a fiery apocalyptic vision like the consuming pillar of fire reminiscent of Exodus, and it signals the "great noontide." God led the people of Israel "through the wilderness" and "went before them by day in a pillar of a cloud . . . and by night in a pillar of fire" (Exod. 13:17, 18, 21), saving and protecting them from destruction. In *Zarathustra*, midway toward that noontide, at the beginning of part three (published in 1884), Zarathustra/Nietzsche tells his heart, "I am a wanderer and a mountain climber." Like the wandering Jews whose destiny was loneliness, Nietzsche's own "wandering and mountain climbing" led him to an insight: "in the last analysis one experiences only oneself." Everything is autobiography.

Nietzsche had experienced "the peaks and the abysses"; they were the same. He relives painful moments of the past; the howlings of dogs at midnight, their moonlight baying at ghosts like that of the father who had died too young and who had come to fetch Nietzsche's two-year-old brother, Josef.

The Old and New Testaments are among the key subtexts of *Zarathustra*. Zarathustra/Nietzsche, like Moses, had descended from the mountain, and within him he was attentive to the voice of Joseph, who said: "Carry my bones hence [out of Egypt] with you" (Exod. 13:9). The stories of God as a leading pillar of fire and of Joseph's bones are tightly joined in the verses of Exodus; and here, too, is the Jewish wanderer Moses who will not inhabit the Promised Land. The wanderer Zarathustra comes across a young shepherd, writhing and choking as a black snake dangles from his mouth. Is the scene real, a hypnogogic fantasy-dream, an inspired riddle, or a vision? It is all these. Here is the serpent that caused humans to make false dichotomies of good and evil in the Edenic story. A voice tears itself out of Zarathustra and urges the shepherd to "Bite, bite its head off . . . my horror, my hate, my disgust, and my pity, all my good and evil cried out of me." One day, says Zarathustra, humanity must bite off and spit out the throat-constricting inheritances of guilt feelings imbibed since Eden and look beyond to a transformation that will bring joy and make them laugh, like the relieved shepherd: "Never yet, had any man on earth laughed as he laughed." It is a Dionysian laughter, and a desire for it that consumes Zarathustra.[8] That is the key to the snake riddle and parable.

THE WANDERING JEW

In the fourth and last part of *Zarathustra* (written in 1885 but not published until 1892), Zarathustra is reunited with his shadow from whom he had parted at the end of *All-Too-Human*. At that point in the parable, the wanderer had expressed love for his shadow and the "light" which the shadow hates. Although the shadow is always present when the sunlight of knowledge appears, it disappears with darkness. Commentators have not been able to do much with this Nietzschean shadow, but we note that the wanderer asks him questions that can only be answered by the other side of reason, that is, intuition which springs from the unconscious. This parable also retells Plato's allegory of the cave in which knowledge is gained indirectly and the shadow is cast by the sunlight of knowledge. Allegory and parable, however, are linked with autobiography. Zarathustra expresses dislike of the shadow that has dogged his heels. And his shadow responds with his own dislike of constant wandering, being without a home, and without a goal—close to being the "Eternal Jew," yet being "neither eternal nor a Jew" (Z, IV, "The Shadow"). And who was as close to Nietzsche as his own shadow for some seven eventful years, if not Paul Rée? And who would be less likely to acknowledge or attribute any significance to being Jewish than Rée? Bayreuth turned a cold shoulder to Nietzsche, blaming Nietzsche's "betrayals" on the shadowy Rée. From then on Nietzsche became the solitary wanderer, but still pursued by his shadow. As for Zarathustra's opprobrious remarks directed against women, they had Lou Salomé as a target, with the reminder not to forget the whip when going to women. The German phrase is worse: it suggests going to whores.[9]

It was Zarathustra-Nietzsche's burden to relive with certain recriminations his past and at the same time ready himself, "glowing and strong like a morning sun," for the messianic noontide that had come full circle with the recurrent midnight horrors of childhood memory. The *Übermensch* vision had come to vanquish his father's ghost. Just as Christianity had conquered paganism by absorbing it, Zarathustrianism was about to vanquish Christianity. Just as "Jewish Protestantism," in Jung's phrase, had brought about a reformation of the Old Testament, Zarathustra had broken the old Judeo-Christian tablets and brought new codes from his mountain cave.[10] What does Zarathustra propose instead of the old tablets that are "never gay"? He looks for a "new nobility" that opposes despotism, the rabble, and the mentality of worshipful courtiers (who dream of an afterlife). The new nobility of procreators and cultivators will inscribe the word "noble" on their new tablets and they will subscribe to a divine belief in many gods but never in "one God." Zarathustra's sermon tells the nobles of the future that he does not praise "the spirit" that led their ancestors and the crusaders into the Promised Land because *there* the worst of all trees grew—the cross. In the new world, the sowers of the future will not revere the Fatherland ("Exiles you shall be"), but "your *children's* land" which will be ruled by "the best." Nietzsche, like Moses, however, intuitively knew that he would never reach the Promised Land, the Utopia of the *Übermensch*. Zarathustra's new codes and goals were far-reaching in religious and social domains. If humans were to develop from an embryonic stage toward the status of the *Übermensch*, there would have to occur a complete overhauling of goals and orientations. Jewish Old Testament legalism would have to yield to new psychological realities, as would Christian ethics derived from Judaism.

In his notes Nietzsche was even more frank than Zarathustra in advocating state-enforced measures to sanitize breeding of offspring. German official "certification" or "licensing" restrictions imposed on Jewish marriages and births in the nineteenth century possessed uncivilized features that found little public reproach, and Nietzsche was to provide *no* sanctions for those bureaucratic practices. His criterion was to bring together the "best"—even if that meant polygamy or incest (on the ancient Egyptian model). Nietzsche was to become a strong proponent of racially mixed marriages, melding the Jew and the Prussian, for instance, but still under stringent rules. While working on the four parts of *Zarathustra* he kept some of his most radical views private in order not to become a complete pariah in the eyes of potential readers. Intermarriage between Gentile and Jew posed problems and created divergent reactions. Goethe, for example, had no objections to church demands that intermarital offspring be baptized in the Christian faith, but felt that church sanctions of Jewish-Gentile marriages undermined morality; he opposed Jewish emancipation. Nietzsche, however, had no wish to overtly offend Jews on so sensitive an issue. But although Nietzsche opposed the Christian state during his time, he was somewhat of a "statist," advocating power in the hands of the state rather than in democratic consensus. Ultimately, however, Zarathustra elevated noble individuals to be above and beyond the "New Idol": "Only where the state ends does there begin the human being who is not superfluous: there begins the song of necessity, the unique and inimitable tune" (Z, I, "On the New Idol").

Friedrich Naumann especially, together with the Jew-baiting court preacher and state-church leader Adolf Stöcker, a most influential spokesman of Christian socialism, achieved notoriety from Berlin to Baghdad.[11] Stöcker's evangelical preaching also targeted Catholics more viciously than even Wagner did to prohibit Protestant/Catholic marriages. In 1881, he preached in Basel churches, and his black-cross banners, radical socialism, and attacks on Jews offended Nietzsche. According to Nietzsche, "state" is the name of the coldest of all cold monsters: "Coldly it tells lies, too; and this lie crawls out of its mouth: 'I, the state, am the people.'" Zarathustra claims that it was creators rather than the state who created peoples and thus served life: "Everything about it [the state] is false; it bites with stolen teeth, and bites easily" (Z, I, "On the New Idol"). In one of his "madness notes," to Meta von Salis in 1889, Nietzsche had ordered Stöcker shot.

It was *Zarathustra*'s fate to have a strange, subsequent history.[12] Almost none of Nietzsche's friends or enemies understood the book during his lifetime. Some saw it as a mishmash of esoteric poetry and peculiar evangelism. Lou Salomé, who was afforded a close look at its author's tone and temperament, found—quite prematurely, I believe—the book to be a disturbing indication of Nietzsche's incipient madness.

Nietzsche, unlike Wagner, could not stomach the coarse aims of the nationalist *Kreuzzeitung* paper and the revolutionary Christian socialism preached by propagandists like Stöcker. The publishers of the *Anti-Semitic Correspondence* bulletin claimed that Nietzsche belonged to their party, and they consistently referred to him as "influential" in their thinking. This misperception had been encouraged by a former publisher of Nietzsche, Ernst Schmeitzner, who increasingly gave priority to anti-Semitic and religious publications—delaying, in Nietzsche's opinion, the publication of his works. Nietzsche complained that the bulletin gave the false impression of secret complicity by Nietzsche with anti-Semitic views; he was "sickened" by their use of his *Zarathustra* to bolster their aims. Even worse was the state of affairs Nietzsche mentioned in confidence to his friend Overbeck, "The cause of a radical break with my sister is the damned anti-Semitic meddlings" (letter, April 2, 1884); "I wish it were possible to restore good footings with Dr. Rée and Fräulein Salomé [a relationship] ruined by my sister" (April 7). A reconciliation was not in the cards, however. A "semi-truce" did emerge between brother and sister: "my sister is a superb little animal," Nietzsche concluded.

Nietzsche could not dissuade his Llama from marrying Förster after she told him that she no longer wished to serve as a surrogate in *his* search for a wife. In the past Lisbeth had been torn between accommodating either her mother or brother; Förster offered a way out, and grudgingly Fritz had to let his Llama escape to the enemy camp. In Nietzsche's words, Förster was riding two horses: anti-Semitic propaganda and his plan to found a racially pure New Germania in the pristine wilds of Paraguay. On May 22, 1885, Förster and Elisabeth were wed, and Nietzsche, in absentia, had his mother report to him every detail of the wedding on a date that also, to Nietzsche's annoyance, had been deliberately chosen to commemorate Wagner's birthday. Franziska relished the ceremonial descriptions: candles, crucifix, an altar, tiger rugs from Paraguay, and cushions for the bridal pair kneeling before priests. The pious mother who had sternly warned her son never to disgrace his father's grave (precipitating a crisis that was almost fatal) now closed her letter with the certainty that peering through the flowers the family's "sainted Papa looked upon the bridal pair to place a hand of blessing upon them." The reappearance of his father's ghost was a chilling vision for Nietzsche and he fled to his favorite retreat in Sils-Maria. In February 1886, Elisabeth traveled to Paraguay to join her husband's colony which Nietzsche christened "Llamaland"; she was not to see her brother again until early in 1889 after his lapse into comatose madness.

The four parts of *Zarathustra* were completed and signaled Nietzsche's search for new codes to fill the void created by the death of God "who had disappeared into the sepulcher of churches." New moral values were needed to give human existence its meaning. One thing was clear to Nietzsche: the *Übermensch* or higher human of the future would be a new Dionysus. And the new moralities would be based on new conceptions of good and evil.

BEYOND GOOD AND EVIL

During his seclusion in Sils-Maria in 1885 and a winter stay in Nice, Nietzsche composed *Beyond Good and Evil: Prelude to a Philosophy of the Future*, intending to give modern dogmatism experimental, Socratic scrutiny. He found no absolutes in such moral judgments as implied by "good" and "evil" and even doubted the mechanical dialectics of posing one against the other, for much of human behavior lies in perspectives and shadings without reference to metaphysical absolutes. His freewheeling thinking asserted itself in irreverent banter—he had no intention of boring himself and readers—when stating, for instance, that only as "immoralists" can we free ourselves from dogma and prevalent prejudices. With a slap at Förster and his fanatical followers, Nietzsche suggested that "it would be useful and just to banish the anti-Semitic crybabies from the land." Among Nietzsche's new valuations was his aim of striking at theological anti-Semites and their bogus treatments of Old and New Testament relationships and interpretations. Nietzsche could never understand the sycophantic attitude toward the New Testament by Jews like Heine, baptized but hardly converted, and his recent ambiguous acquaintance with Siegfried Lipiner, a self-eradicating Jew. Nietzsche's preference for the "Old" over the "New" Testament was greatly guided by G. E. Lessing's view that the former emphasized this life and the latter opted for the afterlife. Yet he parted with Lessing's affirmation of God's existence.

Nietzsche early on believed that civilizations, history, and culture were created by great human beings as exemplified by the range of Old Testament figures from the Patriarchs to Moses and the prophets.[13] In one section, he sets up the Old Testament as a criterion of taste and as an educative exemplar. Nietzsche took his own road with a panegyric that would have been called chauvinistic had it been written by a Jew: "In the Jewish 'Old Testament,' the book of divine justice, there are things and accounts of such grand style that Greek and Hindu writings cannot equal them." ". . . This New Testament, a kind of rococo of taste in every respect," was glued onto the Old Testament in an act that perhaps constitutes "the greatest audacity and sin against the spirit that literary Europe has on its conscience" (J, 52; cf. GM, III, 22).

Nietzsche's defense of the Old Testament and rejection of Christian claims to it and other appropriations goes to the heart of a major nineteenth-century cultural problem vis-à-vis Jews, Christian laypersons, theologians, anti-Semitic politicians, and denigrative historians. Arnaldo Momigliano puts matters squarely: "the Jews whom [Ulrich von Moellendorff-] Wilamowitz, [Julius] Wellhausen, and [Eduard] Meyer were prepared to admit into their own picture of civilization had all been dead before Cyrus King of Persia allowed their descendants to go back to Jerusalem. It was the age of the prophets which belonged to the West—not what we call normative Judaism, which was [Jacob] Bernays's Judaism . . . German historians and theologians went [to great lengths] in trying to eliminate Judaism from civilization."[14]

Nietzsche did not regard Jews as the fossils subjectively portrayed by theologians and historians but as a people with a "normative" continuity from the loss of a homeland, exile, and life as the "other" in foreign host and hostile lands. Nietzsche identified with their strenuous will to survive and transcend. As independent of academically biased biblical exegesis and "higher criticism" was his refusal to go along with many stereotypical views about linkages of feminine and Jewish "characteristics and debilities," unflattering and denigrating of both Jews and women. Radically new for German audiences—and perhaps astonished Jewish readers as well—were the "untimely" thoughts such as those presented in a lengthy passage in *Beyond Good and Evil*:

> About Jews, for instance, just listen! I have not met a German who was favorably disposed toward Jews . . . and one should not be deceived . . . about sentiments that say that Germany has vastly more than enough Jews. . . . The Jews, however, are, without doubt, the strongest, toughest, and purest race now living in Europe. They know how to surmount even the worst circumstances (even more than favorable ones), all by means of virtues that today one readily would call vices, thanks to their resolute faith that does not have to apologize to "modern ideas." . . . It is certain that the Jews—if they wanted to or if they were forced to, as anti-Semites apparently wish—already now could have dominance . . . over Europe; that they are not working toward this end or have any such design is equally certain. Meanwhile they want and wish, instead—even with importunity [*Zudringlichkeit*] to be ingested and absorbed in and by Europe; they finally thirst for respect and want to be granted a haven that would end their nomadic life and status as "the eternal, wandering Jew."

> Combine these then with the Jewish genius for money, patience, and intellectuality. Here, I find it seemly to break off my blithe Germanic-clowning and patriotic oratory, for I have now touched on my serious *topic*: the European problem, as I understand it, is the breeding of a new European caste that is to rule Europe. (J, 251)

The serious and the mischievous blend in this passage is packed with opinions that would raise the hackles of anti-Semites: wedding the Prussian and the Jew and breeding a super-caste that would dominate Europe. Anti-Semites were fearful enough of Jewish domination and battle for "power" without needing the futurist Nietzsche's vision of an *Übermensch*, a wandering Jew who finally ends his nomadic life in order to participate creatively and genetically in Europe's destiny. By denying that Jews desire "lordship" over Europe (as if he were their spokesman), Nietzsche inadvertently feeds anti-Semites' worst fears and their hysterical propagandistic myths. Such statements that do border on the "clowning" he mentions can have effects other than the satire intended. Again, he strongly urges the dropping of national barriers in favor of "good Europeanism," earning for such advocacy the loaded charge of "cosmopolitanism" that fascists tar opponents with. It is noteworthy that here Nietzsche does not share the feeling of Heine and Jews who, wishing to be accepted into the mainstream of host nations, had urged that the "gates be locked" to Eastern Jews; Nietzsche would rather that anti-Semites be ushered *out of* the gates. Jews reading such passages would not, by and large, be unhappy with Nietzsche's undercutting of anti-Semitic puffery and his attribution of "genius" to Jewish intellect. His mentioning their genius for money in the same breath, however, could cause discomfort; there were vast European communities of "Jews without money" who were living in dire straits yet helping each other to survive communally.

Nietzsche was particularly incensed by xenophobic historian-politicians like Heinrich von Treitschke and Heinrich von Sybel (1817–1895), director of the Prussian archives. Sybel aimed for public support for a Prussian power-state of superior Germans which excluded "inferior Jews." Treitschke (1834–1896) was influential as a former professor of political science who turned to politics and professional historical writing. He single-mindedly advocated Prussian territorial expansionism and its enlargement as a "national state." Nietzsche harbored no illusions about such academic blindness; indeed, Treitschke went overboard in 1879 with his anti-Semitic public writings that condoned hooliganism against Jews and explained it as the expression of a deep, long-standing German anger against "foreign" elements, Jewish "cosmopolitan liberalism," and "internationalism." He explained that there was no other course to take since folkish, Germanic feelings had as yet been insufficiently developed, rendering Germans helpless in the face of the "shameless, arrogant, and impudent Jewish rabble";[15] ironically, the propagandist for Germanism himself had Slavic origins. A pre-Nazi ideologue, Treitschke's slogan, "The Jews are our misfortune," unfortunately became a murderous rallying cry for gullible people during subsequent decades, echoing the prototypical Wagnerisms that would not die. Anti-Jewish attacks that had begun on religious bases were now being launched on racial, political, and pseudo-scientific ones. How renegade Jews could be so injurious to themselves was a riddle exemplified by the journalist Wilhelm Marr, who founded the *Antisemiten-Liga* (the Anti-Semite League), in 1879, and he was joined by Otto Glagau whose hate-mongering was centered on attributing the disastrous stock-exchange crash of 1873 on the Jews and their domination of the industrial complex. Eugen Dühring (1833–1921), a philosopher whom Nietzsche called the "Berlin revenge apostle," "the premier big-mouth . . . among like-minded anti-Semites . . . (GM, III, 14), distributed diatribes against Judaization and Jews as self-chosen egotists damaging to the culture and customs of nations. He belonged, as Nietzsche put it, in the "Wagner sump" (*EH*, Wise, 4). Against such xenophobic and anti-Semitic voices as these, Nietzsche could do little except express his disgust consistently. The historian Theodor Mommsen wryly noted that the unity of Germany depended upon the designated common external enemy typified by France and the ostensible "internal" enemy: the scapegoat Jews. Government authorities and politicians of every class found anti-Semitism useful in deflecting attention from real problems requiring solution. A modern historian of religion, Ismar Elbogen, puts this phenomenon in perspective:

> Above all, the daily literature of the nineteenth and early twentieth century refutes the oft-voiced view that the murder-politics of the Nazis appeared suddenly between the two world wars and was invented and carried out by a small criminal clique and just as suddenly disappeared

in 1945. The aim of destroying Jews, or, in any case, of shunting them aside—be it through baptism, "obliteration within Germanism" or "forcible immigration"—was expressed much earlier in a thousandfold ways. . . .[16]

That Wagner's and his Nazi successors' ideology was spawned in the same Bavarian "sump" is a historical tragedy of great human and socio-political proportions. One thing that Nietzsche would affirm was the fact that Jews were agents for change. In calling for the "good European" to replace the fanatical/racial nationalists, Nietzsche knew what he was talking about; the attitudes prevailing against Jews largely stemmed from cultural and political provincialism. The historian Solomon Grayzel sums up the situation that Nietzsche not only deplored but inveighed against: "[pseudo-scientific publicists] agreed that the Semites, who by definition were called non-Europeans, had contributed nothing to civilization. . . . All of this pseudo-science was summed up by Houston Stewart Chamberlain [the English son-in-law of Richard Wagner] . . . in his notorious book *Foundations of the Nineteenth Century*" (1899 and continuous editions to 1935, extolling the "creative Aryan Volk" and condemning Jews as "non-creative").[17]

Nietzsche's stand against such torrential abuse of Jews in all the particulars cited here surely merits credit for intellectual and personal courage and combativeness, although he had no public forum comparable to that of the Sybels or Stöckers. In his *All-Too-Human*, he had already emphasized Jewish contributions to Western culture and repeats his views strongly toward the end of *Beyond Good and Evil*: "What Europe owes to the Jews? A variety of things good and bad but principally one thing that combines both at once: the grand style of morality. . . . On that account, we artists, among observers and philosophers, are grateful to the Jews" (J, 250). As for Jesus, Nietzsche never denied his Jewish origins but applied to him as well principles beyond clichés of good and evil: "Jesus says to his fellow Jews: 'the law is for slaves; love God as I love him, as his son! Of what concern are morals to us, the sons of God!' " (J, 164).[18]

The ambiguity of this statement allows a variety of interpretations and meanings, above all, Jesus' Jewish genius for taking exception to values ascribed to inherited laws and his aim to revalue them. Nietzsche likes Jesus' presumptuousness but implies that, since "sons of God" have

privileges of sorts, Jesus slyly associates himself with that legion. On the
other hand, revolt and revolting are approximate in a moral sense, so
that not all revaluations and rebellions gain Nietzsche's approval: motivations and consequences need to be taken into account and truth is to
be regarded as relativistic, if contradictions are to be avoided. In the following passage, "The Jews," Nietzsche sounds a theme that will become
ever more harsh in condemning the forces of Judaism that vanquished
the pagan world:

> —Although the Jews believed themselves to be the chosen people
> from among all others in the world, Tacitus and the whole world of
> antiquity said of them that they were a people [Volk] "born for slavery."
> But the Jews wrought a miraculous reversal of values that for thou-
> sands of years resulted in a dangerous fascination for life on earth.
> Their prophets have melted into one meaning the ideas of "rich,"
> "godless," "violent," "sensual," and for the first time have coined the
> word "world" as odious [pagan] currency. This inversion of values (that
> includes making "poor" synonymous with "holy" and "friend") denotes
> the significance of the Jewish people: here begins the slave revolt in
> the sphere of morals. (J, 195)

To understand what Nietzsche is saying here would require a résumé of
many passages in which he develops his concept of "master morality" and
"slave morality." These coinages have sometimes led to the mistaken
notion that Nietzsche was making racial or national distinctions.
Instead, he saw "slave" and "master" as both a sociological phenomenon
("slaves" being the lower, impoverished, and powerless strata—the
resentful "herd" whose interests were in conflict with that of the wealthy
and powerful) *and* a psychological state of mind.[19]

WAGNER'S DEATH

After the death of Wagner in Venice on February 13, 1883, Nietzsche
heard from Malwida that Cosima wished to shut out the world and close
friends as well, to live like a nun—only for her children's sake and
Richard's memory. Nietzsche immediately wrote to his most trusted
friend Overbeck that he was similarly inclined to vanish from sight.

Overbeck became a trifle alarmed because he knew of the emotional grip Wagner had exerted on Nietzsche. Cosima and Nietzsche were under tremendous stress concerning the Meister's death. If we remember the last line of the opera *Tristan und Isolde*, faithful Isolde lovingly promised to follow her Tristan into death. Its *Liebestod* music could trigger powerful suicidal impulses. In conversations Cosima and Richard had wished for simultaneous death and burial in the common grave set aside for them at Wahnfried.[20] And in regard to Nietzsche, the biographer Janz notes that Overbeck feared Nietzsche might foolishly "cross the line" and conclude an Oedipal drama.[21] But Nietzsche's thoughts took other convoluted directions, one of which surfaced openly when he wrote Overbeck that with Wagner's death, he was beginning to receive followers, "As I had long prophesied of becoming Wagner's heir" (April 7, 1884), something vaguely hinted at by Wagner during their better days. That dream and the supplanting of Cosima were unrealizable objectives.

Nietzsche's condolence letter to Cosima—as well as most of Nietzsche's letters to her—were destroyed, but from surviving drafts we discern patches of platitudes that disguise his inner feelings. He praises her self-sacrifice to Wagner's immortal ideals, which will link their names forever. But he still could not resist linking his name to that of the Wagners: "We are not opponents in small things" (but certainly in "great ones," he implied). He called Cosima the most deserving of veneration in his heart (letter, mid-February 1883). Lisbeth wanted the world to believe in her brother's normal infatuation with a worthy woman-designate, Cosima-Ariadne (the mythological name her abandoned husband von Bülow had given her); but it is altogether more demonstrable that the love and fatal attraction were vested in the effeminate bully Wagner: Nietzsche wanted to be loved without condescension by an ideal father.[22]

Nietzsche identified and associated himself with a long line of figures but with none more strenuously than Dionysus, Jesus, and Wagner. From the last two he had to break radically, especially from the Jesus who said, "I am not of this world."[23] To Lou Salomé, he wrote:

> I would like you to read my little essay "Richard Wagner in Bayreuth"; friend Rée certainly has a copy. In regard to this man and his art, I have lived through a great deal—it was a very long PASSION—I can find no other word for it. The renunciation, finally made necessary by a redis-

covery of myself, belongs to the hardest and most melancholy moments of my fate (c. July 16, 1882).

Lou Salomé memorably recounts a haunted scene she lived through with Nietzsche during a retrospective visit to the old Wagner estate in Lucerne's Tribschen in May of 1882: "For a long, long while he sat silently on the banks of the lake and was deeply immersed in heavy memories; then while making tracings in the moist sand with his cane, he softly spoke of those times past. And when he looked up, he cried."[24] One would be hard-pressed to find another moment in Nietzsche's Spartan life when he let down his guard to another human being so sentimentally and sincerely. Coincidentally, there is an uncanny, almost posed resemblance between Jesus writing nonjudgmentally in the sand (John 8:6f.) and Nietzsche's writing in the sands of Tribschen's lake. In another pose, Zarathustra, like Jesus, enjoined his disciples not to search for him because they would not find him. The Nietzsche-Zarathustra message calls for following one's self and not in the steps of another. And that is precisely Nietzsche's aim: to strike out for himself. Nietzsche wrote to Overbeck (on February 11, 1883): "Zarathustra, my son," represents "an image of myself in sharpest focus; it is poetry and not aphoristic."

NOTES

1. Johann J. Abel, *Historisches Gemälde der Lage und des Zustandes des weiblichen Geschlechts unter allen Völkern der Erde, von den ältesten bis auf die neuesten Zeiten: . . . Ein Lesebuch für Töchter der hoheren und mittleren Stande* (Leipzig: A. Schumann, 1803).

2. This spitefully accusatory labeling was false and the sad part is that it should have made no difference. But for better or worse many writers have accepted, without checking, Lisbeth's defamation of Lou (though without accepting her bigotry), as late as F. A. E. Lea's *The Tragic Philosopher*, 1957. As background readings for the Lou Salomé-Nietzsche relationship one must first of all rely on Lou's own memoir, *Lebensruckblich*, 1968; *Looking Back, Memoirs*, Breon Mitchell, trans. (New York: Paragon House, 1990); the massive examination in Rudolph Binion, *Frau Lou, Nietzsche's Wayward Disciple* (Princeton, N.J.: Princeton University Press, 1968); H. F. Peters, *My Sister, My Spouse* (New York: Norton, 1962); Lou Andreas-Salomé, *Friedrich Nietzsche in seinen Werken* (Vienna: Carl Konegen, 1894); and Lou Salomé, *Nietzsche*, Siegfried

Mandel, trans., with an introduction (Redding Ridge, Conn.: Black Swan Books, 1988).

3. Throughout her life, Lou carried with her Nietzsche's insults to her femininity. Some fifty years later when she had to undergo surgery and needed to pad her breast, she sadly recalled Nietzsche's words and said that he had been right after all.

4. "My dears, Lou and Rée! Don't be too disturbed about 'my delusions of grandeur' or my 'wounded vanity' . . . forgive me everything" (letter fragment December 20).

5. Z, I, "Of the Thousand and One Goals."

6. For a discussion of Nietzschean tables of values of Greeks, Persians, Jews, and Germans see C. G. Jung, *Nietzsche's Zarathustra*, ed. J. L. Jarrett, vols. 1 and 2 (Princeton, N.J.: Princeton University Press, 1988), vol. 1: 650–51; and W. Kaufmann, *Nietzsche* (Princeton, N.J.: Princeton University Press, 1974), pp. 201–202. Jung regarded the New Testament as a form of "Jewish Protestant Reformation of the Old Testament."

7. Jung, *Nietzsche's Zarathustra*, vol. 1, pp. 13–71, persuasively and intermittently discusses the incarnations of Zarathustra, and he reminds us of Nietzsche later telling a friend that the book could have been called "The Temptation of Zarathustra" in parallel with Christ's and St. Anthony's.

8. Nietzsche's chapter "Of the Vision and the Riddle," Z, III, is given a stimulating reading by H. Miles Groth, "Nietzsche's Ontogenic Theory of Time: The Riddle of the Laughing Shepherd," *American Imago* 37 (1980): 351–70. I have not summarized any of its points here.

9. Cf. Z, I, "Of Old and Young Women."

10. The inversion of Old Testament teachings in *Zarathustra* and the mock-New Testament sermonizings are so rampant as to make discussion of them prolix. For example, see Z, II, "On Old and New Tablets"; Z, I, "On Voluntary Death," in which the difference between the two preachers—Jesus and Zarathustra—comes when Zarathustra says, "I want to die so that you may love the earth [not heaven] more for my sake"; and Z, IV, "Conversations with the Kings," sec. 1, which tells of Christianity's conquest of Rome and the ascendancy of a "Jewish" divinity: Jesus.

11. Salo W. Baron, *Modern Nationalism and Religion* (New York: Harper Brothers, 1947), pp. 143–44.

12. Lisbeth saw a great opportunity to promote the book decades later as a trench Bible to be carried into battle and to inspire German warriors during the First World War. She put together an inexpensive "Kriegsausgabe," a war edition, published by Kroner Verlag, Leipzig, which was widely distributed. Her

patriotic foreword set the tone with "Nietzsche-Sayings for Peace and War" snipped from his writings. Emphasized is the will-to-power slogan and the vision of the new breed of Übermenschen—both were used to fuel the war fervor, although an even greater preponderance of Nietzscheanisms (not quoted by his sister) give unmistakable evidence of his denunciation of nationalism as "mania and patriotic stupidity." But nothing could stem the waxing nationalist appetite: appeals were even addressed to the millions of Germans settled in foreign lands to aid in the Fatherland's expansion. The cacophony of Pan-German, racialist, anti-Semitic propaganda included the voices of religious leaders.

13. Freud's Moses derives from Nietzsche's assumption.

14. Momigliano, *Jacob Bernays*, p. 24. Mohammedans and Catholics, to a lesser extent, received analogous treatment, Momigliano notes. For validation of his view, he recommends Hans Liebeschultz's study, *Das Judentum im deutschen Geschichtsbild* (Tübingen: Mohr, 1967).

15. Elbogen, *Die Geschichte der Juden in Deutschland*, p. 254.

16. Ibid., p. 256.

17. Solomon Grayzel, *A History of the Jews* (Philadelphia: The Jewish Publication Society, 1947), p. 643.

18. What Nietzsche attributes to Jesus is not necessarily endorsed by Paul: "Slaves, be obedient to your earthly masters [emphasis mine], with fear and trembling . . . as to Christ" (Eph. 6:5).

19. Cf. J, 260; GM, I, 7, in which Nietzsche ascribes the slave revolt in morality to priestly Judea as inherited by Christianity.

20. Although Cosima was prone to fits of guilt feelings, any thoughts of following Richard-Tristan into oblivion probably were minimized by the fact that she and Richard had had a horrendous row shortly before his heart attack: it centered on his alleged attentiveness to one of the Rhinemaiden. To the end, Wagner sought inspiration in the tensions created by his own sexuality and the asceticism of his alter egos in operatic dress.

21. Janz, *Friedrich Nietzsche*, 2: 187–88.

22. The psychoanalyst Wilhelm Stekel develops the point that Nietzsche's unreciprocated love for Wagner turned into the revenge motif and a homosexual component for the religious and other inner conflicts that created Nietzsche's neurosis. See, "Nietzsche und Wagner: Eine sexual psychologische Studie zur Psychogenese des Freundschaftgefühles und des Freundschaftsverrates," *Zeitschrift für Sexualwissenschaft und Sexual Politik* 4 (1917): 22–28, 58–65.

23. John 8:23.

24. Lou Salomé, *Nietzsche*, p. 54.

8

Conversations with Paneth and The Innocence of Becoming

THE JEWISH CONNECTION

Of all the intellectual links between Nietzsche and the ten-years younger Sigmund Freud, the Jewish connection was to be most coincidental and strange. Freud was responsible indirectly for putting Nietzsche in touch with the language and ideas of the great British empiricist John Stuart Mill. Freud had translated some of Mill's essays into German and Nietzsche took appropriate note of the ringing defense of individualism in the essay "On Liberty," the idea that human well-being is linked to "the internal culture of the individual," that one must not give in to "the despotism of culture." Mill's attack on the "collective mediocrity" of "tyrannical majorities" in democratic nations pressuring for conformity was a sentiment both Freud and Nietzsche agreed with, though they parted with Mill's idealized, romantic view in the essay "On the Subjection of Women."

In the mid-seventies a young scientist, Dr. Josef Paneth[1] (born in Vienna in 1857), publicly reviewed for the Viennese Reading Society of the German Students of Vienna Nietzsche's essay "On the Advantage and Disadvantage of History for Life" (1874). Very likely Paneth met Siegfried Lipiner at that lecture and other reading sessions of the club. Paneth was readily fascinated by Nietzsche's enticing philosophizing on humanity's memory-perspective of history, and its part in history as a "becoming." Nietzsche struck a chord with his autobiographical lament, "God preserve me from myself, that is, from the characteristics of my upbringing." Like other young Jews striving for emancipation from a heritage they knew little of, except by way of Gentile or renegade Jewish denigration, Paneth was trying to acquire a mainstream identity; the accidental Jewish origin of young Viennese-Jewish intellectuals was an embarrassment to be atoned for somehow or, at the very least, to be avoided. Like his university classmate Sigmund Freud, Paneth suffered from low self-esteem as an ethnic Jew, though Freud later converted that feeling into subversive and stubborn pride. Paneth soon gained recognition in medical and histological researches with the discovery of what were named the intestinal "Paneth cells."

From November 1, 1883, to the end of the following March, Paneth did laboratory research at Nice's Riviera in Villefranche. The scientist was eager to meet Nietzsche, a philosopher he had admired for almost a decade. When Nietzsche learned at the post office about Paneth's inquiries, he left a visiting card and his address at the science laboratory, Paneth's place of work. Prompted by curiosity as to what the reclusive Nietzsche looked like and how he lived, Paneth began to visit. From extensive correspondence with his intended bride, Sofie Schwab, relatives, and his colleague Sigmund Freud (correspondence missing), it is clear that during the Nietzsche-Paneth conversations the most recurrent topics were Judaism and the natural sciences; in the former area, Paneth displayed unembarrassed ignorance and personal evasions, while Nietzsche sought information about both Judaism and science. Paneth noted Nietzsche's deficiencies in the natural sciences and made him a gift of a book he valued highly, Sir Francis Galton's *Human Faculty and Its Development* (1883), engrossed in problems dealing with heredity and eugenics.

Paneth respected Nietzsche's strenuous work in progress and attributed his physical problems to the half-blind philosopher's stomach cramps and headaches. Paneth wrote that Nietzsche was

> uncommonly friendly, and without a trace of false pathos or the prophet-mongering I had suspected in his last book [*Zarathustra*]. . . we then talked about Lipiner and since Nietzsche was long finished with him, I was free to say as much that was unfavorable about him as I wished . . . in many questions of religion we shared the same viewpoints

and skepticism. In Nietzsche's thinking, man could be influenced and shaped morally by physical [eugenic], nutritional, and similar means; regretfully, I could not agree. . . . In tandem, we deplored today's fashionable tendencies that favor the bogus piety of a Paul Lagarde.[2]

Nietzsche ascribed his own talkativeness to his long stretch of solitary living. Paneth writes:

We spoke much about Sicily and Italy . . . and agreed that the unconscious life of every human being is so infinitely more rich and significant than hitherto suspected by anyone. Nietzsche considered *Zarathustra*, with the completed third part, to be perhaps the most blasphemous book ever written . . . with the aim of launching a frontal assault on German obscurantism . . . I wished him luck.

Paneth cautioned Nietzsche against excessive use of chloral hydrate for his insomnia. The scientist felt somewhat discomfited by Nietzsche's very personal "method of much dancing as did the Greeks" and his notion of the efficacy of laughter. For Nietzsche, Greek dance was a religious and social ritual, a model for the man of the future, the *Übermensch*, and the new culture.

Paneth saw in Nietzsche much that was "original and great," and communicated his impressions in detail to Freud and his own uncle Samuel Hammerschlag, a Jewish educator of religion, who was Freud's idolized mentor. "As for any imputations of anti-Semitism," Paneth wrote, "Nietzsche is, above all, a lofty person completely free of any such meanspiritedness and prejudice . . . and he is grounded in pure humaneness . . . he is inclined, though, to voice hyperboles and lacks the ability to differentiate among important and unimportant ideas in his works."

When discussions turned to the subject of anti-Semitism, Paneth—who apparently had followed even Nietzsche's minor writings—asked Nietzsche why he permitted his poems "Idylls from Messina" to appear in his publisher Schmeitzner's anti-Semitic periodical. Nietzsche countered that initially the publisher seemed to belong to the "good European" type and later, along with his contributors, turned anti-Semitic; Nietzsche said of himself that he was a stranger to such hostility and had tried from youth on to distance himself from prejudice against race and religion and judge things and people on individual merit. "He wanted to learn from me," wrote Paneth,

> what kind of expectations and hopes exist among Jews. I replied that I and others who shared my views did not wish to be regarded as a race or as Jews but as distinct individuals; that the belief in being a chosen people depended strictly upon one's acceptance of the [divine] origin of the five books of Moses [the Torah]; that nowhere do we find a Jewish entity or centrality; but that it is impossible nowadays not to acknowledge being a Jew unless one wished to court accusations of cowardice.

Here, Paneth's psychological explanation is as good as any as to why some Jews, despite advantages to be gained in religious conversions and baptismal certifications, rejected conversion as did Freud and Paneth, for instance, while at the same time rejecting Judaism. "Nietzsche at first," wrote Paneth,

> wanted to defend the influence of race but then dropped that position and totally agreed with me that there are no pure races; and, Germans, least of all, could lay claim to racial purity. In projecting a book on German obscurantism, anti-Semitism would certainly have to be taken into account. Slowly it emerged [in conversation] that during the recent course of years, he had been pressed hard to submit to the embrace of this anti-Semitic "piggery," and that he felt his whole existence to be threatened by it; that his own sister and a close family friend, Dr. Bernhard Förster, participated in such a movement; indeed, if he had committed suicide at the time, it would have been largely caused by the tortures he had endured through an anti-Semitism that had terribly embittered his life.

Paneth's account of his conversations with Nietzsche perfectly matched what Nietzsche had written in letters at the time to various correspondents, and it also explains why Nietzsche feared for his reputation among those he thought counted, especially when Paneth, like other nominally Jewish intellectuals, questioned his association with the anti-Semitic publisher Schmeitzner. According to Paneth, Nietzsche told him that

> a number of people of Jewish origin had behaved badly toward him, and that was something that could not be held against their race. (He was

not more specific than that, but it is clear that somehow he is submissive to his publisher [Schmeitzner] who expected anti-Semitic materials from him.) Naturally, I [Paneth] did not avoid noting how much all such matters embittered life among us [Jews]. Nietzsche said that his publisher as anti-Semite called himself a "practical Christian" and that he [Nietzsche] was a *practicus* but no practicing Christian; when the publisher asserted that the Socialist workers are totally dominated by the Jews, [Nietzsche] answered Schmeitzner that one cannot blame the Jews for not resisting the stirring up of the workers. When we spoke about the influence of nationalism, he said that it was an undeniable factor—like the French Revolution that assertively lay in the blood of every Frenchman. He himself is a Pole; his name is Niecki—the "destroyer, nihilist, the spirit that always denies"; this is a designation that gives Nietzsche pleasure. Often, also, Poles address him in Polish because of his looks. . . . Not long ago, Dr. Förster in a pamphlet "What is German?" had equated German with the word "decent" but he omitted precisely those characteristics that Goethe regarded as eminently German: receptivity for the foreign.

In his conversations with Paneth, Nietzsche tentatively shaped the design his thoughts were to take. To preserve the gist of their conversations accurately, Paneth habitually kept a record in his correspondence. He noted Nietzsche's personal wish that

> Jews connect with the best and noblest families of all countries and transmit their best characteristics; something that all nations ought to be concerned with at any rate. And then, with unique and sole vindication, they should produce numerous great men ever of note—Heine and Lassalle [Ferdinand Lassalle, 1825–1864, a Jewish-German founder of the Social Democrat movement] were not sufficiently pure. To use the word Semite as a term of insult is impertinent; never in Europe's history [for instance] was there anything like Spain's Moorish culture.

Nietzsche here repeats his two-sided view of Heine in whom the "best and worst" of Jewish characteristics are embodied: the brilliant stylist, farceur, mimic, and ironist but also the renegade capitulant "not sufficiently pure in lifestyle and motivations." Nietzsche gave Paneth a brief history lesson on the "unique beauty" of Semitic contributions to Spanish culture. Paneth's ignorance of Jewish-Spanish achievements was as painfully obvious as his dismissive attitude toward Jewish questions. Except for the anti-Semitism both deplored, Paneth refused to yield to favorable views that Nietzsche expected Paneth, as a Jew, to corroborate. Specifically, according to Paneth, Nietzsche felt that

> the Jews possessed special ideals as a nation. When I displayed indiffer-
> ence to such an idea, he was disappointed and disappointed as well at
> my rejection of any claim to exclusivity. The restoration of Palestine [as
> a Jewish realm] through peaceful or violent means, I decidedly brushed
> aside.

The implication here is strong that Nietzsche sympathized with the restoration of a Jewish nation while Paneth firmly resisted. As for the generally offensive charge that the press was dominated by numerous corrupt Jewish journalists, Nietzsche said that this phenomenon was a natural development toward the creation of an open marketplace for the exchange of ideas. Paneth then contended defensively that Jews who shared his own inclination

> had indeed lost their Jewish tradition. For me the fact of having worked
> in [Dr. Ernst] Brucke's [the famous physiologist and mentor to both
> Paneth and Freud] laboratory is more decisive than my Jewishness.

Nietzsche, who was plagued by identity questions, demurred: "Yes, but intellects cast loose from all moorings are very dangerous and sus-ceptible to corruption. "But," Paneth responded,

> isn't this what your free-spiritedness demands? One is what one can be
> and not necessarily what one should or wants to be; if one is free, one
> cannot bind oneself to a stake without being hypocritical. That would
> mean to be free—and only free—from the traditional and the conven-
> tional. One would be free to pursue one's choices and one's own
> laws. . . . And for those things an independent spirit and a strong will
> to life are essential. Such was the substance of our conversations that
> were mutually beneficial and agreeable.

Yet, Paneth did not disguise some of the dark hues in Nietzsche's person-ality when he recorded the philosopher's claim of having acquired the gift of being able to decipher humans, to look right through them, and, like Wagner, "an expert in all such matters conceded," he had the gift of killing them, metaphorically, that is. As for philosophical systems, Nietzsche repeated his own conviction that "they are nothing more than their authors' memoirs." Contrary to Schopenhauer, even the most minute in life retains great value. Of all the friends estranged by Nietzsche's isolation, the most difficult was the case of Wagner; but isolation also gained for him an immense power of concentration.

"Anti-Semites," Nietzsche said summarily, "only pretend hypocritically that they are Christians." Of other psychologically discussable subjects, Paneth mentioned the question that was to engage Freud, namely, that of wish-fulfillment. Nietzsche thought that if wishes could kill, no person would any longer be secure; Paneth added his opinion that no one would be alive any longer, and he added that everyone possesses something in life that makes it worthwhile. "For me," said Paneth, "things were going swimmingly and I could afford casual statements. Formerly, it was necessary to ameliorate humans' fear of death, but nowadays it was almost necessary to ameliorate their fear of living." "Nietzsche," Paneth observed, "is possessed of many contradictions but is a thoroughly honest man, a man of moods, and of an inspired prophetical nature." Paneth found Nietzsche's demolition theories congenial. A new ethos and new religious constructs need to be born. Nietzsche explained that one can assume different viewpoints about anything except for the necessary act of thinking and the will to dominate: "all other gods can be destroyed." Paneth complimented Nietzsche's mental vigor and believed that every one of his ideas deserved an audience, particularly those that dealt with the will and self-consciousness, pleasure and displeasure. Paneth did think that Nietzsche's writings and opinions about women were weak and stemmed from his seclusion. "We also talked about the relationship of genius and madness and of the fact that many minds of the first rank were epileptics—Caesar, Napoleon, Mohammed, St. Paul, Byron." Nietzsche may have told Paneth, as he did others, that during his younger days he had experienced epilepsy without loss of consciousness. The poet Friedrich Hölderlin, the nomadic, exotic bard Nikolaus Lenau, and the romantic composer Robert Schumann were figures Nietzsche identified with at various earlier times, figures beset by "the threatening ghost" of madness that drove fragile persons of genius to the brink or "bourne" from which Hamlet shrank. Nietzsche was attracted to the book *Genius and Madness* (1864) by the Jewish-Italian professor of forensic medicine, Cesare Lombroso of Turin, who was to follow Nietzsche's writings with signal interest.

Among Paneth's last communiqués to Vienna detailing his encounters with Nietzsche, opinions are offered that tell of shared sentiments:

> Both of us lamented the swindle perpetrated in the name of nationalism, and I said that to me those Jews who preen themselves as fanatic Germans, Czechs, or Hungarians are particularly ludicrous; Jews should be loyal adherents of the state to which they belong but should not be overzealous nationalists. Nietzsche thought it fortunate that there are people . . . who are good Europeans—they should never permit that identification to be taken from them. . . .

Paneth thought that while Schopenhauer projected his own pessimism upon the world, Nietzsche projected a more positive view, with the expectation that a utopian phase would succeed a nihilistic one. There is no doubt that Paneth was deeply touched by the fact that he could talk candidly with a great mind about social and cultural subjects that were troubling him and he was pleased to find a philosopher he respected and who was free of the "race swindles" engendered by the anti-Semitism popular among *all* social and political classes in Austria and Germany, as well as among anti-liberal Protestant and Catholic clergy.

When Paneth and Nietzsche became too preoccupied with personal and professional affairs, their contact lapsed. Yet Paneth was reluctant to take complete leave of Nietzsche without wanting to write something about his philosopher-friend. In a farewell letter of early May 1884, Nietzsche expressly discouraged any bio-critical forays as premature by at least fifty years; only at the end of that time would some genius realize "what had been wrought through him." Nietzsche, one may assume, was torn between wanting recognition and shunning exposure to criticism. In the meantime, he wished Paneth to retain their conversation only in memory: "My *work bides its time.*"

OVERBECK AND PANETH

Of extraordinary import is a well-intentioned but skewed account of the Nietzsche-Paneth encounter in the memoir of Nietzsche's most dependable university colleague and protector, Franz Overbeck, who had shared bachelor quarters with Nietzsche until he married in Basel. The Overbeck reminiscences directly show that Nietzsche's concern, his identification with Jews and Jewish problems were greater than even his friends—with their limited sympathies for or social antipathies toward Jews—had wanted to realize. Overbeck, with his generous but possessive attitude toward Nietzsche, was loath and late to realize how much attention his friend paid to Jews. Condescension toward the Jewish scientist Paneth in Overbeck's account is not atypical of the attitudes that Nietzsche chose to ignore—or, rather, not to challenge—in his friends. Overbeck writes:

During the winter days of December 26, 1883, to the following March 26, Nietzsche had exchanges with a modern Jew named Dr. Paneth from Vienna. Truly, this encounter of all recountable ones in his life is of the most negligible of its kind. They had something to do with each other and then they "finally parted" not ever to make contact again [during the six remaining years of Nietzsche's sanity]. About the encounter, Paneth at the time corresponded with his intended in Vienna [Sofie, who may have met Nietzsche on a visit to Paneth on the Riviera in 1884]. The year 1884 was a time during which Nietzsche was mired in personal conflicts with anti-Semitism. This movement was distant from his views—if not repulsive to him. . . . In view of what Paneth reveals about himself, he is a very odd Jew, of the Spinoza variety, namely, related to that worldly [secular] sage and mainly with a very rare degree of emancipation from all traditions of his tribe in respect to religious and nationalistic thinking. Also, Paneth is completely alienated not only from the synagogue but also from contemporary Zionism . . . with decisive and unyielding provocation. Paneth lets no other "school" than the scientific take precedence; he had studied in the physiological laboratory of Dr. [Ernst] Brucke in Vienna. Here then was a Jew Nietzsche could not have been indifferent to . . . [in seeking scientific information at the time of his *Zarathustra*].

Purely from a historical perspective did Nietzsche have reason to take a closer look at a Jew of his type. Without investing impassioned or insistent interest, both of us—Nietzsche and I—as historians could not help but give special attention to the tenacious relation of Jews to their folk-tradition and to admire the uniqueness of this tenacity. Related to our exchange of ideas about Jewry, especially during our Basel days, I do not disguise my lack or sparseness of knowledge of

Paneth in my Nietzsche letters. But it was important for Nietzsche to let me know more about Paneth.

In our thinking about anti-Semitism, Nietzsche and I were particularly like-minded, I do believe. Fanaticism of any kind as well as religious hatred were far distant from us . . . so that we had no reason to agree with anti-Semitism. Not that our reservations separated us particularly from other Europeans. . . . In our area everyone actually, and the educated, at the very least, was unfavorably disposed toward Jews and their presence among us. All those in our "society" experienced this as something inborn and gave nuanced voice to their disinclinations; a few used nuances to hide behind and a few did not care to preach aloud. It may be that Nietzsche's and my own displeasure with anti-Semitism expressed itself partially as a form of spite against [endemic social] views; our conversations [about the subject] were infrequent and were never pursued with passion nor ever regarded as "important" but thought of as a passing social mode. Consequently, there reigned a silent and mutual understanding between us on the subject.

And yet, in Nietzsche's writings it is abundantly clear that the heavy dose of anti-Semitism he had cause to experience, as personal vexation, was endured with a mild form of philo-Semitism. As a friend of Nietzsche, I wished neither him nor myself contact with anti-Semitism, and I was spared it even in my old age when a Jew married a niece of mine, a niece I did not idealize though I loved her honestly and considerately. Fate was to deal heavily in matters of the kind.

The notes that Nietzsche dispersed to the world at the outbreak of madness are in many respects signs indicative of how greatly anti-Semitism increasingly occupied his thoughts, more than had been apparent. Among the manifestations was one of the last notes he sent to me and my wife [January 7, 1889: a note telling them that Nietzsche was having all anti-Semites shot].[3]

Overbeck, perplexed by Nietzsche's anti-Judaic language in his later writings, ended his account of Nietzsche and the Jews with the following observation that itself has gained proponents and critics:

Nietzsche is a hearty adversary of anti-Semitism in the form he had experienced it; he viewed "defamation and destruction madness" as one of the most dishonest forms of hatred. . . . Yet that does not obstruct his judgment; when he speaks honestly about Jews, he outdistances all anti-Semites with his sharpness: his anti-Christianity is decidedly rooted in anti-Semitism.

Overbeck's interesting conclusion previewed opinions of critics who claimed to see at the heart of Nietzsche's attitudes a secret or latent Christian who contended with but could not rid himself of his heritage (Karl Jaspers), or a quasi anti-Semite who scorned Christianity as a disguised form of Judaism portrayed by Overbeck. As we shall see, Overbeck's own indigestible antipathy toward Jews was exacerbated by one deeply traumatic experience.

Walter Kaufmann calls for a better reading of—what one must admit—are some tortuous Nietzschean texts; he notes that Nietzsche envisages Christianity "as the dross of Judaism, arising from its lowest elements,"[4] the *pariah* of Judaism (A, 27), as Nietzsche phrased it. Nietzsche, indeed, loathed with a passion what he targeted as the rabble resentful of the nobility, but excoriated equally the "priestly" element that stood in polar contrast to the awesomeness of the Old Testament's wrathful and holy Jehovah.

Jewish priests, says Nietzsche, turned the great epoch of Israel's history into one of decay. As for the negative aspects of Jesus, he embodies that Jewish-priestly instinct which reverses higher values and "has its roots in the worst aspects of Judaism," from which grew Christianity, the great, "unholy lie" (A 24–28, 199, 200).[5] Nietzsche will continue to wrestle with the question of who and what is responsible for the fall of paganism and Rome and bemoan the corrupting roles of Judaism and Christianity.

The church historian Overbeck declined to enter the labyrinth of subtleties erected by his friend Nietzsche and was satisfied with simplifications that, at any rate, were radical enough for his own times. It is clear from his long account that *he* was personally uncomfortable with the "Jewish question" and with the distinguished scientist Paneth of the Jewish "tribe." He knew that Nietzsche was hoping for some usable scientific and ethnic information from Dr. Paneth. And aside from speculations about whatever vindictive emotions surface in Nietzsche's *Genealogy of Morals* (and the *Antichrist*), it is unmistakably clear that he had no reservations about castigating anti-Semites, such as Ernest Renan and Eugen Dühring, for their perversion of morality, self-hate, and their drum beating nationalism.[6]

After the ugly rumors circulated by Lisbeth about her brother's perverse relationship with Lou and Rée, Nietzsche phrased his anguish deliberately in Othello's language: a filched "good name," unlike a stolen purse, is cause for concern. He had wanted to sustain his good name especially among Viennese Jewish intellectuals. Paneth had raised the question of Nietzsche's anti-Semitic publisher and Nietzsche with all good conscience could report that he had risked a break with Schmeitzner by telling him, "In fact, I no longer fit into your Wagner-Schopenhauer-Dühring-and other party-line literature.—But for that we need not be angry with one another!" (postcard to Schmeitzner, June 19, 1881).

Nietzsche was torn between his dependency upon Schmeitzner and his own displeasure. On the list of people to receive complimentary copies of part IV of *Zarathustra*, published in 1885 at his own expense, was Dr. Paneth. Although communications had ceased in the intervening years, the topics they had broached kept appearing in ruminative, speculative form in Nietzsche's notebooks for a work to be titled *Die Unschuld des Werdens* (*The Innocence of Becoming*). Some of the notes, either in toto or with modifications, Nietzsche incorporated into his final works; eventually they were published separately from the collected notes in *The Will to Power*. Although his thoughts roamed far and wide, an exceptional proportion kept returning to familiar topics involving Judaism, Christianity, "race," and ideational spinoffs. From among the kaleidoscopic notes for *Die Unschuld des Werdens* are many that engage Jewish matters. Nietzsche never tired of comparing Jews and Germans to the detriment of the latter, above all the Bayreuthians.

PANETH, NIETZSCHE, AND FREUD

Paneth enjoyed intellectual involvement with the writings of other philosophers as well and his letter-reports to Samuel Hammerschlag and to Freud put him in the maieutic role of midwife, assisting in the delivery of ideas. Years earlier, Freud was indebted to Paneth when Paneth inherited some wealth and was among those people who assisted Freud financially with medical school tuition and saved him from social embarrassment. At the time of Nietzsche's death, Freud wrote to an intimate, Dr. Wilhelm Fliess, that he had acquired a Nietzsche book, *Beyond Good and*

Evil most likely, in which he hoped "to find words that have remained unspoken within me, but I have as yet not opened the book." Throughout the following decades Freud was ambivalent about reading Nietzsche, whether in acknowledging the relatedness of, or assigning priority to, their ideas. In the thirties, he told the novelist Arnold Zweig that Paneth had written him extensively about Nietzsche, but that he and his friend Lou Salomé would in no way be interested in helping him [Zweig] with a fictionalized biography of Nietzsche. Underlying his disinclination was the fact that there were too many similarities in psychic autobiography and revolutionary psychological thinking between himself and Nietzsche.

Nietzsche was pressed into service by Freud dissidents. When Jung broke with Freud, he reminded Freud of what Nietzsche's Zarathustra had said to his disciples: ". . . Whoever remains a student does disservice to his teacher. . . . I bid you to lose me and to find yourselves; and only when you have all denied me will I return unto you . . ." (Z, I, "Of Bestowing Virtue," sec. 2). Of course, this was Nietzsche's Jesus pose, but Freud well understood Jung's message and sent a conciliatory reply acknowledging Nietzsche's prerequisite of freedom for independent thinkers. The same message was embodied in Otto Rank's birthday gift to Freud of a leather-bound edition of Nietzsche's works. It may well be that what Freud resented most about what he called his "unsolicited" biographer, though an undeniably close friend, Fritz Wittels, was that he characterized Nietzsche as a "forerunner" of Freud. Others attributed to Nietzsche a priority of thought about sublimation, repression, conscience, ego, sadism, and the like. Yet all this "anticipatory" attribution is greatly exaggerated. Both men gained great insights by relatively exacting self-observations. Nietzsche's thoughts were intuitive, Freud's were less philosophical and grounded more in clinical and patient-verification analysis. Nietzsche's aphoristic thinking could arrive at some generalized truths but also at new forms of bigotry and half-baked conjectures and visionary programs. At best—and this is not negligible—Freud was enormously stimulated by the venturesome thinking of Nietzsche, but systematized his approaches to psychological problems and carried them much farther and with greater elegance. It gave Freud pleasure to know, on the other hand, that Nietzsche himself was indebted to Professor Bernays, a relative of Freud's wife, in matters of Greek and Aristotelian speculations on drama, tragedy, and catharsis as medical purgation rather than religious purification.

Paneth and Nietzsche were sequestered in Freud's unconscious and afforded the occasion for one of Freud's celebrated dream interpretations, a dream that, for all its complexity, he called "lovely." The dream included Paneth, who (in reality) had died young, at age thirty-three, of tuberculosis, and coincidentally in the same year as Nietzsche, 1900. In the dream, Josef Paneth engages in conversation with Freud's friend Fliess and eventually "dissolves" before their eyes, in which Freud rejoices greatly. If we remember Paneth's discussion of wish fulfillment possibilities, Freud's wish takes on additional interest. Freud himself had expressed admiration for but also envy of his gifted friend and colleague. He states this honestly in the section on "Dreamwork" in *The Interpretation of Dreams* and makes the puzzled admission, "My hostility toward my friend P[aneth] has so little foundation in reality—he was greatly superior to me." As university students they had been brought close by readings and discussions of Ludwig Feuerbach's attack on doctrines of immortality and the bold denial of God's existence except as a creation in humanity's consciousness; they shared mentors and laboratory experiences. Unacknowledged in Freud's analysis was the tension stemming from ambiguous emotions and latent hostility and resentment at Paneth's accomplishments, earlier than his own; indebtedness to Paneth's financial generosity; and, above all, the Nietzschean influences clearly derived from the communications from Paneth about Nietzschean ideas which put Freud severely on the defensive. Freud's anxiety was a feeling that Nietzsche explained in a major way as *ressentiment* as it applied to persons and peoples in their social and historical responses. Freud's associates, at various times, more than implied Freud's indebtedness to Nietzsche, much to Freud's annoyance and even anguish. One upshot of the "*non vixit* dream,"* when it was published, was the refusal of Paneth's young widow to have anything more to do with Freud.†

Josef Paneth's epistolary accounts of his relationship with Nietzsche were brought to the attention of Kröner publishers in 1932, but they

---

*In the dream, Paneth is conversing with Fliess, a friend of Freud. At one point Fliess turns to Freud to ask him to clarify a statement by Paneth. Freud replies, *non vixit* ("he did not exist"). When this interpretation of the dream was published, Paneth's widow regarded the statement as a gross insult to her husband.

†As a family postscript, Friedrich Adolf Paneth (1887–1958), a world-class professor of chemistry in Vienna, one of Paneth's three sons brought up as Protestants by their Jewish parents, was fortunate to leave steps ahead of the Nazi hordes.

permitted the academic Nietzsche editor and Nazi Alfred Bäumler to tailor selections ideologically in "documenting" Nietzsche's life (see Baeumler's *Friedrich Nietzsche*, 1932) and editorially explaining away any of Nietzsche's fundamentally sympathetic attitudes toward Jews in the Paneth letters.

NOTES

1. Dr. Joseph Paneth, 1857–1900, is remembered in biomedical fields as the discoverer of the "Paneth cell," technically a zymogenic, i.e., enzyme-producing, cell found at the bottom of the glandular intestinals.

2. The absence or loss of Paneth's letters to various correspondents about his thoughts and discussions with Nietzsche are a source of real regret if one judges them by the ones that have survived. Some were first printed by Elisabeth Förster-Nietzsche, *Das Leben Friedrich Nietzsche* (Leipzig Naumann, 1895–1904), vol. 2, p. 481 ff.; then reprinted in *Nietzsche in seinen Briefen und Berichten der Zeitgenossen. Die Lebensgeschichte in Dokumenten*, ed. Alfred Baeumler (Leipzig: Kröner, 1932). Additional letter material appeared in contributions by A. Venturelli, *Nietzsche-Studien* 13 (1984). This was considerably augmented by R. F. Krummel, "Josef Paneth über seine Begegnung mit Nietzsche in der Zarathustra-Zeit," *Nietzsche-Studien*, 1984, pp. 478–95. See also Janz, *Friedrich Nietzsche*, 2: 254–57.

3. All quotes by Overbeck are drawn from Carl A. Bernouilli, *Franz Overbeck und Friedrich Nietzsche*, 2 vols. (Jena: Diedrichs, 1908).

4. Kaufmann, *Nietzsche: Philosopher, Psychologist, Antichrist*. p. 299.

5. The *pia fraus* (unholy lie, pious fraud) is a phrase taken from Ernest Renan. See also G, "Improvers of Mankind," sec. 5.

6. Cf. GM, II, 11, 14; III, 26; A 17, 29 (Renan), and 55: "[O]f necessity, the party man becomes a liar. . . . This is *our* conviction: we confess it before all the world, we live and die for it. Respect for all who have convictions! I have heard that sort of thing even out of the mouths of anti-Semites. On the contrary, gentlemen! An anti-Semite certainly is not any more decent because he lies as a matter of principle." See also Isaac Goldkorn, "Renan and Racism," *Midstream* (November 1986).

9

Nietzsche's Ressentiments, the Jews, and the Will to Power

RESSENTIMENTS

One might wish that Nietzsche had devoted an entire book to the theory of *ressentiment*—only the French word harbors some of the many nuances of its foliating meanings—instead of scattered essay passages. Rarely being able to squarely face his own resents, Nietzsche quickly noted them in others. In fact the resentment theory invites parody:

> ... [T]he big news in *The Genealogy of Morals*, crucial to its whole argument, is the world-historical role of the Jews, a sly priestly folk with a genius for rancor, who, subjugated by Rome, incited the slaves of the Empire to moral revolt against their masters, thereby determining a unique historic reversal of values with modern nihilism as its final consequence—pending a transvaluation of values. Even in applying Lou's [Lou Salomé's, actually Nietzsche's originally] dictum on philosophy as a personal confession, Nietzsche had complied with it, for this news was a subtle parable of the Trinity drama of 1882. The villain of the piece was Rée, the "priestly Jew, an ex-master who had instigated the "unclean" slave (disciple) to convict the "distinguished" master of evil

purposes beneath his grand egoism and to infect him with compassion and vengefulness such that his only deliverance lay in a prodigious stunt of self-surmounting. Lou was—subsidiarily—Jesus presented to Rome by Paul as "a martyr from earliest infancy" crucified by his people and hence received by Rome as a godsend: the bait swallowed by "the whole world" [GM, I, 8]. Yet that bait had been temptation in its most sinister form, so that Nietzsche, tempted, was subsidiarily Jesus.[1]

This strange psychodramatic scenario is not as farfetched as it might seem if we note that Nietzsche deliberately staged the famous—or infamous—Trinity photo in which the camera-shy Rée and his friend Nietzsche were holding the handle of a large cart upon which Lou stood brandishing a lily-stalk whip over the two men.* Shortly before, according to her memoirs, she had rejected Nietzsche's marriage overtures. Nietzsche's penchant for shape-changing identifications are at play. Is not the Trinity drama an uncanny replication of Nietzsche's euphorian drama, now featuring Lou as the nun and Rée her brother in a bisexual configuration? There is a further level of interpretation: the figures of the two Pauls, two Jews, Rée and the New Testament Paul. Ironically, Rée was close to Christianity ideationally, while Nietzsche was eons removed. In his book on the origin of conscience, Rée lauded Christianity as the high plateau of humankind's moral evolution toward ethical ideals. It was coincidentally symbolic for him to have found refuge in a stall at St. Peter's to work on his book while Nietzsche first met Lou von Salomé nearby.

Aside from speculations about whatever vindictive emotions surface in Nietzsche's *Genealogy of Morals*, it is unmistakably clear that he had no reservations about castigating anti-Semites, their perversions of morality, self-hate, and their drum-beating nationalism:

> . . . Said confidentially to psychologists, if they are at all inclined to study *ressentiment* up close: this plant now blossoms at its best among anarchists and anti-Semites, and, at any rate, where it has always bloomed—in hiding like the violet, except that it has a different odor. (GM, II, 11)

---

*This is reproduced as a frontispiece in *Nietzsche* by Lou Salomé, edited by Siegfried Mandel. The Trinity photo is an example of Nietzsche's "penchant for shape-changing identifications." It is a parodic response to the brouhaha against his unfortunate aphorism: "Thou goest to women? Remember thy whip!"

I remind readers again of that apostle of revenge in Berlin, Eugen Dühring, who in the Germany of today employs the most indecent and repulsive moralistic trash [*moralischen Bumbum*]; he is the prime moral big-mouth in existence, even among like-minded anti-Semites. All of them are people of *ressentiment*, of these worm-eaten physiological mishaps (who with their self-hate wish to undermine the happiness of the healthy and to plant in them feelings of guilt about their happiness and to infect them with a sense of misery). (GM, "What Do Ascetic Ideals Mean?" III, 14)

. . . All honor to the ascetic ideal [the disciplined, and sometimes cruel, mastery of one's impulses] *insofar as it is honest!* . . . But I do not at all like the coquettish bedbugs whose insatiable vanity prompts them to sniff out the infinite [*das Unendliche*] until finally the infinite reeks of bed-bugs. . . . I do not like the agitators dressed up like heroes that wear magic caps of idealism on their heads filled with straw. . . . And I do not like the latest speculators in idealism—the anti-Semites—who nowa-days roll their eyes heavenward in a Christian-Aryan petty-bourgeois mode that exhausts one's patience already abused by their moralistic propaganda tricks designed to arouse all the horned cattle in the popu-lace. (*Every* kind of intellectual swindle is not without success in pre-sent-day Germany and is attributable to the almost indisputable and evi-dent stultification of the German mind; this I attribute to an altogether exclusive diet of newspapers, politics, beer, and Wagner-music, without forgetting the preconditions of this diet as the national exclusiveness and vanity, the strong but narrow principle of "Germany, Germany, above everything" ["Deutschland, Deutschland über Alles"—the patri-otic anthem], and finally the palsy of "modern ideas.") . . . (GM, III, 26)

Ressentiment, in brief, is a powerful force that can work revaluatively—constructive or destructive—in terms of subjective goals.

ERNEST RENAN

While taking notes for *The Genealogy of Morals*, Nietzsche intensified his focus on what he felt to be the psychological, backstage history of early Christianity. Quite striking, it turns out, are views that strongly parallel those of Ernest Renan even more closely than those of Gibbon. The noted French historian and Orientalist had engaged in extended discussion during Nietzsche's Tribschen evenings with the Wagners. As for Renan's attitudes toward Jews, they pose the same conundrums as Nietzsche's—both praised Jews with extreme flatteries and also dispraised them with the basest calumnies while at the same time sincerely professing no religious or ethnic disparagement.

How can such contradictions be seen as anything but neurotic? The Renan biographer Richard M. Chadbourne reasons that such Hegelian and seemingly insoluble antinomies,[2] contradictions, are all part of an emerging order of things—a major theme of Renan's works and dictum: "The life of humanity, like that of the individual, rests upon necessary contradictions."[3] Further, Renan theorized that the delicate nature of moral truth denies that anything is either black or white but instead depends upon some shade of meaning relativized between polarities; this is very much the notion developed by Nietzsche in *Beyond Good and Evil.* Just as Nietzsche had rebelled against his pastoral home and religious upbringing, Renan also discarded theological pursuits and education gained at Catholic seminaries and turned to secular and philological vocations. His academic career reached its apex and decline simultaneously: appointed to the chair of Hebrew at the Collège de France as Professor of Hebrew, Chaldaic, and Syriac, he gave an inaugural lecture that praised Jesus as an incomparable *man*: shortly thereafter, he was deprived of his position. Without a fixed income but proud of his independence, he had his academic post restored in 1870. Renan said that he accepted the penalty of being excluded from the "great [Christian] religious family" and being regarded as "corrupt." In response, however, he had unbounded contempt for the masses, the herd. With a tone of "calm contempt," he noted that "most men are not human beings at all, but apes." And this, like similar Nietzschean remarks, was not intended to be unflattering to simians who, after all, did not attack him for his "heresies." Renan rejected universal suffrage and proposed that anyone with fewer than fifteen years of education was not to be trusted with cultural or political activities; he pressed for reforms in schooling to obtain such objectives as the replacement of politicians and religious leaders (mainly the French Catholic clergy) by philosophers and other cultural elitists. In that respect, he was more specific about whom he wanted to take charge of the nation's future than Nietzsche was with his incomplete depiction of the *Übermensch.*

In his comparative study of Semitic languages and cultures, as early as 1847, Renan practically invited readers to choose between his own two states of mind about Semitic and Aryan "races":

On the one hand,

> I am . . . the first to recognize that the Semitic race, compared with the Indo-European race, really represents an inferior combination of human nature. It has neither that height of spiritualism which only India and Germany knew, nor the sentiment of measure and perfect beauty that Greece bequeathed to the neo-Latin nations, nor that delicate and profound sensibility which is the dominant trait of the Celtic peoples. (*Histoire générale et système comparé des langues sémitiques* 1855, pp. 4–5)[4]

On the other hand, he avers:

> . . . the Semitic and the Indo-European races, examined from the viewpoint of physiology, do not show any essential difference. . . . [T]he Semites and the Aryans are only one race, the white race; seen from the intellectual side, they are only one family, the civilized family[; further], the Semites contributed to mankind refined religious ideas, poetry, and the instinct of infinity. (*Histoire générale*, p. 504)[5]

Renan's antipodal views of Jews are echoed and matched by Nietzsche's as we have already seen. Pertinent here is Renan's refrain:

> We have insisted often on this [bifocal, bipolar, oppositional] singular character that makes the simple Jewish people include in their bosom the extremes, and if we may say so, the fight between good and evil. Nothing in fact equals Jewish wickedness; and yet we have drawn from their bosom the ideal of goodness, sacrifice, and love. The best of men have been Jews; the most malicious of men have also been Jews. A strange race—truly marked by the seal of God—who has produced the nascent church and the fierce fanaticism of the Jerusalem revolutionaries, Jesus and John of Gischala, the apostles and the assassin zealots, the Gospel and the Talmud. . . . (*L'Antéchrist*, 1873, p. 130)[6]

Chadbourne, unlike some other critics, does not believe Renan to be guilty of anti-Semitism on the grounds that "understandable retributive 'fanatics' of Judaism and Jerusalem will exact their 'revenge' by the eventual triumph over Rome by their Jewish offspring, Christianity. Hence the triple conflict—Judea-Rome-Christianity."[7] In Nietzsche's writings Gibbon's and Renan's Judaic revenge theories mushroomed into his *ressentiment* polemics and psychology. In closing the "cycle of religious history," a task Renan set for himself, he also paid tribute to the Jewish publisher Calmann-Lèvy whom he admired.[8] Personal relationships do count unpredictably in developing attitudes toward Jews. Voltaire pilloried modern and ancient Jews in his *Dictionnaire philosophique* in retribution for unpleasant money experiences with a Jewish person in Berlin. Wagner in Paris was guided by a modest Jewish-German philologist, Samuel Lehrs, to the riches of medieval literature and folklore but lampooned him nevertheless. Nietzsche never made Jewish identity the main criterion for evaluation.

Though praising aspects of Judaism, Renan also gives credit to French life and culture for having assimilated Jews and "weeded out their worst characteristics." Nietzsche would achieve the same by wedding Jews and Prussians, as he noted. The mutual enmity between Rome's pagan world and the Jews is a question Renan defuses by avoiding apportioning blame; he calls it a matter of action and reaction, but puts the onus for "Jewish hatred of the world" upon those who padlocked Jews in ghettos and enchained them. "And yet," as with Nietzsche, there always is a "yet"—a nuanced qualification—Jewish clannishness, condescending aloofness, and exclusiveness as a chosen people prevented them from civilized contact with those peoples in whose presence they felt themselves soiled, according to Renan in his rationale of Jewish "resentment."

Such "even-handed" praise and condemnation of Jews and their hosts or enemies neutralize and perhaps even emasculate history as practiced by Renan and Nietzsche. In effect, can one in all good conscience call Renan-Nietzsche pronouncements even-handed in regard to Jews when those judgments—more subjective than factual—veer freely from the ridiculous blame of Jews to sublime praise of them to the height of meaningless hyperbole? On two issues, Nietzsche drastically differs with Renan: the French historian overpraised the New Testament at the expense of the Old and was a cultural Germanophile beyond Nietzsche's endurance.

Nietzsche's writing plans envisioned four books under the rubric of

Der Wille zur Macht: Versuch einer Umwertung aller Werte (*The Will to Power: An Attempt at the Revaluation of All Values*); instead, much of the material he wrote from about 1883 to the summer of 1888 was included in some form in other books and culminated in the *Antichrist* of 1888, reminiscent in title and some ideas of Renan's earlier *L'Antéchrist*.

THE WILL TO POWER

The "will to power" has been taken to mean a drive for political and social power, but a judicious summary of what it meant to Nietzsche takes us in a different direction; it has positive and negative qualities. He goes beyond Schopenhauer's notion of a will to life and posits a will or drive for quasi-divine self-satisfaction in living and creating, achieving mastery over one's self, a power to change and transcend the self, to love one's capabilities, the glorying in one's being, the lusting for life and gaiety. However, there is a power that he warns against:

> History shows: the strong races decimate one another through war, thirst for power, adventurousness, wastefulness [of strength]; their exis-
> tence is costly . . . they ruin one another. (*WM*, 864)

In some cases the notes were modified, rarely rethought, when readied for publication; but in all instances they present ideas in their first, and often unpolished, existence, and derive their value from that raw state. Again, Nietzsche's thinking about Jews has the patterns we recognize from his earlier publications. The collected notes—many quite fragmentary—that comprise *The Will to Power* contain material that fairly lends itself to a thematic grouping of Nietzsche's thoughts about Jews and relative assessments of Judaism, Christianity, Hinduism (Manu's lawbooks), and Buddhism.[9] His valuations do shift from time to time:

> What a blessing a Jew is among Germans! Of Germans, see their obtuseness, the blond head, the blue eye, the lack of "esprit" in their faces, language and bearing; the lackadaisical stretching of limbs, a habit that comes not from overexertion but from the hideous excitation brought on by alcoholism. . . . (*WM*, 49; January–Fall 1888)

While of little comfort to Jews and less to Germans, Nietzsche's anger points at Germans who, unlike a number of Jews, failed to do him or his work honor. The bilious comparisons do no justice to the Jews, Germans, or Nietzsche.

RELIGIONS

The reversal of social ranks [Die Umkehrung der Rangordnung]. The pious counterfeiters, the priests, are replacing *chandalas* among us; they occupy the position of charlatans, quacks, counterfeiters, sorcerers: we account them as debilitators of the will, as the great slanderers and revengers upon life, and the *rebels* among the underprivileged [those disgruntled with life]. We have turned the servant caste, the Sudras, into our middle class, our "folk" [*Volk*, people] that has decisive political power in its hands.

By way of contrast, the chandalas of ancient times are now on top, they are the *blasphemers*, the *immoralists*, free-wheeling thinkers of every sort, the artists, the Jews, the nomadic minstrels—and basically all *disreputable* elements of society. . . . We determine what on earth is "honor" and "nobility." Today, we *immoralists* constitute the strongest power [as advocates of life]: we reconstitute the world in our image.

We have transferred the *chandala*-concept to the priests, teachers of the beyond, and that entwined *Christian society* of common origin with pessimists, nihilists, the romantic advocates of pity, criminals, heretics, and the whole collective among whom the concept of God, the savior, is imagined. . . . (WM, 116, January–Fall 1888)

Nietzsche identifies with the lowly of yesterday who have become the subversive immoralists of today. Of course, he praises the latter just as he condemned Judaic-Christian "subversions" of earlier times.

Toward a critique of the Book of Manu [Zur Kritik des Manu Gesetzbuches]. The entire book rests upon a holy lie. . . . This priestly species of man wills its own superiority and invents the idea of "improving mankind"—the source of the holy lie is the will to power. . . .

. . . We have before us the classical form in the model of the specifically Aryan form . . . a lie copied almost everywhere: the Aryan influence has corrupted the entire world. . . . (WP, 142, January to mid–1888)

Manu is a semi-historical lawgiver who in 1200 B.C.E. was said to have received a code of ethics from the supreme being of the Hindu pantheon, Brahma; all the other gods are only his manifestations. His priests are of the highest hereditary Brahman caste, an exclusive cult. For some 2,500 years it thrived at the expense of an oppressed and low-caste Sudra class and maintained a privileged, stable, autocratic society and culture. Although strict prohibitions against caste intercourse, socially and eugenically, preserved "pure family strains," Nietzsche here sees it as an Aryan will to power and as a universal, corruptive influence. The concept of "pure blood," he wrote in *Genealogy of Morals*, is "the opposite of a harmless concept" (VII, 5). He did not approve of the taming or emasculation of the Sudras or give any ideological support to notions of racial superiority. If anything, he placed "Aryan humanity" on a lower scale of esteem than the Semitic. Nietzsche expands his basic view:

> Nowadays one talks much about the *Semitic* spirit of the *New Testament*: but this is only another name for the priestly—and in the racially purest lawbook ["founded upon a holy lie," *WM*, 142; in Manu the Hindu progenitor of the human race and human wisdom] this kind of "Semitism," i.e., the *priest mentality*, is worse than anywhere else.
>
> The development of a Jewish rule of priests is *not* original: they learned this pattern in Babylonian [exile]—it is Aryan: When this again gained dominance later in Europe through Germanic blood, it was compatible with the spirit of the reigning race. . . . The Germanic Middle Ages aimed at the restoration of an Aryan caste-hierarchy.
>
> Mohammedanism subsequently learned from Christianity mainly how to use the "beyond" as an instrument of punishment.
>
> The system of an unchanging communal order headed by priests, the oldest and great product of Asian culture in the realm of state organization, naturally prompted extensive reflection and imitation—certainly, Plato, but above all the Egyptians. (*WM*, 143; March–June 1888)

Nietzsche could not ignore the cohesive order that priests imposed upon societies, and at times admired their self-possessive powers and authority. But whenever priesthood or priests—not to be confused with pastors, shepherds—came to mind, he condemned them explosively. Priests of any religion were anathema to him, as anathema as purveyors of false values, prurient asceticism, intrusive mediators between man and God, and manipulators of the so-called God's will. Nietzsche was self-conscious about the hereditary pastor-blood in his veins but neither priest nor pastor would have a place in the Utopian vision he vaguely painted for mankind's future.[10]

> What a *yea-saying* Aryan religion, the offspring of a *ruling class* looks like: see the law-books of Manu. (The deification of the feelings of power in Brahma: it is interesting that it originated with the warrior caste and then was taken over by priests.)
>
> What a *yea-saying* Semitic religion, the offspring of a *ruling class* looks like: see the law-book [Koran] of Mohammed which resembles the earlier parts of the Old Testament. (Mohammedanism as a religion for men despises the sentimentality and deviousness of Christianity that to them is a woman's religion.)
>
> What a *nay-saying* Semitic religion, the offspring of an oppressed class looks like: see the New Testament (regarded from Indo-Aryan viewpoints as a *chandala* [a low-caste] religion).
>
> What a *nay-saying* Aryan religion that has matured under *ruling auspices* looks like: see Buddhism.
>
> It is entirely proper that we do not have a religion of oppressed Aryan races because that would be a contradiction in terms: a superior race [*Herrenrasse*, dominant, master race] either is on top or it perishes. (*WM*, 145; mid-1888)

Nietzsche's coinage of the word *Herrenrasse*—"master race"—has been as vexing as the insidious use to which it has been put and the horrors perpetrated in its exploitation. Nietzsche would have been appalled that the lowest species of humans, the Nazis as political types, had arrogated to themselves a superiority relative to their European neighbors with the intent of exterminating or enslaving them. Readers of Nietzsche need to be reminded that although he took the ancient Greeks as cultural models, he did not subscribe to certain of their self-conceptions that prompted them as "a breed of masters" to brand as "barbarian" non-Greek foreigners fit to be slaves,"[11] nor did Nietzsche entertain anything except revulsion for doctrines that arose from the Förster-Wagner-Dühring "sump." He appears to suggest that the retention of power through pretensions to superiority is precarious: historically, powerful nations have decimated each other, he noted. What is desirable is a *yea-saying* attitude toward all life and a leadership that combines power with benevolence.

As Nietzsche had said aphoristically in *Beyond Good and Evil*, "Fear is the mother of morality" (201); he had a horror of all punitive or prescriptive religious or secular "morality":

> In itself, religion has nothing to do with morality: but both offsprings of the Jewish religion [Christianity and Mohammedanism] are essentially moral religions of kinds that prescribe how one ought to live, and they exact obedience through reward and punishment. (*WM*, 146; 1885–86)

Nietzsche's comparisons of Jewish, Christian, and Buddhistic thought and faith hold not only intrinsic interest but also reemphasize a key idea: he places blame mainly on certain classes within ancient Judaism for the objectionable elements he felt to have been inherited by the Jewish Paul and passed along into the mainstream of Christianity.

> In Buddhism, the following idea prevails, "All passions and everything that creates emotions and stirs the blood to action are *warning* signals of evil." Action makes no sense because it shackles one to existence: but all existence has no meaning. Buddhists see in evil the spurring on to something illogical: the affirmation of means whose purpose one rejects. They search for other ways to nullity, and for that reason they shun all action-prompting impulses of the emotions; so that they enjoin one, for instance, in no way to seek revenge! in no way to be hostile to anyone!—the hedonism of the weary became the highest measure of value here. Nothing is farther from the thinking of Buddhists than the Jewish fanaticism of a St. Paul: Nothing is more contrary to their instinct than the tension, flame, and restlessness of the religious person, and above all, this sensuality which Christianity hallows with the name of love. Moreover, it is the educated and even those of the super-religious strata who find repose in Buddhism: a race that became weary and besotted after centuries of long philosophical quarrels but did not sink *beneath all culture* like those classes out of which Christianity arose. . . . In the ideals of Buddhism, essentially, there is an emancipation from good and evil: they have dreamed up a super-subtle aloofness from morality that is absolutely compatible with the essence of perfection so

that *occasionally* even good actions become necessary if only as a means of being rid of *all* activity. (WM, 155; Spring–Fall 1887)

Nietzsche felt compatibility with what he claims inspired Christianity at its beginnings and with the words of the "primitive Jesus" free from doctrinaire theology and the whole apparatus that laid guilt upon humans:

> Jesus goes directly to the point with the idea that "the Kingdom of Heaven" is in the heart, and he does *not* find the path to it in the observances of the Jewish church—, he even deems the reality of Jewry (its compulsion [*Nötingung*] to preserve itself) to be of no consequence; he is purely *inward*.—
>
> Similarly, he pays no attention to the collectively coarse formulas of discourse with God: in other words, he strains against all of the repentance and atonement teachings; he demonstrates how one must live in order to feel "deified" and [advises] that one does not overcome one's sins with teeth-grinding and contrition; his chief verdict is that "*sin is of no account.*"
>
> Sin, repentance, forgiveness—none of it belongs to Christianity . . . is it Jewish interference [*eingemischtes Judentum*] or is it pagan interference? [Those non-Jews ready to be converted to Christianity and those whose ideas were amalgamated.] (WM, 160; November 1887–March 1888)

Disturbing here is the echo of Wagner's canards of Jewish "interferences," as Nietzsche adopts an accusatory tone in regard to detrimental Jewish involvement in nascent Christianity.

> Paul: He seeks power *against* the ruling Jew, his effort is too weak . . . revaluation [*Umwertung*] of the concept "Jew": "race" is put aside—but that means a negation of the entire *foundation*. The "martyr," the "fanatic," the value of all *strong* beliefs. . . .
>
> Christianity is the form of decay [*Verfalls-Form*] of the old world in its deepest impotence so that the most sick and unhealthy elements and needs become the surface layer.
>
> *Consequently, other* instincts had to come to the foreground in order to create an integral defensive power; in brief, here is a necessary condition of calamity that resembles the one from which Jews derived their *instinct for self-preservation.* . . .

> Invaluable in that regard were the persecutions of Christians—
> [creating] communal unity in the face of danger, mass conversions [to
> Christianity are necessary] as a sole means to put an end to persecution
> of individuals. (WM, 173; Spring–Fall 1887; revised a year later)

Here and in subsequent notes, Nietzsche makes a case for the emergence
of aggressive instincts in response to persecution: "we owe the triumph of
Christianity to its persecutors" (WM, 174). What he finds decadent in
Christianity however is a "hypochondriacal torturing and vivisection of
the soul."

Nietzsche's recurring animus toward Paul deserves an entire book,
but his psychological premise turns on the idea that Paul's vision of punished sinners (similar to those pictures derived from him later by Dante
and Calvin) is the feeling of "voluptuous power" like that enjoyed by a
"God of love" who created suffering and sinning man for his own divine
enjoyment, a kind of ascetic delirium (WM, 113). Nietzsche comes close
to saying that Paul's view of God and Paul's identification with God are
basically rooted in sadism. There is no one to whom Nietzsche gives
greater credit as an improviser of theological mystiques than Paul.

> Believers feel that they are infinitely indebted to Christianity and thus
> they concluded that its founder was a person of the first rank . . . this
> conclusion is false but it is typical of believers. . . . The figure of Chris-
> tianity's founder grew in proportion to the rise of the church, but even
> this spectacle of veneration permitted the conclusion that somehow
> this founder represents something uncertain and doubtful; at the begin-
> ning—one recalls with what free-invention Paul treated the person of
> Jesus and almost juggles [eskamotiert] with the problem of Jesus—as
> someone who had died, and who after his death was seen again,
> someone who was delivered up to death by the Jews . . . a mere motif
> for which Paul provided the music. . . . (WM, 177; January–Fall 1888)

> The Christian-Jewish life: Here ressentiment did not prevail. Only the
> onset of the great persecutions could have elicited the passions (of
> ressentiment) as well as the ardor of love as well as hate. . . . (WM, 174;
> Spring–Fall 1888; revised a year later)

Nietzsche characterizes Christianity as "a form of emancipated
Judaism," but urges that one reject the idea that Christianity in antiquity

was an expression of a new national youthfulness and racial vigor. Instead, one must understand its psychological dynamics: the emergence of Christianity reads like a Russian novel (by the Dostoevsky Nietzsche admired)—Christianity grew and took root in the soil of the lowliest Jewish people, of a "mishmash population without a sense of duties, grown weary, disoriented, neurotic, morally hypersensitive, aimless, and ready to rally around a master-seducer; shorn of instincts the herd became docile and decadent. On the other hand, by comparison,

> . . . the power and a feeling of certainty about the future [*Zukunfts-gewissheit*] of the Jewish instinct, the enormity of its tenacious will to existence and power [*seines zähen Willens zu Dasein und Macht*] resides in its ruling class; however, *those* social strata raised up by primitive Christianity are defined by nothing more distinct than their instinct-*exhaustion* [being tired of life and possessing smug self-satisfaction]. (*WM*, 180; November 1887–March 1888)

The foundation upon which Christianity was able to build was the reality of the small *Jewish family* of the Diaspora [Jewish exile and dispersal], with its warmth and tenderness and readiness to assist its members—things unheard of and perhaps incomprehensible to the entire Roman Empire; with its pride, concealed under the cloak of "the chosen people"; they pretended not to envy inwardly the socially superior and powerful by outward signs of humility. Paul *recognized in all this* blissful condition a *power* transferable to pagans, as seductive, as something infectious—this awareness constitutes Paul's genius. He understood how to exploit the latent energy and cautious happiness for purposes of a "Jewish church of free confession" and he knew how to use all of Jewish experience and mastery in *community self-preservation* while under foreign domination. Jewish propaganda as well, he sensed to be of advantage. He found that precisely the absolutely unpolitical and the shunted-aside *little people* could assert themselves and could prevail. . . .

From the small Jewish community comes the principle *of love*: a *most passionate soul* glows under the ashes of humility and poverty, a passion that is not Greek or Hindu and certainly not Germanic. The hymn in honor of love authored by Paul [I Cor. 13: "Make love your spiritual aim . . ."] is not a Christian but a Jewish stoking of an eternal flame that is Semitic. If Christianity has done anything significant from a psychological perspective, it is the *heightening of the soul's temperature* in the bodies of the more cool and noble races at the time; it was a discovery that even the very impoverished of lives could become rich and invaluable through . . . heightened temperature. . . .

It is self-evident that such a transference could *not* take place in respect to the ruling classes: Jews and Christians possessed the most self-defeating bad manners—a power-display of the spiritual passion of the soul coupled with bad manners has a repellent effect and almost arouses disgust (—I *see* these bad manners when I read the New Testament). One would have to empathize by stooping to lowliness and would need to be lowly in order to relate to the low class of people and to understand what is attractive to them. One's attitude toward the New Testament is a test of one's classical taste, if one has it in one's bones [like Tacitus, see his tirades—says Nietzsche—against superstitions] and whoever is not revolted by the New Testament nor feels defiled by its abominable superstitions is not being honest and does not know what "classical" means. One must feel about the cross as Goethe did. (See his *Venetian Epigrams*, for instance No. 67: "Four things, though, revolt me like poison: tobacco smoke, garlic [invariably associated with Jews], vermin, and the cross.") (WM, 175; March 1887–June 1888)

The persistence and continuity of Judaic features in Christianity are things Nietzsche harps on and characterizes as going against nature, a "holy unnaturalness." Beneath his assertions lies his affinity for Greek "naturalness" and nature worship, physical exhibitionism that he continually poses against Judeo-Christian "artificial reality":

The symbolism of Christianity is based upon *Jewish* symbolism that has already dissolved [*aufgelöst*; resolved] *all reality* (history, nature) into a holy unnaturalness and unreality [*Unnatürlichkeit und Unrealität*, artificial reality] . . . that no longer wished to take account of real history and the natural course of things. (WM, 183; November 1887–March 1888)

The "Christian ideal" is put on stage with Jewish cleverness [*jüdish klug*; astuteness, subtlety]. The basic psychological drive is its "nature": the revolt against the ruling spiritual powers; the attempt to make those virtues that further the *happiness of the lowly*, a chivalrous ideal [or standard] for all values, to call it *God*; the survival instinct of the most impoverished classes. . . . (WM, 185; Spring–Fall 1887)

There are problems with Nietzsche's speculations, for speculations they are in the absence of scholarly presentation of events, textual evidence, and other supporting documentation. It was the priesthood (every mention of which puts Nietzsche into a tantrum) that "knew how to compel obedience by presenting precepts as divine commands . . . under the name of God" (*WM*, 182). Was it this against which "a popular uprising among a priestly people—a pietistic movement from below (sinners, publicans, women, the sick)—was directed and made Jesus the sign of their own identification with discontent? Just as the Jewish priest falsified Israel's history by theological transformations," says Nietzsche, so did the followers of Jesus falsify their leader in making him the "son of God" and creating a new faith that could "only have arisen on the soil of Judaism . . . that linked the idea of guilt to misfortune and sin against God." Christianity, Nietzsche repeated, escalated this into a major precept.

If indeed the priests introduced commands that preserved Jewish identity throughout millennia, how can they be condemned without, at the same time, condemning Jewish survival? By calling early Christianity a low-caste pietistic movement, Nietzsche was reflecting less nineteenth-century scholarship and knowledge of the ancient Jewish world and the emergence of Christianity than his own detraction and rejection of the pietistic atmosphere of his own milieu and upbringing.

Nietzsche's comparisons between the treatment of Jews in the Hellenic world and in nineteenth-century Europe has a greater validity than is at first evident. It could have been expanded into panoramic, illustrative historical and culturally piquant essays. As it is, they do make the point that the Jews in Nietzsche's contemporary world were—ironically—as maltreated as were the early Christians. Modern Christians with anti-Jewish attitudes adopted the role of their own historical tormentors.

> The *deep contempt* with which the Christian was treated in aristocratic areas of the world of antiquity is replicated by today's instinctive aversion to the Jews: it is the hate which independent and self-confident classes feel toward those classes *who eke out their existence* [*Stände . . . welche sich durchdrücken*, who push through despite resistance] and combine shy and awkward gestures with a ridiculous sense of self-worth.
>
> The New Testament is the gospel of a completely *ignoble* species

with pretensions to higher values—yes, in regard to all values—that, indeed, is something that provokes indignation—even today. (WM, 186; Spring–Fall 1887)

Then, too, *Christians* did exactly what the Jews had done. They put into the mouth of their master what they thought to be something necessary for their own existence [*Existenzbedingung*], innovatively encrusting Jesus' life with those teachings. They credited him, as well, with all the wisdom of the proverbs—in brief, they represented their everyday life and activity as forms of *obedience* and in that fashion sanctified them for purposes of propaganda [i.e., miracles, resurrection etc. . . .] (WM, 190; Spring–Fall 1887)

Christianity accommodated itself to already existing and endemic anti-paganism and to those cults that Epicurus had fought against . . . accommodating itself to *the religion of the lower classes*, the *women*, the *slaves*, the *non-noble* segments [and creating . . .] a churchly hierarchy with priests, a theology, cultism, sacrament; in brief, everything that Jesus of Nazareth had *fought* against [pervasive beliefs in miracles, superstition]; . . . the distinguishing feature of Judaism and earliest Christianity consisted of repugnance toward miracles and adherence to a relative *rationality*. (WM, 196; November 1887–March 1888)

In essence, Nietzsche condemns both the priests of early Judaism and their "successors" in Christianity and praises those distinctive elements in ancient Judaism and Jesus "and earliest Christianity" which rejected superstitions, miracles, and the like. Yet, it is a rebellion against "the noble minority"—a conflict Nietzsche sees unfavorably reduplicated some eighteen hundred years later in the French Revolution, whose ignoble rabble he despises.

The Jews attempted to accomplish their goal pertinaciously despite having lost two of their castes [classes]—that of the warrior and the agricultural.

In that sense they are the "clipped" people [*die Verschnittenen*], for what remains are their priests [perhaps Nietzsche means "rabbis" since there were no priests in Judaism after the destruction of the Temple] and the chandala [the low caste]. As might be expected, a disturbance breaks out between them and leads to a revolt by the chandala: the origin of *Christianity*.

Because the Jews only knew the warrior as their master they brought into their religion an enmity toward superiors, the noble, and the proud, against the *reigning* order—: they are pessimists impelled by a sense of indignation—.

And with that they created an important new approach: the priest at the head of the chandala—poised against the *noble* orders. . . .

From this movement, Christianity drew the ultimate conclusion: even within the Jewish priesthood it still sensed a caste of the superior and the noble—and it eliminated the priest—

The Christian is the chandala who rejects the priest . . . he chooses to redeem himself [without intermediaries].

For these reasons the *French Revolution* was the daughter and continuator of Christianity . . . it retained the instinct against [the higher] caste, superiors, and against ultimate privileges—(WM, 184; March–June 1888)

In rough outline here are Nietzsche's ideas on the origin of Christianity out of the turmoil of Jewish religious and political life. But what also surfaces is wicked wordplay that Nietzsche could not resist—wordplay that harbors anti-Semitic buffoonery. Having lost their priestly and agricultural class, says Nietzsche, Jews in a sense were "mis-clipped" people. His jocular word for Jews as "die Verschnittenen"[12] admits of this translation, although he appears to be distancing himself from it by putting it in quotes and not overtly using the word "Beschnittene" for circumcised Jews. From graphic wall sculptures dating as far back as 2300 B.C.E. in dynastic Egypt we find ritual circumcision operations on males across all social lines—pharaohs, priests, shepherds—just before adolescence, whereas in Jewish tradition it also was a symbolic blood covenant with God, mandated and ritualized on the eighth day after birth. Circumcision was not an uncommon pagan rite from Mesopotamia to Polynesia. It was regarded differently, however, by the Greeks and Romans who ridiculed the circumcised organ as an unnatural disfiguration; circumcision was a cause for denigrating Jews and their religious practices. Hellenic Jews were obviously uncomfortable in a Greek gymnasium or Roman bath where they could be identified ethnically. Often such meeting places served the same exclusive or exclusionary functions as modern country clubs in conducting business—anti-Semitism in that respect is ageless. Excellence in athletics, practiced in the nude, was a step up the social ladder. Many Hel-

lenic Jews took protective commercial and social measures in a hostile
environment by resorting to painful surgical epiplasms or infibulations to
cosmetize circumcision, or to neglect the practice altogether and fade into
the mainstream culture. In all, it was as difficult to be a practicing Jew in
ancient as in modern environments.

By tenaciously clinging to their traditions, it was impossible for Jews
not to offend their neighbors, and the more they detested paganism and
were abused for it, the more they exhorted their fellow Jews to stand fast.
However, despite mutual antagonisms, on the days of the Bacchanalia,
Greek Jews had to join the ivy-crowned throngs who wildly celebrated
with song and drink the God Dionysus, Nietzsche's adopted fantasy-pro-
totype. The first of the Hebrew Books of the Maccabees relates that
Jewish women who had their babies circumcised were at times singled
out and put to death with their offspring—so much for Nietzsche's and
other myth-romancers' "noble" pagans. The Jewish resisters memorial-
ized in the Books of the Maccabees were the models for Christian mar-
tyrology and the saints, though minimized by Gibbon and disparaged by
Nietzsche. The abuse of imperial power, territorial overexpansion, licen-
tious lifestyles, administrative corruption, and oppression led to the
moral and political decadence contributing to Rome's decline as much
as, or more than, Nietzsche's Judeo-Christian *ressentiment* theory.

Notwithstanding the tracing of Christian fanaticism to Judaic origins
by Gibbon and previous historians as well as followers like Nietzsche, one
should not ignore the fact that among the pagan Roman populace the
Judaic idea of a merciful God, the examples of communal living that
placed premiums on charity, ethics, neighborly codes of living, and the
attractiveness of a sabbath day of rest, study, and contemplation did impress many in the pagan world and made them receptive to Paul's teachings. These were augmented by romanticized mystiques and promises of
an afterworld immortality. Mainly, Paul eliminated difficult Jewish ritual
demands; the apostle even assured Jewish converts that they need "not
seek to remove the marks of circumcision. . . . For neither circumcision
nor uncircumcision counts for anything, but keeping the commandments
of God" does (1 Cor. 7:18, 19). Paul subverted Old Testament injunctions whenever his new gospel would smooth the way for proselytes. But
Jews who retained tradition and belief in being a "chosen people," iden-
tifiable by the mark of the covenant, were willing to the point of perse-

cution to accept religious demands that were to contribute to their isolated status, survival, and tribulations. While consistently admiring the
survival aspects, Nietzsche remained irritated by the "chosen people"
designation, although both—chosenness and survival—were inextri-
cably entwined:

> [Apostles and saints would appear impudent to the Greeks of Athens]
> . . . the *Jewish instinct of a "chosen" people*: without further ado, they lay
> claim to *all* virtues and account the rest of the world to be their oppo-
> sites; this is a profound sign of *vulgarity of soul* [*Gemeinheit der Seele*]. . . .
> (WM, 197; Spring–Fall 1887)

Nietzsche sees the self-appointment to chosenness as a claim to superiority, an entitlement he reserves for the ancient Greeks and not for
Judeo-Christians.

> The founder of Christianity had to atone for the fact that he addressed
> the lowest strata of the Jewish community and intelligence. Their view
> of him coincided with their own limitations. . . . It was a real disgrace
> to see fabricated a story of salvation, a personal god, a personal
> redeemer, a personal immortality, and to have retained all the mean-
> ness [*Mesquinerie*] of the "person" and the "history" from out of a doc-
> trine that denies all that is personal and historical.
> 　　The legend of salvation takes the place of the symbolic now-and-
> always, the here and the everywhere, while miracles take the place of
> the psychological symbol. (WM, 198; November 1887–March 1888)

Nothing is less innocent than the New Testament. One well knows out
of what soil it grew. These people were possessed of an indomitable will
that worked for them, though they lost all grip on life; and it continued
to exist longer than it would seem possible. Against all odds, they knew
how to survive by means of unnatural and purely imaginary hypotheses
(such as the chosen people, the community of saints, the people of the
promised land, and the "church"): these people handcrafted the *pia
fraus* [holy lie] with such perfection and to such a degree of "good conscience" that one cannot be careful enough when they preach morality.
When Jews themselves appear wrapped in innocence, then danger has
become great indeed: one must always keep a small fund of reasoning,
mistrust, and malice at hand when one reads the New Testament.

People of the lowest origin, in part—a mob, those rejected not only by good society but also by respectable society; they grew up without an *inkling* of culture, without discipline, without knowledge or even a hint of it or the perception that conscience can exist in spiritual matters—in brief, Jews: they are instinctively crafty and able to create an advantage, with every means of superstitious hypotheses and to fashion from these (and even from ignorance) a form of *seduction*. (WM, 199; Spring–Fall 1887)

Here is Nietzsche's seduction theory in brief: a seduction of the lower masses by the instinctively crafty Jews. Though certainly not intended as anti-Semitic labeling, it is only a hair-breadth short of it.

In Section 200 of *The Will to Power* Nietzsche notes that lower-class morality as the measure for all morality was propagated by Christianity in the form of the most seductive, fateful lie in all of history, along with its delusions of grandeur, distortion, and self-serving appropriation of the concepts of God, Judgment Day, truth, love, wisdom, and the Holy Ghost; he concluded that

all such fatalities were made possible by the fact that a similar megalo-mania *already existed in the world*, namely, the Jewish form. (Once the schism between the Jews and the Christians had widened into an abyss, the Christian Jews *had to* adopt as a last resort a measure that had been devised by the Jewish instinct for survival—), abetting all this as well was the Greek moral philosophy that prepared the way for a moral fanaticism even among Greeks and Romans and made it palatable. . . . Plato, the great viaduct of corruption, who first refused to see nature within morality and who had already debased the Greek gods with his conception of "good," was tainted with Jewish bigotry. (WM, 202; Spring–Fall 1887 and revised 1888)

Nietzsche resented Plato's departure from ancient Greek codes and beliefs in religious and ethical matters, saddling him with "Jewish big-otry" and moral fanaticism, a generalization Nietzsche did not carefully work out. In regard to Socrates and Plato, he may have been persuaded by writers who claimed Jewish influence on these philosophers. The historian Solomon Grayzel notes:

The Jews began to write books and pamphlets in which they tried to prove the superiority of Judaism and the truth of God's promise to prefer the Jewish people above any others. So anxious were they for the world to believe that no good could come from paganism and that everything must have a Jewish origin, that they made an effort to prove that the Greek philosophers and the wisdom of the biblical books were in perfect agreement. Some of them even went further, and asserted that Socrates, Plato, and Aristotle had been influenced by the writings of Moses.[13]

In succeeding ruminative notes, Nietzsche raises other questions and claims: that the millions of Jews among the population of the Roman Empire led an "absolutely unpolitical life" as parasites; that Judeo-Christian non-utilitarian demands go against "nature"; and that a "natural" (instinctive) utilitarian, rational morality is superior to a prescriptive theological God-centered morality when in psychological conflict. He seems to have put aside for the moment the idea of morality as relativistic prejudgment, the "immorality of morality" itself, the "unimportance" of morality, the phenomenon of morality as a "herd instinct" in the individual. The implication that one type of morality is superior to another is not convincingly presented in the following assertions about Buddhistic, Jewish, Christian ethics and religion. One senses something that is struggling to reach the surface in Nietzsche's notes: his feeling that it is undesirable to extirpate aggressive instincts and substitute false and sentimental ideals instead of purposively harnessing "instinctive morals":

[*Utility* dictates the retention or discarding of warring or peaceable dispositions. . . .] This was the case, for instance, when Buddha appeared among a very peaceable and spiritually (intellectually) exhausted society. . . . This was also the case with the earliest Christian (as well as the Jewish community) whose principal promise consisted of an absolutely *unpolitical* Jewish community. Christianity could grow only upon the soil of Judaism, that is, only among a people that already had renounced the political life and lived parasitically within the Roman sphere of things. Christianity took one step *farther:* one needed to "castrate" oneself even more drastically: circumstances favored this.— *Human nature is simply ignored* by a morality that says, "Love your enemies": whereas nature enjoins us to "love your neighbor and to hate your enemies"—but even that injunction has become meaningless in law and nature because this law (and instinct) requires that the *love a person feels for his neighbor* must first be based upon *a sort of love for God*. God is inserted everywhere while the idea of *utility* is discarded; everywhere, the natural origin of morality is denied while the veneration of nature, which lies precisely in acknowledging a natural morality is *destroyed* roots and all. . . .

From where does the seductive charm of this emasculated ideal come? Why are we not disgusted [*degoutiert*] just as we are disgusted at the thought of a eunuch? . . . The answer is obvious: the voice of the eunuch does *not* revolt us, despite the gruesome mutilation of which it is the result, because, as a matter of fact, the voice has grown sweeter . . . precisely for virtuous reasons the "male organs were amputated, introducing feminine tones [capable of seducing masculine Corsican and Arab pagans]. . . . The *idealist*, or castrato, subsides into the ideal eunuch who leads a sort of insular happiness as in Tahiti or that of the little Jews in the Roman provinces. Hostility, however, on a grand scale is seen by the example of Paul relative to Judaism and Luther's attitude toward the priestly ascetic ideal. . . . (*WM*, 204; Spring 1887, revised a year later)

Typical of Nietzsche's ambivalence is his deploring the herd *ressentiment* of the "slaves" who inflate their self-defined virtues, while he also gives grudging admiration to the inflation that engenders a *non plus ultra* sense of power [*Machtgefühl*] in those who love danger, adventure, and opposition. Christianity, though a "democratic" herd religion, is both politically submissive in teaching obedience and yet subversive in successfully coercing "the master races" to Christianity. Nietzsche sees here "a form of orgy of the will," a heroic quixotism, as displayed by Saint Teresa (*WM*, 216). He laments certain driving forces that overpowered early Christianity:

The following have gained mastery over [early] *Christianity*: Judaism (Paul); Platonism (Augustine); the mystery cults (the teaching of salvation, the sign of the "cross"); asceticism (enmity against "nature," "reason," the "senses"—the Orient). (*WM*, 214; November 1887–March 1888)

The immoral uses of "morality" and "sin," the rationalized employment of "justice" disturb Nietzsche; "morality" misapplied can poison life:

Morality as a means of seduction. "Nature is good because a wise and good God has created it." If that is so, who then is responsible for the "corruption of mankind"? Rousseau's logic places the onus on mankind's tyrants and seducers—"the ruling classes—they must be destroyed." Compare this to Pascal's logic that places blame on original sin. [Luther's desire for revenge turns against the rulers under the guise of moral-religious duty . . . Israel's sinfulness is the power-seeking ploy of the priests.]

Compare then the related logic of Paul who invokes God's cause. . . . In the case of Christ, the rejoicings of the people appear as the cause of the crucifixion. It was an anti-priestly movement from the beginning. Even with anti-Semites, the trick is the same: to accuse one's opponents with condemnatory judgments and so arrogate retributive justice to oneself. (WM, 347; Spring–Fall 1887)

Nietzsche's concept of power is always related to the uses to which it is put. One must avoid concluding that Nietzsche celebrates mindless power. On the contrary, he warns that *per se*, "Power makes stupid." Power is double-edged.

The concept of power, be it a man's or a god's, always includes the ability both to help and to harm. That is the case with the Arabs, as well as with the Hebrews. In fact, with all strong races. . . . (WM, 352; November 1887–March 1888)

The temptation to reduce opponents to caricature—as did the Romans vis-à-vis the Jews—is strong, and Nietzsche, in regard to Plato for instance, is aware of his own tendency:

Every society has the tendency to reduce its opponents to caricatures— at least in its visualizations—to degrade them and to starve them [into submission]. One such caricature, for instance, is our "criminal." In the midst of the Roman aristocratic rank of values, the Jew was reduced to caricature. Among artists, the bourgeois becomes the "Biedermann" [Philistine]; among the pious, it is the atheist who becomes a caricature,

and among the aristocrats, it's the ordinary person. Among the immoralists, it is the moralist. Plato, for instance, becomes a caricature in
my hands. (WM, 374; Spring–Fall 1887, revised a year later)

GREEK PHILOSOPHERS

The Sophists, as philosophers and teachers, followed in the footsteps of
the pre-Socratics in valuing the ambiguity of language and the paradox
of entertaining opposite, dual, or conflicting meanings. Although
sophistry has come to mean the ability to argue either side of an issue
with equal conviction, it is the enjoyment of discord, logical persuasion,
and the questioning of the conventionally accepted that Nietzsche pursued. He found the contentious—if not confrontational—eristic method
of inquiry to be his unique angle of subversive vision. Nietzsche was to
characterize logic and dialectics as the language of Jewish survival; and,
in that interpretive sense mainly, Socrates and Plato were "Jews":

> . . . The Sophists were Greeks: When Socrates and Plato took up the
> causes of virtue and justice, they were *Jews* if nothing else—. [George]
> *Grote's* tactical defense of the Sophists [in *The History of Greece*, 1856]
> is false: he wants to elevate them to the level of honorable men and
> moral standard-bearers—but to speak in their favor, they did not in-
> dulge in any swindle with big words and [false] virtues—. (WM, 942;
> March–June 1888)

> *Socrates.* . . . Before Socrates' time, all cultured society shunned dialec-
> tical mannerisms . . . also one mistrusted such methods of proof . . . one
> commanded and that was sufficient [dialectics is mob dominance over
> aristocratic ways]; rhetoricians know that dialectics arouses suspicion
> and does little to persuade. Nothing is easier to erase than the effects of
> dialectics. Dialectics can only be the last measure of despair to extort
> one's rights, otherwise there would be no need for dialectics. Therefore,
> Jews are dialecticians, Reynard the Fox was one, as was Socrates. One
> can tyrannize with dialectics [and assume superior airs and make the
> opponent look ridiculous]. The irony of a dialectician is a form of mob
> revenge; the oppressed unload their ferocity through the knifeblade of
> the syllogism. Dialectics . . . as a tool of the will to power. (WM, 431;
> variously dated between 1885 and 1888)

Nietzsche is a trifle off the mark here because Anaximander and particularly Heraclitus—from whom Nietzsche learned the exploitation of ambiguities and to see affinities and similarities between antipodals— were in many respects models for the later Sophists.

Nietzsche courted and counted among his friends and acquaintances many titled people, so that the following comments do carry a tinge of envy. It was a family tradition, one remembers, for the Nietzsches to lay ancestral claim to titled Polish nobility.

> The only nobility is that of birth and blood (I am not referring here to the little [lordly] prefix "von" and the *Almanach de Gotha*[14] (call it Almanac of Asses). Whenever there is talk of "aristocrats of the spirit," there is most of the time no lack of reasons for keeping something secret; "von" is known to be a favorite word [*Leibwort*; password also in the sense of social entrée] among ambitious Jews. Intellect alone does not ennoble; instead, something always is needed to ennoble the mind—what is needed is blood. (*WM*, 942; 1885)

Nietzsche is saying here that "aristocracy of the spirit"—unlike titles— cannot be bought. If, offensively, he singles out Jews who have "bought" the title, he does not spare all the other "von" designates in the *Almanach de Gotha*; some Jews to whom he pays tribute do have the qualities he admires without possessing the "von." An academic Nazi propagandist, Heinrich Härtle, bowdlerized this passage (*WM*, 942) to make the claim that Nietzsche's racial thinking matches that of the National Socialists' demand for pure-blooded Aryanism and the "modern" Nazi way of thinking about race and shares its political conclusions. Härtle, like his cohort Alfred Bäumler, pointed to Nietzsche's alleged view of racial inheritance and to Jews as the antipodes of racial nobility and to "blood" and "birth." For National Socialists, says Härtle, "the question of race is of prime essence."[15] To Nietzsche's statement that "One knows who became the heirs of Jewish revaluation," Härtle adds, "Christianity, Democracy, Marxism,"[16] although Nietzsche never mentions Marxism. Härtle points to what seems to be Nietzsche's agreement with Tacitus that Jews "were born for slavery"—although this is solely Tacitus' statement. And he praises Nietzsche: "Never has anyone attacked Jews more sharply than Nietzsche," but he minimizes Nietzsche's hyperbolic praise of Jews. One does not have to look far to understand why it is possible with a modicum of elision and snipping to present a Nietzsche who is the mirror image of the anti-Semite. Standing by itself, this passage is open to serious objections for its unfortunate lack of clarity. It needs to be considered in context with Nietzsche's other discussions of eugenics and breeding, subjects that at any rate do not display Nietzsche to the best advantage. What should be of consequence, though, is the fact that Nietzsche consistently abhorred anti-Semites.

Many ideas run together in the long section that follows, and what holds interest are Nietzsche's speculations about the psychology of the "weak" and the power derived from the weakness of Jews and women;[17] the relationships of fool, saint, and genius; the anti-Semite and the Jew; and the antagonism between men and women. Again, he overpraises Jews for being a "conserving power" and their essential conservatism in an insecure Europe and attributes to them a power of *esprit* and intellect, the will to the preservation of life. But, at the same time, he raises the warning specter of their latent power, even while excusing their participation in the "liberal" and "socialist" causes he himself despises. Ironically both socialists and liberals in Germany and Austria abandoned Jews when they most needed their political support. Dühring's Christian Socialists, from the start, took Jews to be their enemy.

"The Strong and the Weak" ["Die Starken und die Schwachen"]. *Why the weak triumph.* In sum, the sick and the weak have more *sympathy* [*Mitgefühl*] and are more humane . . . have more *intellect* [*Geist*], are more variegated, changeable, entertaining—more malicious; the sick, exclusively, have invented *malice* (a morbid precocity may be found among the rickety, scrofulous, and tubercular). *Esprit* belongs to the older races: Jews, Frenchmen, Chinese. (The anti-Semites have never forgiven the Jews for possessing "intellect"—and money. Anti-Semite is another name for the "socially lowest people" [*Schlechtweggekommene*, the misfits, the bungled and botched; the so-called underprivileged].)

The sick and the weak in themselves have greater *fascination* and are more *interesting* than the healthy; the two most interesting kinds of people are the fool and the saint, both are closely allied to "genius." The great "adventurers and criminals," and above all, the most healthy, have been sick at certain times of their lives . . . almost every person is decadent for half a lifetime. (WM, 864; March–June 1888)

WOMAN

Finally: woman! constituting half of mankind, is fickle, insecure; she needs a religion of weakness that glorifies being *weak*, loving and humble as divine attributes—she *rules* when she succeeds in dominating the strong. Woman has always conspired with such decadent types as the priests, against the "mighty" and the "strong," against men. Woman reserves her children for the cult of piety, pity, love: the *mother* symbolizes altruism *convincingly.* (WM, 864; March–June 1888)

. . . In *The Flying Dutchman* Wagner preaches the lofty sermon that woman stabilizes even the most restless male, or speaking Wagner's language, she redeems [*erlöst*] him. Here we permit ourselves a question. Suppose that this were true, would it therefore also be desirable? What happens to the Wandering Jew [*dem ewigen Juden,* the eternal Jew] who is worshiped by a woman and who is *stabilized?* He simply ceases to be eternal; he marries and he no longer is of any concern to us. Translated into reality: here is the danger for the artist, the genius—and after all this is what the Jew is—the danger is posed by woman, the worshipful women who cause men's downfall. Almost none of them has sufficient character to resist being ruined—"redeemed"—and once he feels himself treated like a god, he quickly descends to woman's level.—The male is cowardly before the eternal-feminine, and all the darling little women know it.—In many cases of female love and perhaps precisely in regard to the most famous ones [of Wagner's opera heroines] love merely is a more refined form of parasitism, a form of nesting in another's soul, sometimes in the flesh of another—alas! how decidedly often always at the "host's" expense!— ("On Parasitism"; see also UW, II, 862)

[The artist is a species intermediary to the neurotic-psychiatric and the criminal who is restrained from criminality by weakness of will and social timidity, and is not quite ready for the asylum . . . whoever wants to retain power flatters the mob, works with the mob . . . such types as Victor Hugo and Richard Wagner . . . *Result.*—A high culture can only rest on a broad base, upon a strong and healthy, consolidated mediocrity . . . the power of the middle is upheld then by commerce, and above all by monetary transactions: the instinct of the financier goes against anything that is extreme—hence the Jews are the most *conserving* power in our threatened and insecure Europe. They have no use either for revolutions, socialism, or militarism: if they want or need power, say even over the revolutionary party, it is only a consequence of the aforementioned and not its contradiction. Once in a while it is necessary for them to arouse fear against other extreme tendencies by revealing *all that* [power] held in their hands. But their instinct itself is unchangeably conservative—and "mediocre." . . . They know where power resides and everywhere know how to be powerful; but the exploitation of their power always goes in one direction. The honorable term for *mediocre* is the well-known word "liberal." . . . (*WM*, 864; March–June 1888)

It is immediately evident that Nietzschean assertions about Jews are nuanced between the antipodes of good and evil: they have *esprit,* intellect; but they also have money that brings them envy and power. On the threatening side: they have hidden powers—the iron fist hidden in velvet gloves. If one is conservative, one should welcome the Jews' stabilizing power, and if one detests mob revolution—as did Nietzsche—one would also welcome their conservatism or even their "mediocre liberalism" politically.

Nietzsche draws up a peculiar balance sheet without recourse to contemporaneous political specifics, and that is a weakness. He is decisive, however, in his characterization of anti-Semites as the misfits, the botched and underprivileged. Yet even here, Nietzsche is not quite accurate because anti-Semitism was never confined to the impoverished or misfits but crosses all boundaries in the political, professional, academic, and particularly the intellectual and religious spectrum.

The altruistic attributes he ascribed to half of mankind—women—and their insecurity and weakness turned into a conspiracy to dominate the "strong," parallels the Judaic subversion of the Roman world. Thus, the deceptive weakness of women is equated with that of Jews and dovetails with the endemic nineteenth-century German effeminization of Jews. Condemning the "failings" of one automatically condemns those of the other.

Nietzsche's variability of views about women occasionally does take ameliorative colorations despite subordinating women as the sexually "other." In a section called "Will and Willingness," he puts perceptive words in the mouth of a sage:

> Will is the attribute of men and willingness that of women. . . . It is
> men who corrupt women . . . man creates for himself the image of
> woman, and woman shapes herself in the mold of this ideal. . . . All
> humans are innocent of their existence but women doubly so. . . . Men
> need to be educated better. (*FW*, 68)

But, Nietzsche's sage intimates, there is little hope of men taking that
direction.

While Nietzsche's contempt for and condemnation of anti-Semites
remains resolute, he gives unsettling credibility to generalized fears
acquired by the unwary, not excluding himself, about what lurks beneath
the masks of women and Jews—the will to domination that originally
brought Christianity to the fore:

> The *masked* forms of the will to power: (1) The longing for freedom, for
> independence, also equilibrium, peace. . . . In its most elemental form,
> it is the will to exist, the "drive for self-preservation." (2) [Pretended
> subordination to the community's will to power and to those in power,
> with the aim of eventually subverting them and becoming their master.
> . . .] (3) Pretended self-deprecation despite feelings of superiority to
> those in power, the discovery [for purposes of power-seeking] of *new
> codes of morality* (of which the Jews are a classical example). (*WM*, 774)

Nietzsche saw negative and positive "survival" aspects of the will to
power, but mainly saw it in Jews as a hypocritical masking of real and
potential danger of a will that threatened to impose new values.* Ironically, this is precisely what Nietzsche's "son" Zarathustra aimed to do—
to break the Old Tablets. The mask and the act of masking are extensively discussed in *Beyond Good and Evil* from their history on the ancient
Greek stage to their general psychological use as a defensive device by
Jews and others. Climactically Nietzsche comes to the personal conclusion that his face was his own best mask at all times.

It has been suggested that Nietzsche's notes, unpublished during his
lifetime, were shaded differently from their published version. But this
hardly applies if we scan, for instance, two sections he added in 1887 to
a new edition of *The Gay Science*:

---

*Shades of *The Protocols of the Learned Elders of Zion*, that infamous work accusing
the Jews of planning to take over the World!

Of the Origin of the Learned [*Über die Herkunft der Gelehrten*]. . . . The sons of Protestant clergymen and schoolmasters are recognizable by the naive certainty with which—as learned persons—they assume all matters to be proved if they advocate them heartily and with heat: they are thoroughly accustomed to having people *believe* them: that was their fathers' "stock in trade"! This is just the opposite with Jews who are conditioned by their business experiences and the past history of the nation; they are not in the least accustomed to having people believe them: one need only observe learned Jews—they all place great reliance upon logic, that is, aiming to *compel* agreement through persuasive reasons; they know that only by these means can they win, even though racial and class antagonism exists and there is unwillingness to believe them. Nothing, it appears, is more democratic than logic; it takes no account of the person and even takes a crooked nose to be straight. (Incidentally, especially in regard to logical reasoning, and pure clear-headed habits, Europe and above all, Germans (a lamentable unreasoning [*déraisonnable*] race into whose heads sense needs to be knocked even today)—owes no little thanks to Jews. Everywhere that Jews have come into prominence, they have taught more keen decision making, sharper analyzing, and more precise writing: it was always their task to bring reason [*raison*] to a nation. (*FW*, 348)

Nietzsche's acerbic tongue is given unbridled rein here: though Jewish noses are crooked, their logic, unlike that of their hosts, is not. Again compliments for Jews are not given without a price exacted. In the next section, Nietzsche sees acting and dissimulation as genetic, the Heine mask, for instance. Yet, in one way or another, Nietzsche admits his personal dependence upon the mask. And, as a matter of of habit, Nietzsche stereotypically links the characteristics of Jews and women in the next passage.

The Problem of the Actor. [*Vom Probleme des Schauspielers*] . . . imprinted in the flesh of animals is the eternal art of hide-and-seek called *mimicry*. [A similar genetic development, including irrational urges that come to dominate all others] produces the actor, the *artist* (buffoon, pantaloon, clown, and genius). Also under more demanding social conditions and similar pressures arises a similar type of person, except that here mainly the histrionic [the theatrical] is barely reined in by another instinct. Take for example "diplomats." I would, in any case, believe that a good diplomat has the option of playing a good actor on stage, if he lowers his pride. As far as *Jews* are concerned, they are a people [*Volk*] of artful adaptability [*Anpassungskunst*, art of accommodation, chameleon-like blending] *par excellence*, so that, consonant with this idea, one can see that from early on among them existed a universal breeding-ground for actors, a veritable brood in a hatching nest for actors; in fact, the question is timely—which good actor today is not Jewish? Then too, the Jew is a born literary person, the actual lord of the European press that displays his power and play-abilities; in essence, he is an actor, that is, he plays the "expert," the "specialist."—Finally, we come to *women*. If one reflects on the entire history of women [*Frauen*], does one not conclude that first and foremost they *must* be actresses? Why listen to doctors who have hypnotized women [*Frauenzimmer*, a form of, verbal put-down]. In the last analysis, one loves them; we let ourselves be "hypnotized" by women. What is the upshot of all this? Women say that they "give themselves," even as they give themselves. Woman [*Das Weib*, "female"] is so artistic. . . . (*FW*, 361)

NOTES

1. Rudolph Binion, *Frau Lou: Nietzsche's Wayward Disciple* (Princeton, N.J.: Princeton University Press, 1968), p. 137.

2. "The following is the antinomy: Insofar as we believe in morality, we condemn (*verurteilen*) existence." (*WM*, 6)

3. Richard M. Chadbourne, *Ernest Renan* (New York: Twayne, 1968), p. 53.

4. Quoted by Isaac Goldkorn, "Renan and Racism," *Midstream* (November 1986): 40.

5. Ibid., p. 42.

6. Ibid.

7. Chadbourne, *Ernest Renan*, p. 71.

8. Renan described his *History of the Jewish People* "as the arch of the bridge . . . between Judaism and Christianity. In *The Life of Jesus*, I tried to show the majestic growth of the Galilean tree from the tip of its roots to its summit [and] making known the subsoil where the roots of Jesus grew." Chadbourne, *Ernest Renan*, p. 74, and the review essay by Goldkorn, "Renan and Racism," pp. 40–43, for the Renan quotes cited here.

9. The section numerations that follow are those in the popular edition of

Der Will zur Macht. Versusch einer Umwertung Aller Werte, vol. 6, ed. Alfred Baeumler [*Friedrich Nietzsche Werke*] (Leipzig: Alfred Kröner, 1930). The "Afterword," pp. 700–709, proclaims Nietzsche not as a prophet but as a visionary who brought Greek-Germanic educational concepts into a clear, unified reality—a Nazi reading that runs counter to Nietzsche's thinking. The same section numeration is utilized by Walter Kaufmann, ed., *Friedrich Nietzsche. The Will to Power*, co-trans. R. J. Hollingdale (New York: Vintage Books, 1968).

10. A comprehensive overview of Nietzsche's complex feelings about the subject is given by Wolfgang Trillhaas, "Nietzsche's Priester," *NS* (1983): 32–50.

11. Kaufmann, *Nietzsche: Philosopher, Psychologist, Antichrist*, p. 286.

12. The Kaufmann-Hollingdale translation uses the phrase "castrated" people and brings it into line with Freud's theory that "circumcision is the symbolic substitute for the castration" the primal father in the throes of absolute power once inflicted upon the son. This theory, however, has its limitations in view of the inordinate number of *un*circumcised males who find their way to the psychoanalyst's couch.

13. Solomon Grayzel, *A History of the Jews, From the Babylonian Exile to the End of World War II* (Philadelphia: The Jewish Publication Society of America, 1947), pp. 142–43. Grayzel reproduces a mural painting uncovered among the ruins of Pompeii that depicts the Judgment of Solomon.

14. *Almanach de Gotha*, a published register of the titled and upper social levels.

15. Heinrich Härtle, *Nietzsche und der Nationalsozialismus* (Munich: Zentralverlag der NSDUP, 1937), p. 55.

16. Ibid., p. 50.

17. Also see J, 248.

10

Lanzky, Zimmern . . .
Twilight Musings

PAUL LANZKY

On December 25, 1883, Nietzsche wrote to his mother and his not-altogether-overjoyed sister from Nice about another Jew coming into his life meaningfully during a time of depressing memories and physical woes endured without the relief of human company:

> Perhaps soon, I will obtain real help from Herr Paul Lanzky from Florence, who apparently awaits living with me [in Nice], but at the moment cannot [join me]. He is co-owner of the Vallombrosa hotel and for next spring has made plans that would wonderfully suit your hermit and forest-dweller. Herr Lanzky is the first person who addresses me in correspondence as "verehrtester Meister!" [most esteemed Master]— affects me touchingly, as well as with fun and mockery, to start being Wagner's heir. . . .

To Overbeck, Nietzsche wrote glowingly that just in time had a new human being been given him as a gift, a thirty-one-year-old person (eight years younger than Nietzsche), philosophically inclined, "who wishes to link his destiny to mine," an independent thinker and "friend of isolation." Nietzsche spun out the hope that at Vallombrosa a "nest could be found" where his philosophy would take hold. From the contents of a number of letters, we gather that for a time Lanzky did live in the same pension as Nietzsche in Nice.

Nietzsche reported that Lanzky was a former journalist and editor of the *Revista Europea*. Ostensibly Lanzky was the first to review at length, and point to the significance of, Nietzsche's book *Die fröhliche Wissenschaft*. Wagner owned his hagiographical court biographers, but Nietzsche wanted to screen from public view anything private and preferred keying his experiences into his writings, a form of sublimation. He was not keen on having his friends read *Zarathustra* and finding in it a key to *his* biography. And so, just as he had asked Dr. Paneth, "also a great admirer and worshiper," not to write about him, he made the same request of Herr Lanzky. One could hardly call Dr. Paneth a worshiper, but Lanzky came close to fitting the bill; Nietzsche did envy the adoration Meister Wagner received from *his* subjects at Tribschen and Bayreuth. At the moment, however, Nietzsche saw life turning into a charade and told Overbeck grumpily that he preferred being incognito to being lumped with "mediocre enthusiasts." Even so, this did not prevent him from utilizing the compliant Lanzky who played "Joshua" to Nietzsche-Moses in scouting out the dreamland Corsica or St. Raphael as a potential next home.

Lanzky was enlisted on a variety of errands as Nietzsche formerly had been for Wagner; Lanzky went beyond the call of servitude as well by reading three volumes of Stendhal to the near-blind Meister Nietzsche. Lanzky remembered Nietzsche as a modest, unprepossessing, joyful, cultured philosopher, a considerate and noble person. As a matter of affinity, Lanzky said that they shared the illusion of Polish descent, and after the Franco-Prussian war of 1870 could no longer stomach Germans. Lanzky, abandoned by his lover, was deeply wounded and gave up hope of ever hearing of her again; uncannily, though, and quite accidentally he came upon her name on a gravestone in an Italian cemetery. As the biographer Janz surmises, Nietzsche may have intuited a similar fate for himself in regard to Lou Salomé for whose health he had concerns.[1]

Fearing the onset of the annual Christmastime migraine attacks, Nietzsche dispatched a telegram that quickly brought Herr Lanzky to Nice and the Pension Genève; there he presented him with the gift of a leather-bound copy of Rohde's defense of *The Birth of Tragedy*. It does not seem that Nietzsche could discuss in depth with Lanzky, as he had with Rée and Lou, his philosophical ruminations. And hence the very thought of intimately sharing the visionary last part of *Zarathustra* with Lanzky was upsetting to him (although he did send him a dedicatory copy):

> But, my dear Herr Lanzky. . . . Why do you wish to provoke me into saying more than I wish to say? . . . to descend to the ludicrous role of having to explain my *Zarathustra* (or) his animals. . . . Let me ventilate my feelings. . . . You are experiencing the beginning of the most lofty book pregnant with the future that has ever been written. And you have the honor of reading it within your lifetime. . . . What? you do "not fathom my goals"? Well and good; it's not to be wondered at. But is it my fault if you do not have my eyes in your head? Are my goals suitable for everyman? What have you in common with my goals? What with "life"? I would like to hear about the purposes of your life! Had you any, then perhaps you could become the instrument of mine. Away with you, Sir Presumption. . . , Garde votre distance, monsieur! (end April 1884, *KGB* III/l, p. 578)

We do not know how Nietzsche refashioned this draft before sending the letter, but it certainly was prickly repayment for Lanzky's generous companionship; Lanzky overlooked his friend's megalomania. A young man, Baron Heinrich von Stein, who alone of the Wagner enemy-camp had visited Nietzsche out of respect for his work, received a much milder reply when he claimed to have understood only six sentences from the parts of *Zarathustra* he had read.[2] But for Nietzsche, Lanzky perhaps shared—if not typified—the Jewish characteristics of "importunity." Early in January 1885, Nietzsche sent a self-revelatory letter to Naumburg; he admitted that Lanzky was a very devoted and considerate person, tolerant even of Nietzsche's rudeness: "But here begins the old story—when I have need of someone to converse with me, it turns out that I do the conversing. He [Lanzky] is silent, sighs, and looks like a shoemaker and knows neither how to laugh nor show intellect. Intolerable in the long run."

"I would prefer the company of a clown," Nietzsche told Overbeck. It was similar irascibility that reflected a growing and inward gnawing anger at the world's insufferable failure to acknowledge him. And slowly his irascibility and physical instability were to alienate or drive away most of his old friends for the rest of his life. Torn between the company offered by Lanzky and an increasing boredom and utter loneliness Nietzsche could not bring himself to go with him to Corsica or to visit the little Paradise and "refugium" Vallombroso. Lanzky, on the other hand, drew inspiration from Nietzsche. He published a novella and a collection of aphorisms in 1887 called *Abendröte* (*Glow of Sunset*), an obvious play upon Nietzsche's *Morgenröte* (*Daybreak*). To Nietzsche's annoyance, Lanzky—like other contemporary poetasters—gained a greater readership than any of Nietzsche's published works. Nietzsche hid his annoyance defensively. Lanzky recollected that

> Nietzsche reproached me that with my [*Abendröte*] title, I had intended to mock his own *Morgenröte*. In response, I said, "Dear Meister, to your goodness and the riches of your works, I am exceedingly indebted: If you are suspicious of me, then take back all the letters that you have entrusted me with, so that you can be certain that they will not be misused by me." With that, Nietzsche's noble character resurfaced. He told me of being convinced that I would regard the letters as private property and never publish them. That was last thing he said before our parting. I've never released the letters, not even to the emissary Dr. Kogel [Fritz K., a Nietzsche archive editor] sent to me by Frau Elisabeth. I burned the letters as the only way to retain a clear conscience.[3]

The gift of "mockery" Nietzsche ascribed to the Jew Heine, he also attributed to Lanzky. From the beginning of their friendship to the end, Lanzky saw a deterioration and Nietzsche's growing moods of anger and malice. "Even in my presence," said Lanzky in his reminiscences, "Nietzsche was a suffering solitary." Lanzky took pity on the lonely sufferer without instinctively realizing how much Nietzsche loathed pity and commiseration—all of which he felt encouraged demeaning and psychologically untenable relationships. Of other impressions related by Lanzky we learn that climatology and metaphor were synonymous; Nietzsche hated overcast skies as much as unclear thinking in philosophy and psychology, and it accounts for his search for a suitable physical climate. Nietzsche's other fear was of losing his mind as had his father (when he succumbed to syphilis). While on a walk during a moonlit night in the English Garden of Nice, Nietzsche told Lanzky that if he had the power, he would forcefully subvert every European state. But he felt a sense of powerlessness with his meager pension and "a lazy publisher." Lanzky noted the contrast in Nietzsche's inveighing against woolen underclothes and dressing gowns, but then "burdening himself with as much of these as any human could carry." Lanzky did not see that this, in part, also accounted for Nietzsche's compensatory envy and glorification of the sunlit climate and male nudity in ancient Greece, where "gods and heroes danced."

Lanzky insisted that he was almost stoned for saying that Nietzsche was ruined by alcohol and stimulants as well as sleeping powders and possibly narcotics (in moderation), from which Lanzky (solicitously but futilely) wanted to wean him.[4] Although Nietzsche had a temperamental stomach, he drank a good quantity of cognac before meals and double-grog and beer during meals. Lanzky took accurate count of Nietzsche's cognac consumption.[5]

Nietzsche had to struggle with his feelings about Herr Lanzky: On the one hand, Lanzky "has a conception of who I am" and is helpful, but on the other hand Nietzsche tired of "the little journalist" who brought him no intellectual companionship with his "presumptuous" coattail-riding. Nietzsche used the word "Anmassung" (presumption, arrogance) to indicate his displeasure with Lanzky, a code-word for the importunate characteristics he saw in Jews, without overtly saying so, in a letter to Malwida toward the end of July 1887:

> Dear, esteemed friend, you must not confuse me with the feeble-minded and vain Lanzky, a journalist of the tenth rank, and [to] whom I have administered a kick to the backside when I noticed the misuse he began to make of me and my literature. Can you tolerate at all his saccharine wash? It is self-evident that his *Abendröte* of which you write is absolutely unknown to me [a patent lie]: the likes of that, and no less than Herr Lanzky himself, may no longer cross my threshold.

Just as he did not want his philosophy to be confused with Rée's or with Lipiner's dramas, Nietzsche rejected Lanzky's "derivative and imitative" poetry (characteristics which he had even ascribed to the Heine whom he admired). Soon thereafter, he even whistled his dear friend Malwida down the wind, lamented the earlier seven-year stretch of "dog-years" isolation, and also complained furtively about Peter Gast, though an indispensable crutch—"my musician"—and called him an unimaginative

"Klotz" (a sentiment probably true but more worthy of coming from a Wagner than a moral philosopher like Nietzsche). Cast from his home moorings, adrift at Pforta, Basel, and Tribschen, he seemed at first to welcome the possibility of a refuge, a "cloister-solitude" at Lanzky's proffered Vallombrosa which Dante, according to Nietzsche, described as paradise. But actually, it could have been hell.[6] Letters to his mother and sister at that time (1885) reveal deep resentments and fears; at any rate, Nietzsche announced to his family from Nice that he was still alive, and expressed concern about Elisabeth's fate with Förster and their pure Aryan claims:

> I have some thoughts of my own about the future of my sister . . . (if one wishes to escape Germany one need not go as far as Paraguay, take my example). . . . As little as is my enthusiasm for the "German essence," I have even less desire that this "magnificent" race maintain essential *purity*. On the contrary, on the contrary. (To Franziska and Lisbeth Nietzsche, March 21, 1885)

His laments about a lost childhood rarely addressed his specific grievances—a mother to whom he had to prove himself constantly as a surrogate for his father, her coldly disciplinarian and physically Spartan regimentation, and possessiveness oddly mixed with selective solicitude; his need for approbation that mainly came only from his "sentimental" and girlish sister.

Lanzky pointed to contrasts in Nietzsche's personality and was indignant when Nietzsche responded mildly to or ignored deriding attitudes at the Nice pension during mealtimes by table companions who opposed his ferocious attacks on Philistines as presented in Nietzsche's writings. Nietzsche, said Lanzky, "removed his masks for no one," not his mother, his sister, Gast, or Lanzky, "and was always alone." What Lanzky could not have known is that Nietzsche's masking went far back into childhood and that ambiguity, duplicity, and contrasts were all part of his complex personality.[7]

Like Hamlet, Nietzsche had always seen the world as a rank and unweeded garden. During one of his retreats to the Engadine mountains, he told the young medical student Resa von Schirnhofer of his anxiety and of his hallucinations about being engulfed by exotically luxuriating plants: "I never have peace. Don't you believe," he asked Resa, "that this condition is the symptom of the onset of madness?"—a question he had similarly put to Lanzky.[8] Schirnhofer was disturbed by Nietzsche's self-prescribed drugs that Lanzky said were not consumed for pleasure but as palliatives "to survive his moral and physical sufferings."

TWILIGHT MUSINGS

By 1888 Nietzsche's mood had perceptively darkened and after his dissections in *The Case of Wagner*, he turned to work on the gnostic and gnarled Dionysus poems (*Dithyramben*) and *Götzendammerung, oder wie man mit dem Hammer philosphiert* (*Twilight of the Idols, or How One Philosophizes with a Hammer*), written between the beginning of June and the end of November but not published until January 1889. With wry amusement, Nietzsche originally had wanted to title the book *Müssegang eines Psychologen* (*A Psychologist's Leisure Hours*), but Gast did not think it was sufficiently dynamic. About a half dozen entries deal with the Jewish concerns taken up in the previous notes, and some are only slightly reworked:

> When no other means are available, one chooses dialectics. One knows that dialectics arouses mistrust and convinces very few. Nothing is easier to wipe out than the effects of a dialectician: every forum of discussion proves that. It can only serve as a weapon of last resort in the hands of those who no longer have any weapons for defense. At a point of necessity, one must forcibly seize dialectics as a right; not until then does one make use of it. Jews, therefore, were dialecticians; as was Reynard the Fox, wasn't he?, and also Socrates?— (G, "The Problem of Socrates," sec. 6)

Nietzsche peremptorily proposes dialectics to have been a Jewish means of survival if not a weapon, but of course that did not excuse dialectics in the hands of Socrates who used it to spring traps for the unwary, as Nietzsche pointed out. It is an ingenious argument that sheds no light, though, on the exploratory, didactic, and rigorously scrutinizing social and legalistic interrogations of the Jewish Talmud, largely untapped for study in the nineteenth century, and in its educative methods, for instance. Nietzsche hints that the dialectical method goes counter to the instinctive reasoning of the body: the Dionysian intuition that is Greek and not Jewish. Dialectics and logic as a method of reasoning go hand in hand, having a "democratic" tinge, says Nietzsche, something that he clearly does not care for, yet, twisting the argument by the tail, Nietzsche allows that the "lamentably *déraisonnable* race of Germans" could benefit from the cleaner intellectual habits of the Jews" (*FW*, 348).

In August of 1888, during what was to be his last stay in the bracing, crisp air and mountainous beauty of Sils-Maria, Nietzsche was fortunate in finding an old colleague from his days at Basel, the theologian Julius Kaftan. Not since his discussions with Rée and Lou Salomé was he stimulated by intellectual give-and-take as during the three weeks they went for daily walks. Ideas roared through his head and he would often wake up after midnight trying to come to grips with them at his writing desk. Scattered in Nietzsche's correspondence of the time were far-reaching subversive aims of freeing humankind from the tyranny of Christian belief by assuming his most nihilistic guise, the Antichrist. If his message were to be understood, he wrote, it would be "indecent" to remain a Christian or to be an anti-Semite who "lies on principle," or to retain belief in priests with their vested interest in "morality," or to agree with the psychologically unnatural demands of the Gospels and other hypocritical Judeo-Christian valuations. His revelatory teachings were intended "to split mankind in half"—no longer B.C. and A.D. but humankind before and after Nietzsche.

Despite Nietzsche's assault on the roots of Christian ethics in Judaism, he was steadfast in his scorn for modern anti-Semitic manifestations in people of his acquaintance. In a letter to Overbeck on July 29, 1888, he mentioned two instances that angered him. He had been in correspondence with the musicologist-musician Dr. Carl Fuchs, for whose character he lost respect when Fuchs expressed fear that writing favorably about Nietzsche—who was widely regarded as an atheist—might jeopardize his own position as organist at St. Peter's. Fuchs had also dropped Nietzsche after the latter's break with Wagner. And at the time, Nietzsche predicted that Fuchs would "courageously" resume correspondence upon the Meister's death. Fuchs did, and again courted Nietzsche. "Fuchs," Nietzsche quipped, "also is organist at the Danzig Synagogue:

You cannot imagine how he poked fun in the most *scurrilous* way at the Jewish services (—but, he does not disdain *being paid!!*)."

Further, in the same letter, Nietzsche told Overbeck that he had canceled mailings from the periodical *Der Kunstwart* to which he had tentatively promised to contribute. When its young editor, Ferdinand Avenarius, according to Nietzsche, remonstrated, "I bluntly told him the truth (his journal blows the German-mongering horn and has betrayed Heinrich Heine, for instance, in the most vile way. —And yet, Avenarius is a Jew himself!!!)." That Nietzsche came down hard on the "Jew" Herr Avenarius[9] is somewhat surprising, ungracious, and more pejorative than factual. Yet it could be the case that Nietzsche actually thought Avenarius was Jewish and that his remark was not malicious at all: it merely expressed Nietzsche's displeasure at one Jew (Avenarius) excluding or "betraying" another (Heine). Nietzsche had recommended that for his periodical, Avenarius solicit music and belletristic articles from "Signor Enrico" Köselitz of Venice (who desperately needed free-lance income). The editor gave generous space to Gast for a review of Nietzsche's *The Case of Wagner*, and with the review came media attention that Nietzsche only rarely gained. The actual letter to Avenarius was a milder version of what he had written Overbeck. Here is Nietzsche's letter of July 20, 1888, in reply to one—not preserved—from Avenarius:

> . . . something that really disturbed me [about your journal]—the sacrificing of H[einrich] Heine; especially now when an ill-wind blows from German-mongerings for whose condescension I have no lenience . . . the cultural worth of an artist or thinker has nothing to do with national origin . . . Germans have cause to be more thankful for [the freethinkers] Lessing and Heine, than for instance to Goethe. That says nothing against Goethe (on the contrary)—but it does speak for the miserableness and ingratitude now evident against Lessing and Heine.

On October 30, Nietzsche informed Köselitz that during the summer he sent Avenarius an "extremely coarse letter because of the way his publication let down Heinrich Heine . . . coarse letters of mine are signs of gaiety. . . ." The letter, however, did *not* mention that Jews ought to behave better toward Heine.

Evidently, Nietzsche arrogated to himself the right to decide how

Heine was to be treated—with opprobrium or flattery as he had done alternately. It would not be amiss to conjecture that at this point in Nietzsche's life, he had associated himself so closely with Heine as outsider and Jew, that any slight against Heine was one he took to be directed against himself. Avenarius, as Wagner's nephew, could hardly have done other than to defend his uncle, but he behaved like a gentleman toward Nietzsche. Isolation in the last years certainly increased Nietzsche's irritabilities and his delusions of grandeur.

HELEN ZIMMERN

Knowing of Wagner's attachment to Schopenhauer, Helen Zimmern had sent him a copy of her book *Schopenhauer, His Life and Philosophy* upon its publication in 1876. Wagner immediately urged his young friend Nietzsche to send the English German scholar Miss Zimmern his latest book, *Unzeitgemässe Betrachtungen: David Strauss*, in hopes of a hearing in England for his writings. Richard and Cosima invited Miss Zimmern to visit the Bayreuth opera festivities, which she did with alacrity, and the same year also met Nietzsche there, quite fleetingly. In her recollections she admitted to understanding very little of what the professor from Basel had said to her of his philosophy; in Bayreuth she may also have met Malwida von Meysenbug (1816–1903), the author of *Memoirs of an Idealist* published anonymously in 1876, and six years later under her own name when it gained a following for her advocacy of women's rights. Years later through acquaintances in common, Zimmern learned of Nietzsche's vacationing in Sils and joined him for a brief spell in the early summer of 1884. Nietzsche apprised Malwida of the meeting and conveyed Zimmern's wish that Malwida send to London all the books he had written so that Miss Zimmern would author a comprehensive essay to be published in an English magazine.

At Sils-Maria Nietzsche more than hinted that Zimmern consider translating his work. Since he knew that her critical Schopenhauer biography had successfully introduced that philosopher to the English public, Nietzsche hoped for similar attention. He was genuinely taken with her personality, her bilingual proficiency, and literary knowledge, and introduced her in person or in letters as a most intelligent woman—"Jewish as well." Two years later, Zimmern, captivated by Nietzsche's conversation and gentlemanly charm (unlike the polemics of his works), was intrigued by the prospect of translating Nietzsche. She spent nine weeks at Sils to get to know him better as a person and a philosopher. A gracious mutual respect emerged. Only once before had Nietzsche talked glowingly about a woman, and that was when he referred to Lou Salomé as the most intelligent of women. The compassionate Resa von Schirnhofer he judged unfairly as "an entertaining young student from Zurich," yet too ugly for him to even think of marrying, he grumpily told his sister ("I can't tolerate ugly people"). Of the few accounts we have of Zimmern, we note Resa's, who wrote about her impression of Zimmern as a constantly charming person seated at Nietzsche's side, listening courteously and eliciting animated talk from Nietzsche at the dining table of Engadine's oldest inn, the Alpenrose. To Gast, Nietzsche wrote about the Schopenhauer biographer "—naturally, a Jew:—it's fantastic to see how greatly this race now holds Europe's 'intellect' in its hands (at length, today, she conversed with me about her race)" (July 20, 1888).

It would have been valuable to know the substance of their conversations about the Jewish "race." The nineteenth-century use of the word was so elastic as to mean anything one wished: people, nation, bloodline, religion, or gender.

By the time Helen Zimmern was asked to recall her memories in the 1920s, much had paled of what had transpired in conversation some forty years earlier at the Hotel Alpenrose and during walks along the Silvaplana Lake and reverential stops at the rock of revelation where the Zarathustra vision originated. But she still cherished Nietzsche's David Strauss book he had inscribed for her in Bayreuth. She claims that after mornings of writing at Engadine, he would recap his ideas for her, and this, I believe, also accounts for the lucidity of her Nietzsche translations aided by the suppleness of her own cultivated style.

Zimmern took no umbrage at Nietzsche's egocentric consciousness of his own merits and his conviction that in time university chairs and lectures would be given in his honor. He was frightfully lonely and would identify with the Zarathustra character he had created, and repeatedly quoted the Persian prophet. Unlike Lou Salomé, Zimmern saw no signs of megalomania or incipient madness in Nietzsche, either in 1884 or two years later. Nor did she take offense at the warning in *Zarathustra* that one should take along a whip when going to women. She instead countered with her own observation which resembles a Nietzschean aphorism: "Apparently there are men who possess theories about women, but who hardly put them to practice." That was her estimate of Nietzsche who was shy and possessed what the Italians call "gentilezza." In fact he had asked one of Zimmern's friends, a Catholic lady by the name of Fynn, not to read his works because they might injure her feelings. And so, we can infer that the man who warned of his being "dynamite" possessed a core of softness. Zimmern also noted that her English translation of *Beyond Good and Evil* (for which the original German market had been anemic) sold by the thousands in a pirated commercialized American edition, with no protection for those who were being robbed.

In 1887, Miss Zimmern moved from London to the warmer climate of Florence to cultivate her garden and to continue writing on art, literature, and politics, and translating from the Italian and German—more than forty volumes all told. She took great satisfaction in the German translation of her biographical study, *Gotthold Ephraim Lessing*, one of the founders of German literature who also uniquely espoused tolerance for Jews toward the end of the eighteenth century. Zimmern herself was a model of "the good European," Nietzsche's ideal type: she died in 1934, before seeing her ideals destroyed in Germany and the adoption of Nietzsche by some Nazi-oriented academics and political leaders of the new Reich. In reviewing correspondence in which Helen Zimmern is mentioned to others, Nietzsche writes that she also knows Georg Brandes—an association he found eminently appropriate since he saw them as co-religionists. On most occasions he handsomely praised her Jewish intelligence and did this almost aggressively to accent the fact that Germans and non-Jews ought to take note of the discrepancy in the recognition of genius.

Nietzsche's exaggeration becomes patent when we realize the minimal relation of Helen Zimmern to things Jewish. Born in Hamburg on March 25, 1846, she was baptized in the evangelical-Lutheran faith. She was the daughter of the merchant Hermann Theodor Zimmern (of Jewish descent) and of Antonie Marie Therese Regine. Her full name was Helene Adophine Marianne Zimmern, later shortened to Helen Zimmern.[10] As in other cases, Nietzsche's identifications or misidentifications of persons as Jewish was at the mercy of varying purposes. Invention and facticity, and half-shadings, were suited to the occasion. The many summers Nietzsche spent in Sils-Maria were for the most part productive and healing. Ironically it was not in the company of old male friends, as he had envisioned, but with a mix of younger and older women—some of the "titled" variety—whose names he paraded in his correspondence (such as Fräulein von Mansuroff, a countess and *dame d'honneur* of the Russian czarina).

It is remarkable how much reciprocal congeniality they enjoyed— even in playing practical jokes on each other and occasional frankness that reveal much of Nietzsche's psychological state of mind. Resa von Schirnhofer's reminiscences are particularly valuable. I do not believe that there is exaggeration in her describing Nietzsche's anxiety-filled eyes and moods alternating between assertiveness and self-doubting. At moments of emotional excitement, she seemed to see a usually hidden side of him. He actually missed the "ugly" young Resa tearfully when she had to end her vacation, but was compensated by the pert presence of Miss Zimmern. His daily routine varied very little. He lived in the village in a small room in a notion-dealer's house, sheltered from sunlight for the sake of his eyes. He arose early, asked that no one interrupt his writing, and then emerged from behind the locked door at 11 A.M. and took a short walk. After he lunched on beefsteak and fruit at the Hotel Alpenrose, he went for walks in the valley toward the glaciers, returning to his room between 4 and 5 P.M. to work, brewing himself tea before midnight and continued his writing. Throughout the day he consumed vast quantities of apples and grapes bought from itinerant Italians. The innkeeper blamed Nietzsche's digestive troubles on this culinary regimen which nonetheless sustained his work habits.

Moving from place to place—baggage, book crates and all—was becoming more and more difficult for Nietzsche; his diminishing eyesight caused disorientation, and for a while he was able to summon help in the form of "Maestro" Gast or Paul Lanzky to Nice. Some letters to Gast have an anguished air about them. But above anyone else, he missed Rée and Wagner. He admitted that the many letters he was writing— including those to Lanzky—were prompted by his loneliness, restlessness, and his search for locales suitable to his seasonal and health needs. He corresponded with Lanzky on a level reminiscent of his exchanges with Cosima—from gossip to substance. Aside from Miss Zimmern, there were other occasions for Nietzsche's gaining respect for Jews:

> . . . Just now [in Nice] we have had a brilliant convention of astrono-
> mers, le congrès Bisch, named after the wealthy Jew Bischoffsheim—an
> amateur *in astronomicis*, who covers the *costs* of the entire congress;
> people are truly delighted with the festivities he has organized. Nice
> already owes him thanks for his observatory, as well as his support of
> staff salaries, and publications. *Ecco! Jewish extravagance (Luxus) in the
> grand style!*— (Letter to Peter Gast, October 27, 1887)

ECCE HOMO

Nietzsche's *Ecce Homo* requires book-length commentary to do it justice
in ranking it with other major confessional "autobiographies," not so
much in details of his life but in its self-reflections, revisions, and psychological revelations: overcoming all temptations. My purview here
restricts itself to passages that reflect Nietzsche's attitude toward Jews.
Again, Wagner and Jews gain selective attention. Nietzsche could not
shake the feeling that Wagner had damaged himself as much as he had
abused Jews. Nietzsche had cause to put himself in their shoes and he
strikes back at Wagner as no Jew could effectively have done:

> What I really want from music is something cheerful and profound like
> an afternoon in October. It ought to be unique, wanton, tender like a
> dainty little female of charm and roguish disposition. . . . I will never
> agree that a German could possibly *know* what music is. The greatest of
> those now called German musicians are foreigners: Slavs, Croatians, Ital-
> ians, Netherlanders—or Jews, except for Germans of a strong race,
> namely defunct Germans like Heinrich Schutz, Bach, and Händel. There
> is enough of the Pole in me to trade the rest of music for Chopin (exempt
> Wagner's *Siegfried Idyll*, perhaps some Liszt, Rossini, and the music of my
> Venetian maestro, "Pietro Gasti"). (*EH*, "Why I Am So Clever," sec. 7)

By renaming Heinrich Köselitz Peter Gast, Nietzsche felt that he had de-
Germanized him, and de-Germanization was to be a necessary purification for future Nietzsche readers:

> Whoever reads me in Germany today must first de-Germanize himself
> thoroughly, as I have: my known formula states that "to be a good

German requires one to de-Germanize oneself": except if one is of Jewish descent—something that is of no small distinction among Germans—Jews among Germans are always the higher race—more refined, spiritual, kind.—*L'adorable Heine,* they say in Paris. My old teacher Ritschl actually maintained that I devised my philological essays like a Parisian *romancier*—absurdly exciting.—I am the anti-ass *par excellence* and therefore a world-historical monster—I am, in Greek, and not only in Greek, the Antichrist. (*EH,* "Why I Write Such Good Books," sec. 2)

Nietzsche wrote several versions of this passage, of which the above is a draft.[11] In the published passage, Heine and the Jews are omitted, but he does not tone down his resentment that he had been discovered "everywhere in Europe" but not in the shallow land of Germany. The following shots from Nietzsche's rhetorical arsenal are rarely quoted by Wagnerians, anti-Semites, or Germans—or Christians:

I think that I know the Wagnerians, I have experienced three generations. . . . —In truth, a hair-raising company! Not a single abortion is missing among them, not even the anti-Semite. Poor Wagner! Where had he landed! —If he had at least entered into swine! But to descend among Germans! (*EH,* "Human, All-Too-Human," sec. 2)

Another parting shot at German gullibility in regard to anti-Semitism is appropriately recorded in a section on Wagner:

. . . The German nation is becoming ever more lazy and impoverished in its instincts, ever more dishonest, and which continues with an enviable appetite to feed on opposites, gobbling down without any digestive troubles "faith" as well as scientific manners, "Christian love" as well as anti-Semitism, the will to power (to the *Reich*) as well as the *évangile des humbles* [Gospel of the humble]. (*EH,* "The Case of Wagner," sec. 1)

There was no German critic comparable to the Danish critic Georg Brandes (Morris Cohen), who gave Nietzsche great cause for self-esteem and respect in his lifetime. And Nietzsche was grateful to his Jewish discoverer, a "good European," an exemplar of Jewish *délicatesse* (one of Heine's favorite complimentary adjectives) in contrast to Germans.

One lowers oneself by associating with Germans. . . . Except for my association with a few artists—Wagner, above all—I have not enjoyed a single good hour with Germans. . . . In vain do I look for a sign of tact, of *délicatesse* toward me. From Jews, yes; never yet from Germans. . . . Ten years: and no one in Germany had any pangs of conscience about not defending my name against the absurd silence under which it lay buried: a foreigner, a Dane, was the first to show a keenness of instinct and courage, and one who felt indignation at my supposed friends. . . At which German universities is it possible today to hear lectures about my philosophy as it was last spring when Dr. Georg Brandes, who proved his right once more to be called a psychologist, held them in Copenhagen? . . . That does not exclude the fact that I love irony, even world-historic irony. And so I sent into the world the *Case of Wagner* about two years before the annihilating lightning stroke of the Revaluation that will cause earthquakes around the world: By misunderstanding me, Germans commit one more immortal blunder, and immortalize themselves. . . . My compliments, dear Teutons! (*EH*, "The Case of Wagner," sec. 4)

The selections from section 4 just quoted were preceded by a draft version:

And from what side did all great obstructions, all calamities in life emanate? Always from Germans. The damnable German anti-Semitism, this poisonous boil of *névrose nationale*, has intruded into my existence almost ruinously during that decisive time when not my destiny but the destiny of humanity was at issue. And I owe it to the same element that my *Zarathustra* entered this world as *indecent* literature—its publisher being an anti-Semite. In vain do I look for some sign of tact, of *délicatesse* in relation to me; from Jews, yes; from Germans, never.[12]

Notes and fragments written about October 15, 1888, for *Ecce Homo* have been unearthed and serve here to round out Nietzsche's views:

21. [6] Ah, what a blessing to find a Jew among German horned cattle! . . . That is something the anti-Semitic gentlemen underestimate. Actually, what is it that distinguishes a Jew from an anti-Semite: The Jew knows when he lies, the anti-Semite does not realize that he always lies.[13]

Even more salubrious is Nietzsche's next equating of Jews who approve the "chosen" designation with the claims of anti-Semites.

> 21. [7] . . . people, for example, become anti-Semites only because they have a goal that is defined by its outrageousness, namely to obtain Jewish money. Definition of the anti-Semite: jealousy, *ressentiment*, impotent anger as a leitmotif within instinct. The claim of [being] the chosen, a complete moralistic self-deception—a typical sign being constant proclamations of large words turned into virtue. Don't they [Jews] even notice how interchangeably alike they [anti-Semites] seem when making such assertions? An anti-Semite is more jealous and therefore the most stupid Jew.

It is odd, but from none of Nietzsche's Jewish friends and acquaintances could he have derived the notion that Jews held themselves to be a chosen people in the Old Testament sense; on the contrary, all made little of their Jewish identity, and even less of any notions of ethnic superiority.[14] From his definition of the anti-Semite, a very cursory list of attributes, neither the anti-Semite nor the Jew can take any comfort. The one is verbally dismissed and the other hardly exalted. Nietzsche, I think, would have preferred by far to be recognized by German intellectual peers than to be enthusiastically extolled by clever Jews. At any rate, his perception of anti-Semitism is personal and provides an interesting contrast, for instance, to the later French existentialist philosopher Jean-Paul Sartre. While Sartre claims that the Jew exists only because he has been created by his enemies, Nietzsche believes that the Jew exists as an act of will and choice.

Of the men in Nietzsche's life to whom he owed most psychologically and intellectually though in differing proportions, we must note his father, his mentor Ritschl, the *bête noire* Wagner, and his friend Paul Rée. Nietzsche is most likely referring to Rée in the following excerpt as a "pure type"; Wagner falls in the category of an "anti-Semitic gent":

> 21. [8] I may venture to name a scholar of Jewish extraction who gave me at all times a deep feeling of beauty, of cleanliness as I understand it, through his noble coolness and clarity that had become instinctual in him; he never forgot himself for one moment, he was never other than himself and never lost control over himself in or without the company of

bystanders. Attributable to that bearing belongs not only a complete habituation to hardness and frankness toward himself but also a great strength of resistance to being corrupted by the pressure of society, a book, or circumstance. . . . In contrast to this described pure type are, on the average, almost all Germans I know, especially the anti-Semitic gents.

Nietzsche, in revising and reviewing his earlier books, put on a new face and with 1888 hindsight tells us what he had "really meant." Some of the second thoughts are fanciful revisions; others indicate what he wished he had meant at the time; but in still other instances he wants readers to be sure about his proprietorship of ideas. He reminds posterity that although he had praised Paul Rée in one section of All-Too-Human (section 37), it was erroneous for "others" (Wagnerites) to regard the entire work as a "higher Réealism," for there were other points at which he contradicted some of Rée's propositions. "I have always recognized," Nietzsche stated, "who among my readers was hopeless—for example—the typical German professor . . ." (EH, "Human," 6; GM, Preface). Here again appears Nietzsche's caveat that by and large Jews rather than Germans appreciated and understood his work. And yet one major wish dominated his thinking: He did not want the approbation of anti-Semites and Wagner camp-followers, or the common "horned cattle." Quite typical is Nietzsche's open rejection of anti-Semitism in correspondence as firmly seen in exchanges with Theodor Fritsch* (Thomas Frey), the editor of a periodic bulletin for "inner-party" members called Antisemitische Correspondence und Sprechsaal für innere Partei Angelegenheiten, Leipzig. Nietzsche's tone of ridicule toward anti-Semites is undisguised:

> Most esteemed Sir,
>   With your letter, just received, you do me so much honor that I cannot resist adding one more example to yours about Jews in my works although it puts you doubly in the right to talk about my "warped judgments." Please read my Morgenröte, p. 194.
>   Objectively speaking, Jews are more interesting than Germans: their history yields many more fundamental problems. In such matters I habitually disregard sympathy and antipathy in line with the discipline and morality of the scientific spirit, and finally in line with good taste.

---

*This Fritsch is not to be confused with Nietzsche's publisher, Ernst W. Fritzsch.

At any rate, I feel myself greatly estranged from the presently prevalent German spirit, though without becoming impatient with each of its little idiosyncrasies. Along with these I account, in all its oddity, anti-Semitism . . . to this movement I am even indebted for some entertainment, just as last spring I laughed at the books of the puffed-up and sentimental blockhead named Paul de Lagarde! Obviously I am deficient in that "highest ethical position" you attribute to the opposite side. It now remains for me to thank you for your well-meaning assumption that I have not been "led to my warped judgments by any social considerations"; and perhaps it will serve your peace of mind if finally I tell you that among my friends, I have *no Jews*, also no anti-Semites. . . . Your most devoted Professor Dr. Nietzsche.

[P.S.] One wish: [In your news-bulletins] do provide a list of German scholars, artists, poets, writers, actors, and virtuosos of Jewish descent! (It would constitute a valuable contribution to the history of German culture and criticism of it.) (to Theodor Fritsch, Nice, March 23, 1887)

A week later Nietzsche sent an even sharper and dismissive letter to Fritsch,

Herewith, I am returning the three issues of your *Correspondence* bulletin and thank you for the confidence displayed in allowing me to take a look at the muddled principles basic to this curious movement [anti-Semitism]. However, I must ask you not to continue keeping me in mind with your publication: I fear ultimately that my patience may give out. Believe me: this repulsive partying of dismal dilettantes about the worth of people and races, this submission to "authorities," who are rejected by every clear-headed intellect with cold contempt (as should be, for instance, Eugen Dühring, R. Wagner, Ebrard, Wahrmund, P. de Lagarde—who of these in regard to morality and history is the least unqualified and unjust?) their constant, absurd falsifications and cosmetizings of vague concepts—"Germanic," "Semitic," "Aryan," "Christian," "German"—all that if carried on interminably could anger me seriously and lure me out of my mood of ironic toleration with which I have hitherto viewed the virtuous tendencies and Phariseeism of contemporary Germans. —And finally what do you think I feel when the name Zarathustra is mouthed by anti-Semites? . . . Your most devoted Dr. Fr. Nietzsche.

Nietzsche told his friend Overbeck of his latest annoyance with Fritsch and wryly commented,

> . . . By the way, a comic fact of which I've become more and more conscious. I have virtually an "influence"—quite subterranean, as a matter of fact, upon all radical parties (socialists, nihilists, anti-Semites, the Christian Orthodox, Wagnerians) and enjoy a curious and almost mysterious reputation. . . . In the *Anti-Semitic Correspondence* (that is mailed privately only to "reliable party members"), my name appears in almost every issue. . . . There is a uniquely anti-Semitic interpretation of *Zarathustra*, which makes me laugh greatly. (March 24, 1887)

The editor Fritsch went on an abusive counteroffensive in his November newsletter in an article "Anti-Semitism in the Mirror of a 'Philosopher of the Future.'" He condemned Nietzsche's glorification of Jews in *Beyond Good and Evil* and his attack on anti-Semites. Nietzsche, he told party adherents, is a philosophic, shallow fish that has no comprehension of national essence and is a misguided pedant, but fortunately his "books are read by no more than two dozen people."[15] In sad contrast, the *Antisemiten Catechismus*, published by Theodor Fritsch in 1877, became the handbook for anti-Jewish bigots long into the Nazi era.

To his sister's annoyance, Nietzsche viewed anti-Semitism with gleeful distaste; she was distressed when the Bayreuth camp excommunicated him and disrupted the socially good relation she had with Cosima, Richard, and their contingent; after all, she met her husband-to-be in Bayreuth. When she wanted to, Elizabeth could be quite critical of the company her brother kept, especially if it was Jewish. Shortly before and then after her marriage, she became aggressively Germanic like her Bernhard. Although Elizabeth was ensconced in the wilds of Paraguay as the doyenne of the Nueva Germania Colony for the furtherance of pure-bred Germans, in tandem with her hopelessly incompetent husband, she was never out of her brother's mind with her periodic missiles. Nietzsche felt that—even at a distance—the claws of the "Pracht-Tierchen" ("the superb little animal") were as sharp as ever. In late 1888, emboldened by a delirium barely short of the abyss, Fritz told Lisbeth of his meteoric fame: He was about to be translated worldwide. Indeed, he was busy renewing solicitations for Miss Zimmern to take up translations into English. In spite of aversions to "emancipated" women after the Lou episode, Nietzsche nevertheless held fast to the opinion of the Englishwoman "as something of a very sensible Jew," and added: "may heaven have mercy upon the European intellect if the Jewish intellect were subtracted from it!" he wrote to several friends. Other great things were in the offing: Dr. Georg Brandes was spreading his fame throughout Europe, beginning with audience-igniting lectures in Copenhagen, with reverberations being felt in intellectual circles from Paris to Russia's St. Petersburg. In his correspondences, Nietzsche waxed rapturous, and the least spectacular of his claims was that he held the fate of humankind in his hands.

On September 6, 1888, Lisbeth sweetly doused his raptures and sent her "Herzens-Fritz" ("most cherished Fritz") a forty-fourth birthday letter: ". . . I would personally have wished you an apostle other than Herr Brandes . . . who has eaten from too many platters; . . .yet, one cannot choose one's admirers . . ." She suggested that he distance himself strategically and hoped that through Brandes more suitable admirers might present themselves. She closed her letter with her tenderest love and yearning for a reunion, while seriously suggesting that he buy some land in the New Germany and make her husband an executor of his will. Nietzsche felt gored and immediately wrote his friend Overbeck about the deserter, the betraying Llama who had maligned him by writing "what bilge I was associating with—Jews who like Georg Brandes had been licking all plates." He exaggerated Lisbeth's actual words, but not by much.

In November, Nietzsche had hopes that the famous French historian Hippolyte Taine himself would undertake the translation of *Twilight of the Idols*. Also, Gast had published a highly complimentary article on Nietzsche's *The Case of Wagner* in Avenarius's *Kunstwart* belles-lettres journal. To Nietzsche's barely disguised chagrin, Avenarius had appended an editorial note to the article telling readers that he had wished for Nietzsche's work to be more scholarly than feuilletonistic; Nietzsche's book, he wrote, did justice neither to himself nor to Wagner. How Nietzsche could have expected Ferdinand Avenarius, a nephew of the deceased Meister, to react otherwise was self-deluding.[16] In addition to the *Kunstwart* review, Nietzsche expected a feature about his work to appear in the prestigious *Nouvelle Revue*. And to top all good news, the illustrious Brandes had knighted his work with the accolade "aristocratic radicalism." The time was ripe then, he wrote to his friend Deussen,[17] in his need for a large loan, to retrieve his books and rights from the publisher E. W. Fritzsch; further, in a few years the earth would tremble with the lightning blows of his books. *Zarathustra* will be read like the Bible, and historical time will be reckoned differently. Nietzsche was becoming desperate in his solicitations as, among others, he approached Deussen whom he had known for almost thirty years, but for whom he had lesser regard than for the "aristocratic" Rohde and Gersdorff. Behind Deussen's back, Nietzsche had recently praised his young wife and complimented her features as bearing resemblance to Jewish ones. One may surmise that Miss Zimmern had become a new yardstick for Nietzsche's criteria for attractiveness in women. But no matter how greatly he enjoyed being the cock of the walk at Engadine, he yearned for the company of men and minds that stimulated and challenged his intellect. Jacob Burckhardt of Basel (1818–1879), author of brilliant studies on the cultural history of the Renaissance in Italy, was the older colleague Nietzsche consistently looked up to and learned from, especially Burckhardt's love of the Renaissance and his view of it as a rediscovery of Greek antiquity.[18] The historian welcomed the brash intellectualism of the young Nietzsche and mildly encouraged it, but himself remained comfortably ensconced in his ivory tower; Burckhardt kept his distance from Nietzsche's declared war against "cultural Philistinism." He liked the tributes of his iconoclastic colleague and later reciprocated in his *Griechische Kulturgeschichte* (published posthumously, 1898–1902), which accepted Nietzsche's interpretation of Dionysianism in Greek culture. During his acquaintance with Burckhardt, Nietzsche expressed elation at the historian's professional and academic opinion of him (letter to Rohde, October 7, 1875), but he never broke through Burckhardt's private reserve nor criticized his genteel anti-Semitism. As Nietzsche's isolation grew in the late 1880s, Burckhardt, who was always one of the first to receive a copy of Nietzsche's recent works, had become even more put off by Nietzsche's obsession with nihilism and the spiritual demise of the age.

It is clear that during the last few years of Nietzsche's productive life he was openly and publicly at odds with anti-Semites as evidenced in his letters to publishers and others whom he opposed. By the same token, anti-Semites were repulsed that Nietzsche, a former Wagnerian, had "changed" and that his love of Jews wound its way through his works like a red thread.[19] On a personal level, Nietzsche's relations with individuals such as Lanzky and Zimmern were radically different in nature and affectation. However, perhaps it is fair to say that any disrespect for Lanzky on Nietzsche's part was not a result of Lanzky's ethnic or religious background, but because Nietzsche's and Lanzky's eccentric personalities were not well suited to begin with. It is likely that Nietzsche would have viewed Lanzky in like manner even had he not been Jewish. On the other hand, Nietzsche's affection for Zimmern resulted in his extolling her characteristics as "naturally, Jewish."

NOTES

1. Janz, *Friedrich Nietzsche*, 2: 250 – "Paul Lanzky."

2. Nietzsche told von Stein understanding only six sentences was "perfectly in order" and that really experiencing those sentences "would raise one to a higher level of existence than 'modern' men could attain," *EH*, "Book," sec. 1.

Karl Heinreich von Stein (1858–1887) had taken Nietzsche's place in the Wagner entourage as a tutor. He was the only person in the Wagner camp who regretted the breach between Wagner and Nietzsche and felt that there were aspects common to both despite their significant differences. He visited Nietzsche at Sils-Maria and Nietzsche promptly became infatuated with the friendly young man; he lamented von Stein's early death as that of a lost friend.

3. Carmen Kahn-Wallerstein, "Paul Lanzky erzahlt von Nietzsche: Eine Begegnung," *Neue Schweizer Rundschau* (July 1947): 268–74. On p. 271, Lanzky describes the parting.

4. Dr. Paneth had already noted Nietzsche's self-medications and use of chloral hydrate. Pharmacists honored "Dr." Nietzsche's own prescriptions.

5. Apparently, however, at the time (and before) Nietzsche wrote *Ecce Homo*, he changed his alcohol habit: "Later, around the middle of life, to be sure, I decided more and more strictly *against* all spirits: I . . . cannot advise all *more spiritual* natures earnestly enough to abstain entirely from alcohol. Water is sufficient (*EH*, "Clever," sec. 1).

6. The closest Nietzsche came to Vallombrosa was on a visit with Lanzky in Florence. The city and weather did not agree with him and he hurried back to Nice. He did enjoy Lanzky's company on walks. But, as before, he was of two minds about Lanzky's attentiveness. No one except Lanzky, he wrote to Overbeck in December 1885, had really witnessed so close at hand his penurious living and expressed such concern—something Nietzsche could not tolerate for long as unwanted sympathy.

7. Paul Lanzky's brief autobiographical sketch first appeared in *Unsere Dichter in Wort und Bild*, F. Tetzner, ed., vol. 4 (Leipzig: Robert Claussners Verlags-Anstalt, 1896), pp. 14–16. He was born in 1852 in Weissagk, near Dresden, and was orphaned early. He "instinctively" took to mathematics and the natural sciences to counter a sickly disposition. Later he studied philosophy and Romance philology at the universities of Zurich, Pisa, and Rome. Not intending to make a living at academic work, he broadened his studies and writings into generalistic areas of art, history, and economics. For reasons of health he sought the warmer climates of southern France and Italy, leading a nomadic life. His first Meister was Spinoza, then Schopenhauer and in 1881, Nietzsche, who helped to release the poet lurking inside of him. Lanzky admits to a mask, to discourage anyone from prying with curiosity into what lay underneath. "Everywhere I have found helpful people but have no friend. Young girls and women have given me loving attention but I have no wife nor lover . . . every one of my actions lies in the aim of 'being a somebody'"! The need for self-identification proved difficult, being rooted in neither a Jewish tradition nor any other definable one. He was the Wandering Jew *par excellence*. Whatever reputation Lanzky earned with his poetic, aphoristic, and journalistic writings faded very rapidly and finally sank into oblivion. Deprived of his property during the later period of fascism under Mussolini because of his Jewish origin, Lanzky was forced into exile. He found refuge in Swiss Lugano as a hotel bookkeeper and was liked for his kindly personal attitude and professional abilities; he died about 1940, an octogenarian who in his earlier life closely resembled Nietzsche as a learned itinerant, a loner, with similar traumatic sorrows and experiences. Lanzky's biographical essay, "Friedrich Nietzsche als Mensch und Dichter," appeared in volume 4 of the series *Unsere Dichter*, edited by Tetzner, pp. 19–31. His first letter was directed to Genoa in September 1883 and then to Villefranche sur Mer, where Nietzsche had met Paneth. And soon, to Lanzky's delight, a correspondence was encouraged with the Nietzsche he called the "Rektor magnificus of Basel." It was impossible to live with Nietzsche for any length of time, as he found out from 1884 to 1886 because of the Meister's strong mood swings. What struck Lanzky in particular was Nietzsche's inability to cope with the memory of Wagner and the fact that Zarathustra was Nietzsche's fictive figure and surrogate created to overcome Nietzsche's personal weaknesses.

Lanzky's writings remain literary curiosities and their titles are dedicated to the memory of the Meister Nietzsche he never forgot: *Erlöst vom Leid* (*Release from Pain*, 1887); *Abendröte: Psychologische Betrachtungen* (*Evening-glow: Psychological Observations*, 1887); *Am Mittelmeer* (*On Mediterranean Shores*, 1890); *Herbstablätter* (*Autumn Leaves*, poems, 1891); *Neue Gedichte* (*New Poems*,

1893); *Aphorismen eines Einsiedlers* (*Aphorisms of a Hermit*, 1897); *Sophrosyne* (poems, 1897); *Auf Dionysospfaden* (*On Dionysus-Paths*, poems 1898, two editions); and *Amor Fati* (his last volume of poems published in the early 1900s).

8. Resa von Schirnhofer, "Vom Menschem Nietzsche," *Zeitschrift für Philosophische Forschung* (1968): 248–60. The article contains good anecdotal material and remembered conversations.

9. Ferdinand Ernst Avenarius (1856–1923) was a son of Richard Wagner's beloved half-sister Cäcilie (née Geyer) who married Eduard Ludwig Friedrich Avenarius in 1840 and was employed by the Brockhaus publishing firm in various sales and managerial capacities. Ferdinand's brother Richard, named after Wagner, was a distinguished professor of philosophy at the University of Zurich. Nietzsche did not accurately inform himself about Avernarius who, as a twenty-five-year-old in 1881, had published a volume of poetry, *Wandern und Werden*, and chose as his mentor the lyricist Heine! His tasteful anthologies provided first forums for many respectable poets. Was it distemper or fact that caused Nietzsche to chide Avenarius as a "Jew"? The *Neue deutsche Biographie* (1952) and Peter von Gebhardt, *Geschichte der Familie Brockhaus* (Leipzig: Brockhaus, 1928), contain no tangible genealogical information to verify Nietzsche's claim. Nietzsche may have had in mind the persistent rumor (unfounded) that father Geyer had a Jewish background and that the Avernarius line had converts among its ancestors.

Professor Curt Janz, in correspondence dated January 13, 1993, informs me that the original letter in the Overbeckiana at the Basel University library contains the phrase "the Jew Herr Avenarius," but as a sign of caution or to protect Nietzsche, the editor, Bernoulli, in his published edition replaced it with dashes; the Montinari edition of Nietzsche's letters retains the original.

10. The registry information on Helen Zimmern was kindly sent to me by Herr Ulf Bolmann of the Hamburg Staatsarchiv. Born in Hamburg and then taken to England when a child, she later became a British citizen; she chose to live in Florence from 1887 on, and was a leading figure in the British colony there. She died in Florence. For other scant biographical information see: the *British Who Was Who*, vol. 8 (1929–1940); *The New York Times*, January 13, 1934, p. 13 (obituary); "Memories of Nietzsche," *The Living Age* (October 1, 1927): 272; Sander L. Gilman, *Begegnungen mit Nietzsche*, 2d ed. (Bonn: Bouvier, 1985), pp. 497–500; and Janz, *Friedrich Nietzsche*, vol. 2, passim.

11. The draft versions are retrieved and discussed in Erich F. Podach, *Friedrich Nietzsches Werke des Zusammenbruchs* (Heidelberg: W. Rothe, 1930), pp. 254f.

12. See the discussion by Kaufmann, ML, pp. 795–80, of Nietzsche's draft versions and editorial contexts.

13. Sections 21 (7, 7.8), quoted here, ostensibly were written between October 15 and part of November 1888 and were first published in facsimile by Karl-Heinz Hahn and Mazzino Montinari, *Ecce Homo: Facsimileausgabe der Handschrift* (Wiesbaden: Ludwig Reichart, 1985).

14. Yet many Christians anti-Semites, such as Nietzsche's sister and her husband, regarded themselves as the chosen, relegating the Jews to a despised status as Christ killers. When referring to the anti-Semite as a stupid Jew, Nietzsche is most likely referring to negative Jews or Christians. Calling Christians anti-Semite Jews would annoy them immensely; see for instance GM, I, 16, where he refers to *three Jews . . .* and *one* Jewess. (Jesus of Nazareth, the fisherman Peter, the rug weaver Paul, and . . . Mary). Nietzsche often pits positive Jews (ancient Hebrews and modern Jews) against negative Jews (Christians/anti-Semites).—Ed.

15. Quoted in R. F. Krummel, "Josef Paneth über seine Begegnung mit Nietzsche in der *Zarathustra*-Zeit," pp. 65–66. Another contributor, W. Hentschel, divested himself in the newsletter, two years later, of the lament that Nietzsche the former advocate of Wagnerian music had changed and that, instead, "his love of Jews winds its way through his works like a red thread," quoted in Krummel, pp. 75–76.

16. The lengthy Gast article and Avenarius note are included in Janz, *Friedrich Nietzsche* vol. 3, Dokument no. 10.

17. Deussen, one of Nietzsche's sincerest friends since Pforta days, but of whom Nietzsche was neglectful, had already given him a large sum the year before, as did Meta von Salis, to defray publication expenses.

18. *Die Kultur der Renaissance in Italien*, 1860; *Geschichte der Renaissance in Italien*, 1867.

19. Ibid., p. 214, footnote.

11

Last Days and Friendships: Brandes, Mendès, and the Birds of Prey

GEORG BRANDES

By 1887, Nietzsche needed Georg Brandes's approbation even more than Burckhardt's or anyone else's. Who was Brandes and how did the Jew scorned by Frau Förster enter the scene at the most critical period in her brother's life? It has been suggested that Nietzsche's Viennese-Jewish friends had advised him to contact Dr. Georg Brandes, in Copenhagen, whose reputation had gained him the unofficial title "Europe's Pope of letters." One might compare the influence he wielded in his time to that of Edmund Wilson in ours. Brandes, with refreshing candor, acknowledged receipt of *Beyond Good and Evil* and *Genealogy of Morals*: "I do not yet fully understand what I have read. . . . But I find much that harmonizes with my own ideals and sympathies: the depreciation of the ascetic ideals and the profound disgust with democratic mediocrity; your aristocratic radicalism." Brandes confided that Nietzsche's contempt for the morality of pity was not yet clear to him; that "some reflections on women in general" did not agree with his own line of thought; and that Nietzsche, despite his universality, was "very German" in his mode of thinking. Yet, Brandes accepted Nietzsche: "[Y]ou are one of the few people with whom I should enjoy a talk . . ." (November 26, 1887).

257

Brandes apparently had taken lightly Nietzsche's disclaimer about being German and rooted in Polish ancestry, but took seriously Nietzsche's allegiance to "good Europeanism" and his liberal though complex attitude toward Judaism and the Jews. He knew of Nietzsche also through Paul Rée and Lou Salomé, whose friendship, struck up in Berlin, he valued and in later letters and critiques he almost defensively stood up for Rée. Very quickly Brandes, with a wry sense of humor, sketched out what he and Nietzsche had in common: ". . . I see with astonishment that you are a professor and doctor. I congratulate you in any case for being intellectually so unlike a professor." Brandes also stated that, as with Nietzsche, his own country had ignored *his* work: ". . . I have my best public in the Slavonic countries. . . . I have lectured in Warsaw for two years in succession, and this year in Petersburg and Moscow in French. Thus I endeavor to break through the narrow limits of my native land . . ." (November 26, 1887).

During his reading at Nice, Nietzsche had come to appreciate the quality of mind Brandes displayed in his published essays, particularly on French literature; but with Brandes's letter in hand, he was struck by their affinities as beleaguered iconoclasts, their outsider roles, their rejection by those whose esteem they sought most. Again, here was a Jew—this time one of real academic influence—who intelligently, open-mindedly, and in the spirit of debate praised Nietzsche for his "new and original" spirit.

Brandes was born in 1842 in Copenhagen to a non-Orthodox Jewish merchant family (Cohen), and as a young man studied law and philosophy. Befriended and encouraged by Ibsen, he was in the forefront of pan-European cultural, anticlerical radicalism in Scandinavia. That cost him dearly. When a chair and professorship of aesthetics opened at the University of Copenhagen, opponents led a campaign against the candidate as an "atheistic Jew," and so he moved to Berlin in 1877. As for Nietzsche, one remembers that after his retirement from Basel, it was made clear to him that he was not acceptable any longer for an academic post at Leipzig or elsewhere. In short, Nietzsche was a Jewish Brandes, just as Brandes was a Jewish Nietzsche—almost. Brandes in his new Berlin environment frequently met with other intellectuals, including the experimental psychologist Hermann Ebbinghaus and Ferdinand Tönnies, a pioneer in sociology.[1]

It is a pity that the two independent and strongly opinionated thinkers had not established contact earlier, a meeting that would have satisfied their hunger for stimulating, creative companionship, as evidenced in their rapidly growing correspondence and Brandes's three critiques: "An Essay on Aristocratic Radicalism" (1889), which was translated into German for the *Deutsche Rundschau* a year later, and two all-too-brief critiques in 1900 to memorialize Nietzsche's death.[2] Sharp but not flamboyant, respectful but incisively critical, Brandes's "Aristocratic Radicalism" still remains a nonpedantic yet scholarly introduction to Nietzsche's works up through part IV of *Zarathustra*. He is at pains to state Nietzsche's position with extreme clarity and also to express objections he felt warranted with uncompromising firmness and historical explicitness. For instance, with polite reasoning he argued that Nietzsche needed to nuance his "master and slave morality" more finely and prune it of untenable exaggerations—obviously in regard to Judeo-Christian and Greco-Roman experience.

Brandes thought of Nietzsche as a brilliant propounder of psychological theses with "excess of personal passion," yet also faulted his lack of "scholarly accessories." He rightfully calculated that Nietzsche's attacks on the female sex and its assumed dangerousness pointed to Nietzsche's own painful experiences: "[Nietzsche] does not seem to have known many women, but those he did know, he evidently loved and hated, but, above all despised."

Brandes chides Nietzsche not only for masking his intellectual stimulation and debts to Rée in theorizing about the origin of conscience (and consciousness of debt and guilt), but also for his reluctance to thank Ernest Renan "for his conception of culture and hope of an aristocracy of intellect to seize dominion of the world." Brandes, through conversations with Lou, could only guess at the psychological complexities about "love" that haunted Nietzsche: his view of love as parasitical and as a woman's display of pity; of love as bedded in absolute trust; or, of love as the soul's overflow when a lover's needs and weaknesses move and offend the lover, prompting an embrace of the body (VM, 287). Brandes also chides Nietzsche for adopting the abusive tone of Eugen Dühring (1833–1921), although Nietzsche severely condemned Dühring, whose atheism was only exceeded by the stridency of his anti-Semitic and anti-Christian rantings. Dühring's main harangues condemned Christianity as the off-

spring of Judaism; he attacked the foreignness of the Jew as a racial inferior who was depraved, uncreative, and eager to destroy and corrupt.
Dühring's slogans went one defamatory step farther than Wagner's[3] and
became a prime source for Hitler's later diatribes. Brandes, as a secularized Jew, drew back from assailing anti-Semitism as bluntly as did Nietzsche; he combined the qualities of a civil liberties proponent and an
elitist; and he stood up for Dühring's right to free expression. Ironically,
had both Dühring and Brandes lived another decade, the hate-monger
Dühring as propaganda minister of the Third Reich would have sent the
tolerant Brandes-Cohen up in smoke in one of the Nazi crematoria.

Nietzsche called Dühring an imitator and "ape" of his own writings,
but regarded such imitations as insulting rather than flattering. There is
some thought that Nietzsche developed his ideas of the eternal return
and the nature of conscience as an extreme antithetical reaction to those
of Dühring. To construct "Gegen-Ideen" (counterideas) is in the nature
of philosophy, says Brandes, but they ought to be properly credited
without resentment. Brandes, however, did not know the root cause of
Nietzsche's fears that no doubt would have given him a closer understanding of Nietzsche. Going back to 1885, Nietzsche's earlier publisher,
Ernst Schmeitzner, was becoming the owner of a firm with a growing list
of anti-Semitic authors. A Leipzig bookseller confirmed for Nietzsche
that his books, too, were assumed by the public "to fall into the category
of anti-Semitic literature." Nietzsche became concerned: "Your and my
writings," he told Overbeck on December 6, 1885, "lie completely buried
and nonresurrectional in this anti-Semitic hole." The juxtaposition of
the names Dühring, Nietzsche, and Zarathustra roused Nietzsche to fury:
"anti-Semitism ruins everyone's finer taste buds, even those that were
originally uncoated."

Nietzsche never waffled over whose allegiance and influence he preferred: Jews' or anti-Semites'. Bernhard Förster, during his courtship of
Elisabeth, also wooed her brother with favorable mention of him in public
lectures in Berlin. That Nietzsche lost his useful Llama to the enemy camp
only added to his already firm antagonism against nationalists, and political and religious racists. In fact, at one point he seemed peeved that more
Jewish readership (as compared with Wagner's huge Jewish following) had
not materialized for him. As is clear, however, he did not cater to specific
audiences. In the spring of 1886, Nietzsche wrote his mother and Over-

beck that he had found a letter under his door, read its contents, and despite the fierce cold, danced a jig in his nightshirt. From Leipzig, Hermann Credner of Veit, an Imperial Court publisher, had written and asked to be numbered among Nietzsche's admirers. Nietzsche exclaimed: "I have never yet found such faith among Israel." Actually he had a good number of Jewish admirers in Berlin and Vienna aside from Credner. Perhaps Jesus was right in thinking that "salvation comes of the Jews" (John 4:32). And was not Zarathustra-Nietzsche a new prophet among all peoples?

It is sad that in all of the correspondence between Nietzsche and Brandes there is no overt discussion of Judaism and Jews as if both were avoiding the subject as too personal. Brandes was assimilated to European culture and completely secularized—neither asserting nor denying his Jewish identity. He regarded his origin in the Jewish community to be "of little consequence," as he wrote in an article for the *Frankfurter Zeitung*, and would have "conveniently forgotten" it if the Gentile community had not constantly reminded him of his being Jewish.[4]

In an exchange of compliments, Brandes explains that the "aristocratic radicalism" he attributed to Nietzsche well expressed his own political convictions; Brandes accepted the "good European" designation but rejected Nietzsche's designation of him as a "missionary" of culture: "I have a horror of all missionary effort—because I have come across none but moralizing missionaries—and I am afraid I do not believe in what is called culture . . ." (December 27, 1887).

Brandes had asked for a brief biographical résumé and a photo so that he could better visualize his new-found intellectual colleague. Nietzsche obliged with carefully sketched highlights: he was of Polish aristocratic lineage, despite three generations of German mothers, so that his facial likeness might be seen in the famous Polish paintings of Matejko; his grandmother belonged to the court circles of Goethe's Weimar; he described Bonn and Leipzig with "old Ritschl" after the venerable Pforta schooling; he told Brandes of the war, the flattering call to Basel, friendships with Burckhardt, intimacy with Richard and Cosima Wagner, companionships with von Meysenbug "and the sympathetic Dr. Rée"; and he wrote of physical illnesses but no mental disturbances ("my pulse was as slow as that of Napoleon").

Brandes reported on the successful lectures about Nietzsche's works that he gave to large crowds at the University of Copenhagen, and he asked Nietzsche to send his books to a number of people who could spread the word about the philosopher throughout Europe. Brandes had a teasing humor and was not averse to blasphemy:

> Do you know Bizet's widow? You ought to send her [*The Case of Wagner*] . . . She would like it. She is the sweetest and most charming of women, with a nervous tic that is curiously becoming, but perfectly genuine. . . . I could get you her address, unless it does offend you that she has not remained true to her god [Georges Bizet]—any more than have the Virgin Mary, Mozart's widow, or Mary-Louise [Napoleon] to theirs.
>
> I have given a copy of your book to the greatest of Swedish writers, August Strindberg, whom I have entirely won over to you. He is a true genius, only a trifle mad. . . . (October 6, 1886)

In a later letter, Nietzsche told Brandes that he, too, had been uncompromisingly honest even with friends when it came to issues he deemed important, notwithstanding injury to old friendships, as with Baron Reinhardt von Seydlitz and Judge Gustav Adolf Krug, who had become prominent Wagner proselytizers. He also reported a break with his brother-in-law, Förster, and "my respected friend Malwida von Meysenbug . . . who continues to confuse Wagner with Michelangelo . . ." (October 20, 1888). Brandes took much of what Nietzsche said as mock levity, including Nietzsche's genial disclaimer: "The report has been put about that I had been in a madhouse (and indeed that I had died there); nothing is farther from the truth." Not until Nietzsche sent his *Antichrist* to Princess Anna Tenicheff and she protested to Brandes at the weird appellation of the sender—"The Antichrist"—did Brandes begin to wonder about his friend's deranged sense of propriety. It was not so much a lapse in tact as the fact that Nietzsche's profound self-absorption tinged every subject he touched. Had Brandes known of the notes Nietzsche was acidly sketching, he would have understood the new dimensions of his thinking and the identity crisis developing into climactic horror: his divided self. From criticism of Judeo-Christian dogmas, he was turning toward the psychodynamics of religion as developing from without one's personality. In a sense, he was linking the Dionysiac experience explored in *The Birth of Tragedy* with that of the Old Testament prophets, Zarathustra's, Paul's on the road to Damascus, and his own. The demons and antithetical forces within his psyche, and alien oppression from without, are stunningly portrayed in the following autobiographical rumination, leading him to believe that religion is a (psychological) self-induced power:

> Among intelligent, strong, invigorated races, it is mainly the epileptic[5] who arouses the conviction that an alien [supernatural] *power* is at play here; add to that the related involuntary states of the enthusiasts, the poets, the great criminals—whose passions like love and revenge serve their discovery of extra-human powers. . . .[6]
>
> In other words, the subjective psychological concept of God is personified as an [exterior] cause. . . . The psychological logic is this: the feeling of power—when it suddenly and domineeringly overcomes a person (as is the case with all great emotions),—arouses in him a doubt about his own person: he dares not think of himself as the cause of this astonishing feeling—and so he conjectures that a stronger person, a divinity, is its [exterior] cause. (*WM*, "Genesis of Religions," 135; *KS*, III, 747, March–June 1888)

Nietzsche's tragedy lies in his inability to heal himself with his theoretical self-analyses and to see that his nightmares were indeed self-induced in the same sense that he perceived the origin of religions to be.

Nietzsche's biographically important years 1888 and 1889 have suffered intentional or rationalized falsifications, and have seen only sporadically truthful reconstruction. Lisbeth's forgeries of letters, ink blottings, erasures, destruction of originals, and other tampering with transmitted materials were systematically exposed first by the scholar Karl Schlechta.[7] Lisbeth's aim was to falsely claim that there was a firm and loving reconciliation between brother and sister and that he actually wrote that *she* understood him "more than anyone else." These alleged words of her brother became her claim as the legatee, chosen heir, and interpreter of Nietzsche. How were these distortions possible? First, she was able to use the metal-monster typewriter, delivered to Nietzsche by Rée years earlier, to produce letters she ascribed to *him*. Second, she produced the "only remaining" transcripts that she claimed to have made of letters subsequently "lost." Scholars and conscientious critics have adopted the principle that if no original exists, Elisabeth Förster-Nietzsche's "productions" are to be regarded as unreliable. Her aim, as well, was mythographic: to present her brother as a chaste, German warrior possessed of physical and intellectual manliness. Nietzsche's most compassionate friends, however, wanted to keep as long as possible a protective cover on the satyriasis of a shattered friend and colleague.

TURIN (CLAUSEN AND LOMBROSO)

At the beginning of 1888, Nietzsche was particularly restive, and hearing reports from Gast of a dry and pleasant climate in Turin, he left Nice. But first he stopped in Genoa where he "walked about like a mere shadow among memories"; it was a necessary pilgrimage in time, and the last for him there. Turin, as a city, was serious and dignified, princely with aristocratic calm; its seventeenth-century environment was replete with castles and nobility, and above all, it was affordable. For the first time in ten years, Nietzsche was fitted by a friendly tailor who chided him for his unstylish habits. From his third-floor apartment on Via Carlo Alberto, facing the "grandiose" Carignano palace and overlooking the Piazza Astello, he wrote home that his physical malaise was greatly lessened. To Gast he raved: "The evening on the Po Bridge—stupendous! Beyond good and evil"! What buoyed him was the continuing correspondence with Brandes, the completion of *The Wagner Case*, and what he said was the warm personal recognition accorded him on the local scene. To Overbeck Nietzsche reported in May that he had been visited by philosophy professor Pasquale d'Ercole at the behest of a gentleman, Carlo Clausen, who was the manager of Turin's fabulous Loscher bookstore. Nietzsche described Clausen as a Buddhist who was a quiet, modest person, and who voluntarily informed Nietzsche that he was a Jew who never converted. That delighted Nietzsche; he was always curious about a Jewish person's sense of identity—or lack of it. We remember that Nietzsche had put Gast to work years earlier with the request that he discover if Paul Lanzky was Jewish. One critic, Anacleto Verrecchia, asks the sensible question: "Of what significance was it whether or not Clausen, Lanzky, or Avenarius were Jews?" He then answers his own query: "It is far from my intention to see in it a sign of anti-Semitism, but, on the other hand, I would be cautious to give excessive weight to certain ostentatious philo-Semitic remarks by Nietzsche."[8] Verrecchia does imply correctly that Nietzsche deliberately labeled Jews in order to show his pleasure or displeasure with their person. Nietzsche, one remembers, got the habit of identifying Jews from the persistent and bigoted habits of Richard and Cosima Wagner. The hospitality of Carlo Clausen was, after all, one of the reasons Nietzsche expressed his intentions to return to Turin after his usual summer retreat in Sils-Maria.

In Turin as well resided the famous Jewish-Italian physician and professor of criminology, Cesare Lombroso (1835–1909), who had studied at the University of Vienna and later during thirty years of research wrote two books of especial importance for Nietzsche, *Genius and Madness* and *The Criminal Man*.[9] Haunted by a threatening father-ghost, Nietzsche was terrorized by the thin line dividing sanity from madness: his father's deteriorated state just before death and the line between this life and the beyond from which the "Hamletic mole" came. With concern, he viewed the fragility of genius and its relationship to madness as he saw it in models close at hand: the self-immolated poet Friedrich Hölderlin, Heinrich Heine in his mattress-grave, and Count Giacomo Leopardi whose genius yielded to black depression.

Lombroso vaguely connected madness, epilepsy, and genius. But mainly his studies of diverse human physical measurements and comparative studies of temperaments—passive and aggressive—led him to believe in innate, inherited characteristics possessed by the "born criminal," beliefs he later modified by positing criminogenic factors of pathology and environment. Throughout he held that the "true criminal" was a subspecies of man with an atavistic origin. Nietzsche's "instinctual man" closely resembles Lombroso's, as do Nietzsche's problematic discussions and eulogies of the criminal. Where Lombroso argued for measures of rehabilitation of the criminal, a symbiosis between himself and society, Nietzsche objected to this as the domestication and taming of atavistic impulses. Still, Lombroso was inspired by Nietzsche and collected everything he wrote. He eventually gave his collection to the National Library of Turin. Although their paths did not cross in Turin, it is likely that Nietzsche's work encouraged Lombroso to publish a monograph in 1904 in which he noted that the foolishness of anti-Semites lies in their atavism, their brutality; Nietzsche's tendency was to scorn anti-Semites as cowards.

The "Buddhist Jew" Clausen in conversations with Nietzsche noted his interest in the Vedas and the old laws of Manu and also obtained for him an edition of Louis Jacolliot's *Les législateurs religieux: Manu—*

Möise—Mohamet (Paris: Lacroix, 1876). The book set off an important train of thought in Nietzsche.[10]

Nietzsche enjoyed a stroke of good fortune in having found lodgings near the main post office and the palace with the family of his landlord, David Fino, a newspaper-kiosk owner, who respected and grew to like the strange professor with his even stranger routines. Nietzsche, too, liked the Finos and he procured a stove for them; in turn, they lent him a piano and extended many other courtesies. In June, Nietzsche told his landlord that after his vacation, he would return. That he did on September 21. But here conceivably was his greatest mistake: Turin, whatever else it meant and was to mean for Nietzsche, was strongly impacted musically by a Wagner cult. It was the wrong atmosphere for his work and obsessively he set about to collect, in shortened form, his older writings about Wagner, going back a decade, with the title *Nietzsche Contra Wagner: Records of a Psychologist.* His aim, avowed in a short preface, was to leave no reader in doubt about himself and Wagner: "We are antipodes." Nietzsche stated that his readers were everywhere: "In Copenhagen and Stockholm, in Paris, in New York—but not in Europe's flatlands, Germany . . ." (page proofs dated Christmas 1888). Nietzsche's rivalry with the dead Wagner, the "seraphic father," regrettably never ended, but intensified instead to paranoid proportions. Parallel with that was an escalating self-deification. Select people, such as Helen Zimmern, Meta, and Resa, were shown the rock of revelation at Sils-Maria and the meditation bench sacramentalized with Nietzsche's name plate near one of the Silvaplana lakes. Signs began to offer themselves to the Fino family that their esteemed professor was sliding off track.

One day Nietzsche summoned the Finos and asked that every decorative item be removed from the wall of his room because "it had to be turned into an abode like a temple." When that had been accomplished, he announced a holiday and the lighting of all Turin streets because Italy's king and queen were expected to visit his temple. He asked that telegrams be delivered to their royal highnesses; but Fino and the telegraph office thought better of it. Sometime later Fino took his lodger in tow when two deeply relieved policemen turned the distraught professor over to him, relating a peculiar incident: Nietzsche had weepingly fallen around the neck of a horse he had ostensibly saved from a bashing by its master, and Nietzsche's grip could barely be loosened. Pretending to be a friend of the Fino family, a psychiatrist was invited to the house and in four visits calmed his suspicious patient.[11]

Nietzsche's faculties were not totally impaired as yet. There were, of course, a number of signs of his own dark premonitions, if not a will to the abyss, and others quite horrifying. He had cheerfully written his mother that he was on his way to becoming a great personality in Europe and was treated as "a little prince in Turin"; even the fruit peddler-woman had found the sweetest bunches of grapes for him: "great things will come to pass the next year," he predicted. Nietzsche's need to impress his mother remained unabated, although she was in the dark about his writings; for instance, the title *Twilight of the Idols* (*Götzen*) she mistook for exorcism of the ghosts (*Geister*). But if *he* were honored especially by prominent people, that was something she could cherish, bask in, and accept as bringing credit to her long-dead husband, Ludwig.

MENDÈS AND THE BIRDS OF PREY

Because in previous years Nietzsche had signed letters to his family and friends with titles such as Prince Eichhorn, Prince Vogelfrei, and Prince Friedrich,[12] with the onset of his breakdown years later it was perfectly logical, but not altogether sane, to address a note to Cosima Wagner: "To the Princess Ariadne," elevating her to his rank, and informing her mysteriously that "a certain buffoon has . . . finished the *Dionysus-Dithyrambs*" (January 3, 1889). The Dionysus poems, however, were dedicated *not* to Cosima but to Catulle Mendès, a virtuoso French poet and in origin a Sephardic (Spanish) Jew.[13] The dedicatory notes, referring to Mendès's ballet *Isoline*, came in three rapid stages:

> . . . dedicated to the poet of the *Isoline*, with great esteem/Nietzsche-Caesar/Turin, January 1, 1889.

> . . . for the poet of the *Isoline*, my friend and satyr with great/distinction: may he transmit my gift to mankind/Nietzsche-Dionysus/Turin January 1, 1889.

Here the Jew Mendès is enjoined to play the role Nietzsche had assigned to Jews, not as "originators" but as "transmitters" of ideas; in this case, his own. The connective tissue in Nietzsche's inner thinking is uncanny. Mendès is fantasied as a satyr to Nietzsche-Dionysus and, although critics have been puzzled by the dedication to Mendès, the "madness" note is nothing more than an open riddle easy of solution:

> Granting humanity limitless benefaction, I give it my dithyrambs, I place them in the hands of the poet of the *Isoline*, the greatest and principal satyr living today—and not only today . . . [signed] Dionysus.

"Ariadne" holds multiple meanings for Nietzsche, often involving Cosima. In the dithyrambs she had been vanquished and relegated to Zarathustra's labyrinth; but in Nietzsche's mythologems Ariadne also is a metaphor for the soul abandoned by the hero (Wagner?) and in her dream approached by the over-hero (*Über-Held*, Zarathustra); in the Ariadne poem the figure also undergoes a gender change. Whatever the mystery of Ariadne, it is the Jewish satyr-Mendès—and not Cosima or Llama—who is to be the legatee of the Dionysus poems.

Cosima in an 1870 diary entry noted that Nietzsche came to know Mendès at Tribschen personally as one of the leading French Wagnerians. Mendès was to remain an enthusiast of Wagner's music, but his ardor cooled after Wagner's brutal anti-French vituperations in the wake of the Franco-Prussian war. Catulle Mendès, his wife, Judith (Gautier), and Villiers de L'Isle-Adam paid homage to Wagner at Tribschen. L'Isle-Adam was temporarily welcome, having dedicated a French article to "Richard Wagner, Prince of Profound Music." Judith, a voluptuous woman thirty-three years younger than Wagner and who made Cosima look like a scarecrow by comparison, caused the composer nearly to lose his mind with passion. He was reported to have climbed trees and scaled walls to demonstrate his athleticism in reaching Judith's apartment for trysts among silks and satin with his "*douce amie.*" Judith stoked the fires for the sensuous music of *Parsifal* (an opera Wagner later called the "most Christian" of music), and he tried to countermand King Ludwig's insistence that his royal court conductor, the Jewish Levi, be chosen for any subsidized performance. Catulle Mendès had separated from Judith; Cosima (for the sake of the opera) swallowed her pride, but forbade further correspondence between Richard and Judith. The memory of Judith was to be a thorn in Cosima's side.

In December 1888, in the mind of Nietzsche, the bounds of time had collapsed and many figures and events imperceptly merged. To his mother, Nietzsche wrote a cheerful Christmas note about his well-being, ending with a postscript, "First snows, lovely!!!" In another letter, his mood turned mournful: "Snow. After so many days of dry and lovely weather . . . it was a monotonous snowfall mixed with rain that changed the streets into mud-puddles and left a great sadness in one's soul." The phrasing of the last sentence has an elegiac simplicity that renders a state of mind perfectly. Moreover, the last of the Dionysus poems, the dithyrambs composed in Turin, are magnificently somber and they cascade with expressionistic power. Nietzsche's last poems, notes, and letters reflect autobiographical stages of changing identifications, until Nietzsche finally is metamorphosed into Dionysus. In one of Nietzsche's most riddlesome, knotted, and long poems, "Zwischen Raubvögeln" ("Among Birds of Prey"), he autobiographically expresses the plaint of the "loner"; the one who is terrifyingly "einsam," and he mocks the other loners: the hanged god (Jesus) and the dismembered god (Dionysus). He is a riddle, convulsed like a question mark between two nothings; a question mark to be resolved by birds of prey. That special self-knowledge allows him to be judge and self-executioner. His yearning for a mystical union with the Dionysiac is expressed with tantalizing cryptomnesic force:

Jetzt—	Now
zwischen zwei Nichtse	Between two nothings,
eingekrummt,	misshapen,
ein Fragezeichen,	a question mark,
ein müdes Rätsel	a weary riddle
ein Rätsel für *Raubvögeln* . . .	a riddle for *birds of prey* . . .
sie werden dich schon lösen,	—they will surely "solve" you,
sie hungern schon nach	they hunger already
deiner "Lösung."	for your "solution."[14]

What connects this to the Dionysiac experience? In Nietzsche's *Birth of Tragedy*, the experience is central to his perception of a pre-Homeric symbiosis of tragedy and religion and its communal audience: the need *not* for priestly purification, but for physical purgation in a medically cathartic sense. It was Jacob Bernays, Nietzsche's source decades earlier, who had brilliantly delineated the difference between spiritual *purification* (wrongly assumed to have been Aristotle's view of audience-affect) and the physical *purgation* that Bernays argues was in fact meant by Aristotle's "catharsis."[15] In talking about the dramatic presentation of a terrifying situation that can have an oppressive and painful effect, Bernays explains that since fear itself is not a reasoning emotion, such horror pictures (*Schreckbilder*) will cause the viewer *inner* convulsion, a shrinking into oneself (*zusammenkrümmen*), the "eingekrümmt" of the "Birds of Prey" poem—instead of an empathy that opens up floodgates in the viewer and expands the personal self outward into that of an entire community. Tragic fear comes through release (purgation) and not suppression, when loosened tremors sensually dissolve and stream through humans. This kind of emotional upsurge suggested in the "Birds of Prey" poem seized Nietzsche ecstatically.

Alarums from Nietzsche's flat caused his landlady to peep through the keyhole and to witness a scene she had not bargained for—a nude, prancing, and dancing Dionysian professor totally uninhibited. Similar scenes were quietly and confidentially also reported by the unimpeachable Professor Franz Overbeck, who voiced the suspicion that Nietzsche was hiding irrevocably behind his last, libidinous Dionysiac mask.

Christmases had always been traumatic, migrainous days for Nietzsche and were rooted in his ambivalent feelings—the bliss of Christmases in youth against his later revulsion; sometime early in 1889, he crossed the line into madness. Everyone related to Nietzsche offered self-serving explanations. Lisbeth wanted the world to know that excessive medication and the killing pace of workaholic writing during the past years (indeed they were unmatched performances of blinding speed and fierce, polemic exertions) pushed her brother over the brink. Nietzsche's friend Gast implored Overbeck to subscribe to these views because otherwise all of Nietzsche's works would be invalidated in the public's mind as having been written by a madman. Wagnerites claimed to see signs of madness years earlier in Nietzsche when he abandoned Wagner for the Israelite Dr. Rée. Psychologists subscribed to various types of dementia. Some medical people, upon negligible evidence (and without benefit of definitive medical reports), diagnosed his madness as progressive, tertiary paralysis caused by venereal disease resulting from bisexual, luetic contacts in Cologne during the sixties and Messina in the early eighties.

Since no autopsy was ever performed on Nietzsche, and doctors in his lifetime found no bodily lesions, the physical answers will be as moot as they are irrelevant. In addition, there are suggestions of hereditary mental illness, horrific sinusitis, killer-migraine, or some atypical disease.

With the fervor of ancient apocalyptic prophets and New Testament gospelers, Nietzsche had told Miss Zimmern and a few others, in confidence, that his testaments—*Ecce Homo* and *The Antichrist*—were annunciations of the new kingdom and the advent of Nietzsche's global rule.[16] The translation of his latest works into English, he sardonically suggested, would please the English with the exposures of and attacks upon Germans by a German writer. Delusions of grandeur fueled by megalomania prompted Nietzsche to ask that the publisher ready an edition of 400,000 copies of *Ecce Homo* for a world about to experience a new order.

Jews were to be his most potent artillery to bring about the new revaluation. There was consistent reasoning in this. If Judaism under the mask of Christianity destroyed the pagan world and conquered it, Jews could be enlisted for another explosive purpose. And so, from the submerged dark continent of Nietzsche's mind, an ominous beast was released. A letter especially drafted for Brandes reveals it, in which Nietzsche refers to his notebooks: "Here we possess a blow that will exterminate Christianity; it is quite apparent that the only international power that has an interest-instinct for the extinction of Christianity belongs to the Jews. . . . Consequently we must be sure of securing the decisive capability of this race in Europe and America" (December 10, 1888).

There was mad logic in all this: if the (negative) *ressentiment* of ancient Jews turned the world upside down, the *ressentiment* of the modern Jew could do so again, but this time constructively. All this is quite consistent with what Nietzsche wrote earlier in the year in notes for *The Will to Power*: "The concept of power, whether of God and of Man, always includes the ability both to help and to harm. So it is with the Arabs and so with the Hebrews. And so it is with all strong races" (352).

What to the anti-Semite was the alleged specter and fear of a cabalistic international Jewry was taken by Nietzsche to be a fact or potential he thought to be in need of exploiting. Nietzsche, no anti-Semite, shared negative stereotypical perceptions about Jewry with anti-Semites, despite the fact that the "atheistic" Georg Brandes had given him no cause to believe in any wish for the destruction of Christianity or any other religion.

As in former times, Nietzsche again experienced a state of disembodiment, but this time he saw himself buried—a fearful dreamlike premonition. With dizzying speed in notes and letters, Nietzsche kept changing identities, each one rooted in some explainable logical connection and form of reality or anchored in his mission: "I am the tyrant . . . of Turin," or he would stop pedestrians, telling them, "I am God, disguised in order to approach humans."[17]

The fact that the days with the Wagners still burdened his mind is attested to by the last "mad" notes and cards to Cosima. The only one released for publication by Lisbeth during her lifetime read: "Ariadne, I love you." This was to be taken as proof positive that Nietzsche was passionately fixed on a female, on one woman, though it was Cosima.[18] But in the absence of any verification from the Wagner camp of this alleged note or the original, it needs to be taken as an invention by Lisbeth.

In a pertinent Dionysus poem, "Ariadne's Lament," Nietzsche has vanquished Ariadne, "Ich bin dein Labyrinth"—she is lodged and subject within *his* labyrinth. In another authentic letter, he tells Frau Cosima that he, a divine fool, has just finished the *Dionysus Dithyrambs* and has gone through many incarnations: Buddha, Dionysus, Alexander, Caesar, Lord Bacon (the real Shakespeare, as no commoner could have written so nobly!): "[T]he heavens rejoice at my existence," "I have also hung upon the cross," Nietzsche proclaims. A final note asked her to let all of Bayreuth know about his "glad tidings"—of Dionysus' resurrection. Cosima lost *little* time doing so. But the intriguing feature of Nietzsche's longer note was his implicit avowal of Buddhistic beliefs in incarnations, variations of Schopenhauerian ideologies that praised Buddhism as a Christianity without theology. And in spirit, Nietzsche steered close also to Wagnerian themes.

Much in the text of Nietzsche's mad notes are flashbacks to other ideological and personal patterns. The pathology of devolution is played out over a period of several weeks and for Nietzsche it peaked in a letter to Overbeck and his wife, with some testy remarks:

> To friends Overbeck and wife. Although up to now, you have given only little credence to my ability to pay debts, I hope to prove still that I am a person who can repay debts, to you for instance . . . I am having all anti-Semites shot at once. (Written on the 4th or 6th of January, 1889; received in Basel on January 7, 1889)

Nietzsche was in the mood to repay debts: to shoot anti-Semites he thought had personally done him harm, to reward Jews who had helped him, and to enlist Jews in his revaluative cause. Moreover, he unloaded horrendous grudges. Von Bülow, who years earlier returned Nietzsche's musical compositions with the plea that he not "rape the Muse" ever again—and his similar treatment of Peter Gast—was the subject of Nietzsche's curse: "Herr Hans von Bülow . . . I sentence you to the 'Lion of Venice' [Peter Gast]—that he may devour you . . ." ([signed] Dionysus/ Turin, January 4, 1889). Everything in Nietzsche's mad notes was anchored in autobiographical reality. His rapid change of personalities meant that he was heading for identity confusion and a loss of self.[19]

AN ODD TRIO (NIETZSCHE, OVERBECK, AND DR. BETTMAN)

When Overbeck received Nietzsche's letter, alarm bells rang. He quickly consulted Burckhardt, who had received the "I-am-God" letter, and both sought the advice of a psychiatrist, Dr. Wille; all agreed that a state of emergency existed. Overbeck undertook the eighteen-hour train trip from Basel. What greeted him on his arrival at Nietzsche's flat was something he had to share at once with his wife, in a long, distressed letter dated Tuesday, January, 8, '89, from the Grand Hôtel de Turin:

> Dearest wife, . . . Let me tell you about the horrible moment when Nietzsche fell into my arms and dissolved into tears, having collapsed as well into convulsive shudders and groanings. . . . His mind is completely gone, even the manner in which he recognized me has somewhat of a passionate recollection of things. I would rather tell you, dearest, how things finally fell into place. As a traveling [helper] companion I have only a young doctor who very readily offered his services for monetary remuneration. Up to now Nietzsche is harmless and in many respects like a child, while to other people [the Finos] he appears frightful, but certainly, he is not dangerous. . . . For Thursday evening dinner, please be prepared to receive the young doctor. . . .[20]

Lisbeth later accused Overbeck of having ignored signs of trouble when Nietzsche signed himself "Dionysus" and "the Crucified," and, like other friends, having thought that Nietzsche was indulging in grotesque humor and pranks. Overbeck was unprepared and incompetent to cope with the ecstatic satyr in Turin pounding out Wagner chords on the piano. As a matter of record, it was the solicitous Fino family—and the generous German consulate—that provided the mysterious travel-companion doctor who facilitated Nietzsche's leaving Turin with little uproar. Lisbeth stopped just short of slandering and vilifying the unnamed "adventurer" doctor whose name slipped with Overbeck's mind *because* the adroitness of the stranger contrasted with Overbeck's own ineptness. Overbeck's memory lapse was repaired, however, when interviewed by a Leipzig neurologist, Dr. Julius P. Möbius, for a book, *Über das Pathologische bei Nietzsche* (a deeply flawed work about the nature of Nietzsche's illness published in 1902, which predicted an atypically long period of progressive paralysis). Möbius reported Overbeck as saying that

> In Turin he [Overbeck] found a Jewish man who offered his services as a caretaker (though he was not) for insane people, and whose participation helped him to complete a bold task. Nietzsche lay abed and refused to get up. The Jewish man persuaded him that royal receptions and festivities were being readied for him. Nietzsche arose, dressed, and went along to the railway station. There he wanted to embrace everyone, but the companion explained to Nietzsche that this was inappropriate for such a great personage as himself; and Nietzsche calmed down; with the help of enormous quantities of sedatives Nietzsche was subdued and all three arrived in Basel peacefully.[21]

An odd trio: Nietzsche with David Fino's royal nightcap as headdress and grimacing fiercely, the terrified Overbeck appealing to the Jewish doctor to help control the satyr, and the doctor's flattering acts. They succeeded in warding off any would-be visitors to their train compartment. When Mobius's account was published, Overbeck hastily penned a corrective in his copy of Möbius's book, explaining that any possible anti-Semitic implications in his emphasis on the "Jewish" person involved in Nietzsche's removal from Turin was farthest from his mind. Rather, Overbeck stated that this person had rendered "valuable and most satisfactory services." Still, he did not mention the *name* of the Jewish person, although from a letter in the posthumous Overbeckiana collection there is a letter to Dr. Leopold Bettman (15 Corso Oporto, Turin, from Basel, January 11,

1889), in which Overbeck gracelessly asks that Bettman, who was genuinely solicitous of Nietzsche, desist from any further activity in Nietzsche's business. Overbeck undeniably expressed "satisfaction" with Bettman's services, yet he groused about the high hotel and professional bills that were exacted. The question of money was not inconsiderable for Overbeck, who was concerned that the sources of Nietzsche's pension were running dry.

Dr. Bettman, who had the confidence of the German consulate, was a dentist with some medical background, and he probably was a Prussian citizen with a residence in Turin. It may be that Overbeck, as Verrecchia suggests, feared embarrassment that a Jewish dentist, not a medical psychiatrist, was the one who had taken over the delicate transportation of Nietzsche. Here Overbeck resembled his friend Nietzsche, plagued with all kinds of irritations: certainly he was no categorical philo-Semite nor an anti-Semite, but he apparently resented his indebtedness to Bettman and the Finos whose friendly help was beyond compensation.

JENA AND BEYOND

The rest of the story has been told and retold. Overbeck had learned invaluable psychological lessons from Dr. Bettman and on the 10th of January told Nietzsche that he must enter Basel "incognito." At the asylum, he introduced Nietzsche to Dr. Ludwig Wille and Nietzsche correctly remembered having had a conversation with him years earlier on the subject of religious madness. Nietzsche's mother, with the help of asylum personnel, succeeded in bringing her son to the clinic in Jena (closest to Naumburg) on January 17–18, but not without Nietzsche's terrifying outbursts against her. Overbeck wrote to Gast: "It's over with Nietzsche," surmising that Nietzsche's new mask was permanent; he no longer wanted freedom. And indeed it *was* over.

At Jena University's psychiatric clinic, for the next thirteen months, with partial time off in his mother's care, there was no improvement; on the contrary, there was complete regression into all stages of the past, mentally and physically, even to unweaned toilet habits. When Nietzsche became amenably submissive he was released into his mother's care. Along with a faithful governess, she attended to his everyday needs.

His most soothing therapy was the hour-long release of moods on the piano; Franziska welcomed Fritz back to her bosom, and she was made happy by his willing and passive companionship at church Sunday mornings. *Pace* the Antichrist! Was it flight from reality, or taking flight to a state of Nirvana? The riddle is insoluble.

In the autumn of 1890, Lisbeth returned from Paraguay to engage in propaganda work and financial solicitations for her New Germania; but she soon also took a hand in publishing editions of her brother's works and deviously assuming proprietorship. In 1893, the New Germania venture on the burning-hot plains in the interior of Paraguay collapsed after Bernhard Förster committed suicide; the settlers felt they had been swindled all along.* Lisbeth returned home in 1893 and with incredible tenacity created an archive in Weimar three years later, under her sole control, and transferred their residence. Franziska died in April of 1897 and her son was bedridden until he, too, gave up the ghost and died after a stroke on August 25, 1900.

The millennium Nietzsche promised had not arrived, but Lisbeth choreographed a hagiographic farewell celebration that resembled an ascension ceremony for her brother at the family plot in the village of Röcken. The program called for "the tolling of the old bells that first greeted Friedrich Wilhelm Nietzsche on the day of his birth"; ironically, it had been the sound of those bells that visited Nietzsche in nightmares throughout his life. "Song of Lament" "sung by Frau Förster's *women* friends . . ."; "Klange" by Johannes Brahms; numerous valedictions and community farewells; and people reciting passages from *Zarathustra*, the Persian immoralist who brought "pagan" tidings, were included in the festivities. This fealty-drama took place in the cemetery of a Christian church and makes the biographer Curt P. Janz rightly wonder about the ceremonial improprieties rendered unto the uncompromising Antichrist. If one takes this scene as an exaltation of Nietzsche, it also may be regarded as a denigration of his works and philosophy as he was lowered into hallowed Christian ground: Nietzsche had wanted burial at his "rock of revelation" near Sils-Maria.

Lisbeth, a Llama to the last, also brushed aside her brother's heartfelt

---

*A century later, history mocked the Försters as Paraguayan Indians intermarried with the original colonists, leaving *no* pure-blood Germans; the remnant subsists on charity from far-away ancestral Germany.

wish, expressed to Hermann Levi in October 1887, which stated that he had wanted a *male* choir to sing his "Hymn to Life," with lyrics by Lou Salomé, who was never dislodged from his mind.[22] Lisbeth, however, proved that from her brother's funeral day on she was fully in charge of his reincarnation.

A huge gravestone was put in place similar to the one Nietzsche had ordered belatedly at considerable expense, in the late eighties, for his deceased father's grave. Under Lisbeth's ministrations, within a decade the publication of her brother's works and foreign translations were to proceed at full throttle. After all, that course was legitimized by her cousin Mayor Adalbert Oehler, who at the graveside claimed publicly that Lisbeth was the privileged advocate for her brother's "works, thoughts, honor, fame, and name." He carried the travesty further by also claiming that "Friedrich Nietzsche gently expired in her arms, with the name of his beloved sister, 'Elisabeth,' exhaled through his tired lips."[23]

Finally, at Röcken's cemetery, Peter Gast's parting words for Nietzsche—"My immortal friend"—appropriately did border on blasphemy, and prophecy of sorts: "Peace unto your ashes! Holy be your name unto all coming generations!" The phoenix did rise posthumously from the ashes and soared along with Wagner's—well beyond even the heights of fame and notoriety both had dreamed of in their lifetimes.

NOTES

1. Years later Brandes returned home as a celebrated scholar-critic; in 1902 he was given the university chair previously denied him and he continued his literary reign almost up to his death in 1927.

2. Georg Brandes, *Friedrich Nietzsche*, trans. A. G. Chater (London: W. Heinemann, 1914). This volume contains the correspondence between Nietzsche and Brandes, 1887–1888, and Brandes's subsequent critical Nietzsche essays.

3. Friedrich Engels called Dühring "the Richard Wagner of philosophy— but without Wagner's talents," Gutman, *Richard Wagner, The Man, His Mind, His Music*, p. 402, n. 6.

4. Quoted in part by Maurice Fishberg, *The Jews: A Study of Race and Environment* (London: W. Scott, 1911), pp. 467–68.

5. Nietzsche here refers to ancient Greek belief in the "divine madness" of epileptics and seers.

6. Nietzsche romanticized the atavistic, untamed power-instincts of criminals. This is something Strindberg, to whom Brandes had introduced Nietzsche by way of correspondence, criticized by telling him—as a corrective—to read the work of the physician and criminologist Cesare Lombroso. Nietzsche's obsession with the *Carmen* story also centers on the drama of love and instinctive revenge, the ultimate crime of passion.

7. *Friedrich Nietzsche, Werke in drei Bänden*, ed. Karl Schlechta (Munich: Carl Hauser Verlag, 1956). See the editor's "Philological Afterword," vol. 3, pp. 1383ff.

8. Anacleto Verrecchia, *Die Katastrophe Nietzsches in Turin* (Vienna: H. Böhlaus, 1986), p. 79 (translated from the Italian *La catastrophe di Nietzsche a Turino*, 1978). Verrecchia had difficulty in finding a German publisher for his demythologizing study of Nietzsche's last days, with documentary research and interviews of Turin inhabitants.

9. *Genius and Madness* was translated into German as *Genie und Irrsinn* in 1864; *L'Uomo delinquente*, 1876 (*The Criminal Man*), 3 vols.

10. Cf. The letter to Peter Gast, May 31, 1888; Jacolliot's books, especially his *Bible dans l'Inde*, contributed to the Aryan myths prevalent during that time.

In Nietzsche's letter to Gast, after reporting of Jacolliot's work, he writes that the Jews are "transmitters" ("they invent nothing") of ideas. Although this remark appears to dilute much of what Nietzsche had praised in Jewish history in his writings, something more subtle than ruminations over the laws of Manu and the Vedas is at work here, I [Mandel] think. It could be that Nietzsche, who appreciated Brandes but felt indebted to him, was expressing an underlying hostility toward Brandes as a "transmitter" of Nietzsche's own philosophy.

[It could also be that Nietzsche, at the end of the letter in which he is referring to Jacolliot's work, is simply *describing* the role of the Jews as presented in Jacolliot's book, which upheld the myth of the Germanic Aryan race. Nietzsche writes: "The medieval organization looks like a wondrous groping for a restoration of all the ideas which formed the basis of primordial Indian-Aryan society —but with pessimistic values which have their origin in the soil of racial *décadence*. Here, too (in Jacolliot), the Jews seem to be merely transmitters—they invent nothing."—Ed.]

11. Verrecchia, *Die Katastrophe Nietzsche in Turin*, pp. 260 ff.

12. In 1882, he had styled himself "Prinz Vogelfrei" (a free-as-a-bird wanderer) and had composed homoerotic poems for *The Gay Science*, and during his days in Nice he had signed letters to his family "Your Prince" . . . "Prinz Eichhorn" (recalling dramatic figures he and Lisbeth had invented in childhood). When Lanzky's courtship in Nice inflated Nietzsche's ego, he also signed off as "Prince Friedrich."

13. Catulle Mendès (1843–1909). R. J. Hollingdale believes that the dedication to Mendès was "already close to the region of the irrational," *Dithyrambs of Dionysos* (Redding Ridge, Conn.: Black Swan Books, 1984), pp. 11–12. Others surmise that Nietzsche had placed the poems in the hands of the Parisian Mendès because he had written the satirical novel *Le roi vierge* (the virginal king, Wagner's royal benefactor, King Ludwig). Plausible is Ernst Podach's surmise that Nietzsche in Turin regularly read the *Journal des Débats* and saw a notice about a Paris premiere of Mendès's ballet *Isoline, contes de fées* (tales of the fairies), in ten scenes, Podach, *WZ*, 372. Nietzsche also drafted letters to Mendès, January 1, 1889, quoted here.

14. Cf. Philip Grundlehner, *The Poetry of Friedrich Nietzsche* (Oxford: Oxford University Press, 1986), for further commentary. See especially Nietzsche's parable of the lambs and the birds of prey in GM, I, 13. Lambs clearly refer to Christians, "birds of prey" quite likely refer to Jews.—Ed.

15. Jacob Bernays, *Zwei Abhandlungen über die aristotelische Theorie des Drama* (Darmstadt: Wissenschaftliche Buchgesellschaft, 1857, 1876; reprinted 1968). The influential essays by Jacob Bernays are models of scholarship and elegance.

16. In a retrieved draft passage Nietzsche wrote: "Final Consideration: If we could dispense with wars, so much the better. I can imagine more profitable uses for the twelve billion now paid annually for the armed peace we now have in Europe; there are other means of winning respect for physiology than field hospitals—Good; *very* good even: since the old God is abolished I am prepared to rule the world—." (Kaufmann, *ML*, 800).

17. Lest Nietzsche's transformation into God be thought apocryphal, we see, in retrospect, assertions toward self-deification. In *Ecce Homo*, he mockingly assumes the tone of a theologian: "it was God himself who concluded his labors [Nietzsche's completion of *Twilight*] and lay down as a serpent under the Tree of Knowledge: in this fashion he recuperated from being God . . . the Devil is merely the idleness of God on the Seventh Day . . ." (*EH*, "Beyond Good and Evil," 2). Elsewhere he writes: On September 30, "a great victory [completion of the *Antichrist*]; seventh day; a god takes his leisure on the banks of the Po" (*EH*, "Twilight," sec. 3). And a letter to Nietzsche's esteemed older colleague Burckhardt opens with the regret that he would rather have remained a Basel professor than have become God (January 5, 1889).

18. Verrecchia, *Die Katastrophe Nietzsches in Turin*, p. 228, makes this point emphatically.

19. Although Nietzsche wrote and thought a great deal about the assumption of masks—"my face is my best mask," he said in *Ecce Homo*, he showed no sign of being aware of how dangerous identity confusion, exchange, or loss could be nor did he realize the possible fatality of willed or unconscious states of dis-

embodiment. Rainer Maria Rilke, Lou Salomé's later lover, knew Nietzsche's work and could hardly have escaped knowing Nietzsche's fascination with masks and identity associations, particularly in *Beyond Good and Evil*. In his novel appropriately translated by John Linton as *The Journal of My Other Self* (1910), Rilke in the guise of his alter ego, Malte Laurids Brigge, postures and dresses in different masks before a mirror as the mirror becomes the stronger and he becomes its image. It is a lengthy and imagined—but psychologically real—horror event and it may be Rilke's vision of the Dionysian figure by which Nietzsche was transfixed.

20. Verrecchia, *Die Katastrophe Nietzsches in Berlin*, pp. 284–85.

21. Janz, *Friedrich Nietzsche*, 3: 42.

22. One of his drawings in the Jena psychiatric clinic shows himself and Lou embracing.

23. Janz, *Friedrich Nietzsche*, 3, document 20.

Appendix I

Nietzsche and Anti-Semitism— A Survey

Of anti anti-Semitic matters. The Jew, in an absolute sense, is clever: to meet a Jew is a pleasure, given the fact that one lives among Germans. Their cleverness [*Gescheitheit*, sensibleness] prevents them from becoming foolish after our fashion, that is, in becoming nationalistic. They themselves are an antidote against the ultimate sickness plaguing European common sense. From long ago they have been inoculated all too well—even bloodied somewhat—to fall victim to the rabies of nationalism.

In the midst of an unstable Europe, they are perhaps the strongest race: they are superior to all of Western Europe, something that is attributable to the length of their development. Their [societal] organization presupposes a richer "becoming" and a greater number of stages [in their history] than other nations can give evidence of. But that, almost, is a formula for completeness. . . .

A race, like any kind of organic creation, can only grow or deteriorate: there is no standing still. A race that has not deteriorated is a race that has grown continually. Perhaps here as well, growth is synonymous with an achievement of completeness. The duration of its existence then is decisive in regard to the level [*Höhe*, height] of its development. The oldest must become the highest.

In modern Europe, the Jews grazed the border of the most supreme intellectual form: the form of genial buffoonery. With Offenbach, with Heinrich Heine, the potency of European culture is really transcended: the option of his kind of intellectuality is not available to other races. . . . The oldest and latest European culture has Paris: but the most pampered Parisians, such as the brothers Goncourt, have accorded honor to Heinrich Heine along with the Abbé Galiani and the Count de Ligne as the most sublime form of the Parisian spirit—curiously enough, three foreigners! (*UW*, II, 1113)

Among Nietzsche's declared distastes for anti-Semitism—that is, anti-Jewish activities and persecutions—is his contempt for the practitioners' essential cowardice and lack of character (as he put it in *UW*, I, 676). He counterattacks anti-Semitic charges *without* abandoning his criticism of certain features of Judaism. The tight wording of some passages has a tart tone whose irony requires careful reading:

That the Jews have been adjudged the worst people on earth perfectly coincides with the fact that precisely among the Jews originated the teaching about the total sinfulness and corruption of mankind—and because they rejected this [Christian] teaching. (*UW*, II, 912)

In his notes, Nietzsche does not tire of horrendously ridiculing Germanic, Teutonic, Aryan, Christian superior attitudes vis-à-vis Judaism; but neither does Judaism escape his stereotyping:

It would be extremely imprudent to assert that the Teuton was preconceived and predestined for Christianity, because not only is the opposite true but also demonstrably false. Why should it be that the inventions by probably the two most Jewish Jews ever—Jesus and Paul—are so congenial to Germans—more so than to others? (Both Jesus and Paul thought that the destiny of every human in all times past and future, as well as the fate of the earth, the sun, the stars, depended upon a Jewish event [*Genesis*]: this belief is the Jewish *non plus ultra*.) How does the highest moral subtlety honed not by an oafish bearskin mentality but by a rabbi [who proclaimed a divine God, sin, slavish subjection . . .] rhyme with the lazy but warlike, predatory Teutons—mentally bland, lovers of the hunt and beerdrinkers—who had not progressed beyond a rudimentary Indic religion and who had not discarded the long-standing practice of butchering humans on altars built for sacrifices? (*UW*, II, 908)

How much Swiftian satire or risible burlesque does one allow Nietzsche before judging it meanness of spirit? It is difficult to say, if we follow the humorous logic adopted, for instance, toward Prussians and Jews. What he is saying is that not only would their intermarriage be desirable but also necessary to engender offspring that would partake of their strongest qualities. In order to qualify Jews for such a union he must first accede to the stereotyped charge that they are objects of degeneration (*Entartung*, a term that was to become a vicious slander in the verbal arsenal of anti-Semites) and then fall back on his standard defense of Jews as having acquired unfavorable characteristics in hostile if not unsavory environments that distorted and disfigured them as human beings:

[Jews, Prussians, actors, and Greeks]: If it were to depend solely upon intellectual qualities, industriousness, and employability, Prussian Jews would already occupy the higher governing offices, particularly in administrative fields: in brief, they would already have been in possession of power (something that in terms of manifold evidence they already have sewn up). What excludes them from such positions is their inability to fulfill the duties of power—in their own Fatherland [biblical Israel], they were themselves never a *ruling* caste: their eyes are not persuasive, their tongue is much too glib and trips over itself, their anger does not invoke a deep, honest roar as that of the lion, their stomachs cannot retain great banquets nor can their power of reason tolerate strong weeping—their arms and legs permit them no proud gestures . . . , and even the way in which a Jew mounts a horse (or a Jewish composer discovers his theme—the "Jewish pouncing-upon" [*Ansprung*]) is not without prior thought [i.e., not spontaneous] and gives us to understand that Jews never were a *chivalric* race [*ritterliche Rasse*]. If Jews have been regarded as unsuited, in many respects, for judiciary honors, it is not their morality that is condemned but only the uncertainty of their being able to fulfill the duties of that morality. All this instantly yields the conclusion that the Jew of Prussia necessarily is a run-down and stunted type of Jew: [but] in and of itself, the Oriental understands incomparably better the official duties of representation than perhaps a North German. The degeneration [*Entartung*] of the Jew is attributable to a wrong environment and the proximity of unlovely and oppressive slaves, Hungarians, and Germans: amid the Portuguese and Mauretanians the higher Jewish race was able to maintain itself; yes, altogether there is perhaps the ceremoniousness of death and a kind of sanctification of earthly passion not even up to our time more beautifully portrayed than by certain Jews of the Old Testament: The Greeks, too, could have learned from them!

The dangers of the Jewish soul: (1) it likes to nest itself somewhere parasitically; (2) it knows how to "adapt itself," as experts in the natural sciences [Lamarckians] would say: and with that they have become born actors like the polyp, poetized by Theognis,* who borrows the color of the rock to which he clings. Their talent and tendency [toward parasitism and acting, dissimulating] seems to be enormous; the habit of spending much patience and rationality to achieve the smallest gain has left a fateful furrow in their character: so then, even the most noted high-financiers of the Jewish money mart cannot refrain, when circumstances allow, from coldbloodedly letting their fingers reach out for small, mean cheating, the likes of which would make a Prussian finance official blush with shame. (*UW*, II, 1185)

Nietzsche is able to say all these things about the adaptive and excusably "parasitic" Jew without himself blushing! Almost in the same breath, he explains that Jews are essential for the task of building a ruling caste: one needs to focus or centralize their adaptive capability, their acting, dissimulating, and abilities at mimicry. Does Nietzsche mean that once Christianity is gone, one can forgive the Jews for what they have wrought, or does he call for an enlistment of the Jews for the power they demonstrated in having brought Christianity into existence? Perhaps he means both.

Nietzsche's advocacy of the type of intermarriage—of body and minds—described here certainly has no equal among either Jews and Prussians or other Germans at the time or since. Statistics certainly record a substantial increase of Jewish-Gentile/German intermarriages for widely differing financial, social, romantic, or other reasons during the late nineteenth century. Overbeck's embarrassed reaction to the marriage of his niece to a person of Jewish descent, as we have seen, would more likely match the reality of the given situations. Nietzsche's views that Jews never soiled their hands with work or rode horseback, of course, did not match reality either. Moreover, Jews in Eastern Europe worked by the sweat of their brows as farmers and laborers before many of them

---

*Sixth-century B.C.E. Greek aristocrat and poet.

made their way into the middle class and out of degraded positions. Nietzsche, who lived most of his life in either the ivory tower of academia or sheltered by a pension from the University of Basel, had no intention of supporting himself by the labor of his hands; he left that to others. And, like Miniver Cheevy,[1] he harbored dreams and wished that he had lived in times past, in ancient Greece when, as he wistfully noted, philosophers had their slaves to whom their social standing and nobility entitled them. In the absence of slave-owning philosopher-entitlements, Nietzsche had to content himself with fond memories as a self-styled cavalier on horseback within a Prussian volunteer cavalry regiment during a brief period in 1868. The closest he came to owning a domestic was the occasional servitude of his sister.

In order to extol Jews and their cultural achievements, Nietzsche resorts to disquieting apologias. He feels no such need when he attacks the invulnerable institution of Christianity. It would have been a bullying and cowardly tactic to attack helpless Jews, but Christianity was indeed a most formidable and "worthy" opponent:

> . . . Christianity as the greatest mob-movement within the Roman Empire represents the elevation of the backward, uneducated, oppressed, sick, demented, poor, slaves, old women, cowardly men, in brief all those who would have had reasons for committing suicide but lacked courage for it; with deepest zeal, they sought means for making their life tolerable and worth holding on to. And they found the means that offered the world a new kind of happiness. The fortuity of its origin constituted the greatest paradox of antiquity. Avoiding education at the time, people hungered for a paradox such as "Salvation is from the Jews" [John 4:21, Jesus to the woman of Samaria as he confirms that he is Christ, the Messiah]; that was an assertion [however] that no intelligent age could maintain for long. . . . (*UW*, II, 900)

Nietzsche's pretensions to elitism prompted such snobbish views as well as his assessment of Christianity as a resentful, herd- or mob-inspired revolutionary movement. On the other hand, Nietzsche will propose that the *ressentiment* of the herd can of itself become a creative morality in its negative reaction to undesirable institutions and will serve to revalue values; slave morality needs the stimulus of a yea-saying power to struggle against. In that sense, *ressentiment* is capable of creating new values (GM, 10). Here is an argument that justifies Nietzsche's own *ressentiments*!

Nietzsche in less than subtle ways kept reminding Christian anti-Semites of their origin in and descent from the least desirable strata of ancient Jewish life, and that the Gospels, notably that of John, should remind them not only of their debt to Jews but also that salvation allegedly comes from Jews. Nietzsche, as we know, decried the salvation-redemption-sin mechanism. In Christianity, Nietzsche found residual "Jewish characteristics":

> Christianity proceeded from Judaism and from no other source: but it grew into the Roman world and bore fruits that were Jewish as well as Roman. This "crossed" [*gekreuzte*, crucified; hybrid] Christianity found its form in Catholicism in which the Roman element became preponderant; while it found in Protestantism another form in which Jewish elements dominated. This has nothing to do with the fact that the Germans—carriers of the Protestant persuasion—are more related to the Jews but that they stand at a greater distance from the Romans than the Catholic population of southern Europe. (*UW*, II, 909)

Unacknowledged, too, says Nietzsche, is Europe's indebtedness to the morality of the Old Testament's Judaism, and Nietzsche is intrigued by this as well as the adoption of this religious, Semitic book by the "Germanic race"—"race" being used in a loosely cultural context:

> In our schools, Jewish history is taught as being sacred: for us, Abraham amounts to more than any personage of Greek or German history, and that which we derive from David's Psalms is so different emotionally from that which we gain from a reading of Pindar or Petrarch; they differ from each other as does for us the familial from the foreign. This pull toward the achievements of an Asiatic—and very distant and peculiar race—in the midst of the desolateness of our modern culture is perhaps one of the few stable phenomena that stands serenely aloft from education and miseducation: the strongest ethical aftereffects of Christianity were directed not toward nations but toward people and therefore did not have the onus of putting into the hands of the Germanic race a religious book belonging to a Semitic people. If one takes into consideration what efforts were made by a non-Semitic Europe to

place close to its heart this small, curious Jewish world, and if one does not wonder any longer about this but instead wonders about oneself and Europe's own alienation, it becomes clear that Europe had to overcome itself strenuously to gain an inclination toward Jewish literature. The present European feeling for the Bible is the greatest victory over the limitation of the race. . . . This feeling is so mighty that whoever wishes to acknowledge and pay tribute to the history of the Jews, that person will have to make great efforts to distance himself from Jews . . . in order to characterize Jewish elements as alien. This comes from the fact that Europe has immersed itself roundly in the Bible and, by and large, had to do something similar to what the Puritans of England did by discovering that their contemporaries, their wars, their small and large fatalities had been prophetically foretold in the Jewish Book.— What, however, does the European say who is asked about his preference for ancient Jewish literature beyond those of other ancients: "Is there more morality in it?" meaning, however: is there more in it of the morality now professed in Europe; and that in turn means nothing else than: Europe has adopted Jewish morality and regards it as a better, a higher one than any contemporaneous ethics and knowledge and more fitting than the Arabic, Greek, Indic, Chinese.—What is the nature of this morality? By dint of this morality are Europeans really the principal and reigning people on this globe? But with what measure does one delimit the rankings of the multifarious moralities? And what are the non-Europeans, such as the Chinese, likely to say about European alleged distinctions in the realm of morality? Perhaps it belongs to the nature of Jewish morality to regard itself as the principal and highest: perhaps it is pure conceit: Yes, one can ask: is there at all a way of ranking moralities, is there a canon that rules over everything and defines the ethical, without regard to nation, time, circumstances, degrees of knowledge? Or is one ingredient common to all moralities, namely, the degree of adaptation to knowledge—perhaps that makes rankings of morality possible? (*UW*, II, 910)

Aside from briefly touching on the question of Germany's and Europe's failure to acknowledge how much of their own tradition drew from Judaic sources, Nietzsche questions the propriety of assigning rankings to moralities. His philosophical and cultural relativism prohibited deification of absolutes. Intentionally, Nietzsche scorned cultural ingratitude, yet he reserved the right to criticize Christian adoption of Jewish values.

Nietzsche's previous characterization of Jewish "parasitism," "Judaiza-tion"; the talk of sex and "Jewish moneybags" have offensive anti-Jewish implications. Nietzsche's ideological elitism and what he thought to be practical idealism prevented him from anticipating that doctrinaire eugenics could be used as a pretense for extermination: euthanasia as a means of enhancing Aryan racial purity. Hitler's *Mein Kampf* carried for-ward the bogus specters that "parasitism" and "Jewification . . . of our spiritual life and mating will destroy our offspring." Wagnerian thunder discharged itself in a firestorm during the Third Reich. Such events were far from Nietzsche's mind despite his declaration that words had the power to kill. Nietzsche's *Strauss* was one example of verbal assassination, and his words aimed at Wagner had the same intentions. There was more dynamite than cleverness in his slogans and diatribes.

It seemed, at times, that he wished to goad and antagonize rather than educate Germans. The fear of Jews, sexual miscegenation, and race purity that were drummed into the popular mind were exceeded only by accusations of unpatriotic internationalism or cosmopolitanism; Niet-zsche ridiculed such fears but at the same time indirectly fed them. He did not say who made him a spokesman for Jews when he soothingly told his readers that Jews could but were not minded to take over the rule of Europe. Nor did he allay the fears people had about Jews when he deliv-ered himself of the following opinion common in his later writings:

> Germans should engender a ruling caste: I admit that Jews possess indigenous capabilities that are indispensable to a race involved in world politics. The feeling for money is to be learned, inherited, and inherited thousandfold: even now there is this common trait between the Jew and the American. (*UW*, II, 1191)

Red-alert words flash out among intended compliments: "Jews . . . race . . . inherited money capabilities . . . world politics." Neither Jews, Ger-mans, nor Americans could take joy in such indiscriminate and hollow pseudo-encomia. If some biographers explain that Nietzsche's disaffection for Germans and petulant praise of Jews stem from German disesteem of him in the 1880s, they do not know that already in 1874 with his mono-graph *Vom Nutzen und Nachteil der Historie für das Leben* (*Of the Use and Disadvantage of History for Life*), the second in the series *Unzeitgemässe*

Betrachtungen (*Untimely Meditations*), he claimed that the provincial nature of German education caused "Germans to have no culture at all." At the heart of his hyperbole was the argument that Germans, unlike the Greeks, had not learned to "know themselves" and to master the inheritance of a chaotic past. Greek culture was an aggregate chaos of "foreign, Semitic, Babylonian, Lydian, Egyptian forms, concepts, and religions," including the Oriental gods. Nevertheless, the Greeks, Nietzsche reasoned, *organized* the chaos, after a difficult struggle, and enriched themselves with inherited "foreign" treasures and achieved victory over all other cultures through ethical strength. Conquest through amalgamation of the "foreign," Nietzsche suggests, would lead to a *true* rather than a "decorative" culture. This seems to be what he is saying a decade later when he talks—although somewhat crudely—about the wedding, for instance, of the Jewish and the Prussian. I can think of no philosopher— or historian, theologian, or politician—who would brave general outrage with such bold sentiments. In addition to the cultural transcendence he proposed in 1874, he added the idea, a decade later, of eugenic transcendence. If both culture and eugenic breeding were to be achieved, the day of the *Übermensch* would not be far off. It was Nietzsche's Utopian vision—poorly thought through but honestly conceived. Even Nietzsche's personal friend Overbeck could not face Nietzsche's amalgamation proposals vis-à-vis Jews and rationalized his way around them.

> It is an obligatory task to create a *ruling caste*, with the most encompassing spirits capable of assuming the most varied tasks of ruling the earth and centralizing all former individual capabilities into one essence.
>
> The Jewish position relative to this: they have great previous practice in *adaptation*. Formerly they have been the greatest actors because of that capability; also as writers and artists they have been the most illustrious imitators and empathizers. Only when Christianity is properly destroyed will one be more *just* towards the Jews, even though they were the originators of Christianity and created the highest moral pathos up to our time. (*UW*, II, 1112)

Nietzsche's prickliness and proclivity, at least in print, for antagonizing even those generally well disposed toward Jews may be seen in the

convoluted praise heaped on Jews at times and the brusque dismissal of
Christianity most of the time. Generosity and mockery jostle each other;
for example, in the last sentence of this passage in which, among other
things, Nietzsche even forgives Jews for having been "the originators of
Christianity." It takes a sense of black humor to find a silver lining in the
murkiness of anti-Semitism as Nietzsche discovers it:

> The value of anti-Semitism: to drive the Jews toward aiming for higher
> goals and to have them find it unworthy to dissolve in nationalistic
> states. (*UW*, II, 1187)

Contrary even to the moderate Wagnerian anti-Semites, Nietzsche proposes not that Jews disappear within German society, but that they
instead seek goals higher than those of German nationalism and merge
beneficially. Such hopes were to be in vain on two counts: the aim by
intellectual Jews to integrate by being more nationalistic culturally than
Germans themselves and the arrogant refusal by Germans to allow
peaceful integration.

Nietzsche's favorable vision of things ancient is attributable to the
"earthliness and sense of life," as well as the "great sensuousness among
aged nations, for instance the Hungarians, Chinese, Jews, French (were
not the Celts already a nation of culture!)" (*UW*, II, 1115). The basic
reasonableness of Jews, he was sure, would allow them to see the advantages of adapting themselves to the Germans:

> The imperative of the German instinct commands: "No more Jews!
> And bar the doors to the East!"—an advisable [*kluge*] injunction that
> would commend itself to German Jews themselves as a "self-con-
> straint"; it is their task to grow integrally into essential German being
> and to bring into it a more German type of expression and gesture that
> finally results in a "soul"—for this is the path from outer to inner, from
> illusion to actual being [*von "Schein" zu "Sein"*]. It is a goal that should
> not be made unresolvable or be diverted, once again, by the dreadful
> and contemptible ugliness of a new influx of Polish and Russian, Hun-
> garian and Galician Jews. Now *here* is the point, according to which
> Jews themselves should act, namely, to "set frontiers for themselves: the
> sole and last point that would merge Jewish and German to advantage:
> most certainly, it is time, it is high time! (*UW*, II, 1184)

Nietzsche assumes the role occasionally of self-appointed adviser to the Jews, touching sensitive nerves. Ever since Heine's uncharitable travel reports, German Jews had been fearful that their poor Polish-Russian co-religionists and other Easterners with their medieval ghetto customs and caftans ridiculed by anti-Semites would embarrass them to no end in Austro-German society and give hurtful credence to the foreignness of all Jews. Jews who wanted to assimilate or simply to be left alone in their religious reform and secular ways did not welcome the influx. Bernhard Förster, Nietzsche's brother-in-law, had been able to gather considerable public sentiment for his aim to stop Jewish immigration and to encourage expulsion. In regard to Jews, it was easy to see that the social and cultural atmosphere was tense. Nietzsche's cautionary views had more than a share of ambiguity about them.

In Nietzsche's philosophical "inquiries," Rome and the pagan world were idealized at the expense largely of Judea and Christianity, though the latter prevailed. If one remembers that Nietzsche called philosophy nonsystematized personal confessions on conscious and unconscious levels, it becomes clear not only that he himself was captive to "slave" types of resentments, but that master and slave feelings could be contained contentiously within one soul. Self-overcoming, a constant refrain, was the essence of the ideal person in Nietzsche's quest to acquire a compassionate nobility, a benevolent strength to deal justly with the rabble and to reach a level of aristocratic superiority. In a sense, he outlined the prerequisite characteristics of the future *Übermensch*.

Nietzsche says: it is time to replace earlier genealogical hypotheses with more plausible ones (GM, Pref. 4), hypotheses in which Jews and Judaism figure prominently, including a sampling of sections from GM most pertinent to Nietzsche's revaluations.

> One will already have guessed how readily the priestly scale of valuation departs from that of the knightly aristocratic [the priest versus the warrior caste]. . . . In history, whatever campaign has been waged against the "noble," "the mighty," "the lords," "the all-powerful on earth" pales to insignificance in comparison with what the *Jews* have done to them; the Jews, that priestly people, ultimately took its *intellectual revenge* [geistige Rache, clever or spiritual revenge] upon its enemies and oppressors and sought satisfaction by means of a radical revaluation

of their enemies' values. This was perfectly in tune with a nation possessed of a most severely repressed [*zurückgetretensten*] priestly mania for revenge. It was the Jews who dared with fear-inspiring consequences to reverse the aristocratic equation (good = noble = mighty = beautiful = happy = God-beloved) and to hold fast to the inversions with teeth like the most abysmal hate (a hate derived from helplessness): they declared, to wit, only the poverty-stricken are good—as are the needy, the helpless [*Ohnmächtige*], the socially impotent, the lower classes, the sufferers, the self-deniers, the sick, the loathsome; they are the only devout ones, the only ones blessed by God, only for them is spiritual bliss assured. On the other hand, for you the noble and mighty, in all eternity you will be designated as the evil, the gruesome ones, the lechers, the insatiable, the godless; forever you will also be the unholy, the cursed and the damned! . . . We know *who* has become the heir of this Jewish inversion of values . . . [Christianity]; I remind you of the monumental and in all respects fateful initiative taken by the Jews with their most thoroughgoing of all declarations of war and my earlier observation [in *Beyond Good and Evil*, #195] that, namely, with the Jews began *a slave revolt in the sphere of morals*—a revolt that has a two thousand-year history behind it and no longer is visible to us today because it has been so thoroughly victorious. . . . (GM, I, 7)

Some of the principles delineated in *Beyond Good and Evil* have now come to full flower in *The Genealogy of Morals*: the relationship of good and evil, love derived from hate, the nuances between antipodes, the deceptiveness of what passes for virtue. What, of course, is inflammatory and defamatory is Nietzsche's Judeo-Christian conspiracy theory and his foray into the treacherous area of "mass psychology" and the alleged "revenge" motif. No matter how subtly explained or rationalized, a conspiracy allegation directed at Jews can be taken by a reader—if he is selective by intent—as justified fear of and animosity toward Jews. This was not intended by Nietzsche, although he points to the Jewish roots of Jesus' gospel of love and finds it treacherously gilded. He condemns Christian theology's presumptive redemption myth allied to the crucifixion. Coming close to slander, Nietzsche attributes the spread of Jewish values to the "poisoned Christian bait, Jesus." He ascribes similar dangerous and supersubtle plots to the ancient Jews—"plots" typified by Saul (St. Paul). Such imagined cabals—psychological in nature—lie beyond any historical proof or claim by any reputable historian. Instead, we know that the Jews militarily challenged Rome head on as warriors. Foolhardy or not, they countered the imperial legions' invasion of Galilee and then again in the spring of 67 C.E. when the one million Jewish inhabitants of Jerusalem refused to capitulate. But, weakened by bitter internal conflicts and ruthless military pounding, the city and its people were decimated and all heroic resistance was rendered futile. The Romans burnt the magnificent Temple to the ground; those thousands who survived butchery by the soldiers and who were not crucified, became fodder in gladiatorial arenas and slaves in Roman mines. Simon bar Goria, a valiant Jewish rebel leader, was symbolically sacrificed to the Roman gods by being hurled from the Tarpeian rock to bring the Roman holidays to their close. The Roman emperor Vespasian had the Jewish Torah—the scroll of the five books of Moses—and other war trophies brought to his palace, and he struck a commemorative coin inscribed "Judea capta." Jews who had fought for their God and country had reason to loathe their conquerors and even in the aftermath of defeat, rebellion, and enmity toward Rome were part of their heritage. It was not a menial slave mentality poised against aristocratic, noble masters but a revulsion against pagan brutality. Nietzsche built his revisionist case—the psychology of subversion, its power, and the emergence of Christianity—on very shaky premises:

> . . . But do you not understand this? Do you not see what took two thousand years to blossom into victory? . . . No wonder: all things of *long duration* are difficult to see, to survey. *Here*, however, is the prime event growing out of the treetrunk of revenge: Jewish hate—the deepest and most sublime, that is, an ideal-creating and values-reversing hate, the likes of which had never before been seen upon this earth, and out of which at the same time grew something equally incomparable, a *new love*, the deepest and most sublime of all kinds of love; could it have grown out of any other treetrunk? Let no one assume, though, that this is an honest rejection of the mentioned thirst for revenge or the countergrowth to and the opposite of the Jewish hate. No, the reverse is true! This love grew out of hate as does the crown of a tree, triumphing in the purest and brightest sunlight with its crown unfolding ever more grandly in the purest brightness and sun-filled air. It is invested with the same urge and end-goals sighted by hate, seeking victory at the heights and in the realm of light, looking

for booty, and possessing a seductiveness similar to that of evil; love sank its roots greedily into the depths and into evil. This Jesus of Nazareth as the living embodiment of the gospel of love, this "redeemer" who brings salvation [*Seligkeit*, bliss] and victory to the poor, the sick, and the sinners; was he not seduction in its most uncanny and irresistible form, tempting one to take a misleading detour precisely to those Jewish values and innovative ideals? By these means, has not Israel's indirection and with this "redeemer" (this seeming destroyer) and adversary of Israel, has not Israel achieved the ultimate aim in its lust for revenge? Is there not at play here the secret black magic of a truly *great* politics of vengeance, a far-seeing subterranean, slow, tentacular grasping and calculated revenge? Israel itself had to take the actual instrument of its revenge and nail it to the cross for all the world to see, and then to repudiate it with the pretense that it is something of deadly enmity to itself. Was all this not designed so that "all the world," namely, all of Israel's enemies, would unsuspectingly and promptly swallow the bait? Could any human mind possibly imagine a more extreme intellectual finesse [*Raffinement des Geistes*, supersubtle inventiveness], a more *dangerous* bait? Could anything be more tempting, intoxicating, narcotizing, and debilitating than that unparalleled symbol of "the holy cross," that gruesome paradox of a "God on the Cross," that unthinkable mystery and the last and extreme cruelty of a self-crucifixion by a god—for the salvation of mankind? At the very least, it is certain that *sub hoc signo* [under this sign or symbol] Israel with its revenge and reevaluation of all values, has triumphed over all other values, and once again, over all *more noble* ideals [*vornehmeren* (aristocratic) *Ideale*].

But why continue talk about *more noble* ideals! Let us come to terms with the facts: The people [*Volk*] have conquered—or "the slaves" or "the mob" or "the herd" or whatever you wish to call them—and if this has been brought about by the Jews, so be it! for no other people had a comparable world-historic mission. The [Roman] "lords" have been done away with; the morality of the common man has triumphed. One may at the same time characterize this triumph as a blood poisoning (that has thoroughly mixed the races)—something I do not deny; undoubtedly this in-toxication [toxic injection] has *succeeded*. The "saving" of humanity from "the lords" is proceeding expeditiously; everything is being Judaized [*verjüdelt*] or Christianized [*verkristlicht*] or commonized [*verpöbelt*, mob-ized], the specific words hardly matter!).

The poisoning of mankind's body progresses unimpeded. . . . It is the
Church and not the poison that repels us. . . . (GM, I, 8–9)

In this passage, if ever there was a simplistic propagandistic psychologizing
of history—Jewish hate disguised as Christian love—here it is. The slave
morality of the mob, the common man—all that Nietzsche holds in contempt has triumphed over the lordly. The lowly and the noble are generic
designations for divisions among all societies. Pejorative and ugly, however, are the verbs "verjüdeln" (to Jewify) and to Christify: the former
term became a favorite of Nazi sloganeers, along with the slander of racial
blood poisoning. Nietzsche did approve of "racial mix"—one supposes,
under the state-controlled strictures he had advocated—but bandying
about words and incendiary phrases can provoke serious problems when
precision of meaning is lost in murky psychologizing.

In a subsequent section, Nietzsche ratchets into high gear with his
ressentiment theory that at one and the same time explained and
lamented the triumph of Judaic Christianity over Rome. The sounds of
gleeful irony reverberate in his "reminder" that three Jews—Mary, Jesus,
and Paul—triumphed and one bows down to them. If a Jew were to make
such comments, he would stand accused of Jewish anti-Christian, unec-
umenical antagonism; for Nietzsche to have said this could have been
excused as the strayings of a rebellious pastor's prodigal son.

As for the residue of symbolic relations between ancient Judea and
Rome, one Jewish historian concludes that "the beautiful arch which
[the emperor] Titus erected [in Rome], with reliefs of the candlesticks and
holy vessels of the [Jerusalem] Temple, still stands. Today, it is a monument, not to the Romans, but to the heroic little people who outlived
their conquerors."[2] Nietzsche does—with frequency—express similar
wonderment at Jewish survival through tenacity—a quality he identifies
with and extols in Jews. What did survive of Rome in its Catholic and
Jesuitical form was excoriated mercilessly by Wagner and Nietzsche alike.

In Rome, the Jew stood "*convicted* of hate against the entire human
race": and rightly so, insofar as the welfare and future of mankind was
linked to the unconditional lordship of aristocratic, Roman values.
How, on the other hand, did Jews feel about Rome? One guesses the
answer from thousands of pieces of evidence, but it is only necessary to

remember the Apocalypse of John, the most savage of all outbursts ever recorded, and which has the revenge motif on its conscience. (Incidentally, one should not underrate the far-reaching logic of the Christian instinct that selected precisely this book of hate to be signed with the name of the disciple of love, that self-same disciple to whom is attributed that enamored and ecstatic Gospel: no matter how much false literary coinage may have been employed of necessity, there is some truth in that piece.) The Romans were, in fact, the strong and the noble and no stronger or more aristocratic nation had ever existed or been dreamed of on earth; every one of their remains and inscriptions is a delight, provided one senses *what* is at work. The Jews, on the contrary, were that priestly nation of *ressentiment par excellence*, possessed of a unique genius for moralistic folkways: if one compares them with similarly talented people like the Chinese or the Germans, one soon recognizes the difference between the first- and the fifth-rate. Who has emerged *victorious* temporarily—Rome or Judea? There can be no doubt: just consider to whom one bows down in Rome—and not only in Rome but throughout almost half this world—as though lying at the feet of the epitome of all values. In every place where man has become tame or wishes to be tamed, there one bows to *three Jews*, as is well known, and to *one Jewish woman* (to Jesus of Nazareth; the fisherman, Peter; Paul, the rug weaver; and to the mother of the earlier-mentioned Jesus, named Mary). This is very remarkable: Rome is, without doubt, defeated. At any rate, during the Renaissance there occurred a brilliant and uncanny resurrection of classical ideals, the aristocratic manner of valuation of all things: Rome itself was revived like someone wakened from a deathlike trance and weighed down by the newly constructed edifice of a Judaized Rome that looked like an ecumenical synagogue called the "church"; and immediately Judea triumphed again thanks to that thoroughly moblike (German and English) *"ressentiment"*-movement, called the Reformation. Consequently, there had to be a reconstitution of the church—the paralleled restoration also of classical Rome's old gravesite tranquility. In an even more decisive and deeper sense, Judea once again, along with the French Revolution, gained a victory over the classical ideal: the last political nobility of the seventeenth and eighteenth French centuries in Europe collapsed under the weight of the folkish (*volkstümliche*) *ressentiment*-instinct; at no time was there greater jubilation on earth and more noisy enthusiasm heard on earth! And indeed, amid all this occurred the most monstrous and unexpected: the ideal of antiquity itself appeared *bodily* and with extra-ordinary sumptuousness before everyone's eyes and conscience—and once again, stronger, simpler, and more insistent than ever before—and once again, it stood up against *ressentiment's* lying motto that *the majority is in the right* . . . ; it posed a counter-motto terrible and rap-turous, *the prerogative [Vorrecht] of the few!* Like a final road sign for other directions, there appeared Napoleon, the most unique [*einzelnste*, individualistic] and late-born [*spätestgeborne*, residual, anachronistic] person ever, and with him the incarnate problems of *the noble ideal per se*; one might well reflect upon *what precisely is* the problem posed: for Napoleon is that synthesis of Monster and Superman [*Unmensch und Übermensch*]. . . . (GM, I, 16)

Nietzsche's idiosyncratic reading of history continued to burgeon as the Protestant Reformation and the French Revolution were interpreted as movements fuelled by their Judea-*ressentiment* prototype, the subversion of aristocracy by the herd.

Heine's polemical appellation "the Judaic poison" and Nietzsche's "Judain" or evil-smelling rabbinism are as unappetizing as the grossest anti-Semitic name-calling by German and French racists who adopted the Heine-Nietzsche slogans. One critic tries to salvage matters by noting that actually "Heine referred not to the synagogue and the Jews but to the Church as the Synagogue's successor."[3] That may have been Nietzsche's intent as well, but it was so blurred linguistically that the exclusive onus fell upon Jews collectively. One must add that Heine placed emphasis equally on Rome's decline by pointing to Rome's gross materialism.

For Nietzsche (as for Karl Marx before him), some of Heine's ideo-logical catch-alls proved irresistible for adoption in *The Genealogy of Morals* and later in *The Antichrist*:

[Heine:] . . . Roman history became a slow dying, an agony that was to last for centuries. Was it perhaps the assassinated Judea, which left its spiritual legacy to the Romans, wanted to revenge itself upon the vic-torious enemy . . . ? Truly, Rome—a Hercules among nations—was so effectively consumed by the Judaic poison . . . that its imperial battle-voice deteriorated into a praying cleric's whine and a castrato's trill. (*Romantische Schule*, I, 1833)

Heine's lament that Hellenic love of beauty and celebrative dance festivities yielded to the "overspiritualized" and impoverished Judaism of the Nazarene—Judaism versus Hellenism—was the simplistic contrast taken over by Nietzsche: "Rome vs. Israel, Israel vs. Rome—no battle has ever been more momentous" (GM, I, 16). If Nietzsche sides with Roman "aristocratic values" he also assigns powerful, "ethical genius" to the Jews.

Long before Nietzsche's insistence upon Jewish instrumentality and culpability for the existence of Christianity, the Roman emperors called Judaism a sickness, a "Jewish contagion," to be rooted out by persecution. Roman philosophers, not intimidated by the less than 2 percent of Jews in Roman domains, somewhat phlegmatically regarded Christians as Jewish sectarians or Oriental cultists not to be taken seriously as moral crusaders. Neither the emperors nor the philosophers understood the power of the social ideas and spiritual promises that were forging a major transformation in Europe's religious orientation. From his bookseller, Nietzsche bought a translation of William Lecky's *History of European Morals* (1869) to sort out ideas on Rome and Judea, but his most compelling source in that area remained Edward Gibbon's *The Decline and Fall of the Roman Empire*.

Gibbon's account of the rise of Christianity is derisive and his telling of Rome's fall a veritable dirge. Christianity became a state religion and the emperor Constantine on his deathbed in 337 C.E. was baptized as he accepted the god of the Christians; in Gibbon's view this signaled the triumph of barbarism and religion. Christianity, he asserted,

> had destroyed the old faith that had given moral character to the Roman soul and stability to the Roman state. It had declared war upon the classic culture—upon science, philosophy, literature and art. It had brought an enfeebling Oriental mysticism into the realistic stoicism of Roman life; it had turned men's thoughts from the tasks of this world to an enervating preparation for some cosmic catastrophe, and had lured them into seeking individual salvation through asceticism and prayer. . . . It had preached the ethic of nonresistance and peace when the survival of the Empire had demanded a will to war. Christ's victory had been Rome's death.[4]

Gibbon noted the effectiveness of afterworld visions of fire and terror, and above all, the apocalypse:

The Christian . . . expected it with terror and confidence as a certain and impending event . . . it was unanimously affirmed that those who, since the birth or the death of Christ, had obstinately persisted in the worship of the daemons neither deserved nor could expect a pardon from the irritated justice of the Deity. These rigid sentiments which had been unknown in the ancient world, appear to have infused a spirit of bitterness into a system of love and harmony. The ties of blood and friendship were frequently torn asunder by the difference of religious faith; and the Christians who, in this world, found themselves oppressed by the power of the Pagans, were sometimes seduced by *resentment* [my emphasis] and spiritual pride to delight in their future triumph. "You are fond of spectacles," exclaims the stern Tertullian [a dogmatic apologist, convert, and early Church Father], "expect the greatest of all spectacles, the last and eternal judgment of the universe. How shall I admire, how laugh, how rejoice, how exult, when I behold so many proud monarchs and fancied gods, groaning in the lowest abyss of darkness; so many magistrates, who persecuted the name of the Lord, liquifying in fiercer fires than they had ever kindled against the Christians; so many sage philosophers blushing in red-hot flames with their deluded scholars; so many celebrated poets trembling before the tribunal, not of Minos, but of Christ; so many tragedians, more tuneful in the expression of their own sufferings; so many dancers—" But the humanity of the reader will permit me to draw a veil over the rest of this infernal description [in *De spectaculis,* written about 30 C.E.] which the zealous African [Carthaginian] pursues in a long variety of affected and unfeeling witticisms. (Chapter XV; 15)[5]

Nietzsche is in agreement with the pro-classical Roman, anti-clerical, and anti-Christian views espoused in Gibbon's monumental work of history and shares Gibbon's skepticism, but he lacks the elegant cutting edge of the British historian: "After the extinction of paganism," Gibbon wrote, "the Christians in peace and piety might have enjoyed their solitary triumph. But the principle of discord was alive in their bosom, and they were more solicitous to explore the nature, than to practice the laws of their founder" (opening of chapter XLVII). Gibbon developed a technique of damning with faint praise and ridiculing, with extreme literalness, Christian theology and the Gospels—the immaculate conception, the immaculate birth, and a Jesus freed of replenishing "daily waste"; a

Jesus free of thirst or hunger and sensual concupiscence, and possessing virginal purity. Gibbon adroitly avoided direct criminal offense to English statutes still on eighteenth-century law books that made a person "brought up in the truth of the Christian religion" suffer incarceration for writings that would allege the Christian religion to be untrue. His other strategy in condemning Christianity's "major role" in the decline of Rome and the rapid growth of the Church was not to blame Christianity directly but point to the "inflexible, and, if we may use the expression, the intolerant zeal of the Christians, derived, it is true, from the Jewish religion, but purified from the narrow and unsocial spirit which, instead of inviting, had deterred the Gentiles from embracing the law of Moses" (chapter XV). The "if . . . but" construction displays an unease and convolution of thought that served, however, to evade the law's censure. Gibbon found it convenient in some respects to follow such diverse writers as the ancient Tacitus and the modern Voltaire in their denigrations of Jews. He was acquainted with Voltaire's polemics and had met the French philosopher in 1757. Through his accounts of the "gross and imperfect" faith of the Nazarenes (a name applied to the early Christians and then to a Christian-Jewish sect, the Ebionites), Gibbon's persiflage thinly disguised his aim at the real target—Christianity. James Boswell and others not enamored of Enlightenment historians and philosophers readily identified Gibbon as an infidel.

The parallel views of Gibbon and Nietzsche readily come into view. Gibbon made the valid assumption that the hurt of defeat will cause the humiliated and vanquished *resentment*, but it remained for Nietzsche to make of this the major, revolutionary, vindictive, and revaluative "Jewish mechanism." It has been proposed by numerous other historians that Gibbon's type of cause-and-effect views are simplistic to the extreme because the Roman Empire was already in decline and in dissolution when Christianity became an institutionalized force with wide-embracing syncretic doctrines.

Gibbon came into Nietzsche's ken at a point when he was ready to discard theological studies urged upon him by his mother and pastoral relatives. It was Professor Jacob Bernays—a protégé of the Ritschls—at the University of Bonn, who urged and guided Nietzsche's reading of Gibbon in a contemporaneous German translation. Gibbon transformed history into an art form just as Nietzsche was beginning to transform philosophy and psychology similarly. When Bernays noted that Nietzsche's *Birth of Tragedy* contained his own recognizable ideas but in exaggerated forms, he had a point. With justice it may be said that similarly many of Gibbon's ideas were adopted by Nietzsche and escalated into uniquely Nietzschean shapes.

If one contends that the Bonn years lay too far behind Nietzsche to owe any recollection to Gibbon, one needs to remember Carl Jung's discovery of Nietzsche's incredible memory and mental association network. Jung found passages in *Zarathustra* that were paraphrasings from a book by Justinius Kerner, *Blätter aus Prevorst,* and when Jung inquired of Nietzsche's sister she told him that her brother had indeed read it in his grandfather Pastor Oehler's library when Fritz was about thirteen years old.[6] Nietzsche's anxiety about proprietorship of ideas is a common failing that he shared with other superb egotists like Wagner and Freud.

If Nietzsche ventured into the age of the Caesars and the early Church, he did so not as a scholarly researcher but as a polemicist, an urge that Gibbon had to suppress without discarding his urbane weaponry. In any case, Nietzsche had thoroughly assimilated and absorbed ideas gleaned from Gibbon.

Nietzsche distanced himself from the gospelers for the same reasons as did Gibbon. Both found distasteful to the extreme the resentful attitudes displayed by early Christians toward the pagan Romans—the vindictiveness of the apostles of love who envisioned Christ's enemies tormented in brimstone fire to the delight of all the blessed in the kingdom of heaven as they view the punishments of the damned. Nietzsche takes a cue from Gibbon and quotes derisively from the ordained priest and early convert Tertullian, who exhorts Christians to turn from gladiatorial spectacles of bloodied athletes to the pleasures of the stronger spectacle of the bloodied martyrs and Christ. It is the false spiritualization of morality that Nietzsche attributes to Christianity's "Judaized" heritage (GM, 9). Nietzsche was to see more manliness in the spectacle of bullfighting (the modern version, he felt, of gladiatorial contests) than in the exercise of spirituality. In section 15 of *The Genealogy of Morals*, Nietzsche satirizes Tertullian's diatribes against Rome but takes no umbrage at Tertullian's denigration of Jews; a few sections later, however, he honors the Old Testament with a lyricism that would have made a Rée or a Paneth blush with embarrassment:

...the presumption and vanity of Christian agitators, called the Church Fathers, decreed "that *we* too have our classical literature; *we do not need the Greeks*"—and with that they pointed proudly to books of legends, letters of the Apostles, and little tracts of apologia, reminding one of today's English Salvation Army with similar literature in waging war against Shakespeare and other "heathens." One may already have guessed that I do not like the New Testament; it almost makes me uneasy about my taste in regard to this valued and overvalued writing and to stand up alone (the taste of two thousand years is *against* me): but, it can't be helped, "Here I take my stand; I cannot do otherwise" [a paraphrase of Luther's declaration at the Diet of Worms]—I have the courage of my bad taste. The *Old* Testament—yes, that is something entirely different: All honor to the Old Testament! In it, I find great people, a heroic landscape and something that is of the rarest quality on the face of the earth—the incomparable naïveté of *a strong heart*; and more than that, I find a *people* [*Volk*]. In the New Testament, by way of contrast, I find nothing but petty sectarianism, much rococo of the soul, much involution and many nooks, curiosities exhaling the atmosphere of the conventicle—not to ignore the occasional whiff of bucolic sugariness, belonging to the time (and the Roman province) and being more Hellenistic than Jewish. In close proximity is modesty and pretentiousness; a palavering of emotion that has an almost numbing effect; the trappings of passion without real passion; painful play of posturing; here ostensibly every decent manner of upbringing was lacking. How can one make such an enormous fuss about one's minor trespasses as did these pious, petty little men! No one really cares, least of all God. Finally, they even want the "crown of eternal life." And for what purpose? One cannot drive immodesty any farther. An "immortal" Peter: who could tolerate *such* a *one*! . . . They never tire of involving God even in the smallest pitiable affairs they are mired in. The claim of being on personal speaking terms with God attests to the poorest taste! This Jewish though not exclusively Jewish chumminess [*Zudringlichkeit*] is but a nuzzling and pawing of God! . . .

The despised little "pagan nations" in eastern Asia from whom these early Christians could have learned something—*tactfulness* and reverence by those who, unlike Christian missionaries, will not venture to speak the name of their God.[7] Such reverence, it seems to me, is delicate enough. . . . In contrast later, Luther, "the most eloquent," presumptuous peasant lout with lack of taste, wanted to speak to God without mediation—well, that is what he did! (GM, III, 22)

NOTES

1. "Miniver Cheevy," a poem by Edwin Arlington Robinson (1910).

2. Abram L. Sachar, *A History of the Jews*, 3d ed. (New York: Knopf, 1948), p. 120.

3. See Felix Stössinger, *Heinrich Heine, Mein wervollstes Vermächtnis* (Zurich: Manesse, 1950), p. 611. Stossinger believes that Heine's imprecision, arising from his Jewish self-hate, has had a profound impact on world anti-Semitism and on anti-Pauline Christian sentiments. Goethe, too, had expressed his bias against the "noise" of the Jewish Bible over against Homer and Hellenism.

4. Gibbon's views are succinctly summarized in Will Durant, *Caesar and Christ* (New York: Simon and Schuster, 1944), p. 667.

5. Edward Gibbon, *The Decline and Fall of the Roman Empire* (New York: Modern Library Edition, 1932), 1:341–82.

6. The discovery was first published in Jung's doctoral dissertation (1902) and republished in C. G. Jung, *Psychiatric Studies*, 2d ed., trans. R. F. C. Hall (Princeton: Princeton University Press, 1970), pp. 82–83. Jung was not interested in plagiaristic practice but in the memory-retention process and the cryptomnesiac reproduction of material buried in the mind's past. The young Nietzsche also had written a poem extolling Kerner.

7. This still is an orthodox Jewish prohibition.

Appendix II

Sundry Notes

In trying to avoid duplication of earlier writings, Nietzsche had to rely on memory, and though it was near photographic there was some repetition but also some more forceful focusing. Some lay critics like Karl Jaspers, and some theologians—including the most courageous of the twentieth century, Karl Barth—regarded Nietzsche's *Antichrist* as a formidable but refutable challenge to the retention of Christian belief. In selecting passages in close sequence from this work, interest centers on those in which Judaism intersects critically with other topics.

Although Nietzsche follows some bible exegesists in predicating a historical Jewish God as against a later Christian one, he departs by expressing admiration for the former rather than the latter. As a strong image and model of "the will to power," the "Jewish God" is not an emasculated life-denier:

> ... A nation that strongly believes in itself, also has its own god ... projecting the pleasure it takes in its own being, its own sense of power. ...
> Such a God must be able to help and to injure, must be friend and foe. ...
> The unnatural castration of a god to make him conform only to goodness counters anything desirable. One needs an evil god as much as a good one: for instance, one does not owe one's existence to the milk of human kindness or tolerance ... of what usefulness would be a God who knew

305

nothing of anger, revenge, envy, mockery, deviousness, and violence? and who perhaps had never experienced the rapturous *ardeurs* of victory and of destruction? . . . In fact there is no other alternative for gods: either they are the will to power—and therefore they will endure as gods of nations— or, lacking will to power, they become powerless. (A, 16)

Among Nietzsche's gripping memorabilia are notebook entries of 1875 and 1878: "As a child:—I saw god in his splendor. [My] first philo- sophical writing was about the origination of the devil (God invents him, and he can only do this by the representation of his opposite)." Here is the permanently rooted idea of the jointure of good and evil, their co- existence in degree; much branches out from this basic notion. The strong, primal God admired by Nietzsche is the one who takes command and power over what he has created. Nietzsche's feelings border on those of the baroque mystics who want their resistance to be battered down and overwhelmed by a powerful God. On that point he is quite emphatic. Nietzsche's deeply personal wish and vision demands a strong father- God, not one who presides over a ghetto people. He extols the primal, ancient *national god of the chosen people* and not the later Christian God of the sinners and the sick:

> [Slaves change the god of their masters or conquerors into a devil figure while their own remains a good god. This type of revenge, a dualistic fic- tion, is the abortion produced of *décadence*.] How can anyone today still submit to the simplistics of Christian theologians and assert with them that the evolvement of the god-concept from "the God of Israel" (as that of a nation's god) to that of the Christian god (the quintessence of everything good), represents *progress*?—even Renan assumes this; as if he had a right to simplemindedness. . . . When the prerequisites for an *ascending* life—everything strong, masterful, and proud—is stripped from the conception of God, he slowly declines into a symbol, a staff for the tired . . . a god of the poor and the sinners. . . . Formerly he only had his "chosen" people. Then like his people, he became a wanderer, jour- neying into foreign lands without settling down anywhere and this cos- mopolitan came to feel at home everywhere . . . but he did not become a proud pagan: he remained a Jew, a god of unhealthy quarters all over the world . . . over a ghetto kingdom . . . he became a spider, a meta- physician, spinning the world out of himself—*sub specie Spinozae* . . . an "ideal," an "absolute" . . . deterioration. . . . (A, 17)

With consistent reasoning, Nietzsche criticizes even the Spinoza he admired. In this passage we see Nietzsche's elaboration on his earlier observation that God had become a Jew, namely, a wanderer, an emasculated Jehovah who without his "pagan heart" is now a mere presider over ghetto kingdoms.

The exhortation to face life with all its hardships and without the illusion of hope is a Nietzschean refrain. It would be less misleading to call him a paganistic philosopher than an atheist. As his ideal hybrid he seeks the Greek joy in art with its expression of physical overabundance *and* the spirituality symbolized by the Jew of antiquity—a fusion that envisions the *Übermensch*. What Nietzsche rejects out of hand decisively is any "corrupt conception of God" as a God of the sick or as a metaphysical spider or as one who, turned into a spirit, becomes the deification of "nothingness" and through whom "the will to nothingness is sanctified" (A, 18). Greek religion, in Nietzsche's estimation, was unflinching in its attitude toward the notions of "hope" and "love":

> [Hope, perversely, is a stronger stimulant to life than is happiness.] Sufferers have to be sustained by a hope that resists all realities, . . . by a hope, a belief in a Beyond. (Precisely because of hope's ability to keep some unfortunate person on tenterhooks, the Greeks regarded it as the epitome of evil, as the essentially pernicious evil; for that reason "hope" remained in Pandora's box.)—For *love* to be at all possible, God must be a person so that the lowest strata of instincts shall be able to speak up; God must be young. For the passions of women, a handsome saint is delivered, while for men a [young] Maria is moved into the foreground. [Here, Nietzsche points to feminine-Oriental influences.] All this with the prior assumption that Christianity wants to become master on the very soil on which the Aphrodite or the Adonis cult has already determined the cult-concepts. The requirement for *chastity* strengthens the vehemence and inwardness of the religious instinct—it makes the cult more heated, enthusiastic, more blissful—Love is the condition in which man most often sees things as they are *not*. [A religion had to be invented that allowed one to be oblivious to even the worst in life.] . . . Faith, hope and charity [*caritas* (love)] are not virtues but shrewd bait. (A, 23)

In the next several sections, Nietzsche gives his bird's-eye view of the origin of Christianity from Jewish soil. The scholarly content in view of

research—archeological and textual—and in light of the Dead Sea Scrolls
shows the extent to which Nietzsche and other nineteenth-century
thinkers were fishing in the dark and the utter simplicity to which they
managed to reduce a complex subject requiring the utmost philological
and scholarly rigor. Speculation, however, need not be stopped in its tracks
by facts unearthed since then. Nietzsche certainly would be the last to
admit absolute righteousness: all of one's prejudices and opinions, he
believed, are merely substitutions for those previously held. Of interest is
the passionate subjectivity Nietzsche displays and the discomforting ironies
he forcefully pushes to the surface, as with his observation that a Christian
who is "the ultimate upshot of Judaism condemns himself and his roots if
he is anti-Jewish." He is rephrasing Voltaire's thought, "When I see Christians cursing Jews, I think that I see children beating their fathers." Nietzsche, like Voltaire, took a dim view of the Jewish paternity, but he
declined to follow Voltaire's deracinated attacks on Jews and the Old Testament—personal prejudices acquired by Voltaire's limited experience. At
the same time, Nietzsche is at pains to point to those divergences in
ancient Judea that produced Pauline Christianity and to reinforce his idea
of contention between a "noble" and a "*ressentiment*" morality:

> Here, I merely touch upon the problem of the *origin* of Christianity.
> The first proposition for the problem's solution is this: Uniquely, Chris-
> tianity is to be understood only in reference to the soil out of which it
> grew—it is *not* a countermovement against the Jewish instinct, it is its
> very consequence, a step beyond its awe-inspiring logic. It has the sanc-
> tion of the Redeemer: "Salvation comes from the Jews" [John 4:22,
> Jesus' declaration to a Samaritan woman].—The second proposition
> reads: the psychological type of the Galilean is still recognizable; but,
> only in its complete degeneration [*Entartung*] (that at the same time is
> disfigured by and overloaded with foreign traces—) and thus could be
> used as the typology of a redeemer of mankind.
>
> The Jews are the strangest people in the world's history because
> when confronted with the question of being or not-being they chose as
> preference and with a decisive and uncanny consciousness, life—exis-
> tence at *any price*: this price meant their radical falsification of all
> nature and naturalness, all reality, and the whole inner as well as the
> outer world. Jews defined themselves [*grenzten sich ab*, distanced them-
> selves, established a border] *against* all restrictive conditions under

which, up until then, they had been able to or had been *allowed* to exist. Out of their own resources, they created a concept in opposition to *natural* conditions [walling themselves in]; step by step, they twisted religion, cult, morality, history, and psychology into hopeless contradictions and opposites to inherent *natural values* [*Natur-Werten*]. Once more, we encounter the same phenomenon but in exaggerated proportions, a mere copy though: the church cannot lay the slightest claim to originality in comparison with the "holy people." And with that in mind, the Jews are the most catastrophic [*verhangnissvolle,* fateful] people in the world's history: as an aftereffect, they have made mankind false to the point that even today a Christian can feel anti-Jewish without realizing that he himself is *the ultimate Jewish consequence* [*die letzte jüdische Konsequenz*].

In my *Genealogy of Morals,* I introduced for the first time and from a psychological perspective, the contrasting concepts of a *noble* morality and a *ressentiment* morality, the latter having developed out of a rejection of the former: but this is the Jewish-Christian morality pure and simple. In order to reject everything that tended towards an affirmation of life, the aristocratic, the powerful, the beautiful, and the self-affirmative here-and-now, the instinct of resentment turned into a guardian spirit that had to invent *another* world from whose perspective the affirmation of life had to appear as evil and reprehensible. In psychological retrospect, the Jewish people are a people endowed with the most tenacious life-force and who, when exposed to the most impossible situations, voluntarily and with the deepest sagacity of self-preservation sided with all decadent instincts; they were *not* dominated by these instincts but perceived in them a power through which one could prevail against "the world." Jews are the opposite of all decadents: they had to *give the appearance* of representing decadents. With a *non plus ultra* of theatrical talents they knew how to place themselves at the head of all decadent movements (Paul's Christianity, for instance) in order to produce out of themselves something stronger than any yea-saying participant in life. *Décadence* is merely a *means* for the power-seeking types—in Judaism and Christianity, the *priestly* types; these types have a life-long interest in making mankind *sick* and twisting the concepts "good" and "evil," "true" and "false" into things that endanger life and slander the world.—(A, 24)

It is quite clear that Jewish anti-Semitism is a form of self-hate but Nietzsche suggests that Christian anti-Semitism, too, is a form of unaware self-hatred. Decadence, he assumes to be a kind of masking, for he at varying times associates with or disassociates himself from being decadent. Alarmingly, though, Nietzsche's version of the Jew is that of a subversive in the clothing of Pauline Christianity—a maligning caricature.

Nietzsche goes against the currents of thought that the primal God Yahweh represents all that is cruel and barbaric in the remotest history reflected in the Old Testament. He sees instead a "naturalness," power, and instinctive innocence not yet saddled with strangulating theological dogmas and compares ancient Judaism with the pre-Homeric Greek experience not yet "poisoned by the worm of conscience":

> The history of Israel is invaluable as the typical story of denaturing, a *denaturalizing* [*Entnatürlichung*] of natural values: I point to five factual points in support. Originally, and above all, during the time of the kingdom, Israel did stand in *correct* relation to all things, that is, in natural relations. Its Yahweh was the expression of a power-consciousness, a joy in-and-of-itself in being, a self-confident hope within which lay the expectation of victory and salvation; through him nature was trusted to give the nation what was needed—above all, rain. Yahweh is the God of Israel and *consequently* a God of justice: such is the logic of any nation possessed of power and deriving a good conscience from it. In cultic celebrations, both aspects of a people express a self-affirmation: it is grateful for the great events that gave it ascendency, it is grateful for participation in the seasonal cycle and for success with animal breeding and land cultivation.—This kind of cohesiveness remained an ideal even after the kingdom had been done away with in sad fashion: anarchy plagued the inner life and the Assyrians threatened the outer. But the people clung to its most desired vision of a king—one who is a good soldier and a strict judge, as did that typical prophet (a critic and satirist of contemporaneous times) Isaiah.
>
> But every hope remained unfulfilled. The old God *could* no longer do what he formerly did. Should one have let go of him? But what happened? One *changed* one's perception of him, one *denaturalized* the conception of him: and by paying that price, one was able to hold on to him.—Yahweh the God of "Justice" was no longer in unison with Israel as its expression of a nation's essential being [its self-confidence] but only a God under certain conditions. . . . In the hands of priestly agitators, the idea of God becomes a tool, and they interpret all happiness as a form of reward, all misfortune as punishment for disobedience

toward God and as a form of "sin": here is that most mendacious manner of interpretation with which, once and for all, every so-called ethical world order with which the natural concepts of cause and effect are turned upside down decisively. Once one has dispatched natural causalities from this world, one is clearly in need of an *anti-natural* [something that defies the *natural* order of things] causality; now everything that follows indeed becomes unnatural. A God who *demands* (instead of a God who helps and who basically is a byword for every happy inspiration and self-confidence and courage), [points to a] morality that is no longer the expression of the conditions that foster life and growth of a people; and when no longer a people's life instinct but an abstraction, it becomes the antithesis of life—a morality that is a systematic degradation of the imagination and no more than "an evil eye" for all things. *What* is Jewish, *what* is Christian morality? Chance robbed of its innocence; misfortune dirtied by the concept of "sin"; well-being as a danger, as "temptation"; physiological indisposition poisoned by the worm of conscience. . . . (A, 25)

Upon no other persons than priests—of all denominations and pagans as well—has Nietzsche unleashed such a torrent of fury: the greatest haters of mankind in all of history; the most indecent, lying, degenerative, parasitical, life-poisoners and pious counterfeiters, desecrators of nature, psychological excrescences, enemies of knowledge, leaders of low-castes, self-promoters, destroyers of the soul's health, enemies of sensuality, devaluaters of life, the false asserters of God's existence, neurasthenics, war promoters (A, 42); derivers of power from the "sinfulness" of others, Pauline abortions and, least offensively, beefsteak cannibalizers. Like Voltaire, Nietzsche wished to neutralize their power that came from injuring others under the pretense that their devotees are sinners. For Nietzsche to have gone to such lengths in excoriating priests, presupposes deep personal emotions: reaction against his pastoral heritage, the threatening father-ghost, the horrifying invocations of the retributive father by his mother, perhaps the priestly "dissimulating" figure of Paul Rée, the priestly Mosaic injunctions that haunted his childhood, and his subsequent invention of Zarathustra to counter those figures. All this needs to be understood in the context of Nietzsche's historical interpretation of the Jewish experience. From the time of earliest Hebrew settlements, presumably 1300 B.C.E., to the Assyrian and the Babylonian conquests that destroyed the first Hebrew Commonwealth (the kingdom of Judah and Israel), the Temple of Jerusalem, and meant exile for its population in 597, there lay a history of Israel with its devotion to a powerful Old Testament Yahweh, warriors, prophets, kings, and a thriving civilization. During the lengthy period of Babylonian exile, the priests assumed a powerbroker role as never before, and through claims of divine revelation religious fundamentalists seized power. As Nietzsche put it, these "priestly agitators" rewrote sacred texts to suit their political purposes and by the time Jews returned in 539 to rebuild their temple in Jerusalem, Yahweh had become a "captive" of the priests and their self-arrogated divine sanctions. Nietzsche complained that the priests rewrote Israel's ancient history.[1] It is the *pre*-Babylonian exile period that Nietzsche held in as much admiration as classical Athens. But with the Hebrews' return until the disastrous conflicts with Rome and the rule of Roman procurators from 6 B.C.E. on (the kingdom of Judah was renamed the province of Judea), the priestly *ressentiments* provided the leaven for the origination of Christianity. It is this radicalized view that colored Nietzsche's thinking. "Modern" Jewish history begins figuratively with the loss of national identity, Rome's triumph, the diaspora or the centuries-long dispersal and troublesome wanderings that, in Nietzsche's view, reduced Jews, through foreign intimidation, to caricatures of their ancient glory.

Nietzsche does not repeat here what he has already said about the "priestly species of man," arrogant in its feeling of self-willed superiority, a will to power in which the "holy lie originates." "It is a lie copied almost everywhere: an Aryan *influence* that has corrupted all the world" (*WM*, 142). Like Renan, Nietzsche made no essential brief for either Aryan or Semitic superiority. Renan in his best critical moment saw both groups physically as one race, and intellectually as part of one family—the "civilized family." In Nietzsche's view, the priestly element was disastrous wherever it appeared. What follows, at any rate, is his expressed displeasure with the Jewish priest and his alleged religious and historical role:

> The concept of God is falsified—but the Jewish priests did not stop there. They could not use all of Jewish history and decided to do away with it! They have wrought a miraculous work of falsification, ignoring every tradition and the reality of a historical past which they translated into *religious terms*, which means they turned national history into a

stupid salvation mechanism of guilt incurred against Yahweh and punishment and reward for piety. . . . In the hands of Jewish priests, the
great epoch in Israel's history became an epoch of decay, the Exile, the
long years of misfortune, was transformed into an eternal *punishment* for
the great epoch—an epoch in which the priest had not as yet held sway.
. . . The priest makes himself indispensable . . . and he devalues, *dese-
crates* nature. . . . The priest *thrives* upon sins, it is necessary for him
that people sin. Their supreme principle: "God forgives those who
repent"—simply put—those who submit to the priest. (A, 26)

With a touch of intellectual acrobatics, Nietzsche links the Jewish
"priestly instinct" with Jesus' rebellion and casts him as a "holy anar-
chist." Be that as it may, it underlines Nietzsche's contention that Jesus
died not as a religious redeemer but as a rebel against hierarchical order
and as one whose unrealistic visions exceeded even that of the priests.
Nietzsche's designation of Jesus as a "political criminal" would have some
substance if he meant to say that Jesus as "king of the Jews" made him
liable to criminal prosecution as a political subversive against the Roman
Empire. But there was little to commend the pale Galilean Jew over
against Nietzsche's noble Romans:

> . . . Jesus has been understood or *misunderstood* as the originator of a
> rebellion against the Jewish church. . . . His was a rebellion against "the
> good and the just," against "the saints of Israel," against the hierarchy
> of society—and *not* against its corruption, but against caste, privilege,
> rankings, social norms: it was a *rejection* of [*Unglaube,* disbelief in] the
> "higher order of persons" . . . and every priest and theologian. . . . This
> little rebellious movement, baptized in the name of Jesus of Nazareth,
> represents the Jewish instinct *once more,* namely, the priestly instinct
> which can no longer stand the reality of the priest and invents a still
> more abstract form of existence, a more unreal vision of the world. . . .
> It was an attack on hierarchical stability, the profoundest national
> instinct, on the strongest will to life that the world has seen. This holy
> anarchist who roused up the lowest of society, the outcasts, "sinners,"
> the *chandala* within Judaism; [Jesus] was a political criminal . . . in *an
> absurdly unpolitical* society; this brought him to the cross: a proof of that
> is the inscription upon the cross. He died for *his* guilt. Every proof is
> lacking, though it is often asserted, that he died to atone for the guilt
> of others. (A, 27)

Of Jesus' teachings embodied in early, primitive Christianity, Niet-zsche applauds the rejection of Jewish ecclesiastical and priestly ma-chinery—Jesus required no mediation or rites in praying to and commu-nicating with God. Such teachings were integral to the "glad tidings"; here was a trend that Nietzsche regretted to see reversed after Jesus' demise on the cross. In the following passage, Nietzsche resorts by impli-cation to the lovely ecumenical story of Ruth—an ancient example of neighborliness of Jews and non-Jews. He also touches on the philosophy of not resisting evil, a philosophy he elsewhere condemns vehemently as psychologically false. All this and subsequent passages severely compress thoughts that could have benefited from more discursive elaboration. Yet among this raw material he crafted a phrase that with its nettles has sur-vived in time: "There was only one Christian and he has died on the cross" (A, 39). One modern Christian historian says much the same less aphoristically: "Luke's account of the religion preached immediately after Pentecost does not bear resemblance to Jesus' teaching. Its starting point is the resurrection, but otherwise it is Christianity without Christ."[2]

> In the entire psychology of the "Gospel" ["Evangelium," "evangel"], the concepts of guilt and punishment are absent as is the concept of reward. . . . The true evangelic practice makes no distinction between foreigner and native, Jew and non-Jew . . . neither by word nor deed does he resist the person who does him evil. . . . The life of the redeemer [and his "glad tidings" that brings God and man close, without mediation] was nothing else than *this* practice. . . . He no longer required any for-mulas, any rites for communicating with God—not even prayer. He has settled accounts with the whole penance-and-reconciliation doctrine. He knows that it is through actual practice in life that one feels "divine," "blessed," "evangelical," and at all times to have the feeling of being a "child of God." . . . What was dispensed with by the evangel was Judaism's concept of sin, faith, redemption through faith; the whole Jewish *ecclesiastical doctrine* was negated in "the glad tidings." . . . A new way of life, not a new faith. (A, 33)

Nietzsche is consistent in abjuring theological faith and proposing reconstituted moral and ethical values as preliminaries to a culture of the future.

... I shall now relate the *real* story of Christianity. Already the word "Christianity" is a misperception—basically, there was only one Christian and he died on the cross. The Evangel *died* upon the cross. From that moment on what had been called "evangel" became the opposite of what he had lived: "*bad* tidings," a "dysangel." ... (A, 39)

... Naturally the coincidence of environment, language, and of background, determine the complex of certain concepts: earliest Christianity uses *only* Jewish Semitic concepts (the eating and the drinking at the Last Supper, for instance, like everything Jewish, has been misused so badly by the church). .... (A, 32)

In the history of religious anti-Semitism, and cynically adopted by political anti-Semites, the accounts of Jesus' crucifixion have been critical and inciteful to violence against Jews. The most damaging fiction came from Matthew: After Jesus refused to disclaim being "the Son of God," the high priest, appalled by the blasphemy, tore his own robe and incited the mob to declare Jesus deserving of death; the priests and the Jewish elders delivered him bound to the Roman governor Pilate who acceded to their demand to have the self-proclaimed "King of the Jews" crucified. Pilate, fearing a riot, absolved himself of the death judgment and turned Jesus over to a jeering and abusive battalion of Roman soldiers; the Jews, too, absolved Pilate and condemned themselves fatefully by allegedly saying, "His blood be on us and our children" (Matt. 27:25).

The anti-Jewish version by Matthew proved at first to be quite expedient and then disastrously popular. Proselytizers for the new sect had a choice between fact and fiction. Only the Roman governor, Pilate, was empowered to mete out the death penalty, but the proselytizers did not dare implicate him as morally and juridically responsible for Jesus' death. Instead they chose to implicate the Jews who could not be converted by the new sect anyway. A new and major phase of scapegoating Jews had begun in advancing missionary work within the Hellenistic world. In historical perspective, Jesus was uncongenial as a religious and political rebel to both the Roman Pilate, with his record of rapacity and brutality, and the Jews who loathed Roman lordship and Roman paganism but feared the repressive retaliatory measures a political Jewish rebel could prompt Rome to take. In the eyes of Rome, Jesus lived and consequently died as a Jewish rebel, a false messiah proclaiming cataclysm and the advent of a new age by fomenting a revolution in Judea to free it from Roman domination.

Nietzsche downplays the "mutinous" and combative picture of Jesus and imputes to the Jesus on the cross an unearthly triumph over *ressentiment*. The disciples' own "Jewish-derived vengefulness" created an altogether different Jesus from the one who had lived and taught the glad tidings. Nietzsche came close to paralleling Christian with Dionysian mysticism, without accepting the former. Just as he had conceptualized the Dionysian experience in *The Birth of Tragedy*, Nietzsche was on the verge of theorizing about the psychological origin of monotheism and the idea of a *sole* begotten son of God, but he contented himself with a cryptic suggestion that these imaginings arose from the depths of *ressentiment* against polytheism. In a sense this was true because the Roman—like other pagan pantheons—willy-nilly collected *all* gods tolerantly—feeling that if one god did not work satisfactorily, it would be possible to pragmatically turn to another—and they were ready to acquire a representation of the Jewish God through the figure of Abraham. An intangible monotheistic God, however, could be neither burned nor paraded through Rome as a spoil of war nor worshiped in the Pantheon. Nietzsche's own dismissal of a monotheistic God may have been the fear of a prying and dreaded evil eye, with penetrating omnipotent power, destroying the essential privacy with which Nietzsche hedged his life. Monotheism's implicit social message—abhorrent to Nietzsche's aristocratic sense—envisaged a supreme God who watches over all his children democratically. Polytheism, on the contrary, allows men to become gods, as did the Caesars, and Nietzsche to become Dionysus, ultimately. At any rate, Nietzsche's application of *ressentiment* to monotheism is a precursor of modern psychohistorical interpretations:

> The catastrophic fate of the evangel with the death of the one it put to the cross, usually reserved for the *canaille*, [resulted in] the frightful, enigmatic question, . . . *Who* killed him? who was his natural enemy? . . . Answer given: "*ruling* Judaism, its upper class, Jesus as having been *in mutiny against the social order.*" This negative, warlike trait and image [was newly introduced, but his life in word and deed] clearly contradicted this. Apparently the small community did *not* understand the main point, the exemplary nature of this kind of death as the freedom

from and the triumph *over* every feeling of *ressentiment*. . . . Jesus could not have desired anything from his death except to offer publicly the sternest test and proof of his teachings [death with a gentle peace of heart—but his disciples were overcome by unevangelical feelings of *vengefulness*]. The affair could not possibly be allowed to end with this death: "retribution" was required, "punishment" and . . . a "sitting in judgment." Once more, the popular expectation of a Messiah came into the foreground as a historic moment was envisioned: "the kingdom of God" is coming to sit in judgment upon its enemies. . . . [These disciples, completely unhinged souls, made of Jesus a Pharisee and a theologian]; they could no longer endure the evangelic idea of the universal right to be a child of God as taught by Jesus. It was their revenge to *elevate* Jesus extravagantly and to sever him from themselves, just as Jews out of revenge against their enemies, severed their God from themselves and exalted him. The *one* God and the *one* son of God—both were products of *ressentiment*. (A, 40)

Although Nietzsche found Jesus' message objectionable on psychological, ethical, and personal grounds, he lacked no admiration for anyone's overcoming of human, all-too-human *ressentiments* as he thought them to be dramatized in Jesus' finale; although this may have been Nietzsche's personal aim, it was always to remain incomplete. His dual feelings about Jesus—as conqueror of the vengeful or as Jesus theologized—have perfectly rational explanations. As in earlier writings, Nietzsche, again in high dudgeon, attacks Jews and Christians alike through Paul, his black scapegoat: With the cynical logic of a rabbi, says Nietzsche, Paul exercised psychological depravity in his version of the redeemer's death and resurrection.

The Bible admits no peer. There, one is among Jews and the essence of their race. In Christianity, the art of holy lying comes of Judaism's serious schooling and technique perfected during hundreds of years, and attaining ultimate perfection. The Christian, that *ultima ratio* of the lie, is the Jew once more—even thrice more. . . . The Christian is only a Jew of "more liberal" confession. (A, 44)

Nietzsche's reasoning here—one hesitates to use the word "logic"—proposes that the Jewish Christians turned their acquired Jewish instincts against the non-Jew—hence, the Christian is a Jew in disguise. Syllogisms such as these and dicta like the following are fanciful aberrations without historical corroboration to sustain them. One can hardly argue with the fact that self-serving concepts of "morality" have been abused—indeed, they are the everyday staple of politicians and of some religionists—but to direct this idea against a stereotyped "Jewish race" does Nietzsche no credit.

> It certainly makes a difference for what purpose one lies: to preserve something with a lie or to destroy it. . . . Christianity was the vampire of the *imperium Romanum*. . . . With Paul, *chandala*-hatred against Rome and against "the world" became flesh and genius. Paul—the Jew, the eternal Jew *par excellence*. . . . (A, 58)

For the Jew Paul (or Saul), Nietzsche held as much unremitting scorn as he did for priests. Calling Paul "the eternal Jew *par excellence*" traps Nietzsche in an ambiguity here because he attributed the Jew's longevity to obstinacy in survival and to fiery, justifiable *ressentiments*, Nietzsche was neither the first nor the last to blame Paul for the "invention of Christianity"—if indeed it was blameworthy. In attacking Christianity head on as did the monstrous Nazi anti-Christian propagandists—largely and scandalously unopposed by organized Christianity—they found "the evil rabbi Paul" a convenient target. It has with equal conviction been argued by many that Paul saved Christianity from extinction by giving it a theological-mystical base and pruning away those Jewish elements that failed to attract new adherents to a new, syncretic faith. Prior to Paul, however, is the attribution to Jesus that "The flesh is of no profit, it is the spirit that gives life" (John 6:63). The renowned sixteenth-century Catholic theologian Erasmus of Rotterdam sees Paul's beliefs as crucial extensions of Jesus': "Paul's whole purpose is this: that the flesh be despised as it is the source of contention. . . ."[3] Still, Nietzsche makes Paul his *bête noire*:

> [Paul was the greatest of all the apostles of revenge. . . .] *What follows from this?* One does well to put on gloves when reading the New Testament. One is almost forced to do so by the proximity of so much uncleanness. We would no more choose to associate with the "first Christians" than we would with Polish Jews: not that one would need raise a single objec-

tion [*Einwand*] to them. . . . They both do not smell good. . . . In the entire New Testament there is only one single figure to respect—Pilate, the Roman governor. He cannot persuade himself to take Jew-dealings [*Judenhandel*] *seriously*. One Jew more or less—what does it matter? . . . The noble scorn of a Roman in front of whom a shameless travesty was played out in abuse of the word "truth." . . . (A, 46)

Given this passage, Nietzsche apologists do not have the excuse of saying that Nietzsche did not intend such thoughts for publication or that they constituted preliminary notes. By linking the first Christians and Polish Jews in an odoriferous way, he yielded to unseemly prejudices of his time. That many Austro-Germans and some Jews feared the influx of Polish brethren was a fact that Nietzsche needed not to have acquiesced to by pandering to feelings that such immigration was deleterious.[4] That he implicitly referred to East European immigration (which his anti-Semitic brother-in-law petitioned against) is clear in his deliberate use of the word "Einwand" which, stretched a bit, becomes "Einwanderer" or immigrant. Lest this be thought an uncharitable observation, one cannot avoid the Nietzschean portrayal of Pilate as a "noble Roman" displaying noble Roman scorn toward the "shameless Jew-dealings and travesty" unfolding under his eyes. Nietzsche accused the New Testament of dealing fraudulently with the early history of Israel, but Nietzsche himself did no less. He created a personalized psychodrama miles removed from a historian's scholarly responsibilities.

In the next passages Nietzsche substitutes his sardonic fable for the biblical creation story, with the intent of deriding and exposing its rationale, a rationale that he claims backfired:

Has anyone really understood the famous story that appears at the beginning of the Bible [the Old Testament]—that is, God's hellish fear of *science* [*Wissenschaft*, the quest for knowledge and inquiry into the natural causes of things]? . . . It has not been understood. [Genesis] is a priest-book *par excellence* and bespeaks the great inner difficulty of the priest who senses only *one* great danger, and consequently "God" senses only *one* great danger.—The old God, entirely "spirit," entirely high priest, absolute perfection, pleasantly strolls in his garden but has only one problem—he is bored. Even gods fight in vain against boredom. What shall he do? He invents man . . . man is entertaining . . . but see, even man becomes bored. The unbounded mercy of God extends to all in Paradise who, of necessity, share distress, and he immediately created other animals as well. God's *first* mistake: man; and man soon found animals not entertaining—he lords it over them and even chooses not to be an "animal" and consequently God created woman. And indeed, that was the end of boredom—but of other things as well! Woman was God's *second mistake*. Woman by nature is a snake, "Heva" [Eve etymologically means "life," not snake as Nietzsche would have it] as every priest knows. From woman comes every calamity in the world—every priest knows that, too. In consequence, it is from her also that *science comes*. It was through woman that man first learned to taste of the tree of knowledge. What happened? The old God was gripped by a hellish fear. Man himself had become his *greatest* mistake, he had created a rival for himself—science puts one on a level with the *divine* [*gottgleich*, godlike]—it puts an end to gods and priests when man becomes scientific!—The *moral* of all this: Science is in itself the forbidden. Science is the *first* sin, the germ of all sin, the *primal* [original] sin. *This in itself constitutes morality*. "You shall *not* know"—and the rest follows.—God's hellish fear did not preclude his being clever. How does one *protect* oneself against science? That was to become a persistent problem. Answer: drive man out of Paradise! Happiness, leisure [*Müssiggang*], bring with it thinking—idle thoughts are bad thoughts. . . . Man *must* not think. And "the priest in himself" [Nietzsche's parody of Kant's "thing-in-itself"] invents distress, death, the mortal danger in pregnancy, every sort of misery, old age, tribulations, *sickness* above all—all of these are means intended to battle science! Trials and tribulations do not *allow* man to think. . . . And yet, oh horrors! the work of science [knowledge] begins to build up, storming heavenward, spelling doom [twilight of the gods]—what is to be done? The old God invents *war*, he divides nations, he arranges for men to mutually destroy themselves (priests always have required wars); war, among other things, is the greatest disturber of science! Unbelievable! Knowledge—the *emancipation from priests* is growing despite wars.—And a final decision occurs to the old God: "man has become scientific [knowledgeable] so that there is *no recourse except to drown him*"! [a reference to the biblical flood story]. . . . (A, 48)

With the story of Eden and man's exile, the entire psychology of the priest is revealed, says Nietzsche.

Elsewhere, Nietzsche wrote, "American laughter is good for me in the fashion of sea-pilots like Mark Twain. I've not been able to laugh along with anything said by Germans" (*UW*, II, 1011). Nietzsche's indictment of priests as the ventriloquists of God and his parodistic treatment of God does indeed reflect some readings of Mark Twain, who caustically observed that "Our heavenly father invented man because he was disappointed in the monkey." Indeed, Nietzsche provides a Mark Twain reading of Genesis—blasphemy edged with satire and spiked with backhanded compliments for women. Aphoristically, he noted that priests support religion because religion supports them. Further:

> . . . The beginning of the Bible contains all of the priest's psychology.
> . . . One had to bring man to a state of misery . . . and to suffer in such a fashion that he would be in need of a priest at all times . . . *and in need of a savior*; away with doctors. (A, 49)

> The pietist, the priest of both sexes is false. . . . (A, 52)

An exploration of an aphorism formulated earlier—"convictions might be more dangerous enemies of truth than lies"—forms the basis for insightful psychological differentiations in Nietzsche's next essays. The faithful or the believer who relinquishes his independence not only falls into slavery and self-alienation but also risks becoming a pathological fanatic like Savonarola, Luther, Rousseau, Robespierre, or Saint-Simon. A liar knows the difference between truth and falsity, a person of conviction cannot, in Nietzsche's view. The priest arrogates to himself the employment of the lie as did Plato, the Law Book of Manu (Nietzsche's counterpoint to the Bible), Confucius, the Bible itself, the Christian Church, the Koran, and whenever the priest lays claim to be "God's mouthpiece."

> Ultimately it matters toward what *end* a lie is told. A belief may be necessary to life, yet be false. That "holy" ends [*Zwecke*, purposes] are lacking in Christianity is *my* objection to its means. Only *bad* ends: poisoning, defamation, denial of life, despisement of the body, the denigration and self-abuse of humans through the concept of sin—*consequently*, Christianity's means are equally bad.—With quite opposite feelings do I read the Law Book of Manu, an incomparable spiritual and thought-through work; it would be a sin against the spirit to *mention* it in the same breath as the Bible [the New Testament, in context here].

One discovers immediately that it has a real philosophy to back it up and in itself is not, unlike the Bible, an odoriferous, poisonous Jewish [*Judaine*] mixture of rabbinism and superstition; it offers even the most pampered psychologist something to mull over. *Not* forgetting the main point, namely, *the* basic difference between it and every kind of Bible: here we find the means by which the *noble* ranks, the philosophers and the warriors control the masses; everywhere reign noble [aristocratic] values, a complete sense of well-being, a yea-saying to life, a triumphal satisfaction with self and with life—the whole book is *sun* drenched. All those things upon which Christianity vents its bottomless meanness—for instance, on woman, marriage—are treated by Manu with reverence, with love and trust. . . . And how *may* one be a Christian as long as the idea of the *immaculate conception* Christianizes, and actually dirties, the origin of man?

I know of no book like that of Manu that speaks of women with as many tender and gracious words. These old greybeards and holy men have a way of being courteous to women which perhaps has not been surpassed. "The mouth of a woman"—it notes in one instance, "the bosom of a maiden, the prayer of a child, the smoke of a burnt-offering are always pure." In another passage, we find, "there is nothing more pure than the light of the sun, the shadow of a cow, the air, water, fire and the breath of a young girl." To cite another passage still—that also is possibly a holy lie: "all openings of the body above the navel are pure, and all below are impure. Only in respect to young girls is the entire body pure." (A, 56)

Nietzsche's criteria for the comparative evaluations of religious scriptures in terms of their social, anthropological, and ethical implications may be gathered from these and similar ruminations. The "holy lie" mentioned in the last sentence and frequently elsewhere epitomizes his justification of its use by the nobles and warriors of Manu in guiding and controlling the masses. "Certainly it makes a difference for what purpose one lies: if one sustains therewith or destroys." (A, 58). This becomes Nietzsche's own justification for the "lie." Yet he inveighed against other "lies" such as the emasculated sexuality he sees preached in the New Testament. He responds to the evangelist Mark's injunction, "If thine eye offends thee, pluck it out" (Mark 9:47–48) with the sarcastic rejoinder that "it is not exactly the eye that is meant." Unless marriages are eugenically meaningful rather than mere satisfaction of the passions, Nietzsche not only opts for but advocates honest prostitution and trial marriages. He admires what he calls the cold, calculating, noble, and healthy aristocracy of ancient Athens where the breeding of "race and family" dominated. Nietzsche's many entries for *The Will to Power* advocate the ancient Greek patriarchal families.

Nietzsche valued his independence more than conventional social values and conveniences of marriage. He agreed in principle less with Plato than with Aristotle, who views in his *Politics* "the courage and justice of a man and of a woman as not the same; the courage of a man is shown in commanding, and of a woman in supporting." This is precisely Zarathustra/Nietzsche's warrior attitude. Nietzsche's bisexual inclination and confirmed bachelorhood put him at odds with such "Pauline rabbinisms" as this: "because of the temptation to immorality, each man should have his own wife and each woman her own husband" (1 Cor. 7:2); "if [the unmarried like Paul himself, or a widow] cannot exercise self-control, they should marry. For it is better to marry than to be aflame with passion" (1 Cor. 7:9).

On the question of racial discrimination within a society, Nietzsche sometimes deplores it, as he does the caste laws and segregation system of Manu. Yet in order to make his points about sexual, marital attitudes and unregulated bourgeois procreation to which he objected, he plays selective games with Old and New Testament and Manu texts.

The Antichrist gradually builds toward a grand climax with Nietzsche's calumniation of Christianity and his curse upon it and its evil genius, the "rabbi" Paul, who "with the aid of a tiny sectarian movement on the edge of Judaism, unleashed lower-class hatred against Rome and the world." This Nietzschean gospel has the virtue of not laying blame upon an entire people but only on a fringe of Jews who, as Nietzsche claims, caused more corruption than all the corrupt Roman emperors combined. Harangue and lament alternate: "Christianity was the vampire of the *Imperium Romanum* . . ." and destroyed a slowly emerging civilization of undreamed-of possibilities. Nietzsche erects a tombstone and inconsolably mourns the loss of Rome, its noblesse and manliness, which shared with Greece the prerequisites for great culture. Paul, having been accused of leading Jewish *chandala* elements against Rome, now is additionally charged with amalgamating and "outbidding" the ideas of all pagan cults as well as subverting Nietzsche's idealized Rome. The Renaissance and the Reformation offered a chance for the retrieval of ancient values, but Luther and the Germans botched that opportunity.

With a parting salvo, not inconsistent with what is said elsewhere in *The Antichrist*, Nietzsche posits a view generally taken as anti-Jewish; in choosing between two Semitic peoples, Jews and Arabs, and between Islam and Christianity, he chose Islam and the Arab. If he meant only to denigrate the "chandala" Jew, he was not altogether explicit. In his praise of Islam at the expense of Judaism and Christianity, it did not suit Nietzsche's argument to note Mohammed's syncretic adaptations of Jewish and Christian ideas about God, particularly Jewish monotheism and its Old Testament patriarchs and prophets, and, clearly enough, Christian beliefs in the Judgment Day and heaven and hell.

NOTES

1. It is likely that for purposes of communal cohesion there was a "rewriting" of ancient history and new codifications but also a great deal of cultural activity of Jews in Babylon, of which nineteenth-century European historians and Christian Hebraists, along with the non-philological and philosophizing Nietzsche, were in total ignorance.

2. Paul Johnson, *A History of Christianity* (New York: Atheneum, 1976), p. 32.

3. Quoted and discussed by Cornelis Augustjin, *Erasmus: His Life, Works, and Influence* (Toronto: University of Toronto Press, 1991), p. 47.

4. The Sephardic Jews of Holland, for instance, felt their gains and security threatened by an influx of persecuted co-religionists in the fifteenth and sixteenth centuries much as some German Jews feared that a wave of distressed Jewish foreigners—Eastern Jews—would turn Gentiles against them as well in more recent history.

Select Bibliography

I. PRIMARY SOURCES

Nietzche quotations are principally drawn from the following collected works:

The Basic Writings of Nietzsche, trans. Walter Kaufmann. New York: Modern Library, 1968. Includes: *The Birth of Tragedy, Beyond Good and Evil, On the Genealogy of Morals, The Case of Wagner, Ecce Homo*, and various notes and extracts.

Werke in drei Bänden, ed. Karl Schlechta. 3 vols. Munich: Carl Hanser, 1954–56; with an index in a fourth volume (1965).

Werke. Kritsche Gesamtausgabe, ed. G. Colli and M. Montinari. Berlin: de Gruyter, 1967; ca. 30 vols.

Sources for letters and notes included:

Bernouilli, Carl A. *Franz Overbeck und Friedrich Nietzsche*. 2 vols. Jena: Diedrichs, 1908. (For quotations from Overbeck.)

Die Briefe Cosima Wagners an Friedrich Nietzsche, Pt. I, 1869–1871; Pt. II, 1871–1877, ed. Erhart Thierbach. 2 vols. Weimar: Nietzsche Archive, 1938–40.

Briefwechsel. Kritische Gesamtausgabe, ed. G. Colli and M. Montinari. 18 vols. Berlin, 1975–.

F. Nietzsches Briefwechsel mit Erwin Rohde. Leipzig: Insel Verlag, 1916.

Meysenbug, Malwida von. *Memoiren einer Idealistin und ihr Nachtrag: Der Lebens-
abend einer Idealistin,* ed. Berta Schleicher. 2 vols. Berlin and Leipzig, 1927.

*Nietzsche in seinen Briefen und Berichten der Zeitgenossen. Die Lebensgeschichte in
Dokumenten,* ed. Alfred Baeumler. Leipzig: Kröner, 1932.

Werke und Briefe, Historisch-Kritische Gesamtausgabe, ed. Wilhelm Hoppe and
Karl Schlechta. 4 vols. Munich: C. H. Beck, 1938–1942.

Additional letter material appeared in contributions by R. F. Krummel, "Josef
Paneth über seine Begegnung mit Nietzsche in der Zarathustra-Zeit," and A.
Venturelli, *Nietzsche Studien* 13 (1984).

Ecce Homo drafts appear in Karl-Heinz Hahn and Mazzino Montinari, *Ecce
Homo: Facsimileausgabe der Handschrift.* Wiesbaden: Ludwig Reichart, 1985.

Miscellaneous primary sources (including Wagner material):

Cosima Wagner's Diaries, vol. I, 1869–77; vols. I, II, ed. Martin Gregor-Dellin
and Dietrich Mack. New York: Harcourt Brace Jovanovich, 1978–80.

Grundlehner, Philip. *The Poetry of Friedrich Nietzsche.* Oxford: Oxford University Press, 1986.

Mazzino, Montinari. *Nietzsche Lesen.* Berlin: Walter de Gruyter, 1982.

Richard Wagner Briefe, Die Sammlung Burrell, ed. John N. Burk. Frankfurt a.M.:
S. Fischer, 1950. Trans. *Letters of Richard Wagner, The Burrell Collection,* ed.
John N. Burk. New York: Macmillian, 1950.

Selected Letters of Richard Wagner, ed. Stewart Spenser and Barry Millington.
New York: Norton, 1988.

Die Unschuld des Werdens, Der Nachlass, ed. and comp. Alfred Baeumler. Vols. 1
and 2. Stuttgart: Alfred Kröner, 1956.

Wagner, Richard. *Das braune Buch.* Zurich: Atlantis, 1975.

II. ADDITIONAL RELATED MATERIALS

Baron, Salo W. *Modern Nationalism and Religion.* New York: Harper Brothers,
1947.

Bernays, Jacob. *Zwei Abhandlungen über die aristotelische Theorie des Drama.*
Darmstadt: Wissenschaftliche Buchgesellschaft, 1857, 1876; reprint 1968.

Binion, Rudolf. *Frau Lou, Nietzsche's Wayward Disciple.* Princeton: Princeton
University Press, 1968.

Brandes, Georg. *Friedrich Nietzsche: An Essay on Aristocratic Radicalism*, trans. A. G. Chater. London: W. Heinemann, 1914.

Brann, H. W. *Nietzsche und die Frauen*. Leipzig: Meiner, 1931.

Deussen, Paul. *Erinnerungen an Friedrich Nietzsche*. Leipzig: Brockhaus, 1901.

Duffy, Michael, and Willard Mittelman. "Nietzsche's Attitudes towards the Jews." *Journal of History of Ideas* 49 (1988): 301–17.

Elbogen, Ismar, and Eleonore Sterling. *Die Geschichte der Juden in Deutschland*. Frankfurt, a.M.: Athenäum, 1966, 1988; chapter 7, "Die Restauration." Heinemann, 1914.

Fishberg, Maurice. *The Jews: A Study of Race and Environment*. London: W. Scott, 1911.

Förster-Nietzsche. *Das Leben Friedrich Nietzsche*. Leipzig, Naumann, 1895–1904.

———. *Wagner und Nietzsche: Zur Zeit ihrer Freundschaft*. Munich: G. Müller, 1915. English edition, *Wagner and Nietzsche*, Wilhelm Hoppe, ed.

Gay, Peter. *Freud, Jews, and other Germans*. New York: Oxford University Press, 1978.

Gibbon, Edward. *The Decline and Fall of the Roman Empire*. New York: Modern Library Edition, 1932.

Gilman, Sander L. *Inscribing the Other*. Lincoln: University of Nebraska Press, 1991.

Goldkorn, Isaac. "Renan and Racism." *Midstream*, November 1986.

Golomb, Jacob. "Nietzsche's Judaism of Power." *Revue de études juives* 146–47 (July–December 1988): 353–85.

Grayzel, Solomon. *A History of the Jews*. Philadelphia: The Jewish Publication Society, 1947.

Groth, H. Miles. "Nietzsche's Ontogenic Theory of Time: The Riddle of the Laughing Shepherd." *American Imago* 37 (1980): 351–70.

Gutman, Robert W. *Richard Wagner, The Man, His Mind, His Music*. New York: Harcourt Brace, 1968.

Hayman, Ronald. *Nietzsche: A Critical Life*. New York: Oxford University Press, 1980.

Hollingdale, R. J. *Nietzsche*. London: Routledge, 1993.

Holob, Robert C. "Nietzsche and the Jewish Question." *New German Critique* 66 (Fall 1995): 94–121.

Janz, Curt Paul. *Friedich Nietzsche, Biographie*. 3 vols. Munich and Vienna, 1977–1978.

Jaspers, Karl. *Nietzsche und das Christentum* (1938). Munich: Piper, 1947. English trans. E. B. Ashton, *Nietzsche and Christianity*. Chicago: Gateway Editions, 1961.

Johnson, Paul. *A History of Christianity*. New York: Atheneum, 1976.

Jung, C. G. *Nietzsche's Zarathustra,* ed. James L. Jarrett. 2 vols. Princeton: Princeton University Press, 1988.

Kaufmann, Walter. *Nietzsche: Philosopher, Psychologist, Antichrist* (1950). 4th ed. Princeton: Princeton University Press, 1974.

Klausner, Joseph. *The Messianic Idea in Israel.* New York: Macmillan, 1955.

Lang, Paul Henry. *Music in Western Civilization.* New York: Norton, 1949.

Lea, F. A. E. *The Tragic Philosopher.* London: Methuen, 1957.

Lehmann, Lilli. *Mein Weg.* Leipzig: Hirzel, 1913.

Lessing, Theodor. *Der Jüdische Selbsthass.* Berlin: Jüdischer Verlag, 1930.

Mandel, Siegfried. "Genelli and Wagner: Midwives to Nietzsche's *The Birth of Tragedy.*" *Nietzsche-Studien* 19 (1990): 212–29.

Momigliano, Arnaldo. *Jacob Bernays.* Amdsterdam/London: North-Holland Publishing Co., 1969.

Montinari, Mazzino. "Ein neuer Abschnitt in Nietzsches 'Ecce Homo.' " *Nietzsche Studien* (1972).

Newman, Ernest. *The Life of Richard Wagner.* 4 vols. New York: Knopf, 1933–1946.

———. *Wagner as Man and Artist.* New York: Vintage Books, 1960.

Nietzsche, F. A. August. *Gamaliel, oder die immerwahrende Dauer des Christentums.* Leipzig, 1896.

Peters, H. F. *My Sister, My Spouse.* New York: Norton, 1962.

Pfeiffer, Ernst, ed. *F. N., Paul Rée, Lou von Salomé.* Frankfurt: Insel, 1970.

Rée, Paul. *Psychologische Betrachtungen.* Berlin: Carl Dunker, 1875.

Renan, Ernest. *The Life of Jesus,* intro. John Haynes Holmes. New York: Random House, 1927.

Robert, Marthe. *From Oedipus to Moses: Freud's Jewish Identity,* trans. Ralph Manheim. New York: Anchor Books, 1976.

Sachar, Abram L. *A History of the Jews.* 3rd ed. New York: Knopf, 1948.

Sachar, Howard M. *The Course of Modern Jewish History.* New York: Vintage Books, 1990.

Salomé, Lou Andreas. *Friedrich Nietzsche in seinen Werken.* Vienna: Carl Konegen, 1894.

———. *Lebensrückblick,* ed. Ernst Pfeiffer. Frankfurt a.M.: Insel, 1968. English trans. Breon Mitchell. *Looking Back, Memories.* New York: Paragon House, 1990.

———. *Nietzsche,* trans. and ed. Siegfried Mandel. Redding Ridge, Conn.: Black Swan Books, 1988.

Santaniello, W. *Nietzsche, God, and the Jews.* Albany: SUNY Press, 1994.

Stack, George J. *Nietzsche and Emerson, an Elective Affinity.* Athens, Ohio: Ohio University Press, 1992.

Strauss, David Friedrich. *Der alte und der neue Glauben.* 11th ed. Bonn: Emil Strauss, 1881.

Toynbee, A. J. *A Study of History.* New York: Oxford University Press, 1939.

Verrecchia, Anacleto. *Die Katastrophe Nietzsches in Turin.* Vienna: H. Böhlaus, 1986.

Wallerstein, Carmen. "Paul Lanzky erzählt von Nietzsche: Eine Begegnung." *Neue Schweizer Rundschau,* July 1947.

Werner, Eric. "Juden um Richard und Cosima Wagner: Eine Konfrontation nach einem Jahrhundert." *Oesterreichische Akademie der Wissenschaften,* no. 35 (1984): 139.

Westernhagen, Curt von. *Nietzsche Juden, Antijuden.* Weimar, 1936.

———. *Richard Wagner.* Zurich: Atlantis, 1956.

Zimmern, Helen. *Schopenhauer, His Life and Philosophy.* Rev. ed. London: Allen & Unwin, 1932.

Index